Black Politics
in
Conservative America

Black Politics
in
Conservative America

SECOND EDITION

Marcus D. Pohlmann

RHODES COLLEGE

 LONGMAN

An imprint of Addison Wesley Longman, Inc.

New York • Reading, Massachusetts • Menlo Park, California • Harlow, England
Don Mills, Ontario • Sydney • Mexico City • Madrid • Amsterdam

Publishing Partner: Pamela Gordon
Project Coordination and Text Design: Ruttle, Shaw & Wetherill, Inc.
Cover Design Manager: Nancy Danahy
Cover Designer: Kay Petronio
Cover Photo: PhotoDisc, Inc.
Full Service Production Manager: Joseph Vella
Electronic Page Makeup: Ruttle, Shaw & Wetherill, Inc.
Senior Print Buyer: Hugh Crawford
Printer and Binder: The Maple-Vail Book Manufacturing Group.
Cover Printer: Coral Graphic Services, Inc.

Library of Congress Cataloging-in-Publication Data
Pohlmann, Marcus D., 1950–
    Black politics in conservative America/Marcus D. Pohlmann,— 2nd ed.
      p. cm.
    Includes bibliographical references and index.
    ISBN 0-8013-1732-0
    1. Afro-Americans—Politics and government. 2. Conservatism— United States.
  3. United States—Politics and government.
  I. Title.
  E185.615.P544 1998   98-17996
  324'.089'96073—dc21   CIP

Please visit our website at http://longman.awl.com

0-8013-1732-0

2345678910—MA—01009998

*This book is dedicated to Barbara Pohlmann
with love and appreciation*

Contents

PART THREE
Blacks in American Politics

PART FOUR
Conclusions

Preface

The most notable change since the first edition of this book has been the remarkable acceleration of the postindustrial trends described herein. In particular, the polarization of the American work force has been growing at an astonishing pace, with well-paying jobs for administrators and professionals, minimal wages for more and more workers in the various service industries, and fewer and fewer secure, well-paying jobs in the middle. The postindustrial economy simply seems to be increasingly incapable of gainfully employing a sizable number of America's workers. Because of their vulnerability and visibility, many African American workers are among the most obvious casualties.

Not surprisingly, with the declining position of the American middle class has come a considerable amount of political unrest, manifest among other ways in a very unstable national electorate. Amidst such instability, people of color have found themselves to be convenient scapegoats. That trend has included quite popular attacks on immigration, affirmative action, and various social welfare programs perceived to be abused by these populations.

If the issues raised by the central arguments of this book are correct, however, such political diversions will not begin to address our nation's real underlying structural problems. The private American economy, for example, simply cannot keep many of us sufficiently employed anymore. Sooner or later this will have to be addressed by government.

Yet, the United States of America has always been a conservative country. Among other things, this means that it has been infused with a political-economic culture that has strongly believed in individual enterprise rather than governmental intervention. According to the credo, those who work hard will succeed, and their collective success will mean more investment and resultant job opportunities for others who are willing to work equally as hard. Nevertheless, as more and more exceptions to that rule are exposed and faith in those tenets is subsequently weakened, fruitless scapegoating may diminish and challenges to long-standing political and economic structures follow instead.

As an early indicator of such change, this second edition considers the possibility of an electoral realignment not unlike the one that occurred in the midst of the Great Depression of the 1930s. This time, however, the emerging majority party would be much more likely to resemble the labor parties found in various Western European nations.

Black or African American?

The late 1960s witnessed the term "Negro" supplanted by the term "black," and, by the late 1980s, the term "African American" began to appear more frequently. At the time the first edition of this book was published, however, it was still not clear how universally accepted the term "African American" would become. Thus, the editorial decision was made to stick with the more traditional terms "black" and "black American." Good arguments have been made for the use of both "black" and "African American," as each suggests different emphases in regards to ethnicity, global identity, and the American experience.[1] In addition, the black/African American community in the United States remains divided over its own preference, although a clear majority appears to continue to prefer "black."[2] On balance, then, I have chosen to use the two terms interchangeably, although "black" will still be the primary terminology used.

A Note on "Victimization"

Lastly, the first edition of this text was categorized by some as another in a series of "victimization studies." In other words, by placing emphasis on the structural barriers to black success, the book was seen as contributing to the development of *victim mentalities,* whereby African Americans blame the system for their own personal lack of success, as opposed to taking responsibility for their own lives and overcoming whatever barriers may or may not actually exist.

To such an interpretation, I can only respond that I am primarily an analyst attempting to describe and explain that which I have observed. What the empirical results mean to any particular individual and what he or she attempts to do with

---

[1] For example, see Ben Martin, "From Negro to Black to African American," *Political Science Quarterly,* 106 (Spring 1991), pp. 83-107; Robert Smith, *Racism in the Post-Civil Rights Era* (Albany, N.Y.: SUNY Press, 1995), pp. 100-104.

[2] For example, see Ralph Gomes and Linda Faye Williams, eds., *From Exclusion: The Long Struggle for African American Political Power* (Westport, Conn.: Greenwood Press, 1992).

knowledge is likely to depend a lot on that person's own life experiences and values. And, frankly, I feel it is a bit patronizing to presume that the average African American reader is likely to be so dependent and malleable that he or she is not capable of both understanding the barriers and still be responsible enough to push on despite them.

This brings me to a related goal in writing such a book. If a person is to be successful in the American political economy it would seem essential to have an accurate view of both how the system was designed to work and how it actually does function. No matter what one's personal goals, there is no need banging one's head against institutional barriers, when those barriers can be understood and more efficiently navigated in the short run, and hopefully reduced in the long run. Denying their existence, on the other hand, can lead to people wholly blaming themselves for failures that really are at least, in part, systemically related.

Now, there clearly have been exceptions. A sizable number of African Americans have maintained faith in the traditional American culture and have managed to overcome these obstacles and succeed. Of these individuals, a prominent few have come to forcefully espouse variations of conservatism, with the real poster child for this movement being U.S. Supreme Court Justice Clarence Thomas, one of the most conservative voices on the contemporary court. This phenomenon and these views will be addressed directly in Chapter 10.

For now, holding up a handful of black economic successes as role models for the black community is not unlike holding up John D. Rockefeller, Sam Walton, or Bill Gates as role models for whites. Yes, it is possible for someone to overcome class barriers in the course of his or her (mostly his) lifetime. It can and has happened. But, what proportion of the population will ever succeed at this level? In other words, just how "probable" is it? And, why are the odds so much longer for some than for others? Why do so many talented people work so incredibly hard and not make it, while others fall into wealth and power by the fortunes of birth? At very least, such an "American Dream" seems to serve as a convenient pacifier for the overwhelming majority of the population that is quite simply never going to rise to a position of significant wealth or power no matter how talented they are and no matter how hard they work. In essence, then, it serves to reinforce the existing political economy by diverting attention away from discussion of alternative systems that might more effectively allow the most talented and hard working to succeed, while still maintaining an acceptable degree of input, security, and comfort for every individual willing to try.

Acknowledgments

I wish to express my appreciation to a great many colleagues and students who have contributed to the evolution of this book. George Galster, Ken Goings, James Jennings, and Diane Pinderhughes provided insightful criticisms of the first edition. Bob Blair, Dan Calhoun, Thomas Dye, David England, Edward Greenberg, Ken Hoover, Randy Kesserling, David Levenbach, and Frank Miller contributed useful suggestions at a number of different stages. Walt Vanderbush made an invaluable contribution to the section on the educational system. The following reviewers made thought-ful comments and suggestions:

Janet K. Boles, Marquette University; Yomi O. Durotoye, Wake Forest University; Floyd W. Hayes, III, Purdue University; Richard Keiser, Carleton College; Akwasi P. Osei, Delaware State University; Lewis A. Randolph, Ohio University; Stephen Wiener, University of California at Santa Barbara; Zaphon Wilson, Alppalachian State University; and Louis E. Wright, Jr., Howard University.

I also wish to thank my many students over the years, especially those in my Black Politics courses. I appreciate the confidence and support of both my editors, David Estrin and Peter Glovin, and of the Rhodes College Faculty Development Committee. Betsy Eckert was an incredible help in locating needed government documents. Cullen Weeden and Jean Shunk were extremely helpful in typing drafts. Steve Beckham and Grant Whittle did a terrific job verifying quotations and references. Justin Pohlmann assisted in the construction of the bibliography for this edition and was patient, understanding, and loving throughout the many years his father has been working on this book. I also want to acknowledge Charles V. Hamilton in particular, not only for inspiring me in this field, but also for providing a model of a social scientist who is at one and the same time analytical, compassionate, and dedicated to the cause of human liberation.

Marcus D. Pohlmann

PART ONE

STUDYING RACE AND POLITICS IN AMERICA

Chapter 1

Introduction

John and Sharon Williams are both 30-year-old community college graduates. They work 40 hours every week, 50 weeks out of every year, in order to support themselves and their two children. They have been told since grade school that if they work hard they will get ahead, own a nice house in the suburbs, and possibly even own their own company some day. That is the American dream, and they both were raised to believe in it.

But John and Sharon are black. If the market value of the goods and services they produce together is $26.25 each hour, or $4,374 per month,[1] their paychecks should reflect that. But they do not. Instead, John and Sharon receive $547 less per month because of the color of their skin.[2] An additional $727 goes to government in the form of various taxes so that government can provide their nation with a variety of services.[3] Finally, some $124 a month goes to a small group of wealthy white individuals in what is categorized in Chapter 5 as a form of *tribute* for the privilege of living and working in the nation these individuals own.[4] That leaves John and Sharon with less than $3000 every month with which to pay the landlord; make car payments; buy food, clothing, and insurance; pay other miscellaneous expenses for a family of four; as well as save for emergencies, their family vacation, retirements, and their children's college educations. As for investments, there is simply very little chance of them ever saving enough to purchase much of any corporate stock or to buy a small private business.

For John and Sharon Williams, a black couple in America—the land of opportunity—this may well be all there is ever going to be.

Their country is steeped in the rhetoric of *democracy* and *equal opportunity*, and its government collects hundreds of billions of dollars a year in taxes from men and women like John and Sharon at least in part to help make that dream a reality. Why, then, does the game turn out so unevenly, decade after decade? For example,

3

why does the average black family continue to earn considerably less than the average white family? Why do a small number of white men continue to own the controlling shares of virtually all of the nation's major corporations, facilitating their annual collection of billions of dollars from everyone else? Do John and Sharon really believe that members of this white elite are more talented or hard-working than they are? Or do they simply believe that without white racism, there would be free and open competition for those elite positions? If they believe neither of those, why have such consistent results not driven John and Sharon to oppose the present political-economic arrangement more actively?

To begin to answer such questions, it is useful to look first at the American political economy. In doing so, there are clear indications that this system was designed to impede rather than facilitate fundamental change. Instead of providing mechanisms by which the less privileged majority can forge a future with fewer impediments to equal political and economic opportunity, the system described in these chapters can do little other than help reinforce the inequitable status quo. That status quo embodies a history of individual and institutionalized racism that has left African Americans far behind from the start.

Consider the analogy of a marathon between two equally skilled and motivated contestants. One runner has easy access to the best training facilities, coaches, and nourishment available. She trains full time, eats well, and arrives at the starting line in peak condition. The other runner, through no fault of her own, cannot gain access to those resources and is forced to train after a hard day's work and on weekends. The rules of the race may be the same for both runners once they arrive at the starting blocks, but in fact the race is anything but fair, and the result is all but preordained. There will be an occasional upset; but, in the last analysis, such exceptions will do little more than provide false hopes to the large majority and divert their attention from the real underlying problem.

FOCUS

> Black people are not like other ethnic groups in American society. To begin with, blacks came to these shores, not as immigrants seeking a better life, but as slaves intended for use as forced laborers. The racist ideology erected to justify slavery served after the Civil War to keep blacks oppressed and subservient. . . . Businessmen, infected by their own racist dogma, preferred to import foreign labor. With the advent of the civil rights movement, the monolithic structure of racism began to show cracks, but then it was already too late. Black people were to enjoy the unfortunate distinction of being among the first surplus products of an advanced American technology and economic system.[5]

It is important to recognize at the outset that different white ethnic groups had different experiences upon coming to America, some of which more closely parallel those of African Americans.[6] Nevertheless, the black experience in the United States is unique, and thus analogies between that experience and those of any other immigrant group must be drawn with great caution. The original black population of this country consisted of people who were wrested from their homelands by force and ultimately sold into slavery. Their labor soon became integral to the agricultural economy of the American South, and, consequently, structures arose to protect that arrangement, including social and religious rationalizations for white supremacy and laws prohibiting educating slaves or harboring them if they ran away. Almost two centuries after the initiation of slavery in the United States, slaves were legally emancipated in the aftermath of a bloody civil war, rapidly elevated to a degree of power during Reconstruction, and then abandoned to the vengeance of their former masters with the collapse of Reconstruction. Night riders, lynchings, and sharecropper peonage pushed many blacks to move north in what came to be known as the Great Migration. But unlike the white immigrants who had preceded them into the northern cities, these new arrivals were soon to witness, among other things, the nearly complete disappearance of the political party machine as an assimilation agent, a decline in blue-collar manufacturing jobs, and a continuing exodus of middle-class taxpayers.[7]

The purpose of this book is twofold:

1. to analyze major problems African Americans face as well as related political and economic structures, with the ultimate goal of developing a policy agenda for implementation when political power is achieved.
2. to scrutinize black political experiences over the course of U.S. history in order to develop effective political tactics for achieving policy changes.

Internal differences in class, gender, and region have existed throughout the history of African Americans. In this book, however, I will focus on a number of interests common to virtually all blacks, without losing sight of separable and occasionally conflicting interests within black America. In addition, I will suggest that a number of the problems addressed are not unique to blacks. In particular, the development of the *postindustrial economy*—discussed at greater length in Chapters 2 and 5—has created a variety of socioeconomic dilemmas for middle-, working-, and lower-class whites as well. Ultimately, that reality only adds credence to the book's conclusions.

Finally, note that this book is not primarily a historical analysis of black involvement in the American political system, focusing on events like the Amenia Conference and political entities like the Congressional Black Caucus. To treat those developments as central would be to employ the traditional approach of taking the overall system as a given and focusing on the political process within it. A number of history and political science texts already do that quite adequately. Instead, in this study I will broaden the scope of analysis, putting primary focus on underlying political and economic structures. Specifically, once the socioeconomic results for African Americans are scrutinized, I then work back to see if, and in what ways, basic political and economic structures have contributed to those results—and if they have contributed, how they can be changed.

CENTRAL HYPOTHESES

The central hypotheses of this book are as follows:

1. The American political and economic systems are intricately intertwined, particularly in the postindustrial era.

2. There is an economic class structure in the United States, and virtually all of black America is left out of the ranks of the dominant owning class.
3. The American political system serves to reinforce the economic class structure.
4. The education system, the mass media, and at times even the church are important socializing agents that function to suppress the consciousness of the non-owning classes.
5. The resulting political-economic system, which primarily serves the interests of the white owning elite, must be altered if justice is to be achieved.

The analysis will begin with a historical overview of blacks' positions in American society in general and in the U.S. class structure in particular. It will then present an adaptation of Charles V. Hamilton's "conduit colonialism" model[8] in order to demonstrate how America's governmental policies within a capitalist economy have come to reinforce the subordinate economic positions of the black middle, working, and lower classes. Thus, even as government assistance has helped propel the American gross national product and stock market, the American dream has continued to be an American nightmare for far too many American blacks. Why have concerted political efforts not succeeded in redirecting the thrust of this governmental policy? Specific political arenas will be examined to reveal their inherently conservative functions, virtually regardless of the efforts made within them. Finally, the alternatives section will argue for a tightly organized political coalition of disinherited groups, employing a diversified and multifront strategy from within and outside the existing system, with goals that include altering both the political and economic structures that have long helped to perpetuate their inferior position. Such a development is extremely important for all these groups; focusing on African Americans, it is particularly vital if the vestiges of slavery are finally to be eradicated and justice finally attained.

Before proceeding, it is important to pause and consider what is being meant by the word justice. Would justice have been achieved if class inequities remained, stripped of their racial component? In other words, is the ultimate goal simply to see blacks assimilate effectively into the class structure that now exists? From this author's perspective, the answer to that is no. The goal is not to see blacks, or any other group, assimilate into a system that allows some limited interclass mobility but also a considerable degree of unnecessary insecurity and pain. To opt for a less hierarchical political-economic system, however, does entail a trade-off. It would mean taking a system that allows a few to succeed in exploitive positions and trading it for a less exploitive system with fewer extremes of wealth and power. That flies in the face of many fundamental beliefs long held in America. But when the American dream for a few amounts to an American nightmare for far more and American insomnia for many of the rest, there can be no justice. It is time for a fundamental change in the political-economic structures, so that blacks—and all other citizens currently excluded from the American dream—can find justice and dignity in a system based not on exploitation but on a fair distribution of wealth and power.

Nevertheless, it is also clear that such structural alterations are necessary, but not sufficient, to achieve racial justice in America. Racism would continue to stall progressive change even if major structural alterations could be implemented immediately. Racist individuals in positions of power will continue to find ways to discriminate. Yet these structural changes will still accomplish two very important ends. First, they will help clear the way for far more equal economic and political opportunity if and when racism diminishes. Second, they will take some of the sting out of existing racism by forcibly providing more equity for most African Americans.

CHAPTER OVERVIEW

Chapter 2: Theoretical Context

The mainstream political science approach to studying politics is to separate the political and economic systems and to focus on the political behavior of individuals and groups in a sort of empirical vacuum. Chapter 2 sets out a different theoretical approach, however, one that underlies the analysis throughout the remainder of the book. In particular, it allows for a broader focus that encompasses critical links between the political and economic systems. As a case in point, the chapter concludes by turning to the political realities evolving in today's postindustrial economy, and that overview makes quite clear the integral connection between political and economic structures, the limits of the mainstream theoretical approach, and the need for the theoretical synthesis developed in the chapter.

Chapters 3–5 will outline race and class structures within which African Americans have been forced to operate, while Chapters 6–8 will discuss the ways in which basic governmental institutions function to impede fundamental challenge to those structures.

Chapter 3: Blacks in American Society

Chapter 3 adds basic historical context. It begins by outlining some of the central events in the political history of African Americans, culminating with major victories in the Congress and the Supreme Court of the United States. It then turns to measures of actual political, social, and economic progress. In particular, it looks at trends in black educational attainment, occupations, unemployment, income, poverty, housing conditions, health conditions, neighborhood pollution, crime rates, and casualties in the nation's wars. It concludes by looking at differing black and white perceptions of these trends, as well as enduring prejudicial attitudes.

Chapter 4: The Class Structure

Chapter 4 focuses on the economic class structure that underlies the political process. In particular, it looks at the concentration of wealth in the United States—a concentration that has been growing even greater thanks to some of the largest mergers in the history of the country. It then describes the concentrated ownership of those assets, focusing on the extremely small proportion held by African Americans. Blacks, for example, hold only about 2 percent of the nation's capital stock; and although they also own 3 percent of the businesses, most all of those businesses are very small, vulnerable, and operate on the margins of the economy. Lacking anything resembling a proportionate share of the nation's wealth, blacks—like most whites—are left dependent on the decisions of a small white owning class.

Chapter 5: Functions of a Welfare State

To demonstrate how the functioning of the overall American political-economic system has reinforced the underlying economic class structure, Chapter 5 endeavors to estimate the amount of money that has been transferred each year from the black and white middle and working classes to the investment portfolios of the small white owning class. This transference takes a variety of forms, such as private-sector profits from transactions with government and nongovernment consumers as well as direct transfers from government in the form of grants and credit subsidies.

Then, as capital becomes continually more mobile thanks to the transportation and communications technologies of the postindustrial period, the venture capitalists end up in an even stronger position to extract ever larger shares of the nation's income. For example, employees as well as federal, state, and local governments are essentially warned, "Either grant us the concessions we ask, or we will invest our capital elsewhere." Thus the dominant position of the owning class becomes increasingly more secure, while many of those beneath them have actually been experiencing a real-dollar income decline.

Instead of increasing interracial and interclass solidarity among the non-owners, however, some clear polarization has grown out of their frustrations. This appears to be due in large part to both misperceptions and an underlying faith in the enduring myth of economic fairness and interclass mobility in America.

And why have governmental officials fostered these inequities rather than rectified them?

Chapter 6: The Judicial Arena

Insulated somewhat from the electoral reach of the majority, the federal judicial process has often proved to be the most promising governmental avenue by which oppressed minorities could seek protection and assistance. This has certainly been true at a number of junctures in the history of African Americans, at least as long as the redress sought did not pose a serious challenge to the historic maldistribution of property. Nevertheless, even within those confines, major judicial victories are normally very slow in coming and have at times been stalled or even reversed in implementation or by subsequent court decisions.

Chapter 7: The Electoral Arena

At the founding of this nation, the electoral system was not designed to empower the masses—suffrage was generally limited to propertied white males, and the U.S. Senate was to be elected by state legislators. Those restrictions have since been eliminated, but a number of others continue to institutionalize race and class inequities. For example, the practice of privately funding virtually all political campaigns certainly puts the less privileged at a participatory disadvantage, and requiring presidential candidates to gain 15 percent of a state's primary election vote in order to receive any of that state's delegates to the Democratic party's national nominating convention clearly works to the disadvantage of black Democrats.

The party system as a whole is no less obstructive. A variety of rules and practices have impeded the path of third-party challenges to the inherently conservative two-party system—for instance, the winner-take-all, single-member-district arrangement; petitioning laws; the Campaign Finance Act; interpretations of the equal-time provision, and even a history of overt and covert police harassment of a number of them. As for the two major parties, they have tended historically to be moderate and only minimally ideological due to the very nature of a two-party system, while their decentralization and lack of patronage and nomination control have left them incapable of tightly organizing and disciplining their mass and governmental memberships anyway.

Given an electoral system without a number of strong ideologically distinct political parties to educate and lead public opinion, it should not be surprising that many Americans hold uninformed and internally contradictory attitudes and that voting turnout is lower than virtually anywhere else in the world. It should come as even less of a surprise that, as Chapter 10 will indicate, African Americans are becoming increasingly distrustful of the entire system's ability to respond to their needs. They have done everything right. They are geographically concentrated in strategic locations and, controlling for socioeconomic status, turn out at respectable rates. They also have voted as a cohesive bloc for the majority party in virtually every election from the Emancipation Proclamation to 1996. Unfortunately, for reasons such as those just outlined, the electoral system is simply incapable of providing the means to achieve fundamental change.

Chapter 8: The Legislative Arena

Congress, the presidency, and the bureaucracy are intricately intertwined in the process of writing, passing, and executing federal laws. Thus they combine to form the legislative arena. Like its judicial and electoral counterparts, this arena is conservative by design. Beyond the unrepresentative demographics of its members, its rules and procedures make fundamental change extremely difficult to accomplish.

As a result, although blacks have achieved passage of some major pieces of legislation, those gains have come very sporadically, at a very high cost, and have proved difficult to sustain. Nonetheless, there have been a few hopeful signs. The growth of the Congressional Black Caucus has been a particularly significant development, as has the increasing black presence at the top and bottom levels of the executive bureaucracy.

Chapter 9: The Information Arena

Chapter 9 addresses why the information presented in the previous chapters is not more readily apparent, giving rise to rebellions against both race and class structures as well as the political system that reinforces them. The information arena discussed in Chapter 9 focuses on the educational system and the mass media. Each is seen as impeding consciousness of the realities in some significant ways, while helping to sustain a dominant culture that poses no real threat to these structural relationships.

Chapter 10: Shaping the Future

The book will conclude with the argument that a fundamental altering of basic economic and political structures will have to occur if blacks are ever to escape the vestiges of slavery. To that end, they must be prepared to join a tightly organized coalition of disinherited groups, comparable to Jesse Jackson's concept of a "rainbow coalition." Then, with the numbers and discipline to command attention, they must proceed on a variety of fronts, from education to voting to lobbying to litigation to the crisis-stimulating direct action that seems to be necessary in order to move the inherently conservative political system of the United States. The details of such a movement, however, cannot be prescribed. Instead, they must arise naturally and dynamically from the real-life experiences and circumstances of real people.

TERMINOLOGY

The central argument presented in *Black Politics in Conservative America* is that not only does individual racism persist, but also the historical effects of such racism have been institutionalized in the conservative American political economy. To make that case, it is first important to define some key terms and the ideological foundations upon which the American political economy has been built.

Black Politics

Black Politics refers to politics practiced by people of African descent in the United States, even if they practice ideologically different politics. For example, Supreme Court Justices Thurgood Marshall and Clarence Thomas both have practiced Black Politics, as have congresspersons Maxine Waters and J. C. Watts. In addition, Black Politics is also the sum total of actions, ideas, and efforts aimed at creating better conditions for African-descended people in the United States. In other words, any political efforts aimed at raising the psychological, cultural, or material level of African Americans qualify as Black Politics. Black Politics, then, also becomes an agenda to be carried out, as opposed to merely the physical attributes of those carrying out the agenda. Among other things, this combined definition makes it unnecessary to try to first determine whether race or class is the most important impediment to black advancement.[9] Both exist, and they interact for many African Americans at the lower end of the socio-economic spectrum. But regardless of economic position, as Chapter 3 will indicate, African Americans as a group continue to feel differently from other Americans on issues such as affirmative action, crime, criminal justice, and the role of government in public policy, for blacks of all classes continue to battle racism.[10]

Racism

Individual *prejudice* is defined as

> any set of beliefs that organic, genetically transmitted differences (whether real or imagined) between human groups are intrinsically associated with the presence or absence of certain socially relevant abilities or characteristics, hence that such differences are a legitimate basis for invidious distinctions between groups socially defined as races.[11]

Individual racism entails adding discriminatory actions to those prejudicial beliefs. When such racism gets reinforced by basic societal institutions, this is called *institutional racism*.[12] Of the various institutions that serve to reinforce racism in America, one of the most basic is the nation's conservative political ideology.[13]

The American Political Ideology

As any political community attempts to cope with an ever-changing environment, it must apply political power in order to achieve certain of its goals. The setting of these goals and the application of this power are guided by a set of societal beliefs, or a collective "ideology." Phillip Converse defines ideology as a logically coherent set of principles explaining political reality and justifying political preferences.[14] Kenneth and Patricia Dolbeare define it as the integration of political beliefs into a relatively coherent picture of "(1) how the present social, economic, and political order operates, (2) why this is so and whether it is good or bad, and (3) what should be done about it, if anything."[15] An ideology, then, becomes the value prism through which the world is viewed, as well as a set of guiding principles that helps people make judgments about that world.

> Ideology thus intervenes between so-called "objective" conditions and events and the people who perceive and evaluate them. It is a socially generated and transmitted screen that is consistent with. . . the deeper cultural values and way of thinking characteristic of people in a given society.[16]

In terms of public policy, ideology is crucial, for it guides the choice as to which problems are to be tackled and which options seriously considered—the political agenda. And as E. E. Schattschneider argues, the "definition of alternatives is the supreme instrument of power."[17]

Just what are the primary tenets of the political ideology that has served to filter America's view of reality, justify its goals, and ultimately shape its political output by structuring the political agenda at the input end of its political process? First, it is essential to note three key political values upon which that ideology has been constructed: individualism, materialism, and limited government.

Individualism.   Individualism appears to be the most fundamental of America's dominant values. The individual is viewed as the revered center of the political universe. Tied to this is a belief that human beings are competitive by nature. Accordingly, only by recognizing that fact and promoting this competition can either self-fulfillment or social progress be achieved. Individuals are also seen to be endowed with the inalienable rights to life, liberty, and the sanctity of private property, and these are not to be confiscated without full "due process of law," under which all individuals are to receive equal treatment. In addition, individuals are to be guaranteed the right to participate in the creation of these laws, the majority of equal citizens is normally to prevail, and each person is to be free to express dissent.[18]

Materialism.   Materialism is a value closely related to what is often termed the "Protestant work ethic." The assumption is that salvation is achieved by working hard, using one's talents and opportunities, and ultimately attaining worldly possessions as a measure of those efforts. Thus the society comes to place considerable value on consumption, to respect choices based on profitability, and to measure a person's achievement and worth by his or her accumulation of wealth. C. B. MacPherson also notes that, in the process, people come to see and treat themselves as commodities, selling themselves for a wage.[19]

Limited Government.   To begin with, government is seen as having no inherent authority. As a collectivist enterprise with coercive potential, its sphere of operation is to be tightly circumscribed by the authority granted it by the individual members of the community and by the inalienable rights of those individuals. Primarily, it is to facilitate and referee competition between individuals as they jockey for positions of relative affluence. Beyond this function, government is generally expected to keep its hands off ("laissez-faire"). In a system where private profit and private consumption reign supreme, public spending, whether for schools, highways, or hospitals, is viewed with much more suspicion than are private investments, even if the latter are directed into rather banal consumer items.

Conservatism

The more general ideology that structures these values into both an experiential prism and a judgmental road map can be called either conservatism or "classical liberalism."[20] It begins with a belief that the greatest good for the greatest number will emerge in both the economic and political marketplaces if competition in those arenas can be kept as unimpeded as possible. Individuals should be allowed to compete freely and openly: economic merchants competing for buyers, and political candidates competing for voters. Because governmental regulation is limited, all compete economically as everyone strives for that ultimate symbol of success and salvation, material wealth.

Conservatives are less confident than their modern liberal counterparts that human beings are rational, perfectable, and capable of cooperating for mutual improvement. Thus conservatives put more faith in the economic marketplace than in government. The market provides an ideal arena in which the interests of insecure and competitive individuals can clash, leading to the best approximation of the "social good."

Adam Smith argued that the surest route to social good is when every individual neither intends to promote the public interest, nor knows how much he is promoting it. . . . He intends only his own gain, and he is in this, as in many other cases, led by an invisible hand to promote an end which was no part of his intention.[21]

Government, then, is to play a strictly limited role. It is to referee economic interactions and to protect competitive individuals from threatening each other's lives, liberty, and private property.

John Locke, a conservative by today's standards, spoke of the primary interest he saw drawing people together into a society: "the mutual preservation of their lives, liberties, and estates which I call by the general name, property."[22]

Thus, in the final analysis, conservatism advocates a very minimal use of government. Its primary purpose is to facilitate an environment that will allow individuals the maximum amount of freedom while still protecting people and their property from other people.[23]

The general rules that are to govern the competition—such as laissez-faire and survival of the fittest—come to be viewed as natural, inevitable, and self-evident. Inasmuch as the ideology is taken as dogma, approval becomes unquestioned, and opponents come to be viewed as misguided at best or miscreants at worst.

The Political Result

It should come as no surprise that the prevailing political-economic philosophies of 18th- and 19th-century America are reflected in the fundamental procedures and laws of the land. As will be discussed in detail in Part Three, clashing interests were built into the governmental process, so that it would move slowly and deliberately if and when it should ever decide to move beyond its policing functions. Consequently, legislation has always been much easier to block than to pass. As James Madison put it,

> The great security against a gradual concentration [of power] . . . consists in giving to those who administer each department the necessary constitutional means and personal motives to resist encroachments of the others. . . . Ambition must be made to counteract ambition. . . . If men were angels, no government would be necessary. If angels were to govern men, neither external nor internal controls on government would be necessary. In framing the government which is to be administered by men over men, the great difficulty lies in this: You must first enable the government to control the governed, and in the next place oblige it to control itself.[24]

What happens if a group finds itself needing more than a limited government to help erase the legacy of enslavement and subsequent discrimination? Limiting government would seem to promote the prevailing interests, not the aspiring ones. This certainly has been the case for most African Americans (as documented in Chapter 3).

However, slavery aside for a moment, why is that true for blacks when it did not seem to be so for earlier white ethnic immigrants who also were forced to start at the bottom and face discrimination within the confines of limited government?

Most obvious is the difference in skin color. Educated white ethnics who had acquired the necessary middle-class mannerisms could occasionally change their names, addresses, and hair color and "pass" as a member of a more socially accept-able ethnic group. For blacks, by contrast, skin color generally precludes passing as members of higher-status white groups.

In addition, as mentioned earlier, the urban political machine was declining. Thus in many cities, urban blacks were left to try to assimilate without the degree of assis-tance ward bosses and precinct captains had been able to lend to their white immi-grant counterparts. Progressive era reforms and historical events had come together to wound these institutions fatally just as in-migrating blacks needed them most.

Possibly of greatest importance, however, is the fact that the nature of the econ-omy has changed in some extremely significant ways. In particular, primary-sector jobs in labor-intensive industries are no longer providing nearly as many sturdy bot-tom rungs to the economic ladder. Instead of beginning work for union scale on an industrial assembly line with clear career ladders for skill development and promo-tion, today's aspiring workers are far more likely to begin as part-time employees in nonunionized service positions, stocking shelves at discount stores, for example, or bagging hamburgers at fast-food restaurants. This economic change is discussed fur-ther in Chapter 2.

Nonetheless, despite these historical inequities, polls continue to show consider-able black allegiance to the dominant conservative ideology.

NOTES

1. Based on the median income for a two-parent family where both parents work outside the home. These are 1994 estimates derived from 1993 figures. See 1995 *Statistical Ab-stracts of the United States*, p. 476.
2. See ibid.
3. Derived from estimates in chapter 5 below, showing the black middle/working class pay-ing an adjusted $52.2 billion in taxes on $273.7 billion in income—a 19% tax rate.
4. Chapter estimates that *tribute* figure to be $8.9 billion, which is a little better than 3.25% of black middle/working class income.
5. Robert Allen, *Black Awakening in Capitalist America: An Analytical History* (Garden City, N.Y.: Anchor/Doubleday, 1969), p. 51.
6. For example, see Herbert Gans, *The Urban Villagers* (New York: Free Press, 1962); An-drew Greeley, *Ethnicity in the United States* (New York: Wiley, 1974); John Higham, *Strangers in the Land* (New York: Atheneum, 1963); J. John Palen, *The Urban World* (New York: McGraw-Hill, 1975); Talcott Parsons and Kenneth Clark, eds., *The Negro American* (Boston: Houghton-Mifflin, 1966).
7. For example, see Lerone Bennett, *The Challenge of Blackness* (Chicago: Johnson Pub-lishers, 1972); Stanford Lyman, *The Black American in Sociological Thought* (New York: Capricorn, 1972).
8. Charles V. Hamilton, "Conduit Colonialism and Public Policy," *Black World* (October 1972).
9. For examples of this debate, see William Julius Wilson, *The Truly Disadvantaged* (Chicago: University of Chicago Press, 1987); Richard Zweigenhaft and G. William Domhoff, *Blacks in the White Establishment? A Study of Race and Class in America* (New Haven: Yale University Press, 1991).

10. For example, see Michael Dawson, *Behind the Mule: Race and Class in African-American Politics* (Princeton: Princeton University Press, 1994); Katherine Tate, *From Protest to Politics: The New Black Voters in American Elections* (New York: Russell Sage Foundation, 1994), chap. 2; Franklin Gilliam and Kenny Whitby, "Race, Class, and Attitudes toward Social Welfare Spending: An Ethclass Intrepretation," *Social Science Quarterly* 70 (March 1989), pp. 88–100.

11. Pierre L. van den Berghe, *Race and Racism* (New York: Wiley, 1967), p. 11. Also see David Goldberg, *Racist Culture: Philosophy and the Politics of Meaning* (Cambridge: Blackwell, 1993); Lewis Gordon, *Bad Faith and Antiblack Racism* (Atlantic Highlands, N.J.: Humanities Press, 1995); Robert Smith, *Racism in the Post-Civil Rights Era* (Albany, N.Y.: SUNY Press, 1995), chaps. 1 and 2.

12. Charles V. Hamilton and Stokely Carmichael, *Black Power* (New York: Random House, 1967), p. 4.

13. For example, see Thomas Powell, *The Persistence of Racism in America* (New York: University Press of America, 1992).

14. Phillip Converse, "The Nature of Belief Systems in Mass Publics," in David Apter (ed.), *Ideology and Discontent* (New York: Free Press, 1964).

15. Kenneth Dolbeare and Patricia Dolbeare, *American Ideologies* (Boston: Houghton Mifflin, 1976), pp. 2–3.

16. Ibid., p. 3.

17. E. E. Schattschneider, *The Semi-sovereign People* (New York: Holt, Rinehart and Winston, 1960), p. 68.

18. For an example of some of the problems that can arise in a postindustrial adaptation of such unfettered competition, see Robert Frank and Phillip Cook, *The Winner-Take-All Society* (New York: Free Press, 1995).

19. C. B. MacPherson, *The Political Theory of Possessive Individualism* (New York: Oxford University Press, 1973). And for an analysis of some of the societal risks posed by a hedonistic consumer culture, see Barbara Ehrenreich, "The New Right Attack on Social Welfare," in Fred Block, et al., *The Mean Season: The Attack on the Welfare State* (New York: Pantheon, 1987).

20. For a good comparison of "classical liberalism" and "contemporary liberalism," see Melanie Njeri Jackson, "The Liberal State: What Retreat? An Examination of Philosophical Ambivalence and Continuity in Perspectives and Treatment of African Americans in the U. S. Political System," in Marilyn Lashley and Melanie Njeri Jackson, *African Americans and the New Policy Consensus* (Westport, Conn.: Greenwood Press, 1994), chap 1.

21. Adam Smith, *The Wealth of Nations* (New York: Modern Library, 1969), p. 423.

22. Sir Ernest Barker, *Social Contract: Essays by Locke, Hume, and Rousseau* (London: Oxford University Press, 1960), p. 73.

23. For further references on American conservatism, see Milton Friedman, *Capitalism and Freedom* (Chicago: University of Chicago Press, 1962); Friedrich Hayek, *The Road to Serfdom* (Chicago: University of Chicago Press, 1944); Clinton Rossiter, *Conservatism in America* (New York: Vintage, 1962).

24. James Madison in Clinton Rossiter (ed.), *The Federalist Papers* (New York: New American Library, 1961), p. 322.

Chapter 2

Theoretical Context

What is a theory? Quite simply, "a theory is a set of related propositions that suggest why events occur in the manner that they do."[1] A common example would be Newton's Theory of Gravity. How do we explain the relationship of objects in the universe? In his theory, Newton suggested that a force called "gravity" makes all components of the universe attracted to each other. The level of force depends on the amount of matter in the particular bodies and the distance between them. Thus, with this theory he could explain why a large rock is more difficult to pick up off the face of the earth than a small rock.

A political theory, on the other hand, attempts to explain the various components of the process for deciding how things of value are to be allocated in a society. For example, a political theory explains what factors consistently affect who will sit in decision-making positions, what range of alternatives they will consider, what they will decide, how those decisions will be implemented, and who will benefit from those decisions.

Much political science analysis has been built on two fundamental political theories: pluralism and systems theory. These approaches, however, often have left the discipline incapable of explaining adequately phenomena such as the interrelationship of racism, biases inherent in the U.S. political economy, and the socioeconomic position of African Americans as a group. Even elite theorists, who focus on the disproportionate power held by social, economic, and political elites, tend to ignore the structures that shape their behavior. For example, why have blacks as a group remained in a consistently inferior economic position whether the president was Lyndon Johnson or Ronald Reagan and whether the Congress was dominated by Democrats or Republicans?

The purpose of this chapter is twofold. First, I will briefly discuss the pluralist, systems and elite theory approaches, and some of the shortcomings inherent in them.

Second, I will outline a theoretical framework that allows systematic analysis not only of the governmental decision-making process, but also of the political, social, and economic structures that appear to have served as barriers to the type of meaningful political change discussed in Chapter 1.

My alternative framework melds components of systems, pluralist, and elite theories with Marxian and liberation theory. This more complex analytical construct should allow a fuller examination of the American political process within which African Americans struggle.

PLURALISM

Pluralism involves analyzing political conflict as it is organized around interest groups. Yet, using a traditional pluralist approach to the analysis of politics, blacks as a whole are not recognized as a meaningful political interest group appropriate to study. In addition, the possibility of institutionalized barriers to effective black participation is not considered either. Such myopia springs from key presuppositions concerning what constitutes an empirically relevant interest group and how the political process actually functions. Consequently, the entire concept of black politics is alien to this approach. An overview of the traditional pluralist approach follows.

Interests

Interests are defined as needs people are aware that they have. Thus the word "need" tends to become valuable as a political science concept only when used as a verb, that is, once that person has decided that he or she *needs* something. It is seen as having little empirical value in its noun form, as when the person has a *need* for indoor plumbing whether aware of it or not. The latter are avoided or discounted in traditional pluralist theory because they involve the analyst in projecting a need onto someone else, which is seen as entailing too much chance for observer bias. Thus when a black person writes a letter to an elected official requesting something, that is an expressed political interest appropriate to study. When that same person is laid off work because his or her company has moved overseas, that person's need for government protection from such arbitrary abandonment is not deemed to be an appropriate subject for value-neutral behavioral analysis. Why? Because the analyst has projected a need onto that unemployed worker and has thus become more of an advocate than a purely detached observer.

Interest Groups

Political interest groups are composed of people sharing commonly felt needs who interact for the purpose of affecting public policy. Pluralist beacon David B. Truman defines them this way:

> Interest group refers to any group that, on the basis of one or more shared attitudes, makes certain claims upon other groups in the society for the establishment, maintenance, or enhancement of forms of behavior that are implied by the shared attitudes.[2]

By that definition, African Americans—despite a common heritage of oppression—do not have a common interest appropriate to study. They would not have such an interest until it could be shown that all black people had at least one conscious purpose in common.

In addition, they are not an empirically relevant group either. Truman puts it this way:

> The significance of a . . . group in producing similar attitudes and behaviors among its members lies, not in their physical resemblance or in their proximity, . . . but in the characteristic relationships among them. These interactions, or relationships, because they have a certain character and frequency, give the group its molding and guiding powers. . . . A minimum frequency of interaction is, of course, necessary before a group in this sense can be said to exist.[3]

Truman is arguing that in order to be an interest group, all members must not only be conscious of a commonly held opinion but also get together on a regular basis for the purpose of promoting that shared interest. If that is not the case, they are not an interest group appropriate for study as such.

Power Resources

Power resources available to the various political interest groups—such as time, money, prestige, contacts, media access, and the right to vote and petition elected representatives—are clearly distributed in an uneven fashion. Nevertheless, this uneven distribution is not seen by traditional pluralists as a structural bias worthy of analysis in its own right. First, they argue that those with the largest accumulation of power resources do not automatically have the most political power; for example, candidates who raise the largest amounts of money do not always win their elections. Strategy and circumstances are also important, and the resource-wealthy cannot monopolize these. Second, because everyone has access to at least some power resources, pluralists see any group as capable of becoming competitive if it can effectively pool an adequate number of such resources; for example, the poor can use their numbers to generate a substantial voting bloc and their spare time to swamp officials with messages.

Openness

The political system is considered to be open because of the variety of input channels available to interest groups. Not only do all participants have at least some of the resources necessary to compete, but the political process has so many access points that all voices will be heard if they just speak up. For example, there are elections, thousands of officials to contact, radio call-in shows, and newspaper columns devoted to letters to the editor, not to mention the constitutionally protected "right of the people peaceably to assemble and to petition the government for a redress of grievances."

Government

Government is seen as a relatively unbiased arbiter, refereeing the competition between conflicting groups according to neutral rules. Elected officials will either strive to determine and implement the expressed needs of their constituencies, or they will soon find themselves looking for alternative employment. Therefore, even if these officials are virtually all well-to-do white males, they still can and will respond fairly, for example, to black females who head households—if those black women effectively pool their resources.

Elections

As one might expect, any notion of an abstract public interest is discounted. Its existence would require unanimous consent. Nevertheless, traditional pluralists see elections as an important means for determining the collective wish at any one point in time, recording the outcome of the political competition between individual groups.

Equilibrium

In the end, it is argued that diverse groups flock to the political process to do battle over scarce public resources. That conflict creates disequilibrium within the political system, and it is then up to the elected officials to find a compromise that will appease the various groups and return the system to equilibrium.

Overall, then, traditional pluralists are arguing that the dispersion of power resources and the multiple opportunities for influencing government guarantee that the system will be relatively open to all. Therefore, political scientists need not concern themselves with the possibility that the rules of the game include some and exclude others in any really significant way. If the rules were stacked in that manner, it might make some sense to explore why categories of people, identifiable by nothing other than their consistent deprivation, so regularly fail to receive the prizes bestowed by the political-economic system. But if it is assumed that the system is open and that all people are basically aware of their own interests, the researcher need only focus on the government's efforts to appease organized groups seeking government favor. Therefore, drawing on such pluralist propositions, systems theory concerns itself only with that type of expressed political conflict.[4]

SYSTEMS THEORY

Gabriel Almond and G. Bingham Powell define a system as possessing two distinctive characteristics: (1) separate and distinguishable components (differentiation) and (2) interaction among those components in order to perform certain functions (integration).[5]

A political system, then, would be a set of differentiated units interacting to perform certain political functions, as when the Congress and the president interact to provide for national defense, assist the poor, or regulate interstate commerce. David Easton pictures it as in Figure 2.1. Inputs include popular support (e.g., recognizing the laws as legitimate and obeying them) and popular demands (e.g., the American Medical Association lobbying against national health insurance). Conversion ultimately amounts to public policymaking, where political actors (e.g., the president and the Congress) respond to various inputs by converting them into policies. Outputs are these authoritative decisions themselves (e. g., a decision not to pass national health insurance legislation). Feedback amounts to public reaction to these outputs. That reaction may be positive, settling the matter, or it could be negative, leading to further inputs on the issue or a decline in support of the government officials in power and possibly the political system itself.[6]

These bare bones of Easton's model provide a widely accepted picture of how a political system operates. However, this only scratches the surface of what constitutes a political phenomenon. A more searching question is, What is to be included in the category "politics"? And the obvious corollary is, What is and is not public policy and thus is or is not appropriate for a political scientist to analyze?

Empirical Dilemmas

Easton suggests that politics, or public policymaking, occurs when political officials make authoritative policies for an entire political community.[7] It seems simple, but to appreciate the ambiguities that still remain, consider which of the following acts constitute public policy by this definition.

1. The president of the United States imposes trade sanctions on South Africa.
2. Congress passes the Voting Rights Act.
3. An official at the Board of Elections scrutinizes the nomination petitions of black candidates more closely than those of white candidates.
4. The federal government never seriously considers a substantial compensatory payment to former slaves or their descendants.

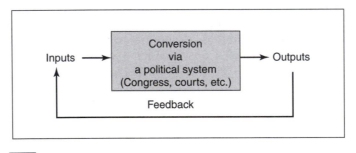

Political system

Political environment

FIGURE 2.1
David Easton's Political System Model. (From *The Political System* by David Easton. University of Chicago Press. Copyright 1953, © 1971 by David Easton. All rights reserved.)

5. The board of directors of General Motors Corporation decides that the auto company will increase its manufacturing abroad instead of in Detroit, a decision with serious implications for thousands of African American workers.

The decisions of the president and the Congress would seem to qualify inasmuch as these are representatives elected to positions of public authority who make authoritative decisions for the political community. By the same logic, the Board of Elections employee has been delegated public authority by elected officials. But what about the last two cases?

Peter Bachrach and Morton Baratz carefully develop the argument that the alternatives government decides against or will not even consider are often every bit as political and important as ultimate decisions to act.[8] The federal government's decision to not even seriously consider compensating former slaves would thus be viewed as an important public policy affecting a large majority of the black political community. It is simply a negative output rather than a positive one, and it may reflect underlying structural biases.

As for the final example, the decisions made in the boardrooms of General Motors, Exxon, Chase Manhattan Bank, and USX—or at the executive meetings of the United Auto Workers, the Teamsters, or the United Mine Workers, for that matter—often are policies that significantly affect large segments of the black political community. They may also be authoritative in the sense that the public accepts these organizations' prerogatives to make such decisions; yet they are not particularly open to much direct popular input.

In summary, systems theory defines the political system as institutions such as the legislative body, chief executive, and bureaucracy interacting to process inputs and emit outputs in a way that will enable them to maintain adequate support from the citizenry. Nonetheless, strict adherence to a combination of traditional pluralism and systems theory leaves the researcher incapable of addressing the type of important policy-related questions raised by the preceding examples 4 and 5. Consider three concrete cases in point that focus on potential structural biases stemming from the interrelationship between America's political and economic systems.

Case 1: Class and Political Participation

Income is distributed quite unevenly in the United States (see Table 2.1). For example, families in the top quintile make nearly as much money as the other 80 percent of the families combined, and this distribution has remained remarkably consistent over time. In addition, many of the families in the lower 80 percent were able to achieve the incomes they had only by virtue of having two or three wage earners or by receiving cash grants from governmental public assistance programs.[9] Thus there appear to be obvious income classes in the United States, and those classes have distinct interests in the degree to which government does or does not reinforce this economic inequality.

In terms of the black community, 40 percent of all black families and a majority of all black children fall into the bottom fifth, a reality that has generally been this bad or worse since slavery. Thus one might reasonably expect to see a rather large

TABLE 2.1

FAMILY INCOME AS A PERCENTAGE OF NATIONAL INCOME, 1950–1994

Population Quintile	1950	1955	1960	1965	1970	1975	1980	1985	1990	1994
Top fifth	43	42	41	41	41	41	42	43	44	47
Second fifth	23	23	24	24	24	24	24	24	24	23
Third fifth	17	18	18	18	18	18	18	17	17	16
Fourth fifth	12	12	12	12	12	12	11	11	11	10
Bottom fifth	5	5	5	5	5	5	5	5	4	4

Source: U.S. Department of Commerce, Bureau of the Census, Current Population Reports, and unpublished data.

group of low-income African Americans becoming quite active politically in an attempt to alter a system that permits—and possibly even reinforces—such a maldistribution of income. Yet, as Lester Milbraith and M. L. Goel conclude,

> it is almost universally true that the more prosperous persons are more likely to participate in politics than the less prosperous. . . . [And] the relationship between income and unconventional political participation is similar to the relationship between SES and conventional political participation.[10]

What do such developments indicate about the political system in America?

A traditional analyst could be expected to argue as follows. If economic injustices are befalling large segments of the population, little precludes these people from seeking political redress by actively participating in the input processes. How can one begin to suggest that the entire system may be structurally biased simply because the conversion process is not responding to interests some analysts claim people have? If these people really felt that certain governmental actions were in their best interests, they would at least be attempting to use the input channels available in order to bring about such policies. For the political analyst to venture into the realm of interest inference is to run an unnecessary risk of introducing bias into the analysis and its conclusions. If political participation is unimpeded, and especially if no single elite dominates these open competitions, there is what can reasonably be viewed as a political system capable of adequately reflecting the community's various political interests.

But what if, no matter how open the procedures, the political race is fixed from the start, making the winners and losers pretty much preordained?

Although technically open to every citizen, the input process certainly does appear to be more open to some than to others. For example, as Milbraith and Goel and numerous other analysts of American political participation have concluded, the poor spend more time eking out a living, leaving less time for politics.[11] Lesser status also makes them less likely to have direct contact with the decision makers, while lower income leaves them less money with which to purchase special consideration by making large campaign contributions. In addition, the dominant American political value system may well be leading the vast majority of American wage earners to accept their subordinate economic position as being a politically irremediable economic outcome. Thus the political system may be far more likely to reproduce, rather than rectify, the inequalities of the economic structure on which it is built. Simply to ignore the possibility of such structural biases seems empirically myopic.

Case 2: Urban Renewal

Under urban renewal, homes in and near the central business district are razed and their predominantly low-income minority residents displaced. The land is then sold below market value to venture capitalists. Meanwhile, the displaced poor are often never relocated. Between 1949 and 1961, some 126,000 housing units were destroyed, displacing 113,000 families and 36,000 individuals, yet only 28,000 new housing units were built in their stead.[12]

Analyzing such an issue so as better to understand who has how much political power in a community, most traditional analysts would once again begin with the proposition that to minimize the introduction of the researcher's own values into a study, there must first be an assumption that people are the best judges of their own political interests. Peoples' political activity, or lack thereof, can thus be seen as a reasonably accurate reflection of those interests. Consequently, the results of a relatively unimpeded competition in the political process again provides an acceptable reflection of the various political interests in that community.

For example, a city council is chosen by means of the standard American electoral process. The council confronts the issue of urban renewal. It proceeds to hold public hearings on the question of whether to raze an inhabited slum block to make way for the erection of a new corporate headquarters. After the hearings, the council votes to raze the neighborhood. Traditional analysts would then approach this political decision by first assuming that the council has effectively refereed a relatively fair competition between various interests in the city. If the procedures are judged to be physically unimpeded, it is assumed that the process was open enough so as not to exclude any interest group from the outset.

But what if the majority of the council members are local business operators or are otherwise beholden to local business owners, either because of their large campaign contributions or the importance of their investments to the community? Is it not possible that the final council decision might primarily be a reflection of narrow elite interests rather than broader interests in the community as a whole? And if such elitism is occurring in most of the city's public policymaking arenas, just how open is the political process in this community?

Case 3: Poletown

Consider the 3,500 lower-income residents of Detroit's half-white, half-black Poletown neighborhood. In 1980, General Motors threatened to locate 6,000 jobs elsewhere if already ailing Detroit would not raze 1,176 Poletown homes so that a new $600 million Cadillac plant could be built there. The city of Detroit had little choice. A number of residents became concerned, however, and formed the Poletown Area Revitalization Task Force. They appealed to the mayor, the city council, and the courts, to no avail. With the help of hundreds of millions of dollars in public subsidies, 465 acres were razed, on which sat 1,176 homes, 100 small businesses, 16 churches, 2 schools, and a hospital; in return, GM promised 3,000 jobs, "economics permitting."

Detroit's black mayor, Coleman Young, author of the $700 million subsidy plan that the Michigan Environmental Review Board termed "incomplete, indefensible, and misleading," summarized it thus: "Jobs are our economic base, the key to our survival and future prosperity." He also termed a court ruling that rejected the Poletown Neighborhood Council's final effort to block the plan a "significant victory" for the city of Detroit. Nonetheless, in actuality, the city government was spending hundreds of millions of dollars out of its very limited budget and destroying an entire functioning neighborhood without a legally binding guarantee of even one job from General Motors.[13]

The most important lesson in Case 3, in terms of the relationship between politics and the underlying economic structures, is that in the Poletown debate, the only realistic alternatives for the city of Detroit concerned how many concessions to make to General Motors. This represented a structural reality, rather than being solely the result of elite preferences or pluralist politics. The municipal government ultimately used eminent domain to condemn and destroy an entire neighborhood. Meanwhile, no one seriously considered using eminent domain to condemn GM property in Detroit and seize it "for the public good." Why did this not occur? Again we confront fundamental political and economic structures. To begin with, the latter type of governmental seizure simply falls outside the present realm of acceptability as established by the dominant political culture in the United States. Beyond that, many local investors could have invested their money elsewhere, literally "freezing out" the economy of Detroit in retaliation. In addition, by withholding capital investments, the owners of capital outside the city would be capable of damaging the economies of both the state of Michigan and the entire United States, if necessary, until such "destabilizing" public policy was corrected.

ELITE THEORY

Elite theorists recognize a certain degree of competition between interest groups; however, they reach very different conclusions about just how open and fair it all is. While power does not always equate precisely with one's amount of power resources (e.g., a resource-laden businessman may not perceive a fundamental interest at stake in a given political decision and thus may not commit his resources to the fray), the two correlate often enough to allow the conclusion that those with the most political power resources generally will dominate governmental decisions.

Thus, a combination of resource-rich corporate elites and governmental officials, most drawn from the white upper stratas of society, will share many interests and work in unison to frame the political agenda in a way that will guarantee that their interests will be served. In addition, they are also capable of manipulating the mass public so that the latter group comes to see these elite interests as what are best for the community as a whole.[14]

Floyd Hunter studied Atlanta in the 1950s and concluded that some 40 such people dominated local politics, speculating that they made their major decisions in hotel rooms, on golf courses, etc.[15] Or, as another example, there is the long-standing rumor that the elites of Houston would meet in Suite 8F of the Lomar Hotel in order to shape the city's crucial governmental decisions.[16]

Although they go beyond the traditional pluralist-systems framework and recognize the significantly unequal distribution of political power, elite theorists continue to focus on the decisions of private and governmental elites. But what if underlying structures all but preordain the decisional results virtually regardless of who holds these positions? For example, in a competitive private enterprise environment, any head of General Motors, no matter how community-minded, will have to continue to look for locations that will reduce production costs. Or, any mayor of Detroit will have little choice but to do whatever is necessary to appease General Motors given the city's reliance on that corporation for its economic well-being.

Most elite theorists also seem reasonably comfortable with the pluralists' operational definition of political "interest groups." Addressing questions of structural bias directly requires some objective determination of peoples' interests, which is an analytical jump most social scientists are unwilling to make. And that brings us to "structural analysis," which allows for the possibility that economic, social, and political rules and relationships may shape the political outcome no matter who lobbies or who actually makes the political decisions.

MARXIAN THEORY

> In the social production of their life, men enter into definite relations . . . of production which correspond to a definite stage of development of their material productive forces. The sum total of these relations of production constitutes the economic structure of society, the real foundation, on which rises a legal and political superstructure and to which correspond definite forms of social consciousness.[17]

Karl Marx hypothesized that societal institutions such as the political system inevitably function to reinforce underlying economic class relationships. Thus if a society is organized under a capitalistic economic system—one in which a small owning class controls business capital and uses it first and foremost to attempt to make profits for itself while everyone else receives wages for working for the owners—the political system will function to help maintain the domination of the capitalist class over the subordinate mass of working people.

Marx's argument can be outlined in the following seven propositions:

1. The evolution and structure of any society arise from the dominant method of economic production, be it feudalistic, capitalistic, or socialistic. In other words, the historical development of a society's social and political relationships—its "superstructure"—reflects and reinforces the domination and subordination existing in the economy.
2. Production under capitalism is accomplished when the owners of the means of production engage workers in wage contracts. As a consequence, human labor becomes a commodity to be bought and sold in the marketplace. When owners sell the resulting products for more than they paid workers to produce

them, providing themselves with a return on invested capital, they are seen to be exploiting the workers by not allowing them to realize the full market value of their work.

3. Products are then distributed via the marketplace, according to the principle of supply and demand. Thus production comes to be determined by the potential profitability of any given product, and consumption is based on one's ability to pay and not necessarily by one's needs.

4. Capitalistic enterprises must continue to expand in order to survive in a competitive marketplace. This requires a relentless search for cheaper labor and materials, the production of as many potentially profitable items as possible, and the cultivation of every conceivable market for those products. Unless government intervenes to temper it, such competition favors the larger enterprises, contributes to the concentration of capital ownership, and proceeds without concern for the actual needs of society.

5. Owners and non-owners end up competing for scarce resources.

6. Paradoxes arise: resources are depleted; industrialization under capitalism has made people both interdependent and at the same time competitive with one another; a maldistribution of wealth and products leaves mansions at one end of town and slums at the other; division of labor and subordination in the workplace mutilate peoples' creative potential and leave them alienated from their work and thus from themselves.

7. The non-owning classes are increasingly likely to become more aware of their common plight, as well as more united and better organized; however, revolution does not occur immediately or automatically. Cultural, social, and political institutions and values in the society's superstructure continue to reflect and reinforce the maldistribution of wealth and power at the society's core; some examples are privately funded electoral campaigns and privately owned means of mass communication (the media) and beliefs that poverty results from one's own inadequacies, that human beings are naturally individualistic and greedy, or that blacks are genetically inferior.[18]

An analogy often used to help explain the relationship between capitalism's political and economic systems is that of a coiled spring. Think of a large and powerful spring being held down by the force of a person's hand. The spring symbolizes the inherent tension in the underlying economic class relations—workers against owners. If the repressing hand—symbolizing superstructural devices—begins to weaken, at some point the spring will be unleashed. That release would represent the class tensions being forcefully resolved as the working class throws off the yoke of the capitalist class.

Two very important premises are in operation here. Marx is suggesting, first of all, that a class structure is inevitable under capitalism. Specifically, not only will there be a small owning class and a large non-owning class, but also there will be societal barriers that all but preclude anyone from crossing those class lines. One is highly likely to remain in the class in which one is born, regardless of talent or hard work. Second, if this class structure exists, it will possess inherent conflict. By this he means that it is in the best interest of the members of the working class to control the means of production themselves, rather than to work for a small class of owners.

Should the workers become aware of this, political conflict will occur, and the political system may no longer be able to keep the workers from seizing a more proportionate share of control over the means of production.[19]

LIBERATION THEORY

But even Marx does not go far enough. For besides the political impact of economic structures such as the economic class system, there are other potentially significant underlying factors that also must be considered. Social structures such as racism or sexism cannot be ignored. Stokely Carmichael and Charles V. Hamilton (black liberation) or Catherine MacKinnon (women's liberation) are among those whose writings remind us that such structural barriers may well shape political outcomes, at least in part, independently of the economic arrangement.[20]

Whether it is the African-American liberation movement or the women's liberation movement, some fundamental concepts are the same. Each begins by noting that regardless of your economic position, your race or gender may limit your political influence. Prejudices imbedded in the dominant ideology, for instance, may predispose people to undervalue what you stand to contribute before you even enter the political arena. The subordinate positions that evolve, then, stem from that imbedded discrimination. Noting the difficulties racism poses for mainstream pluralist analysis, Diane Pinderhughes states,

> When political institutions handle racial issues, conventional rules go awry, individuals react irrationally, and constitutional rules are violated. Incremental frameworks adjudicate explosive, conflictual issues poorly. Thus black historical experience can not be explained by pluralist analysis nor will externally imposed racial status be eroded by incremental bargaining or decision making.[21]

Liberationists attempt not only to unveil and dismantle the external constraints imposed by at least portions of the dominant group, but also to seek to reduce the degree to which their own members have internalized the value structure which helps perpetuate their subordination. In other words, their own members may have come to believe some of the myths about their limitations. African Americans may have come to believe white myths about their own lack of ambition; or women may have accepted the patriarchal notion that men are better equipped to hold positions of power. Thus, liberationists will seek to raise the consciousness of both their own members and those in the dominating group in order to garner more respect from the larger society and to increase their own member's group identity and pride, as well as their self esteem. These goals can be accomplished, among other ways, by noting the historical accomplishments of group members, recognizing current member achievements, and both identifying and celebrating positive aspects of the group's culture.[22]

Focusing first on the black liberation movement, it is important to note that it has taken at least three rather distinct approaches. Charles V. Hamilton defines these as *constitutionalism*, *plural nationalism*, and *sovereign nationalism*. In the first, blacks have joined with liberal allies such as organized labor and civil libertarians in an attempt to attain those civil rights guaranteed to all citizens under the nation's constitution. Organizations such at the National Association for the Advancement of Colored People (NAACP) have led this drive. Meanwhile, plural nationalists have been less convinced that the dominant society will ever deliver on such promises and thus have opted for variations of a black nation within this nation. Instead of attempting to assimilate both politically and socially, these advocates of "black power" have argued for racial solidarity and increased black control of their own institutions of governance. The current Nation of Islam, under Minister Louis Farrakhan, generally advocates such an approach. Finally, sovereign nationalists have gone one step further and worked for an entirely separate African-American nation, whether on the African continent or someplace in the United States. Marcus Garvey and his Universal Negro Improvement Association is one of the better known of these more fully separatist movements.[23]

For black women, however, there is the need to address both racism and sexism. In terms of the latter, feminists were already battling for women's liberation at the time the nation was founded. In 1776, for instance, Abigail Adams noted that if women were not granted a reasonable share of the nation's governing power, "we are determined to foment a rebellion, and will not hold ourselves bound by any laws in which we have no voice or representation."[24] Yet, not unlike the black liberation movement, some feminists have abandoned this constitutionalist approach and pressed for more separatist solutions. While the National Organization for Women presses government for state-sponsored day care, abortion rights, and equal treatment in the work place, *radical feminists* such as Shulamith Firestone and Mary Daly call for women to free themselves from their traditional bonds to men.[25] Meanwhile, women from Sojourner Truth and Maria Stewart to Mary Church Terrell and Angela Davis provided an important black voice to the more general struggle for women's liberation, at times battling both racist and sexist structures simultaneously.[26]

AN ALTERNATIVE THEORETICAL APPROACH

At this point, it is important to return to the Eastonian model. If political analysis is to occur wholly within his original schema, with its inputs, outputs, and feedback, it will be difficult to consider underlying social and economic structures and their relationship to politics. Easton, however begrudgingly, limits his definition of a political system to the operation of the conversion mechanisms, and he proceeds to differentiate his political system from his political environment. Yet, Marx, for example, is claiming that the political system is intricately intertwined with the economic system, functioning primarily to reflect and reinforce an underlying economic class structure. And, the liberation theorists note similar constraints imposed by underlying social hierarchies.

Rather than simply ignoring those possibilities, "political environment" will be defined to include peoples' relations to both the productive apparatus and entrenched social structures. How much wealth does one own? What is one's occupation? What is one's social status? Is one discriminated against because of certain social traits? And so on. The answers to all such questions have potential political relevance.

A political system will be defined to include the entire political environment. This means that a political decision will be any decision that affects the allocation of value, and these political decisions will be weighed in light of various social and economic realities. Thus, in response to the queries posed above, it will indeed be appropriate to study a General Motors decision to increase its manufacturing abroad—a decision with serious implications for thousands of African American workers. And, we will probe why the federal government has never seriously considered reparations for the descendants of former slaves.

Therefore, anything with even remote potential relevance to the authoritative allocation of things of value in a society will be an appropriate subject of political analysis under this empirical framework. Politics simply cannot be separated from economic or social relations.

Easton's revised model is shown in Figure 2.2. The revision allows analysis of any authoritative decision or nondecision that significantly affects the black community, as well as analysis of possible structural impediments to effective black political input into those decisions.

THE POSTINDUSTRIAL POLITICAL ECONOMY

For a better understanding of the link between political, social, and economic systems in late twentieth-century America, it is important to analyze how the development of a postindustrial economy has affected American politics. In a private enterprise system in which economic change normally just happens rather than being governmentally planned, people soon resign themselves to riding the roller coaster of private economic decisions and changes. We will begin by examining some of the most basic private economic events that so profoundly have affected the evolution of the United States.

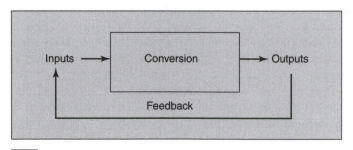

☐ Political system (which includes the political environment)

FIGURE 2.2
David Easton's Political System Model, Revised

Preindustrial Period

In the United States setting, the preindustrial period lasted until the early nineteenth century. The national economy remained predominantly agricultural during this era, with the bulk of the country's population living and working on small farms in the countryside.

The preindustrial economy, then, was based primarily on commerce. Yet without the process of incorporation to allow a number of individuals to pool their capital, most commercial ventures remained rather small. Nonetheless, trading was spurred by developments such as paper currency, insurance, credit facilities, and advertising. Soon these commercial businesses began to grow and diversify. By the late eighteenth century, people also began to manufacture goods for market purposes (e.g., shoes, wagons, etc.), with the work often being done in individual homes either on a contractual basis or sold in small shops run by the producers themselves. Nevertheless, despite the emergence of small-scale manufacturing, commerce remained the order of the day.

Prior to the Revolutionary War, however, commerce was tied to British mercantilism. Americans, for instance, were forced by law and encouraged by tax breaks to export large quantities of raw materials to Great Britain, and they in turn had to import many of Britain's finished products. In the process, Britain gained both economically and politically. Not only did the mother country secure a stable supply of raw materials (especially foodstuffs), as well as a significant market for its products, but also it was easier for the British to maintain political control if American life and trade were centered in a manageable number of places.

Industrial Period

As private entrepreneurs discovered ways to produce and distribute goods on a much larger scale, the prospects of massive profits fueled an economic revolution. From a predominantly agriculturally based society, we would soon be a primarily industrialized and urbanized one.

Howard Chudacoff has defined industrialization as the "coordinated development of economic specialization, mass mechanized production, mass consumption, and mass distribution of goods and services."[27] As the nineteenth century opened, it was clear that economic specialization already had begun, and that the consumption potential existed as well. In addition, the invention of steam power had helped to revolutionize commerce. The adoption of the governmental system established in the United States Constitution helped stabilize commerce by allowing for more trade regulation. Owners of wealth could now pool their resources through the process of incorporation, while at the same time allowing the legal liability of their joint businesses to be separate from that of the individual investors.[28] And, the development of a more formalized and extensive banking system further spurred the accumulation of capital by allowing venture capitalists to borrow and invest other people's money. All of this, ultimately combined with war-inflated profits and protective tariffs, helped to launch industrialization. Soon American manufacturers were mass producing steel, woolen goods, farm machinery, processed foods, and so on; and large cities were providing them with access to labor, materials, ancillary services, and local, intercity, and international markets.[29]

The development of canals and railroads also significantly expanded opportunities for industrialization, as they reduced reliance on existing waterways and thus allowed more resources and finished products to be shipped to and from more places and far more quickly. For example, there were 2,800 miles of railroad track in 1840, some 30,600 by 1860, and 254,000 in 1916. By 1916, trains carried more than three-quarters of all intercity freight (not to mention nearly all the intercity passengers).[30]

The number of people employed in manufacturing jobs increased by 127 percent between 1820 and 1840, as they left their farms or small town trades to work for a wage in the emerging factories.[31] And that was just the beginning, as those working for a wage increased from 7.7 million in 1849 to 48 million by 1929.[32] By the turn of the century, there were some 40,000 corporations, and manufacturing accounted for more than one-half of all commodities produced. Industrial giants were beginning to appear (e.g., United States Steel, General Electric, International Harvester, and American Telephone and Telegraph).

Postindustrial Period

After World War II, technological changes in transportation, communications, and automation had made it possible for increasingly centralized and internationally dominant American corporations to search the United States and abroad for more attractive industrial environments.[33] However, they did not immediately take advantage of these opportunities, striking instead a truce with American labor unions and continuing to make sizable profits by virtue of their international position of superiority.[34] As late as 1960, there was virtually no Third World production of manufactured goods for export; yet, in the face of mounting international competition from Japan and Western Europe in particular, the economic downturn of the mid–1970s seems to have set off what Barry Bluestone and Bennett Harrison have called the "hypermobility of [U.S.] capital."[35] Since that time, many United States–based multinational corporations have launched aggressive searches for production settings that provide cheaper and more abundant resources, less expensive and more pliant labor, and a high degree of political stability.[36] Furthermore, some of the last remaining legal impediments to such mobility have recently been removed by National Labor Relations Board (NLRB) and federal court decisions.[37]

The resulting shifts in capital have come in a variety of ways. The overt physical relocation of an entire plant is relatively rare. Less drastic and more common are such techniques as redirecting profits and depreciation allowances, gradually relocating pieces of physical capital, laying off workers while contracting out their work to cheaper plants, and, of course, shutdowns or bankruptcy.[38]

Regardless of the form they take, such private decisions have an enormous impact on individual citizens, neighborhoods, and the governments involved.

In terms of impact on individuals, take Chicago's South Works as an example. Of the thousands of workers laid off between 1978 and 1984, fully 50 percent found it

impossible to obtain adequate alternative employment. For black workers, that figure was 60 percent. Combining the unemployed and the reemployed, average household income dropped from $22,000 to $12,500; 11 percent were evicted from their
homes; one-quarter felt compelled to find cheaper residences; and an additional one-
third were behind on their mortgage or rent payments.[39]

Beyond losses of income, however, other individual and neighborhood problems
can be found in the wake of such layoffs. Neighborhoods deteriorate. Property values
plummet. Community networks gradually disintegrate, and intergroup tensions increase. Health worsens when medical insurance has been severed. Retirement plans
are curtailed. And suicide rates soar to 30 times the national average. Dr. M. Harvey
Brenner found that for every 1 percent increase in national unemployment, there is a
corresponding increase of 650 murders, 920 suicides, 4,000 admissions to state mental institutions, 3,300 admissions to state or federal prisons, and 37,000 deaths
(27,000 from cardiovascular problems); furthermore, child abuse is three times
greater in families where the breadwinner is unemployed. Brenner also found corresponding increases in automobile accidents, infant deaths, and cigarette smoking and
other forms of drug abuse. He concluded that if unemployment was classified by the
Public Health Service instead of the Labor Department, it would be considered a
"killer disease."[40]

In terms of politics, the increasing mobility of capital has significant implications
for government policy. For example, the nation, state, or locality is well aware that
departing firms will also take with them their share of the tax base, and the new unemployed will no longer be available as a tax source. This revenue loss has obvious
implications for the level of services that can continue to be offered to the population
as a whole, just when the need for social services will have increased as a result of the
layoffs. To remain solvent, therefore, the government would be forced either to raise
taxes or to cut service levels, both of which are likely to be politically unpopular and
to drive away even more taxpayers.

As a result of this understanding, consider the following syllogism:

1. In all political systems, a healthy economy must be government's top priority
   if jobs and taxes are to be generated.
2. Under capitalism, a healthy economy depends on the profitability of private
   corporations.
3. Therefore, governments in capitalist societies must do what is necessary to
   maintain the profitability of their private corporations.

Former New York City mayor Ed Koch put it this way: "The main job of municipal government is to create a climate in which private business can expand in the city
to provide jobs and profit."[41]

The requisites of corporate profitability become the ultimate parameters cir-
cumscribing the political decisions of any government operating in a postindustrial
capitalist economy. And even though many non-owners of capital may gain material
benefits from a healthy economy, the process precludes any serious challenge to
the basic structure of ownership and power. In the postindustrial era, if a government responds to the interests of non-owners by implementing fundamentally re-

distributive public policies, this drives private-sector capital to more favorable locations. Such interests, therefore, must generally be ignored or, at best, occasionally placated.[42]

Yet virtually ignoring all this potential power, the standard political science approach used in testing for the distribution of political power is to try to correlate group voting, campaign contributions, lobbying efforts, and the like with the decisions of public officials. The results have tended to be mixed. This has led to the general conclusion that the corporate elite—normally hypothesized to be the most likely candidate for the position of power elite—are often just another special-interest group, for they do not appear noticeably more likely to win contested decisions.[43] This approach ignores, however, the critical economic role of the large corporate interests and the political power it entails.

With the health of a government unit dependent on the profitability of its private corporations, the corporate elite seldom have to lift a political finger, for the priority of their interests is inherent in capitalism, especially postindustrial capitalism. As capital becomes increasingly more mobile, this corporate power will most likely increase accordingly.[44]

SUMMARY

Today's standard political science approach to public policy-making is to focus on the political behavior of individuals and groups within the existing political apparatus utilizing variants of systems theory. Thus, the political, economic, and social structures get separated, and political activity is analyzed in an empirical vacuum of sorts. The justification is contained in a theory called pluralism, which as traditionally applied presumes enough openness in the political system that the analyst need not be concerned about structural biases favoring some groups of people over others.

This chapter took a critical view of the empirical myopia inherent in that traditional theoretical approach. In its place, a different theoretical framework was suggested, integrating pluralist theory, systems theory, elite theory, Marxian theory and liberation theory. This integration allowed for a broader focus that encompassed potential links between politics and underlying economic, social, and political structures.

The result was a hybrid in which a society's political environment came to be defined to include economic and social structures; and the political system then was defined to include all of that political environment. With this expansion, interrelationships among economic, social, and political structures can now be analyzed as well. In particular, it will allow us to analyze whether social and economic structures bias the functioning and results of the political process from the very outset.

Finally, an overview of the postindustrial economy set the stage for the subsequent analysis of black politics, making clear the integral connection between political and economic structures, the limits of the traditional theoretical approach, and the need to synthesize the three theories discussed. The study that follows will consider African Americans as a political interest group with common objective interests, and it will attempt to test the political process for structural impediments to meaningful black participation and impact. Chapters 3 and 4 will describe blacks' so-cio-economic position in the American "political environment"; Chapter 5 will exam-ine governmental "outputs" that have contributed to that result; and Chapters 6 through 9 will attempt to explain such governmental priorities by looking for inher-ent biases in the nation's "conversion mechanisms"—its various political institutions.

NOTES

1. Kenneth Hoover, *The Elements of Social Scientific Thinking* (New York: St. Martin's Press, 1992), p. 34.
2. David B. Truman, *The Governmental Process: Political Interests and Public Opinion* (New York: Knopf, 1971), p. 33.
3. Ibid., p. 24.
4. For a defense of the position described in the text, see Robert Dahl's articles in the *American Political Science Review* (June 1958; June 1966). For other well-known samples of traditional pluralist thinking, see Arthur Bentley, *The Process of Government* (Chicago: University of Chicago Press, 1908); Earl Latham, "The Group Basis of Politics," *American Political Science Review* (June 1952); Robert Dahl, *Pluralist Democracy in the United States* (Chicago: Rand McNally, 1967): Truman, *The Governmental Process*; Nelson Polsby, *Community Power and Political Theory* (New Haven, Conn.: Yale University Press, 1980).

    For critical analysis of traditional pluralism, see Robert Dahl and Charles Lindbloom, *Politics, Economics, and Welfare* (Chicago: University of Chicago Press, 1976); Charles Lindbloom, *Politics and Markets* (New York: Basic Books, 1977); Robert Dahl, *Dilemmas of Pluralist Democracy* (New Haven, Conn.: Yale University Press, 1982); Michael Par-enti, "Power and Pluralism," *Journal of Politics* (August 1970); John Manley, "Neo-plural-ism," *American Political Science Review* (June 1983); Kenneth Dolbeare and Murray Edelman, *American Politics* (Lexington, Mass.: Heath, 1981), pp. 40–41.
5. Gabriel Almond and G. Bingham Powell, *Comparative Politics: A Developmental Ap-proach* (Boston: Little, Brown, 1966).
6. David Easton, *The Political System* (New York: Knopf, 1953); David Easton, *A Frame-work for Political Analysis* (Englewood Cliffs, N.J.: Prentice-Hall, 1965).
7. Ibid.
8. Peter Bachrach and Morton Baratz, "Two Faces of Power," *American Political Science Review* (December 1962); Peter Bachrach and Morton Baratz, "Decisions and Nonde-cisions: An Analytical Framework," *American Political Science Review* (September 1963).
9. Lester Thurow, *Zero-Sum Society* (New York: Basic Books, 1980); George Sternleib and James Hughes, *Income and Jobs: USA* (New Brunswick, N.J.: Center for Urban Policy Research, 1984).
10. Lester Milbraith and M. L. Goel, *Political Participation* (Chicago: Rand McNally, 1977), pp. 96–97. Also see Sidney Verba and Norman Nie, *Participation in America* (New York: Harper & Row, 1972), pt. 1 and chap. 20.
11. For example, see Milbraith and Goel, *Political Participation*, p. 97.
12. For a more detailed discussion, see the *National Commission on Urban Problems, Build-ing the American City* (New York: Praeger, 1969), p. 153; Martin Anderson, *The Federal Bulldozer* (Cambridge, Mass.: MIT Press, 1964); Bernard Frieden and Marshall Kaplan, *The Politics of Neglect* (Cambridge, Mass.: MIT Press, 1975); Susan Fainstein et al., *Re-*

structuring the City (White Plains, N.Y.: Longman, 1983); Nancy Kleniewski, "From Industrial to Corporate City: The Role of Urban Renewal," in William Tabb and Larry Sawers (eds.), *Marxism and the Metropolis* (New York: Oxford University Press, 1978); Dennis Judd, *The Politics of American Cities* (Boston: Little, Brown, 1984), pp. 273–274.

13. Quotes and information from *New York Times*, September 15, 1980; December 10, 1980.

14. For examples, see Floyd Hunter, *Community Power Structure* (Chapel Hill, N.C.: University of North Carolina Press, 1953); C. Wright Mills, *The Power Elite* (New York: Oxford, 1956); G. William Domhoff, *Who Rules America Now?* (New York: Simon and Schuster, 1983); G. William Domhoff, *Higher Circles: The Governing Class in America* (New York: Random House, 1971); Richard Hamilton, *Class and Politics in the United States* (New York: Wiley, 1972); G. William Domhoff, *The Bohemian Grove and Other Retreats: A Study in Ruling Class Cohesiveness* (New York: Harper and Row, 1975); Jack Newfield and Paul DuBrul, *The Permanent Government* (New York: Pilgrim Press, 1981); Thomas Dye, *Who's Running America?* (Englewood Cliffs, N.J.: Prentice-Hall, 1990).

15. Hunter, *Community Power Structure*.

16. See *New York Times*, October 30, 1989.

17. Karl Marx, preface to "A Contribution to the Critique of Political Economy," as quoted in Robert Tucker (ed.), *The Marx-Engels Reader* (New York: Norton, 1978), p. 4.

18. This outline was drawn from summaries presented in David Gordon (ed.), *Problems in Political Economy* (Lexington, Mass.: Heath, 1977), pp. 3–10; Kenneth Dolbeare and Patricia Dolbeare, *American Ideologies* (Boston: Houghton, Mifflin, 1976), chap. 8; and Tabb and Sawers, *Marxism and the Metropolis*, pp. 3–17. This synthesis originally appeared in Marcus Pohlmann, *Political Power in the Postindustrial City* (Millwood, N.Y.: Associated Faculties Press, 1986).

    For more detailed discussion of Marx's theory of the state and its relationship to capitalism's economic class system, see Karl Marx and Frederick Engels, *Articles from the Nene Rheinische*, tr. S. Rvazanskava, ed. B. Isaacs (Moscow: Progress Publishers, 1964); D. Easton and K. H. Guddat, *Writings of the Young Karl Marx on Philosophy and Society* (Garden City, N.Y.: Doubleday, 1967); Karl Marx, preface to "Contribution to the Critique," Karl Marx, *Die Grundrisse*, tr. Martin Nicolaus (Baltimore: Penguin, 1973); and Karl Marx and Frederick Engels, *The German Ideology*, tr. and ed. S. Rvazanskava (Moscow: Progress Publishers, 1964). For good secondary discussions of these views, see Ernest Mandel, *Marxist Economic Theory* (New York: Monthly Review Press, 1962); David McLellan, *The Thought of Karl Marx* (New York: Harper & Row, 1971) chaps. 4, 6; John McMurtry, *The Structure of Marx's World View* (Princeton, N.J.: Princeton University Press, 1978), chaps. 3, 4; M.C. Howard and J.E. King, *The Political Economy of Marx* (New York: Longman, 1985).

19. See Karl Marx, *The Poverty of Philosophy*, ed. Frederick Engels (Moscow: Progress Publishers, 1966); Karl Marx, *Grundrisse*; Karl Marx, *Das Kapital*, ed. Frederick Engels (Moscow: Progress Publishers, 1965), esp. vols. 1, 3, 4.

    For summaries of Marx's overall thinking, see McLellan, *The Thought of Karl Marx*; Tucker, *The Marx-Engels Reader*.

    For examples of this perspective as applied to the U.S. national government, see Donald Harris, "Black Ghetto as Internal Colony: A Theoretical Critique and Alternative Formulation," *The Review of Black Political Economy* (Summer 1972), pp. 3–33; Dolbeare and Edelman, *American Politics*; Edward Greenberg, *The American Political System* (Boston: Little, Brown, 1983); Ira Katznelson and Mark Kesselman, *The Politics of Power* (Orlando, Fla.: Harcourt Brace Jovanovich, 1987); John Berg, *Unequal Struggle: Class, Gender, Race, and Power in the U.S. Congress* (Boulder, Colo.: Westview Press, 1994); Michael Parenti, *Democracy for the Few* (New York: St. Martin's Press, 1995).

20. For example, see Stokely Carmichael and Charles V. Hamilton, *Black Power: The Politics of Liberation in America* (New York: Vintage Books, 1967); Michael Omi and Howard Winant, *Racial Formation in the United States* (New York: Routledge, 1989); Catherine MacKinnon, *Toward A Feminist Theory of the State* (Cambridge, Mass.: Harvard University Press, 1989); Vivien Gornick, *Essays in Feminism* (New York: Harper and Row, 1978).

For summary overviews of these conceptual frameworks, see Dolbeare and Dolbeare, *American Ideologies*, chaps. 10–11; Kenneth Hoover, *Ideology and Political Life* (Monterey, Cal.: Brooks/Cole Press, 1987), chap. 8; Terence Ball and Richard Dagger, *Political Ideologies and the Democratic Ideal* (New York: Harper Collins, 1991), chap. 8.

21. Diane Pinderhughes, *Race and Ethnicity in Chicago Politics: A Reexamination of Pluralist Theory* (Urbana: University of Illinois Press, 1987), p. 261.

22. For example, see William Grier and Price Cobb, *Black Rage* (New York: Basic Books, 1969); Marilyn Frye, ed., *The Politics of Reality* (Freedom, Cal.: The Crossings Press, 1983).

23. See Charles V. Hamilton, *The Black Experience in American Politics* (New York: Capricorn, 1973).

24. Quoted in Miriam Schneir, ed., *Feminism: The Essential Historical Writings* (New York: Vintage Books, 1972), p. 3. For a fuller early presentation, see Mary Wollstonecraft, *A Vindication of the Rights of Woman* (Philadelphia: Matthew Carey: 1974).

25. For example, see Shulamith Firestone, *The Dialectic of Sex: The Case for Feminist Revolution* (New York: Morrow, 1970); Mary Daly, *Pure Lust: Elemental Feminist Philosophy* (Boston: Beacon Press, 1984).

26. For example, see Marilyn Richardson, *Maria W. Stewart, America's First Black Woman Political Writer: Essays and Speeches* (Bloomington, Ind.: Indiana University, 1987); Mary Church Terrell, *A Colored Woman in a White World* (Washington, D.C.: Ransdell, 1940); Angela Davis, *Women, Culture, Politics* (New York: Random House, 1990). For a more general survey, see Gerda Lerner, ed., *Black Women in White America* (New York: Pantheon, 1972); Elizabeth Stanton, Susan B. Anthony, and Matilda Gage, *History of Woman Suffrage* (New York: Arno, 1969).

27. Howard Chudacoff, *The Evolution of American Urban Society* (Englewood Cliffs, N.J.: Prentice-Hall, 1981), p. 84.

28. See Paul Samuelson and William Nordhous, *Economics* (New York: McGraw-Hill, 1995), chap. 6.

29. For example, see Pred, *The Spatial Dynamics*; and Jeanne R. Lowe, *Cities in a Race With Time* (New York: Random House, 1967).

30. Sam Bass Warner, *The Urban Wilderness* (New York: Harper and Row, 1972), p. 89.

31. Charles Adrian and Charles Press, *Governing Urban America* (New York: McGraw-Hill, 1977), p. 8.

32. Alfred Watkins, *The Practice of Urban Economics* (Beverly Hills: Sage,1980), p. 204.

33. See Marcus Pohlmann, *Governing the Postindustrial City* (New York: Longman, 1993), chap. 3.

34. See Bennett Harrison and Barry Bluestone, *The Great U-Turn: Corporate Restructuring and the Polarizing of America* (New York: Basic Books, 1988).

35. Barry Bluestone and Bennett Harrison, *The Deindustrialization of America* (New York: Basic Books, 1982).

36. For a fuller discussion of this phenomenon, see ibid.; Bruce Stokes, "Multiple Allegiances," *National Journal*, November 11, 1989, pp. 2754–2758; William Goldsmith, "Bringing the Third World Home," in Larry Sawers and William Tabb (eds.),

Sunbelt/Snowbelt (New York: Oxford University Press, 1984); Michael Storper and Richard Walker, "The Spatial Division of Labor," in Sawers and Tabb, *Sunbelt/Snowbelt*, pp. 19–22; Raymond Vernon, *Storm Over the Multinationals* (Cambridge, Mass.: Harvard University Press, 1977); Ernest Mandel, *Late Capitalism* (London: New Left Books, 1975); F. Froebel et al., *The New International Division of Labour* (Cambridge: Cambridge University Press, 1980).

37. *New York Times*, January 25, 1984; April 11, 1984.

38. Bennett Harrison and Barry Bluestone, "The Incidence and Regulation of Plant Closings," in Sawers and Tabb, *Sun belt/Snowbelt*, pp. 368–402.

39. *New York Times*, October 31, 1984.

40. M. Harvey Brenner, *Estimating the Social Costs of National Economic Policy: Implications for Mental and Physical Health, and Criminal Aggression* (Washington, D.C.: GPO, 1976). Brenner found even larger increases when examining data from 1989–1990, as did Mary Merva and Richard Fowles when they analyzed 1976–1990 figures. See Memphis *Commercial Appeal*, October 16, 1992; and Holly Sklar, *Chaos or Community?: Seeking Solutions, Not Scapegoats for Bad Economics* (Boston: South End, 1995), p. 134.

    Also see Douglas Fraser et al., *Economic Dislocations: Plant Closings, Plant Relocations, and Plant Conversion*, report prepared for the U.S. Congress, Joint Economic Committee (Washington, D.C., 1979); articles by Duane Hagan, Dennis Ahlburg, and Morton Shapiro in *Hospital and Community Psychiatry* (May 1983); Bluestone and Harrison, *Deindustrialization of America*.

41. *New York Times*, March 4, 1978.

42. For example, see Harrison and Bluestone, *The Great U-Turn*; Pohlmann, *Governing the Postindustrial City*.

43. For a classic example, see Robert Dahl, *Who Governs?* (New Haven, Conn.: Yale University Press, 1961). For a comparable piece of empiricism built on entirely different ideological premises, see Lynda Ann Ewen, *Corporate Power and Urban Crisis in Detroit* (Princeton, N.J.: Princeton University Press, 1978).

44. For more discussion of this subject, see Kenneth Newton, "Feeble Governments and Private Power," in Louis Masotti and Robert Lineberry (eds.), *The New Urban Politics* (Cambridge, Mass.: Ballinger, 1976); Paul Peterson, *City Limits* (Chicago: University of Chicago Press, 1981); Watkins, *The Practice of Urban Economics*; Barry Bluestone and Bennett Harrison, *Capital and Communities* (Washington, D.C.: Progressive Alliance, 1980); William Tabb, "Economic Democracy and Regional Restructuring: An Internationalization Perspective," in Sawers and Tabb, *Sunbelt/Snowbelt*, pp. 403–416; Pohlmann, *Governing the Postindustrial City*.

PART TWO

BLACKS AND THE AMERICAN POLITICAL ECONOMY

Chapter 3

Blacks in American Society

Race will always be at the center of the American experience.

Michael Omi and Howard Winant[1]

Caught in a spider's web of individual and institutionalized racism, African Americans have pursued power for centuries in an attempt to become free and equal participants in the American political and economic systems. They have often disagreed among themselves about the most appropriate goals and strategies for dealing with specific, day-to-day crises, and some of that disagreement has been grounded in fundamentally different values and world views. But solidarity resides in one simple fact: they share the overriding experience of being black in the United States of America.[2]

To provide a historical context for an analysis of institutionalized racism in America, major events in black political history will be outlined, as will measures of political, social, and economic progress.

MAJOR EVENTS IN AFRICAN AMERICAN POLITICAL HISTORY

The following timeline denotes significant events in the history of African Americans once they arrived in the United States. It should facilitate quick review at the outset and easy reference while reading the chapters that follow.

Needless to say, however, the political efforts of numerous black individuals and organizations mark the years between these developments; for example, the work of the National Association for the Advancement of Colored People (NAACP) in pursuing school integration prior to the 1954 U.S. Supreme Court decision in *Brown v.*

Board of Education. The strengths and limits of those types of activities, both within and outside the formal political process, are discussed in detail in Chapters 6–10.

Beyond that, the outline certainly does not include all the major events in the political history of African Americans. It ignores the rich history experienced on the African continent prior to 1619, besides only scratching the surface of key events that occurred upon arrival in the United States. It is in no way intended as a substitute for a full black history text like John Hope Franklin's *From Slavery to Freedom.* Nonetheless, it does touch on a number of the most important political events as an overview for the purposes of this book.[3]

1619   The first 20 *black indentured servants* arrive (Jamestown, Virginia).

1637   The first American-based slave ship, *The Desire*, begins its ghoulish work of caging and transporting black Africans for sale in the New World.

1641   *Slavery* begins to be sanctioned by American law.

1688   About this time, German Mennonites join British-born residents and others in pressing for the *abolition* of slavery.

1776   The *Declaration of Independence* is proclaimed, but it is stripped of Jefferson's antislavery rhetoric by adamant representatives of southern states.

1776   The *Articles of Confederation* extend citizenship to "free inhabitants," although an effort to limit it to "free white inhabitants" is defeated. Nevertheless, a number of states require blacks to register upon entry and limit their stay, while the State Department issues "travelling papers" but not passports for those free blacks wishing to spend time abroad.

1777   Vermont is the first U.S. territory to *abolish slavery*, followed by the Northwest Territories a year later.

1787   The *United States Constitution* is drafted, with each slave to count as three-fifths of a person for the purpose of determining a state's taxation and representation. The specific criteria for citizenship are left to the states, and Delaware is the only state banning the importation of slaves at this time. However, Article 1, Section 9, does allow the Congress to outlaw U.S. participation in international slave trading after 1808.

1789   *Revolutionary America* finds 92 percent of its roughly 750,000 blacks still enslaved. Free blacks comprise about 2 percent of the national population, and very few of them are allowed to vote.

1793   *The Fugitive Slave Act*, upheld by the Supreme Court in 1842, requires the federal government to assist in returning runaway slaves.

1793   The *Tenth Amendment* lays the legal groundwork for claims of "states' rights."

1796   Richard Allen founds the African Methodist Episcopal Zion Church, as many free blacks begin to form *black churches*—a practice that expands considerably after the Civil War and leads to an infrastructure that has proved politically useful to the present day.

1800   *Slaves* number over one million, reside almost exclusively in the South, face rape and brutal physical punishments at the hands of their slave masters, and are bound by slave codes that strictly limit their rights (to own property, learn to read, etc.). Meanwhile, approximately 60,000 *free blacks* reside about equally in the North and South, and a few of them even own slaves. Nevertheless, their rights have been eroding since the Revolution, and many live in fear of being enslaved themselves as a result of kidnapping or judicial reversal of their status.

1807   Congress rules that there is to be *no further importation of slaves*, although this only increases the domestic slave trade, and the law is so loosely enforced that some 250,000 slaves are still imported after its passage.

1817   Although never very successful, the *American Colonization Society* works to assist blacks in returning to Africa. In part, it helps provide a safety valve for ridding the nation of black "troublemakers."

1819   With the addition of states such as Alabama, Louisiana, and Mississippi, cotton is now "king," and slave labor is in higher demand than ever. The *Missouri Compromise* represents a truce between slaveholders and abolitionists, setting up a boundary line to govern whether newly admitted states are to be slave or free.

1829   Free black David Walker begins publishing *Walker's Appeal*, which calls for blacks to rise up against slavery, using violence if necessary. Soon there are some 50 *black abolitionist groups*.

1831   As *slave resistance* escalates, Nat Turner leads a major slave revolt in Virginia. In just two days, approximately 70 slaves rise up and execute about that many whites. Other forms of resistance include arson, sabotage, work slowdowns, running away, and suicide.

1831   The first *National Negro Convention* convenes in Philadelphia.

1831   With the number of slaves topping the 2 million mark, white reformer William Lloyd Garrison uses his publication, *The Liberator*, to press for the immediate and total end of slavery. Calling primarily for nonviolent passive resistance, the *white abolition movement* is beginning to become a force. A variety of tactics are being pursued, including the formation of the Liberty party.

1834   As black presence increases in northern cities, racism flourishes. In one of the worst *racial riots* of the 1830s and 1840s, white mobs storm black neighborhoods in Philadelphia.

1838   *Frederick Douglass* escapes his enslavement, ultimately to become an important national leader and spokesperson for his race. Besides using his publication, *The North Star*, to press for an end to slavery and later an antilynching law, he also advises presidents and voluntarily recruits blacks for the Union army as the Civil War erupts.

1850   J.W. Loguen, Harriet Tubman, and others organize and operate the *Underground Railroad*, by this time helping roughly 1,000 blacks a year to escape slavery.

1850   The *Compromise of 1850* allows California to be admitted as a free state and ends slavery in Washington, D.C., in return for stricter enforcement of the Fugitive Slave Act. In response, the first serious talk of secession begins in Alabama, Georgia, Mississippi, and South Carolina.

1852   The novel *Uncle Tom's Cabin* dramatizes some of the abject cruelty imposed by slavery.

1853   *Sojourner Truth* rises to speak at the Fourth National Womens' Rights Convention. Posing the question "Ain't I a woman?" and fending off racist jeers, she speaks clearly of what it is to be black and female in the land of the free and the home of the brave.

1853   The National Council of Colored People is formed, conducting some of the many *black political conventions* prior to the Civil War.

1854   The *Kansas-Nebraska Act* nullifies the Missouri Compromise, allowing states to decide the slavery issue for themselves. This leads to some bloody intrastate warfare.

1855   Wilberforce University is founded as an extension of the African Methodist Episcopal Church, and it reflects the growing effort on the part of blacks to provide *education for black children*.

1857   In *Dred Scott v. Sanford*, the U.S. Supreme Court explicitly declares that the now nearly 4 million slaves are property of their masters and not citizens; thus they have no standing to sue, they have no constitutional rights, and their owners' possession of them is protected by the due process clause of the Fifth Amendment. The decision also challenges the federal government's right to regulate slavery in the "territories."

1859   *In the North*, only six states allow blacks to vote; black public schools are generally segregated and inferior; certain states preclude black testimony if a white is a party in the legal case; some states bar black immigration altogether; and so on.

1859   *John Brown* unsuccessfully leads 22 men in a raid on a federal arsenal in Harpers Ferry, Virginia. The goal was to use the captured weapons to help set off a general slave revolt across the South.

1860   The *Civil War* begins following the election of Abraham Lincoln and the Confederate attack on Fort Sumter.

1861   *Federal Confiscation Acts* allow for the expropriation and freeing of slaves, except in loyal border states where even the Fugitive Slave Act is to continue to be enforced.

1863   The *Emancipation Proclamation* is declared for all but the 800,000 slaves in loyal states, although no material reparations are ever forthcoming for the 246 years of forced labor.

1865   The *Thirteenth Amendment* constitutionally abolishes slavery.

1865   The *Freedmen's Bureau* is created in an attempt to provide former slaves with education, relief assistance, and resettlement, as well as to dispose of abandoned property.

1865   President *Abraham Lincoln is assassinated*.

1865   In Savannah, Georgia, General Sherman expropriates 30 miles of southern coastline and grants it to former slaves as an exclusive black settlement. Allotted 40 acres per family, some 40,000 blacks quickly move there. Within months, however, President Andrew Johnson has returned it all to its Confederate owners. Consequently, there and throughout the South, recently freed blacks find themselves *property-*

less and thus forced into virtual peonage at the hands of former slave masters.

1866   Reactionary *race riots* resume with a vengeance. In Memphis, a white rampage leaves 46 blacks and 2 white sympathizers dead, 5 black women raped, and 90 homes, 12 schools, and 2 churches burned.

1867   The Reconstruction Act evades beleaguered President Andrew Johnson and imposes *radical Reconstruction* on much of the South, disenfranchising the bulk of whites as state constitutions are rewritten. Governance is then left to blacks, anti-Confederate whites, and northern "carpetbaggers."

1867   The *Union League* serves as the southern arm of the Republican party.

1867   The Ku Klux Klan is born, one of a number of *violent reactionary white organizations*.

1868   The *Fourteenth Amendment* requires states to guarantee "equal protection" under their laws and to not deprive their citizens of life, liberty, or property without providing "due process of law."

1869   The *National Negro Labor Union* is formed, as blacks are generally excluded from the early white labor movement—a practice that would continue well into the twentieth century.

1870   The *Fifteenth Amendment* bars states from denying anyone the right to vote because of race.

1872   The *Amnesty Act* reinstates citizenship across the old Confederacy, except for the most prominent Confederate officials.

1874   The *Democratic party*, based in the South, wins control of the House of Representatives and makes significant gains in the Senate.

1875   A *Civil Rights Act* outlaws racial segregation in public accommodations and the military; however, it, along with other such legislation passed since 1866, is soon struck down by the U.S. Supreme Court.

1876   *Reconstruction officially ends*, as President Rutherford Hayes trades it for enough southern votes in the House to win an extremely close presidential election over Samuel Tilden. Northern troops will no longer remain in the South to protect the rights of former slaves, although that protection has been less than adequate for some time.

1880   The U.S. Supreme Court, in *Stander v. West Virginia*, declares all-white juries to be unconstitutional if written into state law or the result of overt discriminatory acts.

1884   The U.S. Supreme Court, in *Ex parte Yarborough*, affirms a federal law against interfering with a person's right to vote in federal elections.

1895   *Booker T. Washington*, in his Atlanta Exposition Address, lays out the philosophy that underlies his founding of Tuskegee Institute. Southern blacks were urged to "cast down their buckets where they were," remaining in the South and learning farm, mechanical, and domestic skills before worrying about equal political rights in the larger society.

1896   In *Plessy v. Ferguson*, the U.S. Supreme Court declares that legal separation of the races is not a violation of blacks' constitutional rights. "Separate but equal" is equal.

1900   By this time, all southern states have changed their laws and constitu-tions in order to create the *legal disenfranchisement and segregation* of blacks, 90 percent of whom still reside in the South. In terms of voting, a combination of grandfather clauses, literacy tests, poll taxes, all-white Democratic primaries, administrative discrimination, and outright vio-lence or threats thereof have succeeded in disenfranchising over 95 per-cent of all southern black voters.

1900   Some of the first *direct action* begins to appear as blacks boycott segre-gated streetcars in more than 25 cities over the following six years. Al-though peaceful by intent, some violent confrontations do occur.

1905   W. E. B. Du Bois, Monroe Trotter, and other black leaders organize the *Niagara Movement*, designed to press for equal rights and black solidar-ity. This movement gives rise to a number of black political conferences including a major one in Amenia, New York, in 1916.

1909   Growing out of the Niagara Movement, the *NAACP* is founded to press for black rights by means of lobbying and court cases. W. E. B. Du Bois edits its official publication, *The Crisis*.

1910   The *National Urban League* is created.

1914   Marcus Garvey founds the *Universal Negro Improvement Association* in Jamaica and soon brings it to the United States. It is grounded in the principles of black pride and a separatism that ultimately involves re-newed efforts to help blacks return to Africa.

1915   The U.S. Supreme Court, siding with the NAACP, declares the *grandfa-ther clause unconstitutional (Guinn and Beal v. United States)*. No longer is it to be more difficult for blacks to vote simply because their grandfathers were not registered.

1915   Some 3,600 blacks have been the victims of *lynch mobs* since 1884.

1915   Spawned by acts of violence, the mechanization of southern agricul-ture, and industrial job opportunities in the North, the first major wave of the *Great Migration* has begun, and migrating blacks are as-sisted in their adjustment by the National Urban League and a variety of black newspapers. By 1970, some 6.5 million blacks will have mi-grated to the North, resulting in half of the black population residing there.

1917   *Racial rioting* occurs in East St. Louis, and it is typical of such rioting at the time, with mobs of angry whites storming black ghettos in retaliation for an alleged incident.

1920   The *Nineteenth Amendment* legally enfranchises half the black popula-tion—women.

1921   An *antilynching bill* is finally introduced in the Congress, but it is stopped by a filibuster in the Senate.

1925   A. Philip Randolph founds the Brotherhood of Sleeping Car Porters and Maids, a *black labor union* created in the face of continuing racial dis-crimination on the part of white unions. Such segregation would persist for another three decades.

1929 The *Great Depression* hits blacks particularly hard, leaving them three to four times as likely as other Americans to be receiving public assistance. Yet they even face some discrimination in the relief lines.

1930 The *Black Muslim Movement* emerges in Detroit, later to rise to national prominence under the leadership of Elijah Muhammad and Malcolm X. Its goal is a self-sufficient black nation within the United States, emphasizing self-discipline, thrift, industriousness, pooled resources, and self-defense under Muslim religious beliefs.

1931 For the first of four times, a group of black youths—later to be called the *Scottsboro Boys*—are convicted of raping a white woman. Two of those convictions are ultimately overturned by the U.S. Supreme Court, including the 1932 decision of *Powell v. Alabama*, in which the Sixth Amendment's "right to counsel" was held to be required at the state level too.

1932 The U.S. Supreme Court strikes down *whites-only primary elections* in *Nixon v. Condon* and later in *Smith v. Allwright* (1944).

1934 The newly created Federal Housing Administration openly sanctions *racial segregation in housing* for its first 10 years of existence.

1936 The *shift of black voters* to the national Democratic party, first noticeable in 1928, is cemented as Franklin Roosevelt receives a majority of black votes.

1936 The *National Negro Congress* emerges as an umbrella organization for the civil rights struggle, which would include the formation of groups such as the Southern Conference for Human Welfare.

1941 Despite the beginning of U.S. involvement in World War II, A. Philip Randolph *threatens a huge, all-black march on Washington* to protest racial discrimination. He ultimately calls it off in return for the establishment of the Fair Employment Practices Commission, although that commission can only investigate and make recommendations concerning training and employment in government defense industries, and it all but disappears after the war.

1941 In *United States v. Classic*, the U.S. Supreme Court rules that the federal government can step in and regulate primary elections, as they are an "integral part" of the right to vote.

1942 The Congress of Racial Equality (*CORE*) is formed and is soon organizing freedom rides, sit-ins, boycotts, rent strikes, and other nonviolent direct actions as a way of challenging continuing racial discrimination.

1943 The Detroit riots are some of the most destructive of a series of *black ghetto revolts*, including a major one in Harlem in 1935.

1945 In *Screws v. United States*, the U.S. Supreme Court rules that a Georgia sheriff by the name of Screws could be tried in federal court for violating a black man's Fourteenth Amendment rights by taking his life without "due process of law." The man was beaten to death after being arrested for stealing a tire.

1948 The *Democratic party reaches out to blacks* with a series of moves, including President Truman's creation of a federal Commission on Civil

Rights, his executive order calling for "fair employment practices" in the federal government, and the desegregation of the military after decades of distinguished black service in separate regiments. In addition, the party adopts a civil rights plank at its presidential nominating convention, prompting a number of southern delegates to bolt and form the State's Rights party, nearly costing Truman the election.

1948   The U.S. Supreme Court, in *Shelley v. Kramer*, strikes down clauses in housing contracts that forbid resale of the property to blacks.

1954   In *Brown v. Board of Education*, the U.S. Supreme Court reverses its 1896 decision and strikes down "separate but equal" as "inherently unequal." (Unfortunately, the case would be brought again 32 years later as school segregation continued in Topeka.)

1955   Martin Luther King, Jr., helps organize the successful *Montgomery Bus Boycott*.

1956   The Federal Bureau of Investigation (FBI) launches its "counterintelligence program"—code name: *COINTELPRO*. Conducted until 1971, a major purpose is to disrupt allegedly "dangerous" black organizations ranging from the militant Black Panthers to the very moderate National Urban League.

1957   Out of King's Montgomery Improvement Association is formed the Southern Christian Leadership Council (*SCLC*) to continue to organize direct action against racial discrimination in the South.

1957   Congress passes the first major *Civil Rights Act* since 1875.

1957   Federal troops are sent to Little Rock, Arkansas, to assist in the *forceful desegregation* of its schools.

1960   Black students sit at a segregated lunch counter in Greensboro, North Carolina, touching off a wave of such *sit-ins* across the South. Ultimately, even their arrests and convictions are struck down by the U.S. Supreme Court.

1960   The Student Nonviolent Coordinating Committee (*SNCC*) is formed as the student arm of the SCLC, and it functions until ideological rifts tear it apart seven years later.

1961   NAACP founder *W. E. B. Du Bois*, now a member of the American Communist party, renounces his U.S. citizenship and moves to Ghana.

1961   *School segregation* persists, and South Carolina, Alabama, Georgia, Mississippi, and Louisiana still do not have a single integrated public school.

1961   Federal troops are dispatched to protect civil rights demonstrators engaged in *freedom rides* on interstate buses.

1962   Federalized National Guardsmen escort James Meredith as he becomes the first black student to enter the University of Mississippi. *School desegregation in the South* is beginning to develop momentum.

1963   Governor *George Wallace* stands defiantly "in the schoolhouse door" to prevent black students from enrolling at the University of Alabama.

1963   With more than 200,000 in attendance and capped by Martin Luther King's famous "I Have a Dream" speech, the *March on Washington* is probably the most dramatic of a number of nonviolent protest marches that have been occurring across the South and are beginning to appear in the North as well.

1963   As the world watches black churches being bombed and the dogs and fire hoses being turned on peaceful black protesters, President John Kennedy warns of *impending federal action*. Civil rights activist Medgar Evers is gunned down the day of that speech, and the president will join him within two months.

1964   The *Twenty-fourth Amendment* to the United States Constitution bans poll taxes in federal elections.

1964   The last and most comprehensive of the *Civil Rights Acts* is passed by Congress, directly involving the federal government in the enforcement of black civil rights, especially in the South.

1964   Martin Luther King, Jr. wins the *Nobel Peace Prize*.

1965   A large *ghetto revolt* erupts in the Watts section of Los Angeles, the worst racial unrest since 1943 and one of 164 such outbreaks to occur between 1962 and 1968. These revolts leave more than 100 people dead, thousands wounded, thousands more arrested, and hundreds of millions of dollars' worth of property damage.

1965   Congress passes the first of the *Voting Rights Acts*, involving the federal government even further in forcing stubborn states to allow blacks the right to vote.

1965   President Lyndon Baines Johnson declares a *War on Poverty*, which ultimately leads to the creation of a host of federal programs, including Head Start, VISTA, the Job Corps, and Legal Aid. He also creates the Council on Equal Opportunity.

1965   Black Muslim leader *Malcolm X*, articulate spokesperson for the black underclass, is assassinated.

1966   The term *black power* is coined by Stokely Carmichael and Charles V. Hamilton and is first spoken by Carmichael and CORE's Floyd McKissick. Black Power Conferences begin in Newark and spread to other large cities during the next two years.

1966   The *Black Panther party* emerges, in large part to defend black communities against racist violence. Militant *black workers' movements* are also developing, among them the League of Revolutionary Black Workers (Detroit), the Black Panther Caucus of the Fremont GM Plant (California), and the United Black Brotherhood (New Jersey).

1966   The U.S. Supreme Court's decision in *Harper v. Virginia Board of Elections* eliminates poll taxes in state elections as well.

1967   *Thurgood Marshall* becomes the first African American ever appointed to the United States Supreme Court.

1967   Cleveland's *Carl Stokes* becomes the first black mayor of a major United States city.

1968   *Martin Luther King, Jr.*, is assassinated.

1968   As federal troops guard the Capitol building from the rioting that has erupted following the King assassination, the Congress is inside passing the *Fair Housing Act*. It will bar racial discrimination in the sale or rental of private residences.

1968   Richard Nixon and George Wallace combined receive more than two thirds of the presidential vote, marking what now appears to be the beginning of the *end of New Deal electoral coalition*.

1968   A tent city is erected as part of the *Poor Peoples' March on Washington*; this protest is ultimately dispersed by police force.

1969   The Black Economic Development Conference writes a *Black Manifesto*, which calls for reparations among other things.

1971   In *Swann v. Charlotte* the U.S. Supreme Court rules that busing is a legitimate tool for fighting school segregation, although it is later limited to exclude busing across city-suburb boundaries.

1972   The first *National Black Political Convention* is held the same year that *Shirley Chisholm* becomes the first black candidate to mount a formidable campaign for the office of president of the United States.

1973   James Coleman, whose famous 1968 study helped justify the imposition of busing to improve black educational performance, now concludes that busing is failing because of the *"white flight"* it has helped to generate.

1974   In *San Antonio v. Rodriguez*, the U.S. Supreme Court determines that heavy reliance on neighborhood property taxes is not a discriminatory way to fund public schools, despite tremendous disparities in neighborhood wealth. Although a few individual states have found otherwise and introduced a more redistributive method of school funding, the Supreme Court decision still has serious implications for people living in low-income areas.

1978   *University of California v. Bakke* is the first of a series of Supreme Court decisions clarifying the scope of allowable "affirmative action." The court seems to be saying that race is a legitimate criterion to consider in admission, hiring, firing, and promotion decisions, but rigid quotas are not to be employed unless there is evidence of previous discrimination by that institution or a "clear state need" can be demonstrated. Later decisions will exempt legitimate seniority systems from such affirmative action.

1979   Jesse Jackson launches his *PUSH for Excellence*.

1980   The census confirms *black majorities in large cities* such as Baltimore, Detroit, Newark, and Washington, D.C., and impending majorities in Chicago, Cleveland, Memphis, Philadelphia, and St. Louis.

1980   *Ronald Reagan* is elected president of the United States, with major implications for the enforcement of civil rights laws. For example, not only does his administration all but cease to enforce affirmative action regulations, but it even argues against them in federal court.

1980   *Ghetto unrest* in Miami includes beatings, maimings, burning, looting, and sniper fire, leaving 18 dead, more than 200 seriously wounded, 750 arrested, and more than $100 million in property damage. Smaller incidents occur in Wichita, Chattanooga, and Orlando.

1981   Blacks and laborites join in a massive *March on Washington*, as they do again two years later.

1984   The U.S. Supreme Court, in *Grove City College v. Bell*, declares that the federal government cannot cut financial aid to an entire institution when only one of its branches has violated federal guidelines. The decision poses dilemmas for federal enforcement of a variety of civil rights provisions.

1986   In *Batson v. Kentucky*, the Supreme Court determines that prosecutors cannot use their preemptory challenges to exclude black jurists simply because they feel that blacks are less likely to convict other blacks.

1988   The Congress passes the *Civil Rights Restoration Act* over President Reagan's veto. Its primary purpose is to undo the damage done by the 1984 Grove City decision by allowing entire institutions to be denied federal assistance if any of their parts is found to be discriminating.

1989   Virginia's L. Douglas Wilder becomes the nation's first black governor.

1989   The *Richmond v. Croson* decision severely limits lower courts' ability to require affirmative action quotas on the basis of clear statistical evidence of prior discrimination.

1991   Congress passes another *Civil Rights Restoration Act*, this time addressing portions of eight Supreme Court opinions, most notably requiring employers to justify their job performance criteria if clear statistical evidence of job discrimination is found.

1991   The Supreme Court maintains its single black representative, as its most liberal justice, Thurgood Marshall, is replaced by its most conservative, *Clarence Thomas*, after heated confirmation hearings that came to focus on allegations of sexual harassment.

1992   Los Angeles police are videotaped beating black motorist *Rodney King*, and their subsequent acquittal sets off severe ghetto unrest in South Central Los Angeles.[4]

1993   In *Shaw v. Reno* the Supreme Court challenges the construction of predominantly black election districts as a method of countering years of past discrimination in the drawing of such district lines.

1995   In a highly sensationalized and racially divisive criminal trial before a national television audience, former football great, *O.J. Simpson*, is ultimately acquitted of murdering his wife and a male friend of hers, both of whom happened to be white. (Two years later, he would be held liable for the same event in civil court.)

1995   Louis Farrakhan leads a "Million Man March" on Washington.

MEASURES OF PROGRESS

Emancipation elevated [the black man] only to the position of semi-dependent man, not to that of an equal and independent being.

Harold Cruise[5]

After more than two centuries, the institution of slavery was finally abolished by a civil war. Nonetheless, the legacies of slavery endured. Integration and equal justice met opposition at every turn, and it was nearly another century before even the legal foundations of this discrimination began to be dismantled. Decades of struggle for civil rights did, however, finally begin to succeed following World War II. The right to register and vote came to be enforced directly by the U.S. Department of Justice. Schools were forcibly desegregated. Housing discrimination was outlawed. And not only were employers barred from discriminating openly, but many were compelled to search for qualified black applicants when positions were available. Yet such legal gains have scarcely begun to eradicate centuries of racism and subsequent racial inequities.

Education

An area of marked gains has been education. For example, whereas more than 80 percent of all African Americans were completely illiterate in 1870, very few are today.[6] In addition, racial differentials in school years completed and college enrollment have been reduced considerably. The black high school dropout rate, for instance, has been reduced and is now only slightly higher than the corresponding white rate.[7]

Nevertheless, such progress masks some serious underlying problems. Due largely to the property tax method of public school funding, the historically poorer black community is often left with inferior elementary and secondary educational institutions—clearly a form of institutionalized racism.[8] Test scores indicate that although they are in school and passing from grade to grade, black students are often modal years behind their white counterparts in both reading and writing skills and actual knowledge.[9] Black adult illiteracy is nearly three times that of white adults; more than 40 percent of all black teenagers have serious problems in terms of literacy; and although the gap has narrowed slightly in recent years, average black SAT scores remain some 100 points behind those of whites in both the verbal and mathematics categories.[10] At the college level, the proportion of blacks attending seems to have peaked in the mid–1970s and remains more than 25 percent lower than for whites; a third of all black college students are in two-year schools; and blacks are still badly underrepresented in graduate and professional programs.[11] By the mid–1990s, for instance, some 82 percent of white adults had graduated from high school, while the figure was only 73 percent for blacks; and whites were nearly twice as likely to have graduated from college.[12]

Economics

Although college-educated blacks and younger two-parent black families are now doing nearly as well as or better than comparable whites in terms of the economic indicators discussed herein, the story is not nearly as encouraging for the large majority of black males who are not fortunate enough to have a college education.[13] Black women, by contrast, have begun to approach income parity with white women, but both are in a clearly inferior economic position vis-a-vis men, especially white men.[14] Furthermore, these inferior positions are reinforced by institutions such as seniority systems, not to mention the "old boy networks" used for passing along job opportunities. The results can be seen in the black population's absolute and relative levels of skills, unemployment, income, and poverty.

Occupation.   Whereas a sizable majority of whites held either white-collar or blue-collar jobs in the still largely industrial economy of 1940, only about one-third of all blacks did. Instead, most blacks were employed on farms or at the lower levels of the service sector, often as household workers.[15] These jobs reflected a bygone era.

Much has changed since, but the occupational position of African Americans has continued to lag. The economy has gone from labor-intensive to capital-intensive manufacturing and thus from manufacturing-related employment to jobs in the professions, technical fields, and services. Whites have made that transition: some three-quarters of them now hold either *white-collar* [16] or service positions. Blacks have not: as they hold proportionately more *blue-collar* [17] jobs, and a disproportionate share of their white-collar employment is in sales and clerical positions rather than in management, technical trades, or the professions.[18] In many ways, African Americans seem to be locked at least a generation or more behind whites, left to assume the jobs whites discard, left to be laid off at disproportionate rates, left on the back of the bus of economic change.[19]

Consistent with all of that and despite some impressive gains, blacks continue to find themselves underrepresented in the managerial and professional ranks. By recent accounts, although blacks comprised some 13 percent of the U.S. population, only 6 percent of accountants, auditors, and managers were black, 5 percent of computer systems analysts and scientists; 4 percent of media editors and reporters, engineers, college professors, and physicians, and 3 percent or less of architects, lawyers, judges, realtors, and dentists.[20] But even that does not tell the whole story, for they are even further underrepresented in the nation's top private-sector institutions. For example, blacks make up only 2 percent of the lawyers in the top 100 law firms.[21] No Fortune 500 company is headed by a black, while blacks comprise only 3 percent of the senior managers.[22] Beyond that, approximately one-half of all black managers and professionals are employed directly or indirectly by government[23]—an especially precarious position in times of government retrenchment.[24]

Unemployment.   Prior to 1970, blacks were more likely than whites to work outside the home, making their higher unemployment rates even more noteworthy.[25] That black unemployment rate became approximately the same as the white unemployment rate in the 1930s and 1940s; however, economic changes and the return of white soldiers from the war left blacks behind once again following World War II. Since that time, the black unemployment rate has been roughly twice the white rate across virtually every major category of educational attainment and occupation. And as nationwide unemployment stagnated at recession levels after the mid–1970s, African Americans fell even further behind.[26] The figure has been far worse yet for the burgeoning number of black teenagers, whose official unemployment rate has consistently exceeded 30 percent, and most recently has hovered near 40 percent, more than twice the comparable rate for white teens.[27]

Estimates also indicate that as many as one-half of all black males are presently unemployed, no longer looking for work, or unaccounted for, and that number appears to be increasing.[28] The situation is better for black women, but many remain locked in clerical and domestic positions that offer minimal wages and virtually no skill development, benefits, or advancement.[29] In addition, because black workers are disproportionately likely to be the most recently hired in their particular firm, they are more vulnerable to the economic system's periodic slumps. This reality is made worse by the fact that when they are laid off, black workers are significantly less likely than their white counterparts to be rehired by their former employers.[30] Consequently, it takes a very high rate of substantive economic growth if subemployed and discouraged black workers are to be successfully pulled back into the working fold.[31]

Income.   While official black unemployment seems to have become fixed at roughly twice the white rate, black family income has remained at only slightly more than one-half of white family income during this same period. As a group, black families made 51 percent of what white families took home in 1947. That figure grew to 63 percent by the end of the reform-oriented 1960s, but had slipped back to 55 percent by the 1990s.[32]

Granted, there has been some segmentation within the black community. Black high school dropouts, for instance, have been falling farther behind their white counterparts,[33] while, by contrast, blacks as a group have done much better. For example, whereas black men earned 45 percent of what their white counterparts earned in 1939, they were making some 75 percent by 1990s, while black women were earning approximately 90 percent of what their white counterparts were making[34]—a trend that seems directly related to their increased number of school years completed.[35] In addition, as would be expected, comparable gains can be seen in the median incomes of black working couples. Taking a family income of $40,128 (1993 dollars) to represent the middle class, the proportion of blacks in that group has increased 12-fold over the past 40 years, and relatively speaking, whereas whites were more than five times as likely to be in that category in the early 1950s, they are only about twice as likely to be there today.[36] Even more impressive is the fact that college-educated black couples are presently outearning comparable white couples.[37]

Having noted those gains, however, it also should be remembered that African Americans remain heavily overrepresented at the bottom of the income pyramid, and badly underrepresented at the very top. For example, black households are more than three times as likely to earn less than $5,000 per year, and more than twice as likely to earn between $5,000 and $10,000. Meanwhile, at the pinnacle, whites are more than three times as likely to have incomes exceeding $100,000, and more than twice as likely to be earning between $50,000 and $100,000. Blacks reach parity with whites at around the $20,000 bracket, clearly at the low end of the working class.[38]

There are also a number of reasons not to be overly optimistic about any apparent trend toward black *middle-classification*.[39] To begin with, there is still ample evidence of racism in the job market. For example, African-American men with professional degrees earn only 80 percent of the income made by their white counterparts holding the same degrees in the same job classifications.[40]

In addition, it is important to note that federal affirmative action policies clearly helped accelerate this progress, and the Republican party's battle to turn the clock back on such efforts has made it clear that what the federal government giveth, the federal government can cease to provide. That same principle underlies concern about the fact that so many blacks work for government, where professional positions, antidiscrimination laws, and affirmative action have been more available.[41] Yet such government employment, a major avenue for acquiring middle-income positions, is also very vulnerable to a national change of mood.[42]

Beyond that, other sizable barriers are developing to inhibit the advancement of those who have remained underprivileged despite these new, somewhat tenuous opportunities. To begin with, whereas more than three-quarters of all African Americans lived in the rural South at the dawn of the twentieth century, nearly half now reside in the more urbanized North. This leaves a sizable share of the black population residing in declining industrial cities, lacking the kind of economic opportunities that the proliferation of labor-intensive manufacturing jobs at union wage rates afforded their underskilled white predecessors.[43]

There is also the sociologically complex issue of family disintegration, a nationwide dilemma even more problematic in the African-American community. Whereas 28 percent of black families were headed by a female in 1969, for example, that figure jumped to 40 percent by 1978 and more than 45 percent by the 1990s.[44] Today, nearly one-half of all black children are growing up in fatherless households, a reality compounded by the close correlation between female-headed households and poverty.[45]

Finally, because wages have stagnated nationwide since the growth days of the 1960s, where blacks are making gains, they have been gaining a fairer share of a shrinking pie.[46] Thus, although the education gap has narrowed quite a bit, reducing the income gap between certain segments of the black and white populations, the absolute economic position of African Americans has not actually improved since the 1960s.[47] Black median family income, for example, has not grown at all in real dollars since 1969.[48] Then, on top of that, even the relative gains have pretty much ground to a halt since 1979, as the nature of the national economy has changed and federal efforts have diminished.[49]

Poverty.   In 1994, a family of four was considered poor if their combined income was less than $15,141 in current dollars. As for the extent of poverty in the African-American community, both the absolute and relative figures have improved, but they are still discouraging.

Whereas 55 percent of all blacks were officially poor in 1959, a growing economy and a federal War on Poverty helped reduce that figure to 32 percent by 1969. There is also increasing agreement that this figure has been reduced even further if transfers in kind such as food stamps, Medicaid, and housing subsidies are included as income. However, this trend seems to have stopped, if not begun to reverse; approximately three out of every ten African Americans were still categorized as poor in the mid–1990s, and approximately one-half of all black children found themselves in families living below the poverty line.[50]

Compared to whites, blacks have remained three times more likely to be poor since World War II, and that is true for black children as well.[51] The median income of poor black families is also some 20 percent lower than for poor white families.[52] Consequently, not only are blacks disproportionately poor, but also the black poor are a good bit poorer than their white counterparts.

Overall, then, African Americans are disproportionately likely to be poor. But even more telling is the fact that the black population as a whole is no longer making absolute gains in their poverty status and has not made any relative ones in the entire postwar period.

Housing

Using occupied living units lacking some or all plumbing as an indicator of substandard housing, one can see that blacks have made some progress in recent years but still remain well behind their white counterparts. In 1940, for example, some three-quarters of all black housing fell into that category—twice the white average. Fifty years later, less than 6 percent of all black housing fit that description, but that was still more than three times the white average.[53] Thus their absolute position improved considerably, but they fell farther behind relative to whites. In addition, approximately one in five black children continued to live in substandard housing, while African Americans also comprised nearly half of all Americans who died in fires each year.[54]

Health

In the context of the economic inequalities discussed above, blacks remain twice as likely as whites to lack health insurance;[55] they tend to receive less treatment when hospitalized;[56] and they have a more difficult time collecting disability benefits.[57] Thus, although causality is difficult to pinpoint, there are numerous racial disparities in the nation's various health indices. In the cases of infant and maternal mortality, for instance, although these have been reduced considerably as medicine has advanced in the course of the twentieth century, black rates remain more than two times higher than white rates, and that gap has actually grown considerably over the last 50 years.[58] A disgrace by international standards, one in six black children do not live to see their first birthdays.[59] There is also a sizable black-white differential in rates of contracting tuberculosis, cancer, and a number of other diseases; and the black mortality rate for most diseases is considerably higher, especially for hypertension among black males.[60] Lastly, although life expectancy has increased faster for blacks in the twentieth century, it still lags well behind white life expectancy—some ten years behind for black males; the average newborn black male can scarcely expect to reach 65 years of age.[61] The *New England Journal of Medicine* notes that a black man in Harlem has less chance of seeing his sixty-fifth birthday than does a man in Bangladesh.[62]

Pollution

At least part of these health problems appears related to pollution exposure. For example, the large majority of hazardous waste dumps are located near predominantly black neighborhoods.[63] The Commission for Racial Justice found three out of five African Americans living in communities with relatively uncontrolled toxic waste sites; and, because blacks tend to live in older housing with a greater likelihood of lead in the paint and plumbing, some one-half of all black children under the age of three had lead levels in their blood exceeding the Centers for Disease Control's safety standards when tested.[64] In addition, it appears that lax governmental enforcement of environmental laws has contributed to increased exposure.[65]

Crime

Another major health risk is victimization by violent crime. Blacks are two to three times more likely than whites to be victims of rape, robbery, or assault,[66] and they are seven times more likely to be murdered.[67] One in ten African Americans were victims of a violent crime in 1992.[68] One in 21 black males will be murdered, with murder the most common cause of death for black males between the ages of 15 and 24.[69]

War

Lastly, blacks are also more likely to serve as cannon fodder in the nation's wars. For example, nearly one-third of all Army troops serving the United States in the Gulf War were black.[70] Prior to that, 23 percent of the soldiers killed in the Vietnam War were black, nearly 13,000 young black men—more than double the ratio of blacks to the population in general.[71]

Overall, then, there has been some progress in a number of these areas. This is particularly true today for well-educated blacks. Nonetheless, the United States of America continues to harbor considerable racial inequality, and much of the progress in wiping out the vestiges of slavery appears to have dissipated of late. In particular, recent years have witnessed a relaxation of efforts such as busing and affirmative action designed specifically to address institutionalized racism.

Institutionalized racism has taken many forms. The concept of neighborhood schools, for example, does not appear racist on its face. Students attending schools in the neighborhoods in which they live, and those schools being funded by assessing the parents and neighbors of those children, would appear to be a racially neutral policy. However, if years of racial discrimination have seriously constrained where most blacks are likely to live, neighborhoods will remain segregated, as will their schools. On top of that, years of racial discrimination have also left blacks in some of the poorest neighborhoods in town; there are fewer taxable assets in those areas and consequently fewer tax dollars with which to fund their schools. Thus recognizing that a dogged allegiance to the neighborhood school concept would only help perpetuate long-existing inequalities, the practice of busing was implemented to try to break the grip of this institutionalized racism. Yet the belief in equal opportunity—a truly fair marathon race—has apparently not been enough to create a strong national commitment to desegregating schools on the basis of race and class.

Or consider seniority rules for promotion and retention. Once again, such rules appear racially neutral on their face. The longer a person has worked for a particular employer, the more benefits and protection he or she accrues. But after facing years of overt and covert discrimination, much of it effectively sanctioned by law, blacks are just beginning to have legally protected access to many previously unreachable positions. Nevertheless, seniority rules require that the last hired be the first fired. Consequently, it is very difficult to advance in an economy that experiences periodic slumps. To break that bottleneck, affirmative action was legally established. Yet the

1980s witnessed the chief law enforcement agent in the country, Attorney General Edward Meese, arguing that such practices discriminated against whites with more seniority, and similar arguments were being made by William Bradford Reynolds, head of the Civil Rights Division of the Justice Department.

 None of this is surprising, however, when one turns to the public opinion polls. Blacks and whites seem to be seeing two very different realities.

PERCEPTIONS OF PROGRESS

Perceptions of these trends and developments vary considerably across the American population. Particularly striking are the differing perceptions of whites and blacks. Here are some typical polling results from recent years.[72]

Are blacks as well off or better off than the average white?
      Whites: 58% yes   Blacks: 23% yes[73]

Are blacks generally discriminated against in getting a quality education?
      Whites: 11% yes   Blacks: 37% yes[74]

Compared with whites, blacks have equal or greater educational opportunity?
      Whites: 83% yes   Blacks: 56% yes[75]

Is there a need for any more busing?
      Whites: 17% yes   Blacks: 60% yes[76]

Do blacks receive equal treatment in the justice system?
      Whites: 61% yes   Blacks: 20% yes[77]

Are blacks generally discriminated against in getting decent housing?
      Whites: 20% yes   Blacks: 52% yes[78]

Have job opportunities for blacks improved in the past 5 years?
      Whites: 64% yes   Blacks: 39% yes[79]

Compared with whites, blacks have equal or greater job opportunity?
      Whites: 60% yes   Blacks: 33% yes[80]

Compared with whites, blacks have equal or greater opportunity for promotion to supervisory or managerial jobs?
      Whites: 71% yes   Blacks: 44% yes[81]

Should "every possible effort" be made to help minorities?
      Whites: 25% yes   Blacks: 61% yes[82]

Do you believe that where there has been job discrimination in the past, preference in hiring or promotion should be given to blacks?
      Whites: 28% yes   Blacks: 66% yes[83]

Has the United States gone "too far" in pushing equal rights?
      Whites: 51% yes   Blacks: 26% yes[84]

The majority of the white population seems to see quite different black circumstances than the large majority of blacks who are actually living in them. Thus, although there is certainly no denying some important gains, many more appear to exist primarily in the minds of white people.

PREJUDICE AND RACISM TODAY

To finish setting the context, it is important to assess contemporary levels and trends in white prejudice and racism. To do that, however, it is first essential to review previously discussed definitions of those terms. For the purposes of this analysis, individual prejudice is defined as prejudging people on the basis of a group to which they belong rather than on their individual merits. Individual racism involves adding discriminatory actions to those prejudicial beliefs. Thus, believing blacks to be inferior workers is prejudice, but refusing to hire a black applicant on the basis of that prejudgment is racism.

White Prejudice

Over the course of recent years, the University of Chicago's National Opinion Research Center asked the following questions to a cross-section of American whites and obtained the *yes* responses indicated:[85]

Do you think there should be laws against marriages between blacks and whites?
   1974: 34%   1985: 26%   1994:15%

If your party nominated a black for President, would you vote for him if he were qualified for the job?
   1974: 78%   1985: 79%   1994: 84%

Or, Burns Roper asked whites: *Do you prefer having no blacks in your neighborhood:*[86]
   1978: 28% yes   1990: 21% yes

Meanwhile, white Americans also agreed with the following statements as indicated:[87]

Blacks are inferior to white people.
   1963: 31%   1978: 15%

Blacks care less for the family than whites.
   1963: 31%   1978:18%

Blacks have less native intelligence than whites.
   1963: 39%   1978:25%   1991: 31%

Blacks breed crime.
   1963: 35%   1978: 29%

Blacks are more violent than whites.
   1967: 42%   1978: 34%   1991: 54%

Blacks want to live off the handout.
    1963: 41%   1978: 36%   1991: 59%

Blacks tend to have less ambition than whites.
    1963: 66%   1978: 49%   1991: 47%

In an absolute sense, it is disturbing that a majority of whites still believe that blacks "want to live off the handout" and are "more violent" than whites, while a virtual majority of whites still believe that blacks have "less ambition."

Nevertheless, the trends in polling results are clear. Whites are becoming less prejudiced. Or are they? At very least it is clear that whites have become less willing to display their racial prejudices publicly. However, it has also become less "socially acceptable" to admit them. One is left to wonder just how many whites, safe behind closed doors and in like-minded company, still hold many of the views of this rather candid *middle American:*

> The thing that bothers me about the Negro people is this: they're not like the rest of us. . . . If you ask me, they're slow, that's what l think. They're out for a good time. They want things made easy for them. . . . They actually want relief. They think they're entitled to it! . . . They want all they can get for free. They don't really like to work. They do work, alot of them, l know. But it's against their wish l believe. They seem to have the idea that they're entitled to something from the rest of us. That's the big thing with them: they've suffered and we should cry our heads off and give them the country, lock, stock, and barrel because we've been bad to them. . . . Pity is for the weak, my grandfather used to tell us kids that. But your niggers, alot of them want pity; and they get it. . . . People are afraid to speak out, say certain things, because they know they'll be called "prejudiced," and in fact they are not at all that; they are letting the chips fall where they do.[88]

That view was expressed in the latter 1960s. Not too surprisingly, such sentiments were still around in the 1990s. Mike Royko relates the following letter from a Memphis man.

> Most blacks are immoral and they have an illegitimate kid every year. They don't know who the fathers are and couldn't care less, just so they get their welfare and food stamps and most buy crack and starve their kids. . . It is the black heritage. They come from violent people. The head hunters, cannibals, savages and the Mau Mau tribes."[89]

Racism

> Prejudice is a form of mental illness. . . . Unfortunately it is often a form of mania that results in great hurt to the subjects of its madness. Most people with other forms of mental illness are dangerous only to themselves. Prejudice is different. Its primary symptom is hatred of others, and those who are hated are at high risk of being hurt.[90]

Underlying prejudicial beliefs are quite readily apparent in a host of white literature, including *The Races of Men* by Robert Know, *The Inequality of the Human Race* by J. A. De Gobineau, *Types of Mankind* by J. C. Nott and G. R. Glidden, *The Origin of Races* by Carleton Coon, and more recently in the writings of William Shockley, Arthur Jensen, and Dinesh D'Souza.[91] When those beliefs have gotten translated into action, this phenomenon has proved even more dangerous. Focusing on the American experience, this has included the imposition of slavery, the brutal crushing of Na-

tive Americans, and a variety of imperialistic foreign policies in China, the Philip-
pines, and other nonwhite developing countries.[92]

In the United States, racist acts have continued to plague African Americans for
more than a century beyond the Emancipation Proclamation. They have included
the less visible institutionalized and individual practices that helped create and perpetuate the caste system reflected in the socioeconomic data presented above.[93] Yet,
for reasons that have included intimidation and vengeance, they have often been
quite overt and highly visible, for example, night riders, lynchings, and the storming
of black neighborhoods by white mobs. Although somewhat less frequent, these blatantly violent acts continue and in many ways simply represent the tip of a very large
iceberg of prejudice and racism.[94]

Mobile, Alabama (March 1981)

A black man, accused of killing a white police officer, is set free because of a mistrial. Two
admitted Klan members seek revenge by randomly abducting a 19-year-old black youth.
They beat him with a tree limb as he pleads for his life, and when he is finally beaten into
submission, they strangle him, cut his throat three times, tie a rope around his neck, and
hang him from a tree to demonstrate "Klan strength in Alabama."[95]

Steubenville, Ohio (April 1981)

Another 19-year-old black male is murdered in an apparent act of racist violence. In this
instance, the youth is shot in the head for allegedly dating a white girl.[96]

Detroit, Michigan (May 1981)

For over two years a black woman is harassed by a group of whites for choosing to live in
a predominantly white neighborhood. They throw baseballs through her windows and
paint KKK insignias on her garage. Then three whites, aged 19–23, throw a pipe bomb
through her bathroom window. When she attempts to throw it back outside, it explodes
and leaves her maimed.[97]

Baltimore, Maryland (June 1981)

A black Morgan State University student gets into an argument with a white woman employee where he works. Following the incident, he is attacked by eight whites who beat
him with pool sticks. He suffers a broken left arm, contusions, and swelling of the brain.[98]

Brooklyn, New York (June 1982)

Three middle-aged black transit workers finish their shift at midnight. They stop to buy a
snack on their way home. When emerging from the store, they are harassed by a number
of whites. When their car fails to start, the group of whites swells. Amid chants of "niggers
go home," the car is smashed with blunt objects. Two of the transit workers flee, but the
driver is pulled from the car and beaten to death.[99]

Boston, Massachusetts (June 1982)

A black woman moves into the white neighborhood of Dorchester. As she walks to and
from her home, she endures racial taunts, stone throwing, and hard shoves. Finally, a
gasoline bomb is hurled through her window.[100]

Chicago, Illinois (November 1984)

A black family moves into an all-white enclave called The Island, next to Cicero and Oak
Park. Approximately a dozen whites, armed with guns, spend an entire night hurling
bricks, bottles, pipes, and tire irons through their windows. Unable to call police because
phone service has not yet been installed, the family huddles behind their furniture until
they are able to flee down a back alley at daybreak. Throughout the nightlong attack, no

neighbors came to their rescue, while police cars apparently cruised past on three differ-ent occasions and did nothing to stop it.[101]

Philadelphia, Pennsylvania (November 1985)

A black family and an interracial couple move into the predominantly white area of Elm-wood. Vandalism begins almost immediately, and it culminates in 400 whites congregat-ing outside their homes and chanting for them to leave.[102]

Queens, New York (December 1986)

At approximately midnight, faced with near freezing temperatures, three black men leave their stalled car to seek shelter. As they walk through the all-white Howard Beach area, three white youths shout racial slurs at them, words are exchanged, and gestures are ex-changed shortly thereafter at a pizza parlor. The white youths then proceed to a party and round up eight friends, saying, "There's some niggers in the pizza parlor—let's go kill them." Armed with bats and sticks, they chase and beat the black men; one flees onto a highway and is struck dead by a car.[103]

Peekskill, New York (November 1987)

A black insurance adjuster is confronted by three bat- and pipe-wielding white men on the outskirts of town. He is chased until he is finally rescued by a passing motorist. Five days later, his family's home is firebombed.[104]

Staten Island, New York (June 1988)

A 24-year-old black man is walking home from his job at a Burger King restaurant when a carload of white youths begin shouting racial slurs. The youths then get out of the car, cir-cle the black man, and beat him with a stick and a baseball bat until he is able to break free and run for safety in a nearby pizza shop.[105]

Portland, Oregon (November 1988)

A 27-year-old Ethiopian is beaten to death after being dropped off in front of his apart-ment in southeast Portland. His white assailant, who testified in court that he killed the young man "because of his race," hit him so hard with a baseball bat that the bat split.[106]

Brooklyn, New York (August 1989)

A 16-year-old black youth, having come to all-white Bensonhurst with three black friends to check out a used car he had seen advertised in the paper, found himself surrounded by some 20–30 jeering whites armed with baseball bats and a gun. This group mistakenly thought that the black youths had come to attend a party being hosted by a white woman, and in the course of the confrontation shot and killed the 16-year-old. Standing on a nearby corner shortly thereafter, a white teen stated that "black people don't belong here. This is our neighborhood."[107]

Chicago, Illinois (August 1989)

Two 14-year-old black youths were picked up by police for a curfew violation, taunted, slapped, and then dropped off in the middle of the hostile all-white Bridgeport neighbor-hood, where they were chased down and beaten by an angry group of young whites.[108]

Atlantic Beach, New York (June 1991)

A 17-year-old black man was severely beaten by a group of white youths for talking with a white girl at a graduation party. The youths beat him from behind with sticks and a base-ball bat, leaving him in critical condition with blood clots on his brain.[109]

Brooklyn, New York (October 1991)

A 17-year-old black teen stopped at a Flatbush grocery to buy a soda, when he was attacked by as many as 20 white youths. The victim was knocked unconscious with a baseball bat and cut with a razor, while his friends were pulled from the car and the car nearly demolished.[110]

Philadelphia, Pennsylvania (September 1994)

When a deaf black mother and her two teenaged children moved into an all-white neighborhood, their house was fire-bombed, windows smashed, and she and her son were ultimately severely beaten with metal baseball bats when a group of whites broke into the house.[111]

Lubbock, Texas (October 1994)

Three white men cruise the streets of Lubbock randomly shooting black pedestrians with a shotgun in an attempt to start what they describe as a "race war." In the course of less than one-half hour, they manage to kill one man and seriously injure two others.[112]

Fayetteville, North Carolina (December 1995)

Three U.S. Army paratroopers sought to earn their neo-nazi "spider web tatoos" (indicating that the wearer has killed a black person) by randomly choosing and assassinating a middle-aged black couple out walking in their neighborhood.[113]

Westhampton Beach, New York (May 1996)

A black youth is nearly beaten to death in a nightclub parking lot by a white man wielding a heavy steel bar, while a white off-duty New York City police officer held the youth's friends at bay with a handgun.[114]

Chicago, Illinois (March 1997)

A 13-year old black youth is nearly beaten to death by three white teens when he rode his bicycle too close to the boundary of the all-white Bridgeport area.[115]

SUMMARY

The political history of African Americans has led to some impressive victories in the Congress and the U.S. Supreme Court, but inequities persist. Trends in black educational attainment, occupations, unemployment, income, poverty, housing conditions, health conditions, neighborhood pollution, crime rates, and casualties in the nation's wars are not encouraging overall. In addition, blacks and whites perceive black progress differently, particularly as the divisive policies of busing and affirmative action have been employed to attack forms of institutionalized discrimination. Prejudice and racism clearly linger in the white community.

NOTES

1. Michael Omi and Howard Winant, *Racial Formation in the United States* (New York: Routledge, 1989), p. 6. Also see Gunnar Mydral, *An American Dilemma* (New York: Harper, 1944).
2. For indications of the fundamental underlying unity of black public opinion, see Diana Colasanto and Linda Williams, "The Changing Dynamics of Race and Class," *Public*

Opinion 9 (January-February 1987), p. 53; Frank Gilliam, Jr., "Black America: Divided by Class?" *Public Opinion* 8 (February-March 1986); Michael Dawson, *Behind the Mule: Race and Class in African American Politics* (Princeton, N.J.: Princeton University Press, 1994).

3. The ensuing historical timeline has benefitted significantly from reference sources such as Robert Allen, *Black Awakening in Capitalist America: An Analytical History* (Garden City, N.Y.: Anchor/Doubleday, 1969); Albert Blaustein and Robert Zangrando, *Civil Rights and the Black American* (New York: Washington Square Press, 1968); John Hope Franklin, *From Slavery to Freedom: A History of Negro Americans* (New York: Knopf, 1980); Charles V. Hamilton, *The Black Experience in American Politics* (New York: Putnam, 1973); Manning Marable, *How Capitalism Underdeveloped Black America* (Boston: South End Press, 1983); Howard Zinn, *A People's History of the United States* (New York: Harper & Row, 1980).

4. The officers were subsequently retried in federal court and convicted of civil rights violations.

5. Harold Cruse, *Rebellion or Revolution?* (New York: Morrow, 1968), pp. 76–77.

6. Department of Commerce, Bureau of the Census, *Statistical Abstracts of the United States* (Washington, D.C.: GPO, various years); Department of Commerce, Bureau of the Census, Current Population Reports, P–23, No. 80, *The Social and Economic Status of the Black Population in the United States: A Historical Overview*, 1790-1978 (Washington, D.C.: GPO, 1978); Department of Education, Office of Civil Rights, periodic reports (Washington, D.C.: GPO, various years); American Council of Education Reports (Washington, D.C.: American Council of Education, various years).

7. Department of Commerce, Bureau of the Census, *The Black Population in the United States* (Washington, D.C.: GPO, 1995); Department of Commerce, Bureau of the Census, *Characteristics of the Black Population* (Washington, D.C.: GPO, 1995); Department of Commerce, Bureau of the Census, Current Population Reports, P–20, No. 476, *Educational Attainment in the United States: March 1993 and 1992* (Washington, D.C.: GPO, 1994). In 1996, the *New York Times* reported that the comparative dropout rates were 13.5% for blacks and 12.6% for whites. See *New York Times*, September 6, 1996.

8. For example, see Andrew Hacker, *Two Nations: Black and White, Separate, Hostile, Unequal* (New York: Scribner's, 1992), p. 173; E.D. Hirsch, Jr., "Good Genes, Bad Schools," *New York Times*, October 29, 1994; Ibid., June 4, 1997.

9. James Jennings, "Blacks, Politics, and the Human Service Crisis," in James Jennings, *Race, Politics, and Economic Development* (New York: Verso, 1992), p. 87; *New York Times*, September 19,1985; January 10, 1990. There is some indication, however, that black verbal SAT scores as well as black performance on other national standardized tests actually have been improving more quickly than they have been for whites of late. Nevertheless, black students still remain well behind. See *New York Times*, November 18, 1996.

10. Department of Commerce, *Statistical Abstracts*; Department of Commerce, *The Social and Economic Status*; Department of Education, Office of Civil Rights, periodic reports; American Council of Education Reports; Jennings, *Race, Politics, and Economic Development*, p. 87.

11. Department of Commerce, *Educational Attainment; The Chronicle of Higher Education*, August 28, 1991; Department of Commerce, *Statistical Abstracts*; Department of Commerce, *The Social and Economic Status*; Department of Education, Office of Civil Rights, periodic reports; American Council of Education Reports; *New York Times*, June 8, 1990; January 18, 1994; April 26, 1996;*The Crisis*, May/June 1995, p. 24. It also should be noted that black females comprise 60 percent of those blacks attending college.

12. Department of Commerce, *Educational Attainment* ; Department of Commerce, *The Black Population in the United States*; Lee Sigelman and Susan Welch, *Black Americans' Views of Racial Inequality: The Dream Deferred* (New York: Cambridge University Press, 1991), p. 23; Morton Kondracke, "The Two Black Americas," *The New Republic*, February 6, 1989, p. 18.

13. Department of Commerce, Bureau of the Census, *Money Income of Families: Aggregate, Mean and Per Capita, by Family Characteristics* (Washington, D.C.: GPO, various years); *New York Times*, June 2, 1981; August 7, 1985; Erik Wright, "Race, Class, and Income Inequality," *American Journal of Sociology* (May 1978); Robert Smith and Richard Seltzer, *Race, Class, and Culture* (Albany N.Y.: State University of New York Press, 1992), pp. 34–39.

14. Department of Commerce, *Statistical Abstracts*; Department of Commerce, *Social and Economic Status*; Equal Employment Opportunity Commission Reports (Washington, D.C.: GPO, various years); Department of Labor, Bureau of Labor Statistics, annual reports (Washington, D.C.: GPO, various years); Department of Commerce, Bureau of the Census, *The Black Population in the United States* (Washington, D.C.: GPO, 1995); Department of Commerce, Bureau of the Census, *Characteristics of the Black Population* (Washington, D.C.: GPO, 1995).

15. Ibid.; David Swinton, "Racial Parity Under Laissez-Faire: An Impossible Dream," in Winston Van Horne, ed., *Race: Twentieth Century Dilemmas–Twenty-First Century Prognoses* (Milwaukee: University of Wisconsin Institute on Race and Ethnicity, 1989), pp. 212–217.

16. "White collar" employment includes professional and technical workers, managers, administrators, sales workers, and clerical workers.

17. "Blue collar" positions include craft and kindred workers, operatives, and nonfarm laborers.

18. Department of Commerce, *Statistical Abstracts*; Department of Commerce, *Social and Economic Status*; Equal Employment Opportunity Commission Reports (Washington, D.C.: GPO, various years); Department of Labor, Bureau of Labor Statistics, *Labor Force Statistics Derived From the Current Population Survey: A Databook* (Washington, D.C.: GPO, 1994), Table B–18; Department of Labor, Bureau of Labor Statistics, *Employment and Earnings*, January 1994 (Washington, D.C.: GPO, 1994); Swinton, "Racial Parity Under Laissez-Faire, pp. 212–217; Reynolds Farley, "The Common Destiny of Blacks and Whites," in Herbert Hill and James Jones, eds., *Race in America: The Struggle for Equality* (Madison: University of Wisconsin Press, 1993), 207–209; Alphonso Pinkney, *The Myth of Black Progress* (New York: Cambridge University Press, 1984), pp. 90–91.

19. For example, see Jared Bernstein, "Where's the Payoff?" (Washington, D.C.: Economic Policy Institute, 1995); Timothy Bates, *Banking on Black Enterprise* (Washington, D.C.: Joint Center for Political and Economic Studies, 1993), pp. 7–8.

20. Department of Commerce, *Statistical Abstracts*; Department of Commerce, *Social and Economic Status*; Equal Employment Opportunity Commission Reports (Washington, D.C.: GPO, various years); Department of Labor, Bureau of Labor Statistics, annual reports (Washington, D.C.: GPO, various years); Hacker, *Two Nations*, pp. 111–115; *New York Times*, June 8, 1990; March 16, 1995; *Crisis*, May/June, 1995, p. 24.

21. George Davis and Glegg Watson, *Black Life in Corporate America: Swimming in the Mainstream* (Garden City, N.Y.: Doubleday, 1985); *New York Times*, July 14,1987.

22. Ibid.; *New York Times*, November 23, 1995.

23. For example, see Kondracke, "The Two Black Americas," p. 18.

24. Pinkney, *The Myth of Black Progress* ; Jonathan Krasno, "Black Employment in the Public and Private Sectors," unpublished paper presented at the annual meeting of the American Political Science Association, Chicago, September 3–6, 1992; *New York Times*, December 10, 1991; Smith and Seltzer, *Race, Class, and Culture* , pp. 29–31; Martin

Carnoy, *Faded Dreams: The Politics and Economics of Race in America* (New York: Cambridge University Press, 1994), pp. 162–163.

25. For example, see Swinton, "Racial Parity Under Laissez-Faire," pp. 224–225; Lucius Barker and Mack Jones, *Americans and the American Political System* (Englewood Cliffs, N.J.: Prentice Hall, 1994), p. 37–39.

26. For example, see Department of Labor, Bureau of Labor Statistics, *Handbook of Labor Statistics* (Washington,D.C.: GPO, various years); Hacker, *Two Nations*, p. 103; Paula McClain and Joseph Stewart, *"Can We All Get Along?": Racial and Ethnic Minorities in American Politics* (Boulder, Colo.: Westview Press, 1995), p. 30; Sigelman and Welch, *Black Americans' Views of Racial Inequality*, pp. 24–26; Smith and Seltzer, *Race, Class, and Culture*, pp. 22–24.

27. Department of Labor, *Labor Force Statistics Derived From the Current Population Survey*, Table A–28; Department of Labor, *Employment and Earnings*, A. Rees, "An Essay on Youth Joblessness," *Journal of Economic Literature* 24 (1986), pp. 613–628; Keith Jennings, "Understanding the Persistent Crisis of Black Youth Unemployment," in Jennings, *Race, Politics, and Economic Development*; Pinkney, *The Myth of Black Progress*, pp. 116–133; Smith and Richard Seltzer, *Race, Class, and Culture*, pp. 25–28; Dawson, *Behind the Mule*, pp. 25–27.

28. *New York Times*, May 11,1984; Sigelman and Welch, *Black Americans' Views of Racial Inequality*, pp. 26–27; Billy Tidwell, ed.,*The State of Black America* (New York: NUL, 1994), pp. 220–225; Farley, "The Common Destiny of Blacks and Whites," pp. 209–211; Dawson, *Behind the Mule*, p. 24.

29. Department of Commerce, *Statistical Abstracts*; Department of Commerce, *Social and Economic Status*; Equal Employment Opportunity Commission Reports (Washington, D.C.: GPO, various years); Department of Labor, Bureau of Labor Statistics, annual reports (Washington, D.C.: GPO, various years); Wade Nobles, "Public Policy and the African American Family," in Van Horne, *Race*, p. 105.

30. For example, see *Wall Street Journal*, September 14, 1993, p. A1; Richard Freeman, "Employment and Earnings of Disadvantaged Young Men in a Labor Shortage Economy," in Christopher Jencks and Paul Peterson, eds., *The Urban Underclass* (Washington, D.C.: Brookings Institute, 1991)); Jennings, "Blacks, Politics, and the Human Service Crisis," p. 87.

31. For example, see *Wall Street Journal*, March 8, 1990, p. A1; Mack Jones, "The Black Underclass as Systemic Phenomenon," in James Jennings, *Race, Politics, and Economic Development* (New York: Verso, 1992).

32. Department of Commerce, *Statistical Abstracts*, 1995, p. 476. The figure is 59% when individuals or households are compared. Also see Department of Commerce, *Money Income of Families*; *Christian Science Monitor*, October 18, 1988; McClain and Stewart, *"Can We All Get Along?"* p. 30; *New York Times*, September 16, 1994; Barker and Jones, *Americans and the American Political System*, pp. 34–35.

33. *New York Times*, June 2, 1981; August 9, 1991; William Darity and Samuel Myers, "Racial Earnings Inequality into the 21st Century," in Billy Tidwell, ed., *The State of Black America 1992* (New York: National Urban League, 1992), p. 133.

34. James D. Smith and Finis Welch, *Closing the Gap* (Santa Monica, Calif.: Rand, 1986); Hacker, *Two Nations*, p. 100; Andrew Sum, Neal Fogg, and Robert Taggart, "Withered Dreams: The Decline in the Economic Fortunes of Young Non-College Educated Male Adults and Their Families," (paper prepared for the William T. Grant Foundation Commission on Family, Work, and Citizenship, 1988), p. 43, B–2; Billy Tidwell, ed., *The State of Black America 1993* (New York: National Urban League, 1993); p. 197; Department of Commerce, Bureau of the Census, *The Black Population in the United States* (Washing-

ton, D.C.: GPO, 1995); Department of Commerce, Bureau of the Census, *Characteristics of the Black Population* (Washington, D.C.: GPO, 1995).

35. For example, see Hacker, *Two Nations*, pp. 95–96.
36. Ibid.; National Urban League, *The State of Black America*, 1987 (New York: National Urban League, 1987); Sigelman and Welch, *Black Americans' Views of Racial Inequality*, pp. 30–31; Barker and Jones, *Americans and the American Political System*, pp. 35–36.
37. *New York Times*, October, 31, 1995. Meanwhile, black female-headed households make scarcely more than 60% of their white counterparts. See Department of Commerce, Bureau of the Census, *Current Population Series*, P–60, 1990.
38. Department of Commerce, Bureau of the Census, Current Population Reports, Series P60–188, *Income, Poverty, and Valuation of Noncash Benefits: 1993*, Table G (Washington, D.C.: GPO, 1995).
39. For an interesting analysis of this general subject, see Melvin Oliver and Thomas Shapiro, *Black Wealth/White Wealth* (New York: Routledge, 1995), especially chap. 5.
40. For example, see *New York Times*, November 23, 1995.
41. Department of Commerce, *Statistical Abstracts*; Department of Commerce, *Social and Economic Status*; Equal Employment Opportunity Commission Reports (Washington, D.C.: GPO, various years); Department of Labor, Bureau of Labor Statistics, annual reports (Washington, D.C.: GPO, various years). Richard McGahey, "Industrial Policy," *Review of Black Political Economy* (Summer-Fall 1984), pp. 85–96; Memphis *Commercial Appeal*, June 22, 1987, p. B4; Barker and Jones, *Americans and the American Political System*, p. 37; Smith and Seltzer, *Race, Class, and Culture, p. 20*.
42. *New York Times*, July 14, 1987.
43. For example, see Peter Passell, "Blacks' Setbacks By Association," *New York Times*, August 28, 1991, p. C2; Smith and Seltzer, *Race, Class, and Culture*, p. 22.
44. For example, see Billy Tidwell, ed.,*The State of Black America* (New York: NUL, 1994), p. 232.
45. Department of Commerce, *Statistical Abstracts*; Department of Commerce, *Social and Economic Status*; *New York Times*, May 11, 1984; January 26, 1987; William J. Wilson, *The Truly Disadvantaged* (Chicago: University of Chicago Press, 1987).
46. For example, see Department of Commerce, Bureau of the Census, "Black Population in the United States," (Washington, D.C., GPO, March 1994); Carnoy, *Faded Dreams*, pp. 17–18.
47. For example, see Carnoy, *Faded Dreams*, pp. 72–73.
48. Department of Commerce, Bureau of the Census, *Statistical Abstracts of the United States* (Washington, D.C.: GPO, various years); Department of Commerce, Bureau of the Census, Current Population Reports, P–23, No. 80, *The Social and Economic Status of the Black Population in the United States: A Historical Overview*, 1790-1978 (Washington, D.C.: GPO, 1978).
49. Department of Commerce, Bureau of the Census, *The Black Population in the United States* (Washington, D.C.: GPO, 1995); Department of Commerce, Bureau of the Census, *Characteristics of the Black Population* (Washington, D.C.: GPO, 1995); Carnoy, *Faded Dreams*, pp. 120–122; Tidwell, *The State of Black America 1993*, pp. 158–164.
50. Department of Commerce, *Income, Poverty, and Valuation of Noncash Benefits: 1993*, Tables K and 20; Department of Commerce, *Statistical Abstracts;* Cynthia Rexroat, *The Declining Economic Status of Black Children* (Washington, D.C.: Joint Center for Political and Economic Studies, 1994).
51. Department of Commerce, Bureau of the Census, *Statistical Abstracts of the United States* (Washington, D.C.: GPO, 1949–1995).
52. National Urban League, *State of Black America*, pp. 53–56,135.

53. Department of Commerce, *Statistical Abstracts*; Department of Commerce, *Social and Economic Status*.

54. Jennings, "Blacks, Politics, and the Human Service Crisis," p. 87.

55. For example see *New York Times*, September 16, 1993. Also see GAO study cited in Robert Smith, *Racism in the Post–Civil Rights Era: Now You see It, Now You Don't* (Albany: State University of New York Press, 1995), p. 74.

56. See *New York Times*, January 13, 1989; March 18, 1992; August 26, 1993; April 20, 1994; September 12, 1996.

57. See *New York Times*, May 11, 1992.

58. Department of Health and Human Services, National Center for Health Statistics, *Advance Report of Final Mortality Statistics 1991* (Washington, D.C.: GPO, 1991), p. 11. Also see Smith, *Racism in the Post-Civil Rights Era*, p. 69; *New York Times*, July 10, 1995.

59. Ibid.; *New York Times*, November 29, 1990; March 27, 1992; January 26, 1998.

60. Department of Health and Human Services, National Center for Health Statistics; Vincent Navarro, *Dangerous to Your Health* (New York: Monthly Review Press, 1993); Smith, *Racism in the Post-Civil Rights Era*, pp. 70–71; *New York Times*, February 6, 1991; December 17, 1991; August 26, 1993; January 26, 1998.

61. Department of Health and Human Services, National Center for Health Statistics; Smith, *Racism in the Post-Civil Rights Era*, p. 69; *New York Times*, May 6, 1990.

62. See *New York Times*, December 24, 1990. For a general discussion of recent data and governmental policies, see Robert Hahn, "The State of Federal Health Statistics on Racial and Ethnic Groups," *Journal of the American Medical Association*, 267 (January 8, 1992), pp. 268–271; Leith Mullings, "Inequality and African-American Health Status: Policies and Prospects," in Van Horne, *Race*, pp. 154–182.

63. *New York Times*, December 28, 1983; April 16, 1987; Robert Bullard, *Confronting Environmental Racism: Voices from the Grassroots* (Boston: South End, 1993); Robert Bullard, ed., *Unequal Protection: Environmental Justice and Communities of Color* (San Francisco: Sierra Club, 1994). For case studies see Andrew Hurley, *Environmental Inequalities: Class, Race, and Industrial Pollution in Gary, Indiana, 1945–1980* (Chapel Hill: University of North Carolina Press, 1995); Mark Rose, "NAACP Fumin' Over Rubber Plant Emissions in West Texas," *Crisis*, February/March, 1994, p. 24; Peter Marks, "Issues of Race, Justice, and Pollution Trouble the Residents of an L.I. Town," *New York Times*, November 12, 1994.

64. See *Public Citizen*, September/October 1990, p. 16.

65. See Bullard, *Unequal Protection: Environmental Justice and Communities of Color*.

66. Department of Justice, Bureau of Justice Statistics, *Crime Victimization in the United States* (Washington, D.C.: GPO, various years); *New York Times*, April 23, 1990; Hacker, *Two Nations*, p. 183.

67. National Center for Health Statistics, *Vital Statistics of the United States: Volume II-Mortality*, Table 1–22 and *Final Mortality Monthly Vital Statistics: 1992* (Advance Report), Table 1–25 (Washington, D.C.: GPO, 1994).

68. Department of Justice, Bureau of Justice Statistics, *Crime Victimization in the United States* (Washington, D.C.: GPO, 1993).

69. *New York Times*, December 7, 1990; March 17, 1991; Jennifer Hochschild, *Facing Up to the American Dream* (Princeton, N.J.: Princeton University, 1995), p. 202; National Association for the Advancement of Colored People (NAACP), *The Crisis* (March 1986), p. 26.

70. See *New York Times*, January 25, 1991.

71. Department of Defense figures.

72. Besides the polls cited below, also see Howard Schuman et al., *Racial Attitudes in America* (Cambridge, Mass.: Harvard University Press, 1985); Dawson, *Behind the Mule*, ch. 3;

Sigelman and Welch, *Black Americans' Views of Racial Inequality*; Donald Kinder and Lynn Sanders, *Divided by Color: Racial Attitudes and Democratic Ideals* (Chicago: University of Chicago Press, 1996).

73. 1995 poll by the *Washington Post*.
74. 1989 poll by ABC News/*Washington Post*.
75. Gallup Poll, 1991.
76. 1981 poll conducted by George Gallup.
77. 1988 poll by Lou Harris and Media General-Associated Press.
78. 1989 poll by ABC News/*Washington Post*.
79. 1991 poll in *Time*, May 27, 1991, p. 21.
80. *Los Angeles Times* Poll, 1991.
81. Gallup Poll, 1991.
82. 1994 by Times Mirror.
83. 1993 *New York Times*/CBS Poll cited in *New York Times*, April 4, 1993. And as for the intensity of disagreement on this particular issue, see Paul Sniderman and Thomas Piazza, *The Scar of Race* (Cambridge; Harvard University, 1993).
84. 1994 by Times Mirror.
85. General Social Survey, National Opinion Research Center, University of Chicago. Also see George Gallup, Jr., *The Gallup Poll: Public Opinion* (Wilmington, Del.: Scholarly Resources, Inc., annual series); Floris W. Wood, ed., An American Profile–Opinions and Behavior, 1972–1989 (New York: Gale Research, Inc., 1990); Schuman, *Racial Attitudes;* Dawson, *Behind the Mule* , ch. 3; Sigelman and Welch, *Black Americans' Views of Racial Inequality*; Sniderman and Piazza, *The Scar of Race*.
86. See Burns W. Roper, "Racial Tensions Are Down," in *New York Times*, July 26, 1990.
87. *Newsweek*, February 26, 1979, p. 48. Note that these historical comparisons include both Harris and National Opinion Research Center data, with some of the questions having been asked in slightly different ways.
88. Interview in Robert Coles and Jon Erickson, *The Middle Americans* (Boston: Little, Brown, 1971), pp. 9–10. Also see Studs Terkel, *Race: How Blacks and Whites Think and Feel About the American Obsession* (New York: The New Press, 1992).
89. Memphis man quoted in Mike Royko, "Honesty Leads to Open Wounds," nationally syndicated column appearing in the Memphis *Commercial Appeal*, November 2, 1991.
90. J. David Smith, *The Eugenic Assault on America* (Fairfax, Va.: George Mason University Press, 1993), p. xiii.
91. For example, see Dinesh D'Souza, *The End of Racism* (Washington, D.C.: American Enterprise Institute, 1995).
92. For a well-developed survey of these views as they have evolved over the course of United States history, see ibid.
93. For a wide variety of examples, see Smith, *Racism in the Post–Civil Rights Era*; Margaret Austin Turner, Michael Fix, and Raymond Struyk, *Opportunities Denied, Opportunities Diminished: Racial Discrimination in Hiring* (Washington, D.C.: Urban Institute Press, 1991); Kathryn Neckerman and Joleen Kirschenman, "Statistical Discrimination and Inner-City Workers: An Investigation of Employers' Hiring Decisions" (Paper presented at the annual meeting of the American Sociological Association, 1990); Derrick Bell, *Faces at the Bottom of the Well: The Permanence of Racism* (New York: Basic, 1992); Douglas Massey and Nancy Denton, *American Apartheid: Segregation and the Making of the Underclass* (Cambridge: Harvard University, 1993); *New York Times*, April 30, 1991; October 2, 1992; February 5, 1993; March 17, 1995; *Wall Street Journal*, March 31, 1992; Benjamin Bowser and Raymond Hunt, eds., *Impacts of Racism on White Americans* (Newbury Park, Calif.: Sage, 1996); Carter Wilson, *Racism: From Slavery to Advanced Capitalism* (Newbury Park, Calif.: Sage, 1996).

94. It should be noted that beginning with data for 1991, the FBI has been attempting to estimate the number of hate crimes occurring each year in the United States. See Federal Bureau of Investigation, Criminal Justice Information Services Division; Hate Crimes-1995, *Information Letter 95-4* (Washington, D.C.: GPO, 1996). Sam Vincent Meddis, "Race biggest factor in hate crimes," *USA Today*, January 5, 1993, p. 1. Also see Jack Levin and Jack McDevitt, *Hate Crimes: The Rising Tide of Bigotry and Bloodshed* (New York: Plenum Press, 1993); Eddie N. Williams and Milton Morris, "Racism and Our Future," in Marilyn Lashley and Melanie Njeri Jackson, eds., *African Americans and the New Policy Consensus: Retreat of the Liberal State?* (Westport, Conn.: Greenwood Press, 1994), p. 417.

95. *New York Times*, February 2, 1984.

96. Marable, *How Capitalism Underdeveloped Black America*, p. 241.

97. Ibid., pp. 240–241.

98. Ibid., p. 240.

99. *New York Times*, June 23, 1982; March 4, 1983.

100. *New York Times*, June 2, 1982.

101. *New York Times*, November 18, 1984.

102. *New York Times*, December 1, 1985.

103. *New York Times*, December 24, 1986; January 5, 1987; September 23, 1987.

104. *New York Times*, December 14, 1987.

105. *New York Times*, June 23, 1988.

106. *New York Times*, May 3, 1989.

107. For example, see *New York Times*, August 25–26, 1989.

108. *New York Times*, October 20, 1989.

109. *New York Times*, June 7, 1991; June 10, 1991.

110. *New York Times*, October 15, 1991; October 16, 1991.

111. *New York Times*, September 27, 1994.

112. *New York Times*, October 15, 1991; October 16, 1991.

113. *New York Times*, February 28, 1997; May 13, 1997.

114. *New York Times*, September 28, 1996.

115. *New York Times*, March 27, 1997.

Chapter 4

The Class Structure

"America belongs to the white man." That statement is nearly correct. But to be even more accurate we should say, "America belongs to a very small number of white men." They are the tiny fraction of the population that owns the bulk of the nation's property, corporate stock, and financial accounts.

This chapter focuses on the economic class structure that underlies the political process. In particular, it looks at the concentration of corporate capital in the United States, a concentration that has increased due to some of the largest mergers in the history of the country. It then describes the concentrated ownership of those assets, focusing on the extremely small proportion held by African Americans. Failing to own any significant share of the nation's corporate capital, most all blacks are left dependent on the decisions of a white owning class.

> (Class is) for European democracies or something else—it isn't for the United States of America. We are not going to be divided by class.
>
> President George Bush[1]

THE CONCEPT OF CLASS

A central focus here and throughout the book is the relationship between economic classes. *Economics* describes how a society's goods and services are produced and distributed. *Economic classes* refer to the subgroupings within a society that delineate that society's most basic power relationships as it decides how to produce and distribute its goods and services.

For example, under a capitalistic economic arrangement like the one in the United States, most goods and services are produced by privately owned companies and distributed according to people's ability to pay. The owners of these companies, referred to as capitalists, directly or indirectly hire others to work for them and pay those workers a wage. That wage, however, is not set at the full market value of what the workers produce. Instead, the capitalist sells the fruits of the workers' labors for more than the workers are paid and thus extracts a "profit" in the bargain.

The end result in terms of power is that the workers are dependent on the capitalist for their very livelihood. And out of that dependence comes subordination. In the final analysis, the company belongs to the owner and the owner's interest in maximization of profits is ultimately the interest that controls the workers. Workers' needs to the contrary must be subordinated, or the workers risk losing their livelihood.

Such subordination also has implications for self-expression and security. Ideally, by having control over decisions as to what is to be produced and how it is to be produced, one's work provides an opportunity for self-expression. By contrast, when one must work exclusively to maximize the owner's profits, those opportunities are reduced, and there is a tendency to become alienated from the work and ultimately from oneself.[2] In addition, there is little personal security without the cushion of accumulated wealth, and one can become destitute virtually overnight due to a lay-off, extended illness, or large medical bills.[3]

These economic class relationships become an *economic class structure* when the boundary lines between the classes begin to harden. In other words, in the capitalist context, this would be true when there becomes almost no likelihood that one can move from the non-owning class to the owning class or vice versa. The evidence, then, is in the intergenerational reproduction of existing class positions. One is born, lives, and dies a member of the non-owning class, for example, as does one's children, grandchildren, and so on. That results in large part because class positions are inherited. For example, one inherits one's parents' values, connections, wealth, and other attributes. Thus it becomes highly unlikely that a member of the owning class will slip to the non-owning class, regardless of abilities, efforts, and value of his or her skills to the society. Non-owners are similarly likely to remain non-owners no matter how talented and productive they are. Where such is true, a class structure can be said to exist.

At this juncture, it is important to address two additional points: the number of meaningful class groupings to be found in contemporary capitalist societies and how to categorize the self-employed.

First of all, are there normally more than two economic classes within a capitalist economic system today? Using a Kroger grocery as an example, beyond the obvious class distinction between the major stockholders of the company and those who work there, is there not also a significant difference between the store manager and the checkout clerks? Clearly, the former does have a degree of power over the latter. However, that manager has been hired to maximize profits for Kroger stockholders. Thus decisional leeway is limited, and the manager's personal interests are subordinated to those of the company's owners in virtually the very same way the clerks' are. These employees are playing different roles, but the bottom line is the same for both. They must do what they can to turn acceptable profits for those who own the institution. And if they fail, they lose their jobs. This distinction or lack thereof, will be explored further at the end of this chapter when discussing the contemporary separation of ownership and management.

The second phenomenon, self-employed workers, is conceptually more troublesome. The proportion of the American population that is self-employed, with no non-family members working for them, has shrunk steadily since the nation began and is now less than 9 percent.[4] Yet this is still a sizable number of people, and as a group they remain difficult to categorize. They are clearly not capitalists, as they are not extracting profits from the labor of others. By the same token, they are not really workers either, as they are not having their labor exploited by a capitalist. Thus they end up as a group in between. On the other hand, they also can be seen as a small-scale glimpse of a socialist-type economic arrangement in which all would control the businesses within which they labored.

DISTRIBUTION OF OWNERSHIP

> Widespread accumulation inevitably turns into accumulation by the few. . . . Accumulation, which means, under the rule of private property, concentration of capital in a few hands, is a necessary consequence when capitalists are left free to follow their natural course.[5]

Corporate Concentration

Just how concentrated is the ownership of capital in the United States? To begin with, there are more than 20 million private businesses in this country, and together they make more than $12 trillion in sales every year. Approximately 90 percent of those sales, however, are made by corporations, which number fewer than 4 million.[6] If the focus is narrowed to the approximately 300,000 manufacturing corporations, one gets an even clearer idea of just how concentrated the American means of production has become.[7]

The top 500 manufacturers (0.17 percent of all such corporations) presently employ more than 70 percent of the nation's manufacturing work force and possess more than 90 percent of its manufacturing assets.[8] Even more revealing, however, are the details presented in Figure 4.1. The 200 largest manufacturers—roughly 0.07 percent of all such corporations—possess more than 80 percent of the nation's manufacturing assets, while the top 100 alone control more than two-thirds of the manufacturing capital. This concentration has grown significantly over the course of this century.

Who are the very largest of these industrial giants? Table 4.1 indicates both who they are and just how stable their ranks have been. The lists have consistently been dominated by essentially the same companies. It should also be remembered that many of these corporations have become increasingly diversified conglomerates. A number of the oil companies, for example, have bought up much of the nation's coal and uranium reserves.

The size of these firms is impressive. For example, in 1995 the General Electric ledger looked like this: $194 billion in assets and $65 billion worth of sales. General Motors had $199 billion in assets and $155 billion in sales. The Ford Motor Company

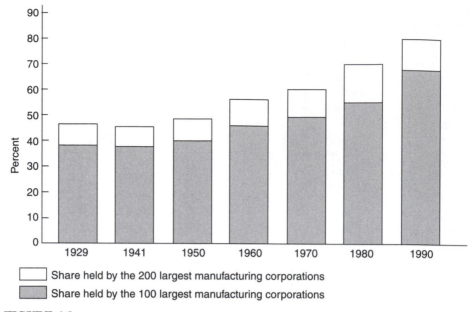

Percent

| 1929 | 1941 | 1950 | 1960 | 1970 | 1980 | 1990 |

☐ Share held by the 200 largest manufacturing corporations

▨ Share held by the 100 largest manufacturing corporations

FIGURE 4.1

Share of Manufacturing Assets, 1929–1990. (Sources: 1929 and 1941 from Senate Subcommittee on Antitrust and Monopoly, "Economic Concentration" [Washington, D.C.: GPO, 1979], p. 173; remainder from U.S. Department of Commerce, Bureau of the Census, *Statistical Abstracts of the United States,* [Washington D.C.: GPO, various years].)

had $219 billion in corporate assets and $128 billion worth of sales.[9] These budget figures are rivaled in size by a limited number of other large multinational corporations and the government of the United States.[10]

And as for market dominance, consider the food industry. Here, 1 percent of the corporations control 80 percent of the industry's assets and make 90 percent of its sales.[11] In cereal production, for instance, six companies (Kellogg, General Mills, Kraft, Quaker Oats, Ralston Purina, and RJR Nabisco) account for 90 percent of the sales.[12] Similar concentration of capital can be found in other industries as well. For example, eight airlines account for more than 90 percent of industry sales;[13] DuPont and Dow dominate the chemical industry; IBM in computers; General Electric in electronics; International Paper, Georgia-Pacific, and Weyerhaeuser in forest and paper products; Caterpillar, Tenneco, and Deere in industrial and farm equipment; Xerox, Eastman Kodak, and Minnesota Mining & Manufacturing in scientific, photo, and control equipment.[14]

The companies that have risen to the top produce the nation's most needed primary products: food, energy, chemicals, transportation vehicles, and communications and information equipment. Their production is essential to the economic independence and prosperity of the nation as a whole, not to mention the number of individual Americans whose jobs derive either directly or indirectly from one of these basic manufacturing industries.

TABLE 4.1

FORTUNE'S TOP 10 MANUFACTURING CORPORATIONS, 1960–1995 (BY SALES)

1960	1970	1980	1990	1995
1. General Motors	General Motors	Exxon*	General Motors	General Motors
2. Standard Oil (N.J.)	Standard Oil (N.J.)	General Motors	Ford	Ford
3. Ford	Ford	Mobil	Exxon	Exxon
4. General Electric	General Electric	IBM	IBM	AT&T
5. U.S. Steel	IBM	Ford	General Electric	General Electric
6. Mobil	Chrysler	Texaco	Mobil	IBM
7. Gulf	Mobil	Standard Oil (Calif.)	Phillip Morris	Mobil
8. Texaco	Texaco	Gulf	Chrysler	Phillip Morris
9. Chrysler	ITT	Standard Oil (Ind.)	DuPont	Chrysler
10. Swift	Gulf	General Electric	Texaco	DuPont

*Formerly Standard Oil (N.J.).

Source: Fortune (*July 1960, May 1970, May 1980, April 1990, May 1995*).

Such tight concentration, mammoth size, and strategic importance are not limited to manufacturing. For example, 50 banks out of 1,400 (fewer than 4 percent) hold two-thirds of the nation's banking assets; while five (Citicorp, BankAmerica, Chemical, NationsBank, and Morgan) control nearly one-fourth.[15] In insurance, the top 50 insurers hold 80 percent of all insurance assets, and two, Prudential and Metropolitan, alone possess 30 percent of them.[16]

Combining manufacturers and nonmanufacturers, then, fewer than 1 percent of these corporations produce more than 80 percent of the nation's corporate output.[17] From a global perspective, a disproportionate share of the world's largest corporations are multinational companies based in the United States, meaning that these largest of American firms also control a hefty proportion of the entire world's corporate capital.

Beyond that, such concentration has been increasing rapidly of late due to a plethora of corporate mergers. Economist Frederic Scherer points out that there was a proliferation of mergers in the years 1887–1904, 1916–1929, and 1945–1968.[18] Those mergers pale, however, when compared to the ones occurring in the 1980s and 1990s, when U. S. corporations actually began to buy more stock than they issued.[19] Mergers and acquisitions came to involve more than $300 billion per year in the United States alone, and to approach $800 billion each year worldwide.[20]

Some of the largest multibillion dollar domestic mergers during this most recent period have been Time and Warner Communications, Gulf Oil and Standard Oil of California, Texaco and Getty Oil, DuPont and Conoco, Coke and Columbia Pictures, Lockheed Martin and Northrop Grumman, U.S. Steel acquiring both Marathon Oil and Texas Oil & Gas, and Phillip Morris subsuming first General Foods and then Miller Brewing Company. Yet, it is in banking where the mergers have been most impressive. For example, recent mergers have involved the nation's third largest bank at the time, BankAmerica, and Security Pacific (No. 6); also Chemical Bank

(No. 4) and Manufacturer's Hanover (No. 7). Or, NCNB, C&S, and Sovran merged to form NationsBank, which then acquired the Barnett Banks and became the nation's third largest banking conglomerate.[21]

Not only are corporate assets highly concentrated, but also these individual corporations often have what are called interlocking directorates.[22] A direct interlock exists when a member of the board of directors of one corporation also sits on the board of another corporation. An indirect interlock exists when two corporations each have a director on a third board.[23]

In a comprehensive analysis of this interlock phenomenon, the Senate Subcommittee on Intergovernmental Affairs found either direct or indirect interlocks between nearly all of America's largest corporations. John de Butts, for instance, was not only chairman of the board of American Telephone & Telegraph (AT&T) but also a board member of fellow corporate giants such as General Motors, Citicorp Bank, and United States Steel (now USX).[24] Other more recent examples include Clifton Garvin chairing Exxon, while serving as a director for Citicorp, Pepsico, and Sperry Rand; Harry Jack Gray chairing United Technologies, while a director for Exxon, Citicorp, Aetna, Carrier Corporation, Otis Elevator, and Pratt & Whitney; Edmund Pratt chaired IBM and directed Chase Manhattan Bank, International Paper, and General Motors; Irving Shapiro chaired DuPont and served as a director for Citicorp, IBM, Bank of Delaware, and Continental American Insurance; Rawleigh Warner chaired Mobil Oil, while a director for AT&T, Chemical Bank, American Express, and Wheelabrator; George Jenkins chaired Metropolitan Life Insurance, while directing Citicorp, ABC, St. Regis Paper, Bethlehem Steel, and W.R. Grace and Company.[25]

For the end result at the corporate level, take AT&T as an example. Its directors created direct interlocks with Cummins Engine, Bristol Myers, Exxon, Pepsico, Coca-Cola, Atlantic Richfield, Johnson & Johnson, Weyerhaeuser, RJR Nabisco, Caterpillar, Springs Industries, International Paper, Aluminum Corporation of America, Smith Kline, Warner Lambert, J.C. Penney, Orion Pictures, Eli Lilly, NCR, BankAmerica, Citicorp, Chemical Bank, Chase Manhattan, Bank of Boston, First National of Boston, CBS, and the New York Times.[26]

There also has been a recent tendency toward joint ventures between major international firms. For example, the American Motors Company (AMC) and France's Renault Corporation combined efforts to produce the Alliance automobile. Political scientist Edward Greenberg found the world's 20 largest oil companies involved in some 2,000 such joint operations.[27] In many industries, the list is long and getting longer. This trend could lead to a slower growth in the size of individual multinational corporations, but in the end it simply adds a new dimension to the interlocking phenomenon.

In many ways, the center of this interlocking web of corporate control is the American financial community.

Beyond sheer size and monopolization of lending, a number of the largest banks also hold the controlling shares of other giant corporations, which means that their stockholdings are large enough to allow them to sway decision making in those other companies. For example, five of these banks—Chase, Citicorp, Morgan Guaranty Trust, Bankers Trust, and the Bank of New York—held controlling shares in three-quarters of the top 324 American-based corporations in 1969.[28] Economists Robert Fitch and John Oppenheimer concluded that "to a considerable extent these 5 banks actually constitute a unified money cartel."[29] A decade later, a Senate study concluded that 15 financial institutions effectively controlled virtually all major corporations.[30] As a specific example, Chase, controlled by the Rockefeller family, has held or continues to hold controlling shares in both CBS and NBC, Union Carbide, General Electric, United Airlines, Safeway, and AT&T.[31] As another example, J.P. Morgan, Inc., holds some $15 billion in stock, including sizable shares of American Express, ITT, IBM, and Citicorp.[32] Actually, there appear to be some 15 industrial-banking complexes so tightly interlocked that they virtually act as single economic entities.[33]

No matter how you choose to configure it, however, it appears safe to conclude that a relatively small number of very large corporations control the bulk of America's corporate assets. Nevertheless, if it can be shown that ownership of these corporations is spread broadly across the American citizenry, those findings will not be nearly so significant. Unfortunately, such is simply not the case.

Concentration of Ownership

African Americans

> "A lot of times, when I'm working, I become as despondent as hell and I feel like crying. I'm not a man, none of us are men! I don't own anything."[34]

To begin with, African Americans own very few of the nation's corporate assets. That leaves them almost totally subordinate to the interests of a white owning class. But before documenting that, it is important to remember the historical context within which this reality has developed.

During slavery, millions of blacks were denied the right to own property for two and one-half centuries. During that period, even free blacks faced a dual wage system and other forms of racial discrimination that made it quite difficult for them to accumulate wealth. Following emancipation, after the promised reparation of "forty acres and a mule" never materialized, black accumulation of wealth continued to be retarded by the nature of available employment. Little could be saved while working as a sharecropper, domestic servant, or leased convict, and employment and wage discrimination continued to plague blacks who attempted to work outside those situations. Many blacks moved to the industrializing North in a futile search for the economic opportunities white immigrants had enjoyed for decades. By the time legally sanctioned discrimination finally began to be struck down, it was essentially too little, too late. The American political and economic systems were undergoing fundamental changes that would seriously reduce the number of bottom rungs on the ladder of upward mobility. In particular, the urban political machine was declining as the assimilating agent it once was for white ethnics, and rapid growth in technology was allowing mechanization of much of the manual and semiskilled work in unionized industries that had been providing decent wages, benefits, and opportunities for skill development and advancement.[35]

It should come as little surprise, then, that significant disparities have developed between the accumulated wealth of whites and the accumulated wealth of blacks. By the 1990s, for example, the median white household possessed wealth worth $44,408; the figure was only $4,604 for the median black household.[36] Thus, although African Americans represented 13 percent of the U. S. population, they held less than one-half percent of the nation's wealth.[37]

In absolute terms, only 1 percent of all black households have accumulated over $250,000 worth of wealth, while more than 30 percent either owned nothing or owed more than they owned. Where wealth had been successfully accumulated, it most often simply reflected a small amount of equity in a house or automobile. Only 6 percent of black households held any corporate stock or mutual funds at all, and the median holding was only $4,013—most likely small Individual Retirement Accounts (IRAs). The mean holding was only $7,841, which indicates some variation in size of holdings but very few large accumulations.[38]

From a different perspective, blacks hold only about 2 percent of the nation's capital stock.[39] And although they own 3 percent of the businesses,[40] those businesses received only 1 percent of all gross receipts. Only 17 percent had even one paid employee, while less than 0.4 percent (189 firms) employed more than 100 people. As telling as anything is the fact that 94 percent were sole proprietorships, most of which operated on capital drawn from the owner's personal savings or borrowed from friends.[41] Although there has been some recent expansion in areas such as heavy construction, professional and business services, finance, insurance, and real estate,[42] black-owned businesses generally continue to be restaurants, car dealerships, laundries, funeral parlors, gas stations, barber shops, hair salons, shoe repair shops, neighborhood grocery stores, and other service-producing enterprises, most of which are small and operate on the economic margin: more than three-fourths of them go bankrupt within three years of opening.[43]

Table 4.2 lists the most successful contemporary black businesses. Although impressive given the historical obstacles they had to overcome, such firms are a mere drop in the very large bucket of American corporate capital. For example, while

TABLE 4.2

BLACK ENTERPRISE MAGAZINE'S TOP SIX BLACK BUSINESSES, 1995 (BY SALES)

1. TLC Beatrice International Holdings (food processing and distribution)	2.1 billion
2. Johnson Publishing Company (*Ebony, Jet, Fashion Fair Cosmetics,* etc.)	316 million
3. Philadelphia Coca-Cola Bottling Company	315 million
4. H.J. Russell (construction, development, etc.)	173 million
5. Pulsar Data Systems	165 million
6. Uniworld Group (advertising, public relations, etc.)	134 million

Source: Adapted from Black Enterprise Magazine, June, 1996.

General Motors was making $155 billion in sales, only one black-owned business in the entire country had sales exceeding even $400 million. With annual sales of $2.1 billion, TLC Beatrice still did not make the Fortune 500, while the second largest black-owned firm, Johnson Publishing, would have had to multiply its sales nearly seven times in order to have entered the ranks of the nation's top 500 manufacturers. And if the sales of the top 100 black firms had been combined, they would still have ranked only 72nd—far lower yet when nonmanufacturers are included.[44]

Overall, then, blacks owned little of the nation's corporate capital as of the late 1970s, and as a group they have made only very limited gains since. However, such inequality of ownership is not a uniquely racial phenomenon; it exists to nearly the same extent in the American society as a whole. And even though white non-owners do not face the double-edged sword of race and class oppression, they still share with their black counterparts a parallel position in the economic class structure.

Americans in General

... rather than being an egalitarian society, the United States has become the most economically stratified of industrial nations.[45]

Compiled from a variety of sources, some of the best available data suggests that fewer than 20 percent of Americans have ever directly owned any stock. Of even more importance is the fact that a far smaller number of them have held nearly all the shares.[46]

The last complete federal survey of stock ownership found that the richest 1 percent of U.S. adults owned nearly two-thirds of all stock, the richest 5 percent held 86 percent, and the richest 20 percent held 97 percent. That, of course, left 3 percent of the stock to be owned by the other 80 percent.[47]

Estimates compiled by economists using publicly available estate tax returns help to put black and white ownership figures into historical perspective. The proportion of all stock held by the top 1 percent of the American adult population seemed to peak shortly after World War II. By governmental estimates, this small group still holds nearly 40 percent of all corporate stock and has done so since at least 1922. The top 5 percent of Americans has continued to hold the majority of all the stock, with the top 10 percent possessing more than 80 percent of it.[48] Other estimates place these figures even higher,[49] while Maurice Zeitlin concludes that all Americans owning more than $1 million worth of stock would fit easily in one average-size professional football stadium.[50]

As for the stock this elite group does not hold, much of it is owned in relatively small amounts, and the size of these shares has shrunk dramatically. Nationwide, for example, the median shareholding was $10,000 in 1992, roughly one-third of what it was as recently as two decades earlier; and a growing amount of this investment is tied up in small, tax-sheltered retirement accounts. Viewed another way, the mean household shares were valued at nearly 7 times more than the median shares, suggesting considerable variation in these holdings and a sizeable statistical skew in the direction of some very large accumulations.[51]

In terms of control, which is the essence of ownership, stockholders theoretically have the ultimate say as to the running of the corporations in which they have invested. This role, however, tends to end up in the hands of a small number of the very largest stockholders.

To begin with, an increasing number of corporations do not even operate by a one-share, one-vote principle. A small group of dominant stockholders own *management shares* that may, for example, allow them 10 votes per share. The ordinary shareholder, in contrast, would only be allowed one vote per share or in some cases none at all.[52] Henry Ford II, for instance, was able to control 40 percent of Ford Motor Company's voting rights (and thus dominate the company) even though he actually owned only 20 percent of the company's stock.[53] Lester Thurow estimates that the $166 billion in business assets owned by the wealthiest 482 individuals and families in the United States allowed them to control business assets worth $2,200 billion, the equivalent of 40 percent of the nation's nonresidential private capital.[54] Consequently, we get the term *controlling shares*, meaning that the person possesses enough shareholder votes to direct company decisions in the direction desired.

But even where there is a one-vote-per-share rule, the vote of the stockholders is still proportionately weighted according to the number of shares owned. Therefore, those with the largest accumulation of shares can still dominate, especially because smaller stockholders rarely band together to counterbalance such power.

Taking the next step and identifying precisely who the dominant shareholders are is much more difficult. Companies are not free with their lists of stockholders. Large shareholders are not generally willing to publicize their precise holdings. And even if this information were readily available, one would still have to track down the roots of all the foundations, holding companies, and trust funds, not to mention names that have changed through marriage, and so on.[55] From the best evidence available, however, one can still get a relatively clear indication of both whom these people are and how little has changed over the years.

America's corporate landscape has long been the domain of large family empires. Robert Sheehan found that either individuals or members of a single family held controlling shares in nearly 150 of the nation's largest 500 corporations. He also found that 70 of the family-named companies on this list were still controlled by their founding families.[56]

The Du Ponts, for example, had controlling shares in 24 of the country's biggest corporations, including General Motors, Coca-Cola, and United Brands; and more than one million people were employed in Du Pont–controlled firms. They also controlled eight of the 40 largest defense contractors, grossing more than $15 billion during the Vietnam War alone.[57]

The Rockefellers held over $300 billion worth of corporate stock, including controlling shares in five of the nation's largest oil companies headed by Exxon and four of its largest banks headed by Chase Manhattan.[58]

The Mellon family also remains significant. They hold controlling shares in such corporate giants as Alcoa, Gulf Oil, and Carborundum.[59]

Beyond all that, William Domhoff warns that even though a good many family corporations have broken up and their stock has been sold on the open market, this has only added to the concentrated control of the wealthiest corporate elites. He reasons that where three families each had their own companies before, now all three may well own stock in each other's companies, giving "the upper class an even greater community of interest than they had in the past when they were more contentiously involved in protecting their standing by maintaining their individual companies.[60]

Thus it appears just as true today as when C. Wright Mills wrote in the 1950s that "the idea of a really wide distribution of economic ownership is a cultivated illusion: at the very most, 0.2 or 0.3 percent of the adult population own the bulk, the payoff shares, of the corporate world."[61]

Beyond their domination of individual firms, however, these white corporate elites also have numerous opportunities to get together in groups, facilitating a more collective exertion of power. For example, they regularly cross paths in trade associations, social clubs, ad hoc groups, political action committees, public and private forums, and the boards of various profit-making and nonprofit organizations.

Recent Developments

Before moving on, four relatively recent developments warrant brief attention. First of all, institutions of various types directly possess an ever greater proportion of all stock held. Second, in what Peter Drucker has termed "the unseen revolution,"[62] the proportion of all stock held by public and private pension funds has increased steadily as well. Third, there has been a sizable infusion of foreign capital into the United States. And fourth, there continues to be considerable discussion about the alleged separation between those who own and the professional managers who actually operate these corporations. Nonetheless, closer analysis of these trends suggests that they have not fundamentally altered class divisions in the United States.

Institutional Investments.   Besides wealthy individuals, large institutions have become important investors. They currently do the majority of trading on the New York Stock Exchange,[63] and they own a near majority of all corporate stock—including the majority of equity in the nation's top 50 corporations.[64] This is not a cross-section of American institutions, however. Large banks, insurance companies, mutual funds, and pension funds comprise the overwhelming majority of the institutions involved in stock ownership.[65] Mutual funds currently hold more than 1 trillion dollars worth of stock,[66] while banks own roughly one-fourth of Fortune 500 common stock.[67] When control of Northwest Airlines was being pursued by billionaire Marvin Davis in 1989, for example, its four largest stockholders were Prudential Life Insurance, Equitable Life Insurance, Wellington Management Fund, and Windsor Funds.[68]

More important, the primary purpose of such institutional investment is to serve the economic interests of the holders of stock in the particular investing company. Thus these institutional investments actually represent investments for individuals, and, consequently, it is not so important that institutions are purchasing more and more of the available stock.[69] The important question is who owns the controlling shares of the investing company's stock, and this, we have seen, is apt to be concentrated in a small number of hands. Thus institutional, as opposed to individual, investment does not alter the class structure significantly.

Pension Funds.   Pension funds differ in that their ownership is widely dispersed across a large number of pensioners. These funds now contain approximately $5 trillion in assets and hold some 17 percent of all corporate stock.[70] Yet, for a variety of reasons, this has not translated into significantly more economic clout for the nonwealthy.

Less than 40 percent of the American work force is currently covered by such funds, down from a peak of 49 percent in 1979.[71] In addition, those who are union members have the more substantial pension accounts, but union membership has been declining rapidly to the point where less than one out of every five American workers is unionized today.[72] And even those who belong to the unionized group are destined to have very small individual shares in their union's pension stockholdings; their shares are often voted for them by union appointees; and such investments are often governed by governmental regulations that limit the investment discretion of the trustees. For example, there is even evidence that trustee demand for efficiency in the companies in which they invest has actually contributed to thousands of worker layoffs.[73] Lastly, as the number of stockholders increases while the relative size of their shares decreases, the little dispersal that is taking place may well be strengthening the hands of the major corporate elites by further diluting the remainder of the ownership pool.[74] Peter Drucker's alarm over "pension fund socialism" in America appears to have been premature at very best.[75]

Foreign Capital.   Foreign acquisitions of U.S. companies appear to have grown to a peak in the latter 1980s, including Shell Oil being subsumed by Royal Dutch Shell, Standard Oil of Ohio by British Petroleum, Firestone Tire and Rubber by Bridgestone (Japan), Federated and Allied Department Stores by Campeau (Canada), Pillsbury by Grand Metropolitan P.L.C. (Britain), and Carnation by Nestle (Switzerland).[76] In the course of the 1980s alone, direct foreign investment in U.S. companies soared from $90 billion to more than $300 billion.[77] Nevertheless, such acquisitions appear to have subsided considerably thereafter.[78] The Federal Reserve Board estimated foreign holdings to be 2 percent of corporate stock in 1965 and still only 6 percent by 1994.[79] Viewed from a different vantage, foreign companies came to own between 3 and 4 percent of American businesses, employing between 11 and 12 percent of the nation's work force.[80]

These foreign investments do help explain why a smaller share of all domestic corporate stock is presently held by the wealthiest Americans. Yet that American owning class still owns the overwhelming majority of all domestic stock, and ownership by foreign capitalists in no way enhances the economic position of the overwhelming majority of Americans.

In addition, one should be very careful not to interpret the overall decline in the proportion of stock held by the American owning class to suggest a decline in their economic well being. Although they do indeed own less of the nation's stock, their share of all national wealth has actually been increasing. For example, where the top 1 percent of Americans owned 24 percent of the nation's total wealth in 1972, that figure had grown to more than 30 percent by the 1990s.[81] Thus the members of the domestic owning class simply have been more inclined to choose investments other than stock in recent years.

Ownership versus Management.   The fourth phenomenon is a development occurring in the upper echelons of this corporate structure and has been labeled the "bureaucratization" of corporate decision making. In the larger publicly owned corporations, stockholders choose a board of directors that then chooses a set of managers to make the day-to-day decisions for that company.[82] If an ultimate concern is with the political power that is inherent in capital ownership, is this power actually shifting from a small group of owners to a larger, fundamentally different group of non-owning managerial elites?[83]

To begin with, in terms of race, African Americans have been no more likely to be top-level managers than to be owners. No black has ever been chairman or CEO of a major industrial corporation, bank, insurance company, investment firm, or communication network.[84] The number of black senior executives among the Fortune 1000 can be counted on one hand.[85] And, blacks make up less than 2 percent of the directors of the nation's largest companies.[86]

As for other possible distinctions between managers and owners, first note that the managerial cadre are often large stockholders as well.[87] Returning to the Northwest Airlines ledger discussed above, as an example, after the four institutional investors and the venture capitalist, the next four largest shareholders were its current chairman, vice chairman, president, and a former chairman.[88]

This results, at least in part, because these top executives may draw as much as one-half of their salaries in stock bonuses and stock options.[89] Besides helping to guarantee that the managers will have vested interests in the profitability of their companies, such arrangements serve to shelter the executives' incomes. In 1984, for instance, Ford chairman Philip Caldwell received over 60 percent of his $4 million remuneration in the form of stock. Chrysler chairman Lee Iacocca received $4.3 million worth of stock that same year as part of a total compensation package valued at $5.5 million.[90]

Yet most obvious is the fact that any manager's career may well rest on the figures found on the bottom line of the company ledger, for without impressive profits, stock prices will decline, borrowing will become more difficult, less capital will be available for innovation and new investment, and so on—all of which will seriously hamper the attainment of any secondary goals the manager might have.[91] It should come as no surprise, then, that Edward S. Mason found the rate of profit to be virtually the same whether a corporation was run by stockholders or managers.[92]

No matter who is at the helm, the corporate ship seems to sail first and foremost for profits, the ultimate interest of the shareholders and the managers. And even if their interests do occasionally diverge in any given company, the managerial elite is simply not large enough, different enough in motivation, or separate enough from ownership itself to alter the size or nature of the small owning class in any significant way.[93] As Thomas Dye put it, "Disagreement among various segments of the nation's elite occurs within a framework of consensus on underlying values. The range of disagreement is relatively narrow, and disagreement is generally confined to means rather than ends."[94]

SUMMARY

Personal wealth may be the only truly stable measure of self-sufficiency in a capitalist economic system like that of the United States. The accumulation of wealth serves as a buffer in times of adversity (disability, temporary loss of income, etc.) and also guarantees that class position can be handed down from generation to generation (through money for college, funds for private entrepreneurship, etc.). Personal wealth also allows greater opportunities for self-fulfilling work, and most importantly, it is usually accompanied by increased economic and political power.

In the United States, wealth is highly concentrated in the hands of a small owning class, which is almost exclusively white. All others—especially blacks—are left in varying states of insecurity, dependence, subordination, and alienation.

NOTES

1. Quoted in Benjamin DeMott, *The Imperial Middle: Why Americans Can't Think Straight About Class* (New York: William Morrow, 1990), pp. 9–10.
2. See David McLellan, *The Thought of Karl Marx* (New York: Harper & Row, 1971), pp.105–121.
3. For a more complete discussion of the value of holding "wealth" (bank accounts, stock, bonds, real estate, etc.), see David Swinton, "The Economic Status of African Americans: Limited Ownership and Persistent Inequality," in National Urban League, *The State of Black America 1992* (New York: National Urban League, 1992), pp. 62–63.
4. U.S. Department of Commerce, Bureau of the Census, *Statistical Abstracts of the United States* (Washington, D.C.: GPO, 1995), pp. 407–410. Also see Michael Reich, "The Development of the U.S. Labor Force," in Richard Edwards (ed.), *The Capitalist System* (Englewood Cliffs, N.J.: Prentice-Hall, 1978), p. 180; U.S. Department of Commerce, Bureau of the Census, *Current Population Reports*, Series P–60 (Washington, D.C.: GPO, various years).
5. Karl Marx, "Profit of Capital," in J. B. Bottomore (ed.), *Karl Marx: Early Writings* (London: Watts, 1963), p. 91.
6. Department of Commerce, *Statistical Abstracts*, p. 543. A "corporation" is a legal entity characterized by joint stock ownership and a continuous legal identity of its own that relieves the stock owners of financial liability. For further explanation, see Paul Samuelson and William Nordhaus, *Economics* (New York: McGraw-Hill, 1995), p. 102.
7. Department of Commerce, *Statistical Abstracts*, p. 543.
8. Ibid., pp. 562–563.
9. *Fortune Magazine*, May 22, 1995.
10. For example, see Paul Kennedy, *Preparing for the 21st Century* (New York: Random House, 1993); New York Times, February 14, 1993.
11. Michael Parenti, *Democracy for the Few* (New York: St. Martin's Press, 1995), p. 12.
12. See *New York Times*, August 10, 1993.
13. *New York Times*, March 12, 1989.
14. *Fortune*, May, 1995.
15. See Thomas Dye, *Who's Running America?* (Englewood Cliffs, N.J.: Prentice-Hall, 1995), pp. 19 and 21; Thomas Dye and Harmon Ziegler, *The Irony of Democracy* (Belmont, Cal.: Wadsworth, 1992), pp. 100–101. Also see Richard Barnet and Ronald Muller,

"The Negative Effects of Multinational Corporations," in David Mermelstein (ed.), *The Economic Crisis Reader* (New York: Random House, 1975), pp. 15–155.

16. Dye, *Who's Running America?* pp. 20–21. For a discussion of the insurance industry's exemption from antitrust laws under the McCarran-Ferguson Act of 1945, see Linda Lipsen, "Insured Firms: Privileged Class," *New York Times*, June 5, 1990.

17. Parenti, *Democracy for the Few*, p. 10. Also see Charles Anderson, *The Political Economy of Social Class* (Englewood Cliffs, N.J.: Prentice-Hall, 1974).

18. Frederic Scherer, *Industrial Market Structure and Economic Performance* (Chicago: Rand McNally, 1980), pp. 119–123. Also see Samuel Reid, *The New Industrial Order* (New York: McGraw-Hill, 1976); *New York Times*, August 5,1981.

19. For example, see *New York Times*, January 30, 1990; January 19, 1998; April 14, 1998.

20. See *New York Times*, October 31, 1995.

21. For a recent discussion of the phenomenon, see Saul Hansell, "Wave of Mergers is Transforming American Banking," *New York Times*, August 21, 1995. Also see the *Multinational Monitor* 7 (February 15, 1986).

22. For one of the more comprehensive contemporary discussions of this subject, see Dye, *Who's Running America?* chap. 6.

23. For example, see ibid., p. 151.

24. *New York Times*, April 23, 1978.

25. See Dye, *Who's Running America?* pp. 155–157.

26. Ibid., pp. 160–162.

27. Edward Greenberg, *Capitalism and the American Political Ideal* (New York: Sharpe, 1985), p. 121.

28. Michael Parenti, *Democracy for the Few* (New York: St. Martin's Press, 1983), p. 12.

29. Quoted in James O'Connor, "Who Rules the Corporations?" *Socialist Revolution* (February 1971), pt. 1, p. 99.

30. Study by E. Winslow Turner for the U.S. Senate Committee on Governmental Affairs, as reported in the *New York Times*, February 5,1981. Also see Beth Mintz and Michael Schwartz, "The Structure of Power in American Business," paper presented at the annual meeting of the American Political Science Association, Washington, D.C., September 3, 1977.

31. Ferdinand Lundberg, *The Rich and the Super-rich* (Seacaucus, N.J.: Lyle Stuart, 1968), pp. 144ff; Robert Lampman, *The Share of Top Wealth-holders in National Wealth* (Princeton, N.J.: Princeton University Press, 1962); U.S. Congress, Senate, Committee on Governmental Operations, *Disclosure of Corporate Ownership*, 93d Congress,1st sess., December 27, 1973 (Washington, D.C.: GPO, 1974), p. 22; David Kotz, "Finance Capital and Corporate Control," in Edwards, *Capitalist System*.

32. Parenti, *Democracy for the Few* (1995), p. 10.

33. Peter Dooley,"The Interlocking Directorate," *American Economic Review* (June 1969).

34. Harlem resident quoted in Kenneth Clark, *The Dark Ghetto* (New York: Harper & Row, 1965), p. 1.

35. For a more detailed discussion of this postindustrial phenomenon, see Marcus Pohlmann, *Governing the Postindustrial City* (New York: Longman, 1993); Marcus Pohlmann, *Political Power in the Postindustrial City* (New York: Stonehill, 1986).

36. *New York Times*, January 26, 1993.

37. *New York Times*, July 25, 1989.

38. U.S. Department of Commerce, Bureau of the Census, *Household Wealth and Asset Ownership: 1991* (Washington, D.C.: GPO, 1994); Department of Commerce, Bureau of the Census, Current Population Reports, Series P–60, No. 179, *Income, Poverty and Wealth in the United States* (Washington, D.C.: GPO, 1992). Also see, for example,

Abram Harris, *The Negro as Capitalist* (New York: Haskell, 1936); Timothy Bates, *Black Capitalism* (New York: Praeger, 1973); Roger Ransom and Richard Sutch, *One Kind of Freedom* (Cambridge: Cambridge University Press, 1977); Melvin Oliver and Thomas Shapiro, *Black Wealth/White Wealth: A New Perspective on Racial Equality* (New York: Routledge, 1995), pp. 62–65.

39. See Jeremiah Cotton, "Towards a Theory and Strategy for Black Economic Development," in James Jennings, ed., *Race, Politics, and Economic Development* (New York: Verso, 1992), p. 13.

40. *Wall Street Journal*, April 3, 1992, p. R6.

41. U.S. Department of Commerce, Bureau of the Census, *Survey of Minority Owned Business Enterprises: Black* (Washington, D.C.: GPO, 1990). This is the most recent comprehensive governmental study of this phenomenon. Also see *New York Times*, July 26,1981.

42. Timothy Bates, *Banking on Black Enterprise: The Potential of Emerging Firms for Revitalizing Urban Economies* (Washington, D.C.: Joint Center for Political and Economic Studies, 1993).

43. Department of Commerce, *Survey of Minority Owned Business Enterprises*. For a specific example, see *New York Times*, August 16, 1989.

44. See *Black Enterprise*, June, 1996; *Fortune*, May, 1995. It should be noted, however, that the combined assets of the top 100 black firms left them at only 110th place in 1988. Thus, although gains are not readily apparent when analyzing the "average" black store, clearly a small number of black firms exhibit increased size, as indicted in Bates, *Banking on Black Enterprise*.

45. Keith Bradsher, "Gap in Wealth in U.S. Called Widest in West," *New York Times*, April 17, 1995. Also see Vincent Navarro, *Dangerous to Your Health* (New York: Monthly Review Press, 1993), p. 22; Peter Lindert and Jeffrey Williamson, "Long-Term Trends in American Wealth Inequality," University of Wisconsin's Research Institute on Poverty, Discussion Paper No. 472,1977.

46. Department of Commerce, *Statistical Abstracts*, pp. 515–517. Department of Commerce, *Income, Poverty and Wealth*; New York Stock Exchange Survey (November 1983), as reported in the *New York Times*, December 1,1983; Gabriel Kolko, *Wealth and Power in America* (New York: Praeger, 1962), p. 51; James D. Smith and Stephen D. Franklin, "The Concentration of Wealth, 1922–1969," *American Economic Review* (May 1974), p. 164; Edward Greenberg, *The American Political System* (Boston: Little, Brown, 1983), p. 36; Neil Jacoby, *Corporate Powers and Social Responsibility* (New York: Macmillan, 1973), pp. 36–37. The reference is to direct ownership, although a large number of people indirectly hold shares through banks, insurance companies, and pension funds. Most of the latter group have not controlled these shares in a way that has threatened the dominant power of those who directly hold large individual holdings.

47. U.S. Federal Reserve Board, *Survey of Financial Characteristics of Consumers* (Washington, D.C.: GPO,1962).

48. U.S. Federal Reserve Board and Internal Revenue Service, *Survey of Consumer Finances* (Washington, D.C.: GPO, 1992). Also see *New York Times*, March 13, 1996; Kevin Phillips, *Boiling Point: Democrats, Republicans, and the Decline of Middle-Class Prosperity* (New York: Harper, 1993), p. 79 and App. B. Earlier figures for the top 1 percent of Americans come from Smith and Franklin, "Concentration of Personal Wealth"; figures for the top 5 percent estimated by taking Smith and Franklin's calculation for the top 1 percent in 1962 and dividing it by a calculation for the top 5 percent from the *Survey of Financial Characteristics of Consumers* (1962). The resulting ratio was then applied to Smith and Franklin's other figures to attain the corresponding estimates for the top 5 percent, extrapolated for the years skipped over in the Smith and Franklin article.

Stock is defined as common and preferred issues in domestic and foreign firms, certificates or shares of building and loan and savings and loan associations, federal land bank stocks, accrued dividends, and other investments reporting equity in an enterprise, as well as stock held in trust (though understated).

49. For example, Samuelson and Nordhaus, *Economics*, p. 204; Parenti, *Democracy for the Few*, pp. 10–12; Keith Butters et al., *Effect of Taxation on Investments by Individuals* (Cambridge, Mass.: Riverside Press, 1953), p. 400.
50. Maurice Zeitlin, "Who Owns America?", *The Progressive* (June 1978), p. 15.
51. Department of Commerce, *Statistical Abstracts*, p. 517; Department of Commerce, *Income, Poverty and Wealth*; *Christian Science Monitor*, December 6,1985.
52. *New York Times*, June 10, 1992; December 17,1986; July 15,1985; March 19, 1985.
53. Lee Iacocca, *Iacocca: An Autobiography* (New York: Bantam, 1984), p.110. Also see Dye, *Who's Running America?* pp. 47–48; *New York Times*, March 19, 1985; July 15, 1985; December 17, 1986; April 12, 1991; G. William Domhoff, *Who Rules America Now?* (New York: Touchtone, 1983), pp. 59–78.
54. Lester Thurow, "The Leverage of Our Wealthiest 400," *New York Times*, October 11, 1984.
55. William Domhoff, "The Study of State and Ruling Class in Corporate America: New Directions," paper presented at the annual meeting of the American Political Science Association, Washington, D.C., September 3, 1977, provides a good example of how family stock control can be hidden. His research focuses on the Weyerhaeuser lumber company.
56. Robert Sheehan, "Proprietors in the World of Big Business," *Fortune* (June 15,1967), pp. 178,182.
57. Gerald Colby, *Du Pont: Behind the Nylon Curtain* (New York: Lyle Stuart, 1985); Dye, *Who's Running America?* pp. 40–49; Parenti, *Democracy for the Few*, p. 13.
58. Peter Collier and David Horowitz, *Rockefellers: An American Dynasty* (New York: Holt, Rinehart and Winston, 1976); Ferdinand Lundberg, *The Rockefeller Syndrome* (Secaucus, N.J.: Lyle Stuart, 1975); Dye, *Who's Running America?* pp. 40–46.
59. Dye, *Who's Running America?*, pp. 40–46.
60. William Domhoff, *Who Rules America?* (Englewood Cliffs, N.J.: Prentice-Hall, 1967), p. 40.
61. C. Wright Mills, *The Power Elite* (New York: Oxford University Press, 1956), p. 122. I have focused on publicly traded corporate stock, but there is no evidence that including privately held or nontraded stock would dilute the concentration of ownership.
62. Peter Drucker, *The Unseen Revolution* (New York: Harper & Row, 1976).
63. *Christian Science Monitor*, December 6,1985.
64. See *New York Times*, December 18, 1990; February 23, 1990.
65. *New York Times*, December 18, 1990; November 2, 1989; Committee on Governmental Operations, "Corporate Ownership and Control," 94th Cong., 2nd sess., November 1976 (Washington, D.C.: GPO, 1971); *New York Times*, January 22,1978.
66. *New York Times*, January 26, 1996.
67. Dye, *Who's Running America?* p. 47.
68. See Memphis *Commercial Appeal*, April 1, 1989, p. A14.
69. Dye, *Who's Running America?* p. 47.
70. Federal Reserve Board, *Flow of Fund Accounts, Assets, and Liabilities* (Washington, D.C.: GPO, 1995). The 1995 figure, including all stock held by a combination of public and private pension funds, is up from 5 percent in 1965.
71. Department of Commerce, *Statistical Abstracts*, 1995, p. 383; *New York Times*, April 13, 1992.

72. The number is only about one in ten in the private sector. See Department of Commerce, *Statistical Abstracts*, 1995, Table 696; Kirk Victor, "Labor's New Look," *National Journal*, October 14, 1995, pp. 2522–2527.

73. For example, see Leslie Wayne, "U.S. Official in Plea to Pension Funds," *New York Times*, October 12, 1993.

74. For supporting evidence, see Gayle B. Thompson, "Pension Coverage and Benefits: Findings from the Retirement History Society," U.S. Department of Health, Education and Welfare, Social Security Administration, *Social Security Bulletin* (February 1978); U.S. Congress, Senate Committee on Labor and Public Welfare, "Welfare and Pension Plans Investigation," 84th Cong., 2nd sess.,1956 (Washington, D.C.: GPO, 1956), pp. 11–14; *New York Times*, February 24,1978.

75. Drucker, *Unseen Revolution*.

76. See Dye, *Who's Running America?* pp. 22–23; Phillips, *Boiling Point*, pp. 139–145; Jonathan Hicks, "Foreign Owners Are Shaking Up the Competition," *New York Times*, May 28, 1989.

77. Jonathan Hicks, "The Takeover of American Industry," *New York Times*, May 28, 1989. Also see Jack Anderson, "Who Owns America?" *Parade Magazine*, April 16, 1989, pp. 4–7; Department of Commerce, *Statistical Abstracts*, pp. 805–807.

78. Department of Commerce, *Statistical Abstracts of the United States*, p. 555; *New York Times,* July 3, 1991.

79. Department of Commerce, *Statistical Abstracts of the United States*, p. 532; *New York Times*, March 30, 1987; *U.S. News and World Report*, August 18,1977. Also see Martin Tolchin and Susan Tolchin, *Buying into America* (New York: Times Books, 1987).

80. Department of Commerce, *Survey of Current Business* (Washington, D.C.: GPO, March 1996), p. 45.

81. For example, see 1980 *Statistical Abstracts*, p. 471; Federal Reserve Board and Internal Revenue Service, *1992 Survey of Consumer Finances* (Washington, D.C.: GPO, 1992). For more trend estimates, see Edward N. Wolff, "Trends in Household Wealth in the United States, 1962–83 and 1983–89," *Review of Income and Wealth* (June 1994); Edward N. Wolff, "The Rich Get Increasingly Richer," Economic Policy Institute, *Briefing Paper*, 1992; or the work of Wolff, Claudia Goldin, and Bradford De Long, cited in Sylvia Nasar, "The Rich Get Richer, But Never the Same Way Twice," *New York Times*, August 16, 1992; Internal Revenue Service, *Supplemental Statistics of Income Bulletin* (Washington, D.C.: GPO, 1983); Lampman, *Share of Top Wealth-holders*; James D. Smith and Staunton K. Calvert, "Estimating the Wealth of Top Wealth-holders from Estate Tax Returns," Proceedings of the American Statistical Association (1965); unpublished estimates by James D. Smith, the Urban Institute, and Pennsylvania State University.

82. For a more detailed discussion of actual management structures, see Dye, *Who's Running America?* pp. 24–30.

83. For an outline of this ongoing debate, see ibid., p. 28. Also see Samuelson and Nordhaus, *Economics*, pp. 171–172.

84. Dye, *Who's Running America?* p. 177.

85. Ibid., pp. 175–179. Also see Edward W. Jones, Black Managers: The Dream Deferred," *Harvard Business Review* (May/June 1986), pp. 84–93.

86. *New York Times*, April 12, 1992.

87. Kolko, *Wealth and Power*, p. 67. Kolko also details directors as managers (pp. 60–61) and as owners of large blocks of stock (pp. 61–65). Also see Paul Blumberg, "Another Day, Another $3,000," in Mark J. Green et al. (eds.), *The Big Business Reader* (New York: Pilgrim Press, 1983), pp. 316–332; *Wall Street Journal*, April 18, 1978; Sheehan, "Proprietors," p. 12; Mills, *Power Elite*, pp. 121–122; D. Villarejo, "Stock Ownership and the

Control of Corporations," *New University Thought* (Fall 1961), pp. 33–77, (Winter 1962), pp. 45–65; Jeremy Larner, "The Effect of Management Control on the Profits of Large Corporations," in Maurice Zeitlin (ed.), *American Society Inc.* (Chicago: Rand McNally, 1970), pp. 251–262; Paul Baran and Paul Sweezy, *Monopoly Capital* (New York: Monthly Review Press, 1966), pp. 34–35; Edward S. Herman, *Corporate Control, Corporate Power* (New York: Cambridge University Press, 1981).

88. See Memphis *Commercial Appeal*, April 1, 1989.

89. Ira Katznelson and Mark Kesselman, *The Politics of Power* (Orlando, Fla.: Harcourt Brace Jovanovich, 1979), p. 79. Also see Ralph Miliband, *The State in Capitalist Society* (New York: Basic Books, 1969), pp. 35–36; Herman, *Corporate Control, Corporate Power*.

90. *New York Times*, April 13,1985.

91. For example, see Samuelson and Nordhaus, *Economics*, p. 172. As an example of what happens when large investors perceive managerial deviation from their interests, see Sarah Bartlett, "Big Funds Pressing for Voice In Management of Companies," *New York Times*, February 23, 1990.

92. Edward S. Mason, "Corporation," *International Encyclopedia of the Social Sciences*, vol. 3 (1968), pp. 396–403. Also see William Darity, Jr., "The Managerial Class and Industrial Policy," *Industrial Relations* 25 (Spring 1986), pp. 217–227.

93. For a more complete critique of the owner-management separation thesis, on both conceptual and empirical grounds, see Maurice Zeitlin, "Corporate Ownership and Control," *American Journal of Sociology*, (March 1974), pp. 1073–1119. Also see Miliband's critique of Galbraith in *The Socialist Register* (1968); Herman, *Corporate Control, Corporate Power*.

94. Dye, *Who's Running America?* p. 196.

Chapter 5

Functions of a Welfare State

In the fall of 1972, Charles V. Hamilton published an article titled "Conduit Colonialism and Public Policy" in which he set out a model that had four basic components: taxpayers, government, welfare recipients, and "welfare beneficiaries"—wealthy individuals who make sizable profits selling goods and services to the welfare-receiving poor. A primary point was to show how governmental welfare programs caused their recipients to function as channels for transferring money from the paychecks of the average taxpayer to the pockets of a group of wealthy elites. This pass-through occurred when the recipients paid inflated amounts of taxpayer-provided money to the welfare beneficiaries: the landlords, doctors, pharmacists, and other vendors who served them. Consequently, the recipient was a "conduit" and was being "colonized" in the process—left dependent on others for subsistence and at the same time absorbing much of the wrath of the average taxpayer.[1]

By using an extended version of Hamilton's "conduit colonialism" model, this chapter attempts to estimate the degree to which America's political economy functions to enrich an "owning class" at the expense of the rest of American society. But whereas Hamilton focused on the systemic functions of the poor as welfare recipients, this analysis will extend his model to focus on the systemic functions of the black and white middle and working classes as well.

In particular, the chapter attempts to estimate the amount of money that has been transferred from the black and white middle and working classes to the bank accounts of the small white owning class. This transfer takes a variety of forms, among them private-sector profits from sales to governmental and nongovernmental consumers and direct transfers from government in the form of grants and credit subsidies.

The chapter concludes that the rich are getting richer and the poor poorer in the United States. That will come as no real surprise to more than three-quarters of the American public, who are already convinced of that.[2] The chapter also concludes that average Americans, black and white, pay a sizable share of their paychecks to government each year and have not been pleased about having that hard-earned money go to many of the existing welfare recipients. Somewhat less obvious is that a significant portion of those paychecks also goes to the owners of corporate capital, as a sort of "tribute" for the privilege of living in the country they own, and that government, welfare recipients, and this owning class interrelate to create that reality. The documentation and explanation of how that happens will be the primary focus of this chapter.

Where is the opposition to this arrangement? The last sections of the chapter present evidence that much middle- and working-class anger is diverted toward the poor. In addition, many in the exploited population are coopted by their faith in a mythology that holds out the hope of interclass mobility as a reward for talent, hard work, and frugality.

Before beginning, however, three methodological qualifications are in order.

First of all, it is clear that the operation of the economic system is a dynamic process. Corporate profits, for example, generally are not hoarded away in the vaults of the owning class. Instead, they are often spun back into the economy in the form of investments, purchases, and the like. What this chapter attempts to provide is a reasonable indication of which class groupings have been gaining and which losing in the course of this dynamic arrangement.

Second, along those same lines, it is important to note that governmental policy is also a moving target in its own right. We are living through a period of considerable political instability, reflected in the varying partisan control of Congress and the White House, and consequently in taxing and spending priorities. Whether the issue is welfare reform, corporate subsidies, or tax rates, it is difficult to accurately describe a process that is changing almost daily.

Lastly, certain definitions and measures have been dictated by the best and most recent data available at the time the book was written.[3]

THE CONCEPTUAL MODEL

The primary components of my adaptation of Charles V. Hamilton's model are presented in Figure 5. 1.

Government

In domestic policymaking, it can be argued that government (meaning federal, state, and local levels combined), as an institution, has come to play three basic roles. Economists call them allocation, stabilization, and redistribution. Allocation is the provision of maintenance, or "housekeeping," services. These include police and fire protection, educating the young, and keeping the streets and highways paved. Stabilization involves government using fiscal and monetary policies to help maintain a healthy, growing economy. If successful, these actions help secure adequate numbers of jobs, goods, and services for an ever-increasing American population. Finally, through redistribution, government attempts to compensate people who suffer significant economic hardship in the course of this process. It does so by using tax revenues to provide public assistance when the breadwinner of a family is unable to

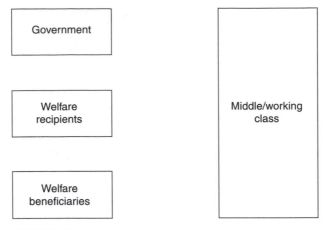

FIGURE 5.1
Welfare State Capitalism: The Participants

work or to earn enough money to provide the family with the essentials of life. Other examples are job training for people who lack marketable skills and unemployment compensation for workers who lose their jobs because their employers shifted production patterns or location in order to operate more efficiently.

Economist James O'Connor collapses these three categories into two and calls them the accumulation and legitimation functions. Government assists the process of capital accumulation by attempting to guarantee an adequate supply of venture capital and productive labor so that the owners of capital can and will invest in ways that will lead to stable economic growth, for example, by providing tax breaks and subsidies to corporations ("social investment"), teachers to educate the corporate work force, road crews to help minimize corporations' transportation costs, police to protect corporate property, and so on ("social consumption"). In legitimation, government compensates people who become economically dislocated, so that the necessary level of social harmony can be maintained, as by providing maintenance services and social-welfare programs ("social expenditures"). As the ownership of capital becomes more concentrated, the capitalist class can coerce the government into socializing even more of the costs of capital accumulation and production, while the benefits remain largely private. This, however, requires that the government also spend more and more on social expenditures in order to retain legitimacy with the nonowners. Thus the role of government continues to expand, and it essentially stabilizes a system that smiles most favorably on the owning class.[4]

The Owning Class (Hamilton's "Welfare Beneficiaries")

> I hate to use the word *class*. We're responsible, fortunate people, old families, the people who have something.[5]

According to economists Paul Samuelson and William Nordhaus, "if we made an income pyramid out of a child's blocks, with each layer portraying $500 of income, the peak would be far higher than Mt. Everest, but most people would be within a few feet of the ground.[6] For our purposes, the *owning class* consists of the people highest off the ground in that income pyramid—or the even steeper wealth pyramid. These are the elite group of people, almost entirely white by race, who assume the chore of accumulating the bulk of the nation's wealth and, ideally, in the process create relatively stable patterns of capital investment. Their discretion in the latter regard adds considerable economic and political power to the personal and family security their wealth provides.[7]

As defined here, this group represents the top 1 percent of American households in terms of wealth,[8] with average assets of nearly $7 million in value.[9] As a group, they have consistently owned a clear majority of the nation's business assets;[10] and, their wealth holdings guarantee virtually all of them enough unearned income to keep them in the nation's top 5 percent of income earners even if they do not work.[11] They make 16.4 percent of all national income,[12] averaging nearly $700,000 per household.[13] By contrast, as we saw in Chapter 4, less than 1 percent of all black households have ever fallen into this category; thus, for empirical convenience, these black households have been included in the middle- and working-class grouping.[14]

Besides wages, interest, gifts, and inheritance, the owning class derives its income from at least three other sources: the work of their employees, direct government aid, and indirect government aid. To begin with, they make profits from investments of their capital by charging more for products and services than employees are paid to produce and distribute them.[15] Direct government aid includes government subsidies like low-interest loans and tax abatements and profits derived from contracts with government for building things like highways, bombers, housing, and other durable goods. Indirect government aid is the profit realized when selling goods and services to the publicly subsidized indigent (called "welfare recipients" from here on).

Welfare Recipients (Lower Class)

> In Brooklyn's grimy Bedford Stuyvesant ghetto, a welfare mother surveys her $195-a-month tenement apartment, an unheated, vermin-ridden urban swamp. The bathroom ceiling and sink drip water on the cracked linoleum floor. There are no lights, no locks on the doors.[16]

If they are aware of its availability and not too proud to accept it, most indigent Americans are eligible to receive at least some form of relief provisions from the state. Those opting to receive such assistance comprise roughly 10 percent of the U. S. population. Meanwhile, as Herbert Gans and others have pointed out, they and the eligibles not receiving this aid—roughly another 10 percent of Americans[17]—perform a number of economic functions. They serve the system, for example, in the following roles:[18]

1. *Marginal work force.* As long as relief payments are kept low enough, the able-bodied indigent are often compelled to accept virtually any job at any wage at any time. This adds a dimension of elasticity to work force supply as demand for labor periodically rises and falls.[19]

2. *Dirty work.* This segment of the population is also compelled to do even the most undesirable jobs.
3. *Rejects market.* Given their low incomes, even after welfare assistance, they are more likely to purchase unmarketable items such as damaged merchandise, stale food and beverages, out-of-style clothing, deteriorating housing and automobiles, and the like.
4. *Pawns.* At home, they have been driven from their neighborhoods in order to make way for urban renewal, new highways, hospitals, and universities. They also have provided a disproportionate number of the foot soldiers who have fought and died in America's wars abroad.[20]
5. *Steppingstones.* Their low status allows other groups, often only slightly better off, to feel superior and thus better about their own circumstances.
6. *Clients.* The programs that are designed to help them also provide jobs for the educated unemployed and underemployed, especially surplus administrators.
7. *Lightning rods.* They are an easily visible and vulnerable target for the wrath of the "middle and working class," members of which often feel overworked, underpaid, and overtaxed.
8. *Conduits.* They allow the capitalist class to squeeze venture capital out of the paychecks of the middle and working class. This is accomplished when government transfers money to welfare recipients, who in turn use it to purchase goods and services. The welfare recipients derive elements of their subsistence from these payments, while an often substantial portion of this relief dollar gets passed along to the owning class as profit from these transactions. For example, the landlord of a welfare hotel charges $1000 a month for a run-down efficiency apartment; the tenant gets barely subsistence-level shelter, and the landlord makes a sizable profit.[21]

Beyond those economic functions, whether rural or urban, young or old, married or single, migrant or stationary, black, white, red, or yellow, the indigents also have much else in common. Many experience hunger;[22] they live in almost constant fear of crime;[23] their health suffers as a result of their poverty;[24] and they are much more likely to die prematurely.[25] They also remain rather hopelessly in debt—often to unscrupulous loan sharks; are more likely to divorce;[26] tend to remain socially isolated;[27] and a growing number have become homeless, with estimates ranging from 230,000 to 4 million.[28]

After a trip to West Africa, *Time* correspondent Robert Wurmstedt concluded:

> The poverty in the black and Puerto Rican neighborhoods on the West Side of Chicago is worse than any poverty I saw in West Africa. . . . [The poor of West Africa] do not live in constant fear of violence, vermin, and fire. You don't find the same sense of desperation and hopelessness you find in the American ghetto.[29]

In addition, although the large majority of the able-bodied indigent are employed at least part of the year,[30] the shift to a postindustrial economy has severely limited many of their escape routes. Instead of full-time unionized factory positions with decent wages, benefits, and opportunities for advancement, they are far more likely to end up working at part-time, low-wage service jobs, without benefits and with very limited opportunity to advance.[31] For indigent blacks in particular, this is doubly distressing. As William Julius Wilson put it, "It's as though racism, having put the black underclass in its economic place, stepped aside to watch technological change finish the job."[32]

For the purposes of analysis, this group (the "lower class") has been defined as the bottom 20 percent of American families in terms of wealth, with the average household owing more than it owns.[33] As a group, they made 3.1 percent of the nation's income, averaging $6000 per household; and, rarely making more than 125 percent of the federal poverty level, they have generally been eligible to receive one or more forms of public assistance from the welfare state.[34] Approximately 40 percent of all black households, and a majority of black children, fall into this category.[35]

Middle- and Working-Class (MC/WC) Work Force and Tax Base

> Middle class is where you can live in a decent neighborhood, drive a decent car and get all your necessities.[36]

The 79 percent of American households in between the owning and lower classes, including 60 percent of America's black households, constitute the "middle and working class."[37] This group has an average net worth of $157,000; but most of this is owned by those at the very top of the group. For example, that amount is nearly cut in half if you omit the top 10 percent of these households, and it falls by nearly two-thirds if the top quarter are excluded. It also should be noted that for most members virtually all of this wealth is tied up in their houses and cars, with very little invested in financial assets like stocks and bonds.[38] Beyond wealth, the group makes just over 80 percent of the nation's income; averaging $43,000 per year;[39] however, increasingly it requires the paychecks of at least two wage earners in the household in order to remain in this category, especially for African Americans.[40]

Working in either the private or public sector to produce the nation's goods and services, the members of this group also find themselves caught in two additional economic predicaments. Most are employees of the owning class, working for a wage that is less than the market value of what they produce. Secondly, taxation deprives them of a significant portion of their incomes; while, as we shall see below, billions of those dollars end up in the pockets of the owning class.[41]

What is left for those who work for a living? Even before taxes are applied, the average family household has an income below what the Bureau of Labor Statistics estimates it costs such a family to meet an "intermediate budget" for food, shelter, clothing, transportation, and personal and medical care.[42] And with African Americans spending a higher than average proportion of their incomes on such necessities, this becomes even more of a problem for the black middle and working class.[43]

Lastly, without a cushion of wealth to fall back on if times get significantly worse, these middle- and working-class people find themselves economically vulnerable. A 5-year University of Michigan study, for example, concluded that 7 out of 10 American families have at least an even chance of spending some years of their lives in "economic distress," most likely the result of the family losing the paycheck of one of its breadwinners.[44]

Much of this should become clearer by examining the "welfare state capitalism" model of Figure 5.1 as applied to the United States. The model contains seven junctures where money is transferred from one group of participants to another: private-sector corporate profits; personal taxes; direct subsidies, contract profits, interest profits (corporate subsidies); public assistance; and conduit capitalism. The model also shows a venting of pent-up frustration, termed "directed wrath."

WELFARE STATE CAPITALISM

> Black people cannot afford the social injustices of capitalism. They cannot afford a system which creates privileged classes within an already superexploited and underprivileged community. They cannot afford a system which organizes community resources and then distributes the resulting wealth in a hierarchical fashion, with those who need least getting most.
>
> Robert Allen[45]

Private-Sector Corporate Profits

When the owning class invests its money in corporations, it expects something in return. What it gets in return are profits (see Figure 5.2). These derive from paying workers less than the market value of what they have produced. In other words, this is a return to capital, not to labor.

These corporate profits have accounted for approximately 10 percent or more of all national income throughout most of this century.[46] Corporate profits from domestic industries alone reached $256.2 billion in 1994, even after subtracting the owners' taxes, adjustments for inventory valuation and capital consumption, and profits from transactions with both government and welfare recipients (considered later in this model).[47]

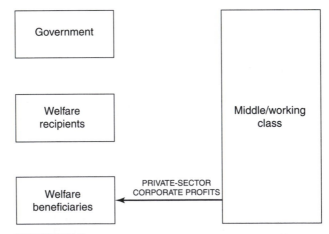

FIGURE 5.2
Welfare State Capitalism: Private-Sector Corporate Profits

Focusing on African Americans, such private profit taking has allowed the white owning class to acquire billions of dollars of income each year as profits from its sales of goods and services to the black middle and working class. In 1994, the white owning class extracted more than $7 billion in profits as a result of these transactions—nearly $128 billion when combined with sales to the white middle and working class.[48]

Personal Taxes

We don't pay taxes. Only the little people pay taxes.

Leona Helmsley[49]

Although Mrs. Helmsley exaggerates the case, when tax burdens imposed by federal, state, and local governments are combined, it is quite clear that the United States does not begin to have a *progressive* tax system. Americans who make most of the money still have most of the money after government is paid. In 1985, for instance, economist Joseph Pechman found the poorest one-tenth of American families making 1.3 percent of all adjusted family income before taxes and 1.3 percent of it afterward. At the other end of the income spectrum, the wealthiest one-tenth made 33.1 percent of all adjusted family income before taxes and had 33.9 percent of it after all taxes had been paid.[50] Ten years later, Thomas Dye continued to note that "before-tax and after-tax income distributions are nearly identical."[51]

Now add the fact that the United States has no wealth tax as such. In other words, besides local real estate taxes, individuals are taxed only on the yearly income derived from their stocks, trust funds, bank accounts, and so on, instead of being taxed annually on the overall value of such wealth. Inheritance and estate taxes are applied once the individual dies, but even those are fraught with loopholes. Prior to death, for instance, a wealthy person may (1) gradually liquidate the estate by giving it away in untaxed annual gifts to each heir, (2) sell property to the inheritor(s) for a nominal fee, or (3) create trust funds that will be taxed only when the inheritors collect their yearly allotment. The entire estate is also granted a $1 million dollar federal estate tax deduction ($1.3 million if farms or businesses are involved), and the estate is subject to inheritance taxation only when first put into trusts. (Unspent trust money can be passed along to the next heirs without incurring any inheritance taxation.)[52] In addition, *lead trusts* can be established that allow wealth to be inherited tax free as long as interest income goes to charitable causes for a fixed period of time.[53] Beyond that, a number of highly wealthy Americans have managed to avoid capital gains and estate taxes altogether by renouncing their citizenship and moving abroad. Tax consultant William Zabel refers to such expatriation as "the ultimate estate plan."[54]

In the end, then, estate and gift taxes have been providing less than 1 percent of all governmental revenues despite the billions of dollars' worth of wealth that exists and is passed on incrementally every year. Thus, huge family fortunes often can be amassed and handed down from generation to generation with little government interference.[55] It also should come as no surprise that thousands of the nation's wealthiest individuals pay few if any personal income taxes either, once all tax breaks have been utilized.[56] Meanwhile, average Americans working for a wage or salary wind up paying the lion's share of the ever-increasing (nonprogressive) government tax burden.[57]

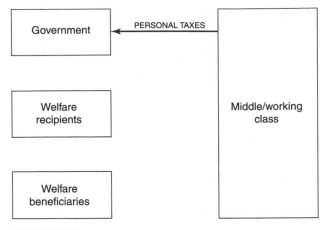

FIGURE 5.3
Welfare State Capitalism: Personal Taxes

By 1994, Americans were paying more than $1.2 trillion in taxes every year (see Figure 5.3). In that year, the black middle and working class paid nearly $54 billion in taxes, while black and white workers combined to pay more than $978 billion.[58]

Corporate Subsidies

> The myth of the self-regulating market has outlived the conditions that gave rise to it . . . In this large sense, it is capitalists themselves, by their demands for state intervention, who have given the lie to the myth that powered their ascendency.[59]

Direct Subsidies.   Each year the *Survey of Current Business* compiles the amount of government subsidies paid to enterprises primarily in the agricultural, construction, and transportation industries (see Figure 5.4). In 1994, the owning class's share of those subsidies amounted to more than $21.5 billion. This meant that the black middle and working class transferred more than $955 million to the white owners by means of these governmental subsidies, with black and white workers combining to contribute more than $17 billion.[60]

Contract Profits.   The owning class is also reaping profits from business transactions with government, as its corporations sell various goods and services to the federal, state, and local governments (see Figure 5.4). These profits were estimated to be more than $7.5 billion in 1994. This cost the black middle and working class nearly $336 million, with the total middle and working class contributing more than $6 billion.[61]

Interest Profits.   Government indebtedness continues to mount into the trillions of dollars, and thus government continues to pay more and more interest to its lenders (see Figure 5.4). In 1994, these interest payments meant more than $6.5 billion in income for the white owning class. As a result of this vehicle, then, the owning

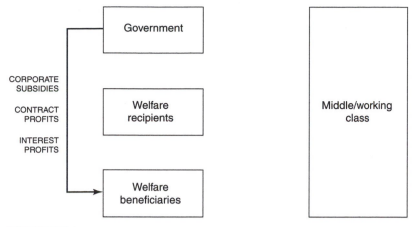

FIGURE 5.4
Welfare State Capitalism: Corporate Subsidies

class extracted nearly $300 million dollars from the paychecks of the black middle and working class that year, and more than $5 billion from the middle and working class as a whole.[62]

Public Assistance

Public assistance refers to those governmental programs designed to ease the load of being indigent in the United States of America, programs such as family assistance, Medicaid, food stamps, rent subsidies, and the Supplemental Security Income program (see Figure 5.5). They provide low-income Americans with money and vouchers with which to purchase necessities like food, shelter, clothing, and medical assistance. Beginning primarily with Franklin Roosevelt's New Deal and accelerating dramatically during and after Lyndon Johnson's Great Society era, such relief payments have grown to sizable proportions. In 1984, for example, some 74 need-based programs provided millions of indigents with over $134 billion worth of "relief."[63] By 1994, the total spent on all "cash and non-cash benefits for persons with limited incomes" exceeded $306 billion.[64] But the story does not end there, for the recipients do not eat, wear, and live under these checks and coupons. They spend them, and in the process, they provide additional profit for the owning class.

Conduit Capitalism

Charles V. Hamilton was one of the first to note the "conduit" function played by nearly all relief recipients.[65] As indicated earlier, this occurs when various proportions of their governmentally funded purchases flow on to the owning class—wealthy landlords, the stockholders of pharmaceutical companies, nursing home operators—as profits from these transactions (see Figure 5.6). Although it is difficult to determine how much money each of these vendors is making by serving the poor, it is possible to estimate what the owning-class vendors as a group have made. For example,

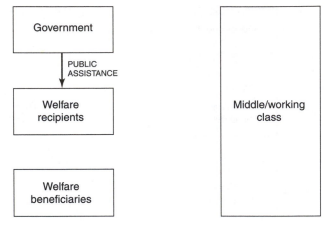

FIGURE 5.5
Welfare State Capitalism: Public Assistance

applying the average corporate profit rates to the billions spent on need-based public assistance programs, the owning class garnered nearly $180 million from the pockets of the black middle and working class, and more than $3 billion from the entire middle and working class.[66]

How does this actually occur? Consider the following examples of this phenomenon—some legal and some illegal.

> **Case 1.** The city of New York houses 2,900 homeless families in welfare hotels, with each family living in a single room, fewer than half of which have refrigerators and almost none of which have stoves or allow cooking facilities. The city pays landlords a monthly average of $1,900 per room for these accommodations.[67]

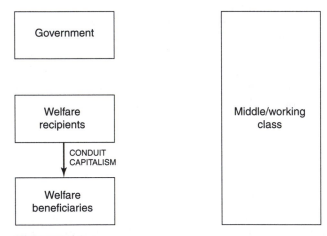

FIGURE 5.6
Welfare State Capitalism: Conduit Capitalism

Case 2. Builders, contractors, and operators in the notorious nursing home in-
    dustry make millions of dollars from government while elderly patients
    reportedly go underfed and underattended and are occasionally even
    being found in shock from cold or dehydration or starving and fighting
    each other for food.[68]

Case 3. Certain hospitals engage in a practice known as "upcoding," in which
    they receive larger than allowable payments from Medicare by inflating
    the seriousness of the illnesses they treat.[69]

Case 4. A group of doctors in New York City get names of Medicaid patients by
    enticing them to clinics with free food, then bill Medicaid for more than
    $1 million in psychotherapy sessions they never performed.[70]

Case 5. A string of *Medicaid mills* writes numerous unneeded prescriptions for
    Medicaid recipients who then fill them and sell the drugs cheaply to a
    series of pharmacies which turn around and sell the drugs at below-mar-
    ket prices making a tidy profit.[71]

Case 6. National Health Laboratories, Inc., one of the nation's largest labora-
    tory chains with facilities in 41 states, agrees to a $110 million plea bar-
    gain arrangement after being caught billing Medicaid for numerous un-
    necessary blood tests.[72]

Case 7. Industries producing health care items—companies like American
    Home Products, G. D. Searle, Merck, Smith Kline, Sterling Drug, Eli
    Lilly, Johnson & Johnson, Miles Laboratories, Pfizer, Squibb, and Up-
    john—reap some of the highest profits in the corporate world. Through
    Medicaid, the American taxpayer has certainly paid a significant share of
    their hefty profits.[73]

Now, none of this is meant to suggest that a considerable amount of good has not
come from governmental relief programs. Public assistance has provided badly
needed items such as food, shelter, clothing, and medical assistance to many who
would have been significantly worse off without it. As long practiced, however, such
assistance also has allowed for a considerable amount of profit taking on the part of
the owning class.

Summary

America's political-economic system does seem to reinforce existing class relationships. This becomes even more obvious when all of the above figures are combined.

In 1994, nearly $9 billion was transferred from the paychecks of the black mid-
dle and working class to the investment portfolios of the white owning class. That figure climbed to nearly $160 billion when considering the black and white middle and
working classes combined. This amounts to a "tribute" of sorts for the privilege of living and working in the country owned by the white elites.[74]

Government was directly involved in one-fifth of this transfer. It was also indirectly involved in the amount transferred through private-sector profits, given its
nonprogressive tax system, economic regulations or lack thereof, many of its maintenance services, and so on.

Most recently, welfare reform efforts have been designed to coerce many of the poor into low-wage employment as a condition of receiving relief. This, too, will enhance the position of the owning class by providing them with an easily exploitable group of workers in what essentially will amount to a condition of indentured servitude. If successful, then, *private-sector corporate profits* will increase as *conduit profits* are reduced, leaving the overall *tribute* levels pretty much unchanged.[75]

The Trickle-down Fallacy

As at least partial justification for such a *tribute* system, both liberal and conservative politicians from time to time have espoused varying versions of *supply-side economics*, an economic theory based on the premise that if the wealthy are allowed to get wealthier, a reasonable amount will *trickle down* to everyone else, making the entire society better off in the long-run.[76]

Reality, however, poses some serious problems for that theory. First of all, there is no guarantee that such increased wealth will necessarily be invested in job-producing endeavors in the United States.[77] Instead, much of it may well be invested abroad or spent here on things such as collectibles or quick-profit speculations.[78] Secondly, even if it is invested in a manner that produces American jobs, there is little guarantee that such new jobs will necessarily pay the kinds of wages and benefits needed to provide middle-class life-styles for the employees.[79]

As a test, it should be noted that the rich have indeed been getting considerably richer by both absolute and relative measures. Looking at families ranked by income, for example, the poorest family among the nation's top 5 percent of families made $92,158 (1993 dollars) in 1980 and $113,182 by 1993. That's an increase of nearly 23 percent. In relative terms, the top 5 percent of American families increased their proportion of all family income from 15.3 percent in 1980 to 19.1 percent by 1993.[80] In addition, at the very top of that group, the number of centimillionaires more than tripled over this time frame, while the period also produced the nation's first billionaires.[81]

Meanwhile, not much appears to have trickled down. The income of the median white family grew some 2 percent, seeming at least minimally to support the trickle-down concept. By contrast, however, it also should be noted that the median income for black families actually declined 3 percent; and, as will be demonstrated below, the gain for white families was far from uniform across the group.[82] In relative terms, as the top 5 percent of American families were increasing their portion of national income, the bottom 80 percent saw their income share decline rather uniformly across the board.[83] Susan Mayer and Christopher Jencks conclude that the distribution of income has become "more unequal than at any time since the Census Bureau began collecting such data in 1947."[84]

Although such *creaming* may well be the natural result of a capitalistic economic system, the postindustrial developments discussed in Chapter 2 appear to be accelerating this trend. Amid the shift from an industry-dominated economy to a service-dominated one, not only is the owning class getting richer, but also a division is developing within the middle and working class. Skilled technicians and professionals continue to do well in the technological era, while much of the rest of the class has slipped into the secondary labor market.[85]

Paul Starobin summarizes it this way,

> Using new technologies and management methods, many large firms have reorganized the production process in ways that have increased demand for a relatively small cadre of well-skilled, well-educated workers—and reduced demand for the much larger cluster of low-skilled workers. It's a trend that began in the manufacturing sector, which has become increasingly automated, and has now spread to the service sector.[86]

George Sternleib and James Hughes note this general phenomenon when analyzing economic indicators between the mid–1970s and the mid–1980s—a crucial juncture in postindustrial development (see Chapter 2). Looking at constant-dollar income distributions, they found growth in the proportion of the population making $35,000, clear shrinkage of the $15,000-$35,000 group, and growth in the percentage making less than $15,000.[87]

The growth at the top of the middle and working class reflects the increase in professional and technical positions integral to an expanding postindustrial service economy. As for the losses in the rest of the class, consider the fact that between 1973 and 1982, for example, the United States lost 1.3 million manufacturing jobs, which paid an average of $17,000 per year, while adding an even larger number of service positions that paid an average of only $12,000 per year.[88] More Americans came to be employed by McDonald's than by General Motors.[89] Not surprisingly, the unionization rate for the private-sector work force slipped to scarcely more than 10 percent,[90] while the number of strikes continues to decline and has reached the lowest level since World War II.[91] The number of involuntary part-time workers doubled.[92] Real-dollar average hourly wages declined for production and nonsupervisory workers as a whole, with roughly one-half of all new jobs created between 1976 and 1985 paying a family head poverty-level wages.[93] Home ownership became significantly more difficult to attain;[94] and the number of persons without health insurance increased markedly.[95]

Noting similar developments into the 1990s, Martin Carnoy found that middle class workers who managed to ride on top of postindustrialism's technological wave tended to be those with educations that allowed them to process and analyze information. Meanwhile, those with manual skills, or few skills at all, tended to miss that wave and sink into the service sector's sea of secondary labor market opportunities[96] where "40 percent of (the nation's) jobs still can be learned in less than one month and are generally low-paying."[97]

As evidence of those who caught that wave, scarcely more than 1 million American families earned $100,000 in income as recently as 1967. Using constant dollars, that number jumped to 2.7 million households by 1980 and 5.6 million by 1993.[98] Meanwhile, most every other group's real-dollar income remained where it was or declined.[99] For example, there has been a relatively steady increase in the percentage of full-time workers working for what the federal government deems to be *low wages*—less than $7.00 per hour.[100]

Since the early 1970s, aggregate Census Bureau data tell us that median family and household incomes have remained relatively steady or stagnant, depending on how you look at it.[101] Either way, these aggregate measures mask the fact that the distribution is becoming *bimodal*—meaning there are increasingly more people at the relatively higher and lower ends, with fewer in the middle.[102]

Now, there is some intergroup movement occurring over time (e.g., households moving from the lower-to-middle group when a wage earner is added or from the middle-to-lower group following a divorce or layoff.) Nevertheless, society as a whole continues to end up with pretty much the same class configuration trends after those movements occur.[103] And, as Greg Duncan et al. conclude, "A middle income adult's chances of falling from the middle to the bottom of the distribution increasingly (have) exceeded their chances of moving from the middle to the top . . . "[104]

Beyond all that, these figures actually understate the declining position of much of the middle and working class for a variety of reasons:

1. The large baby boom generation has begun to reach its peak earning years.
2. The number of multiple-income families has been growing markedly.[105]
3. Individuals are working longer hours at the expense of leisure time.[106]
4. Baby Boomers have married later and had smaller families than their predecessors, allowing for more discretionary per capita income, even when hourly wages were declining.[107]
5. Savings has declined and short-term borrowing increased in an attempt to maintain existing living standards.[108]
6. Welfare reform has cast the working class into competition with former welfare recipients for a variety of low-wage jobs, in an economy where the Federal Reserve Board is inclined to increase interest rates in order to slow growth if unemployment shrinks much below 5 percent.[109]

Thus the present does not appear as bad as it has become, and the future looks even less promising for many in the next generation of middle- and working-class families. But even for the present, this situation only appears to be intensified by the next development.

Real-dollar governmental spending has continued to increase. Therefore, given a nonprogressive tax structure, the corresponding growth in taxes has consumed much of what little the middle and working class gained as a result of any expanded economic pie. The average owning-class family, by contrast, received enough from their disproportionate share of increased income so that they could pay their taxes and still emerge with a sizable increase in after-tax income.[110]

In conclusion, there simply is not much recent evidence to support the supply-side economic theory; in fact, the opposite has seemed to be true of late. As tribute has grown since 1980, the income level of most people has remained where it was or dropped, while income gaps increased. According to Felix Rohatyn, "What is occurring is a huge transfer of wealth from lower-skilled middle-class American workers to the owners of capital assets and to the new technological aristocracy."[111] As Duncan et al. summarize, "the rising tide of economic growth in the 1980s appears to have lifted the yachts, but neither the tugboats nor the rowboats."[112]

Meanwhile, there is reason to believe that tribute will continue to rise. As described in Chapter 2, the advent of the postindustrial economy has further strengthened the bargaining position of the owners of capital. With expanding opportunities to invest virtually any place on the face of the earth, venture capitalists are likely to be increasingly successful at extracting concessions from government. Consequently, wealth and income gaps appear destined to continue to widen. The rich will get richer and more powerful, while most of the remainder of society becomes relatively poorer and more subordinate.

Directed Wrath

> Tax money is collected from the upper-lower and lower-middle classes (black and white)—whom I call the "middies"—and funneled through the conduit system to private hands in another segment of the economy. And all the while the ignorant, unsuspecting "middies" think their money is going to help "shiftless, lazy welfare cheats." Both the middies and the conduits are being pillaged.[113]

Watching its overall standard of living decline since the mid–1970s, much of the middle and working class has become frustrated. It is instructive, however, to note who ends up as a primary target of its wrath (see Figure 5.7).

The words *welfare recipient* seem consistently to conjure up one of two images in the minds of many middle Americans, particularly whites. The first is the black female heading up a household with numerous small or adolescent children, having lived somewhat comfortably on the dole for years and probably receiving more aid than she is legally entitled to receive. The second, even more resented, is the shiftless black male hanging out on the street corner drinking and joking with his friends when he could be working.[114]

A *New York Times* survey, for example, found nearly two-thirds of its nationwide respondents believing that welfare "encourages people to have larger families than they would have had otherwise," while a clear majority were convinced that welfare discourages "pregnant women from getting married."[115] Consequently, it should not be surprising that a near majority favored "requiring welfare mothers to accept contraceptive implants."[116] Meanwhile, when California Governor Pete Wilson signed a

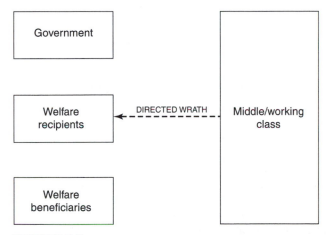

FIGURE 5.7
Welfare State Capitalism: Directed Wrath

welfare payment cut, he asserted that this would mean "one less six-pack per week."[117]

Lurking just beneath the surface of such stereotyping, however, is also the specter of race. After analyzing the "concerted ideological attack" on welfare recipients that has been building in the United States, Frances Fox Piven and Richard Cloward conclude that this "inevitably becomes an attack on minorities. . . . In this sense, the . . . brush being used to tar the welfare state is indeed black."[118]

There is no denying that a disproportionate share of the nation's black population has been on welfare, a reflection of their disproportionate poverty and underemployment.[119] Nevertheless, there is still a considerable difference between public assistance myth and public assistance reality. The reader is encouraged to take the test presented below.

If you answered "true" to any of these questions, you may well be one of Charles Hamilton's misguided *middies*.

The typical AFDC-receiving family was white, with one or two children, had been on the dole less than three years, and had gone on relief because of a divorce or separation.[120] Fewer than one quarter lived in government-subsidized housing;[121] and fewer than one in ten resided in urban ghettoes.[122] The average monthly benefit was $373;[123] and there was no credible empirical evidence that poor women had additional children in order to receive more welfare.[124]

Nonetheless, AFDC remained the lightning rod of the relief package, even though it comprised less than one-tenth of total welfare spending at the time it was eliminated. At least two-thirds of the recipients were children.[125] Most heads of those households were single mothers, and more than one-third of them had been employed during the previous year.[126] The number of able-bodied adult males receiving such relief had been estimated at 1 to 2 percent of the caseload[127]—not a particularly high figure in a period when 5 to 10 percent of those actively seeking work could not find it. In addition, contrary to popular belief, intergenerational welfare dependence was highly unusual;[128] and despite public fears to the contrary, there was very little evidence of actual welfare fraud. Of New York City's 1.1 million recipients, for example, there were only 184 arrests for welfare fraud in 1993—less than 0.02 percent.[129]

TEST

True or False. The typical family receiving Aid to Families with Dependent Children (AFDC):

1. was black?
2. resided in an urban ghetto?
3. received an AFDC check for more than $400 per month?
4. lived in publicly subsidized housing?
5. had been on the dole for more than three consecutive years?
6. went on relief because the mother was unmarried and had a child?
7. had three or more dependent children?
8. had additional children in order to receive more welfare?

If there was waste, it may well have been in the amount of resources expended over-seeing such programs. In Cook County, for instance, Northwestern University's John McKnight found some two-thirds of their poverty funds spent on administration.[130]

There is also the persistent belief that most able-bodied recipients of any type of welfare are simply too lazy to work their way out of poverty. In other words, most end up on welfare due to their own character flaws.[131] There has been little systematic measurement of recipients' desire to work; however, examples like the following do seem continually to reoccur.

> The subway system, about half of which is above ground, needed its track cleared of snow. It put out the word that it would pay people $5 an hour to do the job.
>
> The next morning they began to show up; hundreds at first, then thousands. No easy trick, mind you. Many of the streets weren't plowed yet. Public transportation wasn't running. People had to get up at 4 A.M. or 5 A.M and fight their way through thigh-high snow—sometimes miles—to get this job. Yet thousands did.
>
> The predictable thing happened. The city didn't want thousands. It wanted, at most, a few hundred. So, fist fights broke out over places in line and the people had to claw their way onto the buses. The buses then had to force their way through an angry mob that pounded on them and threatened to overturn them. Left behind, one enraged group of job applicants looted a nearby liquor store . . .
>
> One of the men who made the bus, explaining the riot, said: ". . . Those folks could see the job, they could smell it. They wanted it bad."[132]

There is no denying that personal irresponsibility contributes to some of the un-deremployment and poverty that leads to welfare reliance; yet, despite the monetary disincentives discussed below, a majority of these households have at least one wage earner, and two-thirds of those who leave the relief roles do not return.[133] Lou Harris found what the poor most wanted were (1) better job opportunities, (2) more school-ing, and (3) more job training, while their single biggest regret was not being ade-quately trained to support themselves.[134] And as for welfare, the poor hold virtually the same views as everyone else. For example, 88 percent of them believe the able-bodied should be required to attend school or training in order to receive welfare, and that poor people who have more children should not automatically receive more public aid.[135]

Another myth is that these recipients could live quite comfortably on public as-sistance. To begin with, remember that the median AFDC and food stamp allot-ments combined still left household income at less than three-quarters of the federal government's poverty level.[136] Now look specifically at what was provided in one of the nation's most generous states. In Illinois, for example, a single mother with one child was eligible to receive a monthly maximum of $313 in AFDC payments, $187 in food stamps, and a Medicaid card. That was less than $400 per month, and less than $5,000 per year.[137] Or consider a single mother with 9 children in the city of Chicago, who received Medicaid, $669 in AFDC, $833 in food coupons, and $40 for having infants in the house. Assuming the food stamps covered all food needs, that still left only $700 a month with which to buy clothing and other necessities for ten people besides paying rent, utilities, and transportation costs.[138]

A very real dilemma often develops. Again using Illinois as an example, consider the case of Linda Baldwin and her three children. Linda earned $1040 per month as a counselor, received some very limited health benefits, and still was eligible for $243 worth of food stamps. From that monthly sum, she paid $111 in Social Security and state taxes, $260 in rent for her publicly subsidized apartment, $60 for a transit pass, $20 for work clothes, and $35 for a telephone. That left less than $600 to cover all other expenses. Now, had she chosen not to work, under the previous welfare system she would have received $821 per month in AFDC and food stamp allotments, and her rent would have been only $80, leaving her $741 to cover expenses—not to mention Medicaid for herself and children, providing free dental and medical care, free prescriptions and eye glasses.[139] Rather than indicting the welfare system within which it occurred, this very real dilemma seems to be more of an indictment of the paltry wage and benefit packages in the secondary labor market—wherein an increasing proportion of American workers are left to work.[140]

Nevertheless, polls conducted during a particularly telling period reflect an increased animosity toward "welfare" when times are tough—animosity felt by average Americans, black and white.[141] Amid the real-dollar leveling of the mid–1960s, such attitudes were relatively favorable. For example, a majority of Americans felt that spending on "welfare and relief programs" was either not enough or about right.[142] Yet once those programs proliferated and the real-dollar incomes of middle- and working-class citizens began to plateau or decline in the postindustrial period, this tone changed considerably. By the late 1970s, for instance, some three out of five Americans felt "too much" was being spent on "welfare" and disapproved of most government-sponsored "welfare" programs. Two out of three respondents even mistakenly believed that public assistance costs made up a major part of governmental expenditures.[143] Those attitudes were still pretty much the same by the mid–1990s, despite some variation in sentiment over the intervening two decades.[144]

How, then, does one move to counteract this illusion of lazy, conniving, promiscuous welfare chiselers? A majority of Californians, for example, cited a desire to reduce "welfare expenditures" as their primary reason for supporting taxation-limiting Proposition 13.[145] Nationwide, as postindustrialism took hold, more than 40 percent of Americans favored cutting relief programs "a lot," and an "overwhelming number" of those favoring service cuts cited "welfare and social services" as clearly their most preferred target.[146] As part of the rationale, more than one-third of Americans incorrectly believed the majority of recipients were receiving more than they were legally entitled to;[147] thus, when asked which welfare reforms were most needed, the majority of Americans called for "better screening methods." The second most common response was to get those who can work off the welfare rolls.[148] By the mid–1990s, a large majority even favored cutting off indigent mothers of small children after they exceed a given number of years on the dole.[149]

At the governmental level, in apparent response to such sentiment, the amount of real-dollar expenditures on public assistance quit growing in the 1980s. For example, a combination of governmental assistance and tax policies lifted 30 percent of individuals in single-parent families out of poverty in 1979, but only 20 percent by 1990.[150] The proportion of the poor receiving AFDC shrunk from 55 percent in 1973 to 49 percent by 1992 (81 percent to 63 percent for poor children).[151] The typical state's maximum AFDC benefit was cut nearly in half between 1970 and 1994,[152] while the states also tightened eligibility for unemployment compensation,[153] and

Medicaid cuts meant the poor would have an increasingly difficult time finding medical treatment.[154] Then, in the summer of 1996, Congress passed and the President signed sweeping welfare reform legislation which further reduced the government's commitment of funds, while ending the AFDC program entirely.[155] Not surprisingly, the posttransfer income of the bottom one-fifth of American families has been declining in real dollars.[156]

In absolute terms, the rich are getting richer and the poor are getting poorer, and that reality is both reinforced and enhanced by the functioning of the welfare state capitalism model, summarized in Figure 5.8. So, just what keeps people in the middle and working class and the lower class going in the face of the political-economic realities just described? At least part of it can be explained by a faith in another long-standing bit of mythology.

AMERICAN MYTHOLOGY

> Americans seem willing to tolerate wide gaps between rich and poor so long as they view the door of opportunity as open.[157]

Horatio Alger (1834–1899) was a successful author who inspired generations of American youth with tales such as Ragged Dick, Tattered Tom, and Luck and Pluck, wherein penniless heroes gained wealth and fame through a combination of goodness and courage. Thus the *Horatio Alger myth* comes to read something like this:

> It is possible to go from rags to riches in the United States if one displays the right combination of abilities, hard work, thrift, and wise investment. Conversely, the existence of considerable economic inequality must be taken as a given, the necessary result of healthy competition between free, variably talented individuals.

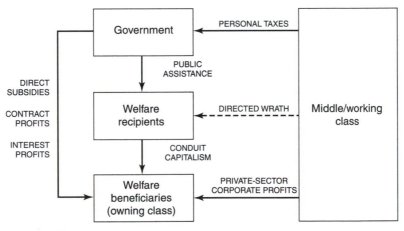

FIGURE 5.8
Welfare State Capitalism Model

A century later, the myth seems alive and well, for rich and poor, black and white. In a Gallup Poll, for instance, nearly two-thirds of all adults under 30 years of age considered themselves at least somewhat likely to be rich someday.[158] Now consider the realities.

Acquiring Riches

To begin with, the ranks of the owning class are not impenetrable. However, how one usually enters these ranks today might well cause poor Horatio Alger to turn uncomfortably in his grave.

> A young reporter asked a leading capitalist how he made his fortune: "It was really quite simple," the capitalist answered. "I bought an apple for five cents, spent the evening polishing it, and sold it the next day for 10 cents. With this I bought two apples, spent the evening polishing them, and sold them for 20 cents. And so it went until I had amassed $1.60. It was then that my wife's father died and left us a million dollars.[159]

Lester Thurow, studying families with incomes of more than $100,000 and wealth holdings averaging $1.5 million, found 57 percent of these families to have inherited substantial amounts of these estates.[160]

In an in-depth study of Connecticut probate records, Paul Menchik found much the same thing. Comparing children's estates to those of their parents, he estimated that some 30 percent of a child's estate will be directly left over from the parents' estate. However, if one assumes that the child invests the inheritance, the figure jumps to 50 percent at bond rates and well over 50 percent if stock market indexes are employed. He also notes that the larger the inheritance, the more of it is likely to survive; for example, if one person's lifetime resources are 10 percent higher than another person's, the first person's estate will be some 25 percent higher because a higher proportion of those resources can be saved and invested. The end result of all this is that the median child dies possessing 85 percent as much wealth (in real dollars) as his or her parents had accumulated by the time they died. The correlation coefficient is .635, meaning that a full 40 percent of a child's wealth is statistically determined by the level of parental wealth. Menchik concludes that if one is born to parents who are 10 times wealthier than someone else's, one is likely to die at least eight times wealthier than the other person.[161] It is also true, however, that more than 40 percent of the "great" and "less great" fortunes have been compiled without the benefit of substantial inheritance, but Thurow has found that this economic success is rarely the result of a lifetime of scrimping and saving. Rather, it comes as virtually "instant wealth." The person gambles or invests and happens to win, which is obvious when one looks at how quickly most of these fortunes were accumulated, often in a matter of a few years and seldom in two or more leaps. Therefore, this success comes to be seen much more as a matter of luck and seldom as the result of life-long hard work and frugality.

Thurow concludes that only about 10 percent of economic success is explicable by how hard one works or how frugal one has been. The rest is determined by a society's population trends, unemployment level, tastes, and so on, leaving some 70 to 80 percent of economic success unexplained by the standard variables such as education, experience, and personality traits. Hard work may be necessary, but it is certainly not sufficient, and there is little indication that it is even necessary. A person may well work hard and even save, but that is not likely to place that person on the path to a great fortune. Rather, the latter tends to be a "random walk": One happened to be fortunate enough to have chosen Xerox or IBM in the 1950s rather than the broad array of other possible investments—and, of course, one was among the small minority that had much of anything to invest in the first place.[162]

More recently, inheritance appears to be increasingly critical to capital accumulation. Looking at 35 to 39 year olds in 1973, for example, some 56 percent of their wealth had been inherited. By the mid–1980s, however, that figure had jumped to 86 percent.[163] And as for its distribution, the richest 1 percent of Baby Boomers stand to inherit more than $2 trillion by the year 2011—some $3.6 million a piece. Each Boomer in the next 9 percent should garner roughly $396,000; while the bottom 90 percent will average only $40,000—and most of that will fall to those at the top of the group.[164]

In sum, it is possible to become wealthy other than by inheritance, but that leap requires luck more than anything else. Alger's goodness and courage seem to play very little part in the process. Consequently, short of inheriting a healthy sum of money from a long-lost relative or hitting a number in the lottery, the odds are that the hardworking, penny-pinching janitor from the ghetto simply has no realistic hope of acquiring a fortune in his lifetime. His children and grandchildren will not see one either. As a matter of fact, they will almost certainly find themselves punching a time clock as well.

If a child's father is in the bottom 5 percent of wage earners, for example, that child has only a one in twenty chance of earning his or her way into the top quintile—let alone the owning class. Except for the normal income fluctuations associated with age, most Americans simply do not move very far up or down over the course of their lifetimes. As for trends, it is actually becoming more and more difficult to fall from the top or rise from the bottom, despite the modicum of mobility apparent in the upper strata of the middle and working class.[165] And, this is particularly true for African Americans.[166]

Focusing on males, both black and white, an earlier Department of Commerce study revealed that nearly two out of three sons will end up working at a job of the same general status as their fathers. And when the white-collar category is limited to professionals and managers, almost three in four sons will remain outside of this group, just as their fathers did.[167]

So, if hard work and frugality do not really help much in scaling the class wall, must the overwhelming majority of Americans be content to "bet on the horses" as their only realistic hope of gaining a share of the means of production? Even though Thurow has indicated that all the abilities in the world are nowhere near the surest ticket to a ride on the wealth train, it seems reasonable to believe that if nurtured, such abilities might help increase income as a step toward attaining wealth. Indeed, as discussed when analyzing postindustrial trends above, there is empirical evidence that schooling helps determine one's job, which in turn should help determine income and wealth.[168]

Education and Mobility

To begin with, financial position is indeed related to educational attainment, regardless of a person's age. A college graduate makes an average of 59 percent more than a high school graduate, and more than three times that of a grade school graduate. The same is even truer for wealth accumulation, where the college graduate has more than seven times the financial assets of a high school graduate and some 32 times that of a grade school graduate.[169]

But who gets the higher levels of education? Looking at Table 5.1, it becomes clear that the more income parents have, the more likely their children will be afforded the opportunity to further their educations.[170] As a matter of fact, even more recent trend data suggest that the gap in educational attainment between the children of the haves and have nots has increased significantly since the late 1970s, especially with rising tuition costs and a decline in government's tuition assistance.[171] Then, when the impediments of race and poverty come together, we find scarcely more than 1 percent of African-American students from the poorest category of households attending college full time.[172] Not surprisingly, weak students from well-off families stand a better chance of attending college than better students coming from poorer backgrounds.[173] And there are some indications that the ante has been going up.

The technological prerequisites of postindustrial success have prompted ever more of the population to both finish high school and find a way to attend college. But as an increasing proportion of the middle and working class has managed to work its way into college classrooms—a veritable elite bastion until relatively recently—a mere college degree is no longer enough to open the most desirable of the postindustrial doors of employment.[174]

In 1960, for example, 29 percent of America's full-time workers had high school educations and another 13 percent had managed to attain college degrees. Those figures jumped to 38 percent and 30 percent respectively by 1990.[175] Meanwhile, the number of high-skill jobs has not kept pace with this proliferation of educated workers, and this has led to at least two important developments. First, in a process called *downward substitution*, better educated workers have displaced those less well educated in jobs requiring few skills.[176] Related to that, it now requires an advanced degree from a prestigious college in order to compete successfully for many of the more desirable positions that used to require only a college diploma. And, not too surprisingly, it is the wealthier who are more likely to attend the more expensive elite institutions.[177]

TABLE 5.1

COLLEGE EDUCATION BY FAMILY INCOME, 1993

Family Income Level	Children Attending College (%)
Less than $10,000	16
$10,000–19,999	22
$20,000–39,999	36
$40,000–74,999	52
More than $75,000	64

Source: U.S. Department of Commerce, Bureau of the Census, "School Enrollment—Social and Economic Characteristics of Students: October 1993," Current Population Reports p. 20–479 (Washington, D.C.: GPO, 1994).

Reflecting the subsequent competition for admission into these more prestigious academic programs, the *New York Times* unearthed the following:

> The rising demand of American youth for the limited vacancies in medical and law schools appears to be creating an increase in questionable and even illegal efforts to gain admission.
>
> Court records and interviews with knowledgeable authorities suggest that payments totaling millions of dollars are being made to these schools by parents and friends of prospective students to assure their acceptance. Covert bids of as much as $250,000 have been made for one place in the freshman class of a California medical school.[178]

Educational attainment does seem to be intergenerationally linked, at least in part, by the socioeconomic position of the student's parents. But looking beneath the opportunity to study a greater number of years, it is just as revealing to note that the quality of the person's elementary and secondary educational experiences may well be affected by the socioeconomic status of that person's parents.

Because nearly one-half of all school funding comes from local property taxes, there are substantial discrepancies in the amount of money available to spend on the public schools. In the state of Texas, prior to judicial intervention, one district spent $2,337 per pupil, while another was able to spend more than $56,791 and still enjoy a much lower tax rate.[179] As a result, the wealthy schools have the latest textbooks, full libraries, science laboratories, state-of-the-art computer equipment, and can attract the better teachers. Meanwhile, at the other end of town, children make do with out-of-date textbooks and other hand-me-down resources, while many teachers eschew teaching there.[180] Then, comparing teacher salaries to student achievement, Harvard's Ronald Ferguson found a considerable correlation. Students at better funded schools simply score higher on such tests.[181]

A Class System

Americans do not like to talk about economic classes and class differences, in large part because they hold staunchly to the belief that there are no fundamental class barriers to advancement in the United States. Any one of us can rise from rags to riches.[182] However, it seems safe to say that in today's real world, a person who is not born in the owning class will almost certainly never end up there, regardless of abilities, hard work, thrift, and knack for making wise investments. When there is nothing left at the end of the month to invest in either the stock market or further education for one's children, the family simply lacks the ante even to get into the game—a reality that appears even more hard and fast for African Americans.[183]

Each generation is likely to have its superrich entrepreneurs (e.g., J. Paul Getty, H. L. Hunt, and Daniel Ludwig [oil]; Howard Hughes, William Hewlitt, and David Packard [aerospace]; Edward Land [photography]; John Kluge [mass media]; Sam Walton [retail]; William Gates, Paul Allen, and H. Ross Perot [computers]). And, in extremely rare cases, a Samuel Newhouse, Henry Kaiser, W. Clement Stone, or a Tom Monoghan will actually rise from rags to riches largely by virtue of his own efforts.[184] Such examples help keep the Horatio Alger myth alive and spur support for the existing system. Stated another way, capitalism's limited permeability serves as an important reinforcing device. Meanwhile, virtually every American will work very hard to make profits for someone else and will remain essentially locked into the class position into which he or she was born. Indeed, there is a light at the end of the tunnel, but for the overwhelming majority of Americans it simply amounts to a false hope, a cruel hoax, as they continue to bite the bullet of their own economic exploitation.[185]

SUMMARY

To what extent does the U.S. political-economic system function to transfer income between classes? The welfare state capitalism model found a system that exploits the middle and working class, struggles to maintain the lower class at subsistence, further enhances the dominant position of the capital-owning class, and leads to an at least temporary diversion of middle and working class wrath toward the lower class while maintaining essentially groundless hopes of interclass mobility.

NOTES

1. Charles V. Hamilton, "Conduit Colonialism and Public Policy," *Black World* (October 1972), pp. 40–45.
2. For example, see Donald Kellermann, *The People, The Press & Politics 1990* (Los Angeles: Times Mirror, 1990), p. 127.
3. It also should be noted that the definitions and measures used in this second edition differ somewhat from those used in the book's first edition. Thus, direct comparisons should not be made between prior findings and those presented here.
4. James O'Connor, *The Fiscal Crisis of the State* (New York: St. Martin's Press, 1973), pp. 6–7. Also see Ralph Miliband, *The State in Capitalist Society* (New York: Basic Books, 1969); Larry Hirschorn, "The Political Economy of Social Services Rationalization," in R. Quinney (ed.), *Capitalist Society* (New York: Dorsey, 1979).
5. Quote from Susan Ostrander, "Upper Class Women," in William Domhoff, ed., *Power Structure Research* (Beverly Hills: Sage, 1980), p. 79.
6. Paul Samuelson and William Nordhaus, *Economics* (New York: McGraw-Hill, 1995), p. 359. For a comparison of just how much steeper the American pyramid is when compared to those of other large industrialized nations, see *New York Times*, October 27, 1995.
7. For a more detailed discussion of the power inherent in capital ownership, see Marcus Pohlmann, *Governing the Postindustrial City* (New York: Longman, 1993), chap. 6. Marcus Pohlmann, *Political Power in the Postindustrial City* (New York: Stonehill, 1986), chaps. 3–4.
8. Many consider the true owning class to be much smaller than this, for example, see C. Wright Mills, *The Power Elite* (New York: Oxford University Press, 1956), p. 122; Michael Best and William Connolly, *The Politicized Economy* (Lexington, Mass.: Heath, 1982), p. 76.
9. Federal Reserve Board and Internal Revenue Service, *1989 Survey of Consumer Finances* (Washington, D.C.: GPO, 1989) where it was reported that the top 1 percent of households (834,000) owned $5.7 trillion in net wealth—which averages out to more than $6.8 million per household.
10. For example, see Federal Reserve Board and Internal Revenue Service, *1992 Survey of Consumer Finances* (Washington, D.C.: GPO, 1992). For trend data, see works such as

Edward N. Wolff, "Trends in Household Wealth in the United States, 1962–83 and 1983–89," *Review of Income and Wealth* (June 1994); Edward N. Wolff, "The Rich Get Increasingly Richer," Economic Policy Institute, *Briefing Paper*, 1992; or the work of Wolff, Claudia Goldin, and Bradford De Long, cited in Sylvia Nasar, "The Rich Get Richer, But Never the Same Way Twice," *New York Times*, August 16, 1992.

11. For example, see John Harrigan, *Empty Dreams, Empty Pockets: Class and Bias in American Politics* (New York: Macmillan, 1993), p. 10. Also note that this presumes exceptionally safe investments. For those wealthy individuals willing to assume even a little more risk, there are investment vehicles such as *hedge funds* that provide substantially larger returns for those with a million or more dollars to invest. For example, see Saul Hansell, "Hush-Hush and for the Rich: Hedge Funds Under Scrutiny,"*New York Times*, April 13, 1994.

12. Wolff, "Trends in Household Wealth."

13. Estimated from 1989 Congressional Budget Office figures reported in the *New York Times*, March 5, 1992. For a higher estimate, see Vincente Navarro, *Dangerous to Your Health: Capitalism in Health Care* (New York: Monthly Review Press, 1993), p. 23.

14. For a visual impression of this phenomenon, see H. Edward Ransford, *Race and Class in American Society* (Cambridge, Mass.: Schenkman, 1977), p. 52. For further discussion of the black class structure in the United States, see St. Clair Drake and Horace Cayton, *Black Metropolis* (Orlando, Fla.: Harcourt Brace Jovanovich, 1945); Thomas Dye, *The Politics of Equality* (Indianapolis: Bobbs-Merrill, 1971); William J. Wilson, *The Declining Significance of Race* (Chicago: University of Chicago Press, 1980); William J. Wilson, *The Truly Disadvantaged* (Chicago: University of Chicago Press, 1987).

15. For example, see Karl Marx, *Value, Price, and Profit* (New York: International Publishers, 1935).

16. *Time*, August 29, 1977, p. 17.

17. U.S. Department of Commerce, Bureau of the Census, *Statistical Abstracts of the United States, 1995*, p. 377. Block, *The Mean Season*, chap. 2; *New York Times*, May 29, 1990; November 15, 1988; May 10, 1988; March 14, 1985. Edward Greenberg, *Capitalism and the American Political Ideal* (New York: Sharpe, 1985), pp. 160–166.

18. Adapted from Herbert Gans, *More Equality* (New York: Pantheon, 1972). Also see Frances Fox Piven and Richard Cloward, *Regulating the Poor* (New York: Vintage, 1971); Charles V. Hamilton, "The Patron-Recipient Relationship and Minority Politics in New York City," *Political Science Quarterly* (Summer 1979); Robert Allen, *Black Awakening in Capitalist America: An Analytical History* (Garden City, N.Y.: Anchor Doubleday, 1969), esp. chaps. 1, 4, 5,7.

19. For a more detailed discussion of the "slump and boom" phenomenon, see Samuelson and Nordhaus, *Economics*, chap. 29; Howard Sherman, *Radical Political Economy* (New York: Basic Books, 1972), chap. 7.

20. For example, see Richard Hope, "Blacks in the U.S. Military: Trends in Participation," in Winston Van Horne (ed.), *Race: Twentieth Century Dilemmas—Twenty-First Century Prognoses* (Madison: University of Wisconsin, 1989), pp. 183–205; Benjamin DeMott, *The Imperial Middle: Why Americans Can't Think Straight About Class* (New York: William Morrow, 1990), pp. 175–181.

21. For a more complete explanation of this "conduit" function, see Hamilton, "Conduit Colonialism and Public Policy."

22. For example, see Jean Mayer and J. Larry Brown, "More Prosperity, More Hunger," *New York Times*. February 25, 1989; Robert Pear, "5.5 Million Children in U.S. Are Hungry," *New York Times*, March 27, 1991; Felicity Barringer, "Whether It's Hunger Or 'Malnourishment,' It's a National Problem," *New York Times*, December 27, 1992.

23. For example, see *National Journal*, April 17, 1993, p. 956.

24. For example, see *New York Times*, July 8, 1993; December 15, 1996.
25. For example, see Robert Pear, "Wide Health Gap, Linked To Income, Is Reported In U.S.," *New York Times*, July 8, 1993.
26. See Robert Pear, "Poverty Is Cited As Divorce Factor," *New York Times*, January 15, 1993.
27. For example, see Cathy Cohen and Michael Dawson, "Neighborhood Poverty and African American Politics," *American Political Science Review* 87 (June 1993), pp. 286–302.
28. This depends in large part on how the term is defined. One group is the "literally homeless," those with absolutely no place to live at that moment. These people end up sleeping either on the streets or in one of a limited number of publicly or privately provided shelters. The other major group is the "hidden homeless," those living in someone else's home because they lack the wherewithal to provide one for themselves. See Mitchell Levitas, "Homelessness in America," *New York Times Magazine*, June 10, 1990; Peter Rossi, "The Urban Homeless: A Portrait of Urban Dislocation," *Annals of the American Academy of Political and Social Sciences* (January 1989), pp. 132–142; *New York Times*, April 12, 1991.
29. *Time*, August 29, 1977, pp. 16–17.
30. For example, see *America's Middle Class Under Siege*, a report by the AFL-CIO Maritime Trades Department (Washington, D.C.: November 1991), p. 9.
31. For example, see U. S. Department of Commerce, Bureau of the Census, *Workers and Low Earnings: 1964–1990* (Washington, D.C.: GPO, March 1992); *New York Times*, April 25, 1995; January 25, 1996; August 1, 1997.
    For a fuller discussion of what the indigent have in common amidst postindustrial developments, see the section on the "Trickle-down Fallacy" below; Michael Harrington, *The New American Poverty* (New York: Viking Penguin, 1984); Pohlmann, *Governing the Postindustrial City*; Pohlmann, *Political Power in the Postindustrial City*; *New York Times*, December 21,1986. *Christian Science Monitor*, February 15, 1985, pp. 1819.
32. Quoted in *Time*, December 1, 1986, p. 27. For a fuller discussion of the unique circumstances that have befallen the black underclass, see Wilson, *The Truly Disadvantaged*; Douglas Glasgow, *The Black Underclass* (San Francisco: Jossey-Bass, 1980); Douglas Glasgow, "The Black Underclass in Perspective," in National Urban League, *The State of Black America, 1987* (New York: National Urban League, 1987), pp. 129–144; Chicago Tribune Staff, *The American Millstone: An Examination of the Nation's Permanent Underclass* (Chicago: Contemporary Books, 1986); Sylvester Monroe and Peter Goldman, *Brothers* (New York: Newsweek/William Morrow, 1988).
33. Wolff, "Trends in Household Wealth," *New York Times*, June 22, 1996.
    Note that the term *poor* has been avoided in describing the lower class. This has been done because the term is normally associated with the hotly debated "poverty" figures published by the federal government. For example, see Julie Kosterlitz, "Measuring Misery," *National Journal*, August 4, 1990, pp. 1892–1896; Wilson, *Truly Disadvantaged*, pp. 170–171; *New York Times*, April 26, 1990; December 8, 1994.
34. Wolff, "Trends in Household Wealth," 1995 *Statistical Abstracts*, p. 373; Mary Jo Bane and David Ellwood, *Welfare Realities: From Rhetoric to Reform* (Cambridge, Mass.: Harvard University, 1994); *New York Times*, November 27, 1985; Chicago Tribune Staff, *American Millstone*, p. 83.
35. For example, see Mack Jones, "The Black Underclass as Systemic Phenomenon," in Jennings, ed., *Black Politics and Economic Development* (New York: Verso, 1992), pp. 53–65; Andrew Hacker, *Two Nations* (New York: Scribner's, 1992), p. 98.
36. Carolyn Milini, a 37-year-old home health aide whose husband is a steel worker, quoted in Peter Kilborn, "The Middle Class Feels Betrayed, But Maybe Not Enough to Rebel," *New York Times*, January 12, 1992.

37. Although he uses a different measure of middle class status, an interesting analysis of the evolution of the black middle class can be found in Robert Hill, "The Black Middle Class: Past, Present, and Future," in Paulette Robinson and Billy Tidwell, eds., *The State of Black America 1995* (New York: National Urban League, 1995). Also see Robert Smith and Richard Seltzer, *Race, Class, and Culture: A Study in Afro-American Mass Opinion* (Albany, N.Y.: State University of New York Press, 1992), pp. 34–44.

38. Wolff, "Trends in Household Wealth."

39. Wolff, "Trends in Household Wealth."

    Although not as skewed as wealth holdings, the income average of $47,000 is inflated by the higher incomes at the top of the group. For example, the average drops to $34,000 if the top 10 percent are excluded, or $29,000 if you omit the top quarter. For more on this phenomenon, see for example, Robert Reich, "The Fracturing of the Middle Class," *New York Times*, August 31, 1994.

40. For example, see Louis Uchitelle, "Moonlighting Plus: 3-Job Families on the Rise," *New York Times*, August 16, 1994; Kevin Phillips, *Boiling Point: Republicans, Democrats and the Decline of Middle Class Prospects* (New York: Random House, 1993), pp. xxi-xxiii and 157–163; Katherine Newman, *Declining Fortunes: The Withering of the American Dream* (New York: Basic, 1993); Juliet Schor, *The Overworked American: The Unexpected Decline of Leisure* (New York: Basic, 1991).

    And as for the special position of African Americans, see, for example, Melvin Oliver and Thomas Shapiro, *Black Wealth/White Wealth* (New York: Routledge, 1995), chap. 5; *New York Times*, November 26, 1990, p. A11.

41. Note that a sizable minority of the "lower class" also work for a wage. (See Bureau of the Census, *Workers and Low Earnings*.) Thus, in a sense, these people also end up in the middle-and working-class category. They too are paid less than the market value of what they produce, contributing to owner profits. And they too pay taxes, some of which find their way to the bank accounts of the owning class. Nonetheless, this total transfer is relatively small, for even counting public assistance, this group earns less than 4 percent of all national income. And owning virtually no property, members of the lower class pay very little in property taxes.

42. The *intermediate budget* was derived by converting the last available Department of Labor estimate to constant 1994 dollars ($41,329). See *Monthly Labor Review* 105–7, pp. 44–46.

    The average pretax household income was taken from the U.S. Department of Labor, Bureau of Labor Statistics, *Consumer Expenditure Survey 1994* (Washington, D.C.: GPO, 1994), Table 7 ($36,838). Average income was used instead of median income even though it is skewed high by the nation's highest incomes. This was done in order to be reasonably conservative with the estimation. It was also used instead of the average middle/working class household income estimated in the previous paragraph as $43,000. That was because that estimate was based on 1989 figures, and even it dropped to $34,000 if the top 10 percent were excluded. [$34,000 in constant 1994 dollars is $40,664, still less than the *intermediate budget*.] Overall, then, the national *average household income* figure seemed the fairest representation.

    Also see Sherman, *Radical Political Economy*, pp. 5–51.

43. Percentages derived from 1994 *Consumer Expenditure Survey*, Table 7.

44. *New York Times*, July 10, 1977. For further discussion of this "vulnerability," see Phillips, *Boiling Point; New York Times*, November 17, 1991, section 3; Andrew Levison, *The Working Class Majority* (Baltimore: Penguin, 1974); Arthur Shostak, *Blue Collar* (New York: Random House, 1969).

45. Allen, *Black Awakening*, p. 274.

46. For an example, see Samuelson and Nordhaus, *Economics*, pp. 202–203.

47. The May 1996 *Survey of Current Business* (Washington, D.C.: GPO, 1996), p. 21, listed domestic corporate profits at $465.3 billion for 1994. Using a corporate income tax rate of .386 (derived from figures in the 1995 *Statistical Abstracts*, p. 564), $179 billion was subtracted at corporate income taxes, $10.5 billion for profits from lending to government (see below), $12.2 billion for profits from government contracts (see below), and $6.5 billion for profits from serving the poor (see below).

48. Adjusted domestic corporate profit figures from the *Survey of Current Business* (March 1996). Interest profit, contract profit, and conduit profit amounts, as calculated later in this chapter, were then subtracted to avoid double-counting. Profits derived from foreign investments and sales were also excluded, as they generally involved extracting money from transactions with foreign workers and consumers. Lastly, corporate taxes were subtracted as well, using a 38.6% tax rate derived from figures in the 1995 *Statistical Abstracts*, p. 564.

Estimates of the percentage of business assets held by the top 1 percent of American households were used to calculate the share of these profits garnered by the owning class. These figures exclude profits made by partnerships and proprietorships, which tend to be small firms with relatively few employees that account for only approximately 10 percent of all sales. Inasmuch as a number of their white owners would fall into the owning-class category, ignoring profits from these firms makes the private-sector profit figure slightly more conservative.

Population statistics were used to calculate African Americans as a percentage of the total middle and working class from whom owning-class profits have been extracted. Because blacks have regularly made less income than their white counterparts, their proportionate contribution to the corporate profit figure was deflated by multiplying it by a ratio of average black middle- and working-class (MC/WC) income divided by average middle- and working-class income as a whole:

$$BD = TD \times \frac{BF}{TF} \times \frac{BI}{AI}$$

where   BD = total black MC/WC dollars involved at this juncture
                   TD = total dollars involved at this juncture
                   BF = black MC/WC families (60 percent of all black families)
                   TF = total MC/WC families (79 percent of all U.S. families)
                   BI = average black MC/WC family income
                   AI = average MC/WC family income

In 1994, domestic corporate profits were $465.3 billion, before subtracting corporate income taxes ($179.9 billion), profits from loans to government ($10.5 billion), profits from sales and services to government ($12.2 billion), and profits made from transactions with welfare recipients ($6.5 billion). That then left $256.2 billion in adjusted after-tax owning corporate profits. The owning class's share was estimated to be $158.844 billion—calculating the owning class's share via their share of business assets that year: 62 percent. The proportion of that share contributed by the total middle/working class was estimated by taking the middle working class share of all taxes paid: 80.5 percent; and the black middle/working class was derived by using the formula above.

49. Quoted in *New York Times*, July 12, 1989.

50. Joseph Pechman, *Who Paid the Taxes, 1966–1985?* (Washington, D.C.: Brookings Institution, 1985), p. 52. Also see Citizens for Tax Justice, *A Far Cry From Fair* (April 1991); *New York Times*, May 29, 1990; *Washington Post*, February 18, 1990; Citizens for Tax Justice, *The Sorry State of State Taxes* (January 1987).

51. Thomas Dye, *Who's Running America?* (Englewood Cliffs, N.J.: Prentice-Hall, 1995), p. 55. Also see Donald Barlett and James Steele, *Who Really Pays the Taxes?* (New York: Si-

mon and Schuster, 1994); Phillips, *Boiling Point*, chap. 5; Robert McIntyre, "Are the Rich Really Overtaxed?" *Washington Post*, July 24, 1995.

52. For some concrete cases in point, see Joseph Ruskay, "Tax Reform: The Loopholes Still with Us," *The Nation* (March 22, 1971), pp. 368–371.

53. See Teresa Odendahl, "A Thousand Pointless Lights?," *New York Times*, July 21, 1990.

54. Karen De Witt, "One Way to Save a Bundle: Become a Former American," *New York Times*, April 12, 1995.

55. 1995 *Statistical Abstracts*, p. 300.

56. In 1993, for example, of those individuals or couples making $200,000 or more, 2,400 paid no federal income taxes at all, while 18,000 paid less than 5 percent of their incomes in federal income taxes. See David Cay Johnston, "More U.S. Wealthy Sidestepping I.R.S.," *New York Times*, April 18, 1994.

57. For a somewhat dated but relatively comprehensive discussion of this subject, see Keith Butters et al., *Effect of Taxation on Investments by Individuals* (Cambridge, Mass.: Riverside Press, 1953).

58. Figures from 1995 *Statistical Abstracts* for all taxes paid were multiplied by middle- and working-class percentage of national income for all taxpayers, with black middle- and working-class taxes derived as done above. Given the nation's nonprogressive tax structure, it seemed safe to assume these middle/working classes were paying taxes in proportion to their national income share.

These figures are conservative estimates, however, not only for the reason cited in the text but also because federal social security payments are not being included as taxes in this study, even though that is a payment that is not optional. For example, see Phillips, *Boiling Point*, pp. 42–49.

59. Block, *The Mean Season*, p. 94.

60. The *Survey of Current Business* "subsidy" figure was used despite the fact that it includes subsidies paid to governmental enterprises. Nonetheless, when considering that the figure excludes items like benefits-in-kind, tax expenditures, loan guarantees, and sales below market value made to private businesses, this best available indicator appears to be a conservative estimate of the amount of tax dollars flowing to private-sector enterprises.

For some specific examples, see Peter Stone, "Street Fight," *National Journal*, March 8, 1997, pp. 453–456; Peter Stone, "Fortune 500 Welfare Queens?" *National Journal*, March 25, 1995, p. 773; Stephen Moore, "How to Slash Corporate Welfare," *New York Times*, April 5, 1995; Kirk Victor, "Takin' on the Bacon," *National Journal*, May 6, 1995; Jonathan Rauch, "You Lose, We All Pay," *National Journal*, April 6, 1991; *Multi-National Monitor*, January 2, 1993; *New York Times*, March 13, 1997.

The precise calculation for 1994 took the $34.7 billion "subsidy" figure, arriving at the owning class's share via their share of business assets, with the proportion of that share contributed by the total middle/working class and the black middle/working class was derived by the same methods used above.

61. *Survey of Current Business* figures on federal, state, and local government purchases of services and durable and nondurable goods and structures, less all money going directly to employee compensation—conservatively assuming that the owning class was not receiving any of this compensation. In 1994, this amounted to $1,175.3 – 602.8 = 572.5 billion (1995 *Statistical Abstracts*, pp. 451 and 457).

An indicator for a national profits-to-sales ratio was calculated using *Survey of Current Business* figures for the combined manufacturing and trade industries—profits from the Jan/Feb 1996 Survey, p. 79 and sales from the Oct. 1995 Survey, p. C–41. As the latest available data was from the 1993 calendar year, those numbers were multiplied by a cost-of-living factor to create a 1994 estimate. The resulting calculation was $174.4 billion (in profits) divided by $8,156.9 billion (in sales) = 2.13 percent profit-to-sales rate. This is a conservative estimate, as a sizable majority of these purchases have been made without competitive bidding; and thus profit rates are no doubt higher than usual in this governmental arena (e.g., see *New York Times*, March 8, 1985; April 9, 1985; May 30, 1988).

Corporate profits were then calculated as a proportion of government purchases each year, and the shares captured by the owning class and paid by the black middle and working class were calculated as done above.

62. According to the 1995 *Statistical Abstracts* (p. 519), federally insured banks earned a net profit margin of 4.36 percent on their loans and investments. This profit margin was then applied to the $241.3 billion in net interest government paid to domestic persons and businesses in 1994 (*Survey of Current Business*, March 1996, p. 12). The resulting profits from lending to government were then reduced to the share gained by the owning class and paid by the black middle and working class as calculated above.

Overall, these too are seen as reasonably conservative estimates in that semi-private corporations like the Farm Credit System do additional borrowing and transferring, while members of the owning class likely make more than 4.36 percent net interest when they personally loan money directly to government via purchases of government securities, as opposed to reaping profits via the bank shares they own when banks do the lending.

63. See Vee Burke, *Cash and Non-cash Benefits for Persons with Limited Income*, Congressional Research Service Report No. 85–194 (Washington, D.C.: GPO, 1984). For a concise history of the evolution of these programs, see Bane and Ellwood, *Welfare Realities*, chap. 1.

64. 1995 *Statistical Abstracts*, p. 377. Nearly one-half of this amount is spent on the Medicaid program.

The federal government did pass significant welfare reform in August of 1996 (e.g., converting Aid to Families with Dependent Children [AFDC] into block grants to allow more state control of this spending.) Nevertheless, as this analysis combines the amounts spent at all levels of government, it is anticipated that these numbers will not change much. In the end, the federal reforms ultimately will do little more than shift the cost burden to the states, as was done during the last major wave of welfare reform in the 1980s (see chap. 8 below).

65. Hamilton, "Conduit Colonialism and Public Policy."

66. Focus is on cash paid to welfare recipients and items and services purchased for them, such as school lunches and medical care. It is presumed that the cash is spent and not saved or invested.

The 1994 public assistance totals ($306,113.28 million) is actually an estimate derived from using the latest available figures (from 1992) and multiplying those times a cost-of-living factor. The estimated 1994 figures were then multiplied by the average corporate profit of 2.13 percent, and the shares going to the owning class and paid for by the black middle and working class and the total middle and working class were calculated as done above.

It is also assumed that the administrative portion of these government expenditures is offset by the higher-than-average profits gained in many of these transactions. In addition, there are some indications that the administrative costs of these programs are actually relatively low (e.g., see *Social Security Bulletin Annual Statistical Supplement*, 1972, p. 57).

There is some overlap between the "conduit profits" and the "contract profits" discussed earlier. Nonetheless, the earlier figures are conservative enough to more than compensate for that.

67. *New York Times*, June 15,1985. For a follow-up article, see John Tierney, "Welfare Priority Is Angering Tenants of Housing Projects," *New York Times*, June 28, 1990. For similar examples, see National Urban League, *State of Black America, 1987*, p. 12; Rochelle Stanfield, "Big Money in Low Rents," *National Journal*, May 7, 1994, pp. 1068–1071; Michael Janofsky, "Faulty Oversight Profited Owners of Public Housing," *New York Times*, June 23, 1997.

68. For one of the best exposes, see *The Progressive* (September 1975), p. 11.

69. For example, see *New York Times*, March 28, 1997; *National Journal*, July 19, 1997, pp. 1458–1460; Memphis *Commercial Appeal*, August 10, 1997, p. A5.

70. "New report tells more health care fraud tales," Memphis *Commercial Appeal,* July 8, 1994, p. A4.

71. Richard Perez-Pena, "50 Admit Guilt in Cheating Medicaid," *New York Times*, November 24, 1992.

72. *New York Times*, December 19, 1992. Also see Warren Leary, "10% of Spending on Health Found Lost Through Fraud," *New York Times*, May 8, 1992.

73. For example, see Phillips, *Boiling Point*, p. 286; Milt Freudenheim, "Pressure Grows for Curbs on Prices of Prescriptions," *New York Times*, May 11, 1991.

74. These numbers are slightly inflated by the fact that some welfare recipients also work for a wage and thus supply a portion of this tribute. Nonetheless, these numbers are conservative estimates for the variety of reasons discussed in the notes and text. Thus they provide a reasonable estimate of the total transferred to the owning class from the paychecks of the middle and working class.

75. For example, see Jason DeParle, "U.S. Welfare System Dies As State Programs Emerge," *New York Times*, June 30, 1997.

76. For example, see Jude Wanninski, *The Way the World Works* (New York: Basic Books, 1978); George Gilder, *Wealth and Poverty* (New York: Basic Books, 1981); Irving Kristol, *Two Cheers for Capitalism* (New York: Basic Books, 1978); Milton Friedman, *Capitalism and Freedom* (Chicago: University of Chicago Press, 1962); Arthur Laffer and James Seymour, *The Economics of the Tax Revolt* (Orlando, Fla.: Harcourt Brace Jovanovich, 1979).

77. For example, see Louis Uchitelle, "Corporate Spending Booms, but Jobs Stagnate," *New York Times*, June 16, 1994.

78. For example, see Kevin Phillips, *The Politics of Rich and Poor* (New York: Harper, 1990), Appendix J; *Washington Post*, January 28, 1985; May 14, 1985.

79. For example, see Thomas Vogy, "Above the Poverty Line-But Poor," *Nation*, February 15, 1993.

80. 1995 *Statistical Abstracts*, pp. 474–475.

    The 1980–1993 time frame was chosen because 1993 family data was the most recent and most complete available, while 1980 was the first year in which the Census Bureau employed a new definition of *family*. Actually, I would have preferred to have used household data subdivided by the wealth categories employed above; however, this was simply the closest existing data would allow me to come if I wanted to do meaningful comparisons over time.

81. Phillips, *The Politics of Rich and Poor*, pp. 157–172. The number of billioniares had grown to 135 by 1996. See *Forbes*, October 14, 1996.

82. For example, see *New York Times*, April 15, 1992.

83. 1995 *Statistical Abstracts*, pp. 474–475; Harrigan, *Empty Dreams, Empty Pockets*, p. 19.

84. Susan Mayer and Christopher Jencks, "Recent Trends in Economic Inequality in the United States: Income versus Expenditures versus Material Well-being," in Dimitri Papadimitriou and Edward Wolff, eds., *Poverty and Prosperity in the USA in the Late Twentieth Century* (New York: St. Martin's, 1993), p. 121. Also see Joel Nelson, *Post-Industrial Capitalism: Exploring Economic Inequality in America* (Beverly Hills, Calif.: SAGE Publications, 1995); Phillips, *The Politics of Rich and Poor*; Leonard Silk, "Rich and Poor: The Gap Widens," *New York Times*, May 12, 1989; Sylvia Nasar, "However You Slice the Data The Richest Did Get Richer," *New York Times*, May 1, 1992; Steven Holmes, "Income Disparity Between Poorest and Richest Rises: Trend in U.S. Confirmed," *New York Times*, June 20, 1995; January 9, 1997. Albert Hunt and Alan Murray,

"Rich Man, Poor Man," *Smart Money*, May, 1998. For further evidence from within the black community, see Wilson, *Declining Significance of Race*, esp. p. 173.

85. For example, see Pohlmann, *Political Power in the Postindustrial City*, chaps. 1, 3, 6; Robert Reich, *The Work of Nations: Preparing Ourselves for 21st Century Capitalism* (New York: Knopf, 1991); Paul Starobin, "Unequal Shares," *National Journal*, September 11, 1993, pp. 2176–2179; Sylvia Nasar, "Puzzling Poverty Of the 80s Boom," *New York Times*, February 14, 1992.

86. Starobin, "Unequal Shares," pp. 2176–2177. Also see, for example, Nelson, *Post-Industrial Capitalism*; Jeremy Rifkin, *The End of Work* (1995).

87. George Sternlieb and James Hughes, *Income and Jobs: USA* (New Brunswick, N.J.: Center for Urban Policy Research, 1984), chap. 5; *New York Times*, July 31,1987; Jonathan Rauch, "Downsizing the Dream," *National Journal*, August 12, 1989, pp. 2038–2043. And see *Los Angeles Times*, April 2, 1988, for statistical evidence of this trend in black America specifically.

88. Sternlieb and Hughes, *Income and Jobs*; Congressional Research Service, *Measures of Racial Earnings since 1970* (Washington, D.C.: GPO, 1988); Frank Levy, "The Vanishing Middle Class and Related Issues," *PS* (Summer 1987), pp. 650–655; Frank Levy, *Dollars and Dreams: The Changing American Income Distribution* (New York: Norton, 1988); *New York Times*, April 16, 1992; Phillips, *Boiling Point*, pp. 195–197.

89. See Sternlieb and Hughes, *Income and Jobs*. And for evidence of fast food pay scales, see *New York Times*, November 19, 1990.

90. 1995 *Statistical Abstracts*, Table 695; Kirk Victor, "Labor's New Look," *National Journal*, October 14, 1995, pp. 2522–2527. Also see Sklar, *Chaos or Community?: Seeking Solutions, Not Scapegoats For Bad Economics* (Boston: South End, 1995), pp. 28–29; *New York Times*, September 15, 1993; December 13, 1991.

91. See Steven Greenhouse, "Strikes Decrease To A 50-Year Low," *New York Times*, January 29, 1996.

92. Nancy Green Leigh, *Stemming Middle Class Decline: The Challenge to Economic Development Planning* (New Brunswick, N.J.: CUPR, 1994); Steve Lohr, "Steady Business in Temporary Jobs," *New York Times*, December 4, 1992; *New York Times*, July 6, 1993; March 10, 1994; December 1, 1994.

93. See Sternlieb and Hughes, *Income and Jobs;* Jean Mayer and J. Larry Brown, "More Prosperity, More Hunger," *New York Times*, February 25, 1989; Alan Krueger, "The Truth About Wages," *New York Times*, July 31, 1997.

94. For example, see Oliver and Shapiro, *Black Wealth/White Wealth*, p. 27; Phillips, *Boiling Point*, pp. 159–161; *New York Times*, October 8, 1989; November 3, 1991.

95. See Sternlieb and Hughes, *Income and Jobs*; *New York Times*, July 30, 1989; Robert Pear, "More Are Lacking Health Insurance," *New York Times*, December 19, 1991; Peter Kilborn, "Illness Is Turning Into Financial Catastrophe for More of the Uninsured," *New York Times*, August 1, 1997.

96. Martin Carnoy, *Faded Dreams: The Politics and Economics of Race in America* (New York: Cambridge University Press, 1994), pp. 99–103. Also see Robert Reich, "The Fracturing of the Middle Class," *New York Times*, August 31, 1994; Peter Kilborn, "Even in Good Times, It's Hard Times for Workers," *New York Times*, July 3, 1995; Keith Bradsher, "Technology and Income Gap Are Linked, Greenspan Says," *New York Times*, August 27, 1994; Guy Gugliotta, "The Minimum Wage Culture," *Washington Post National Weekly Edition*, October 3–9, 1994, pp. 6–7; *New York Times*, November 27, 1990; May 27, 1992; July 26, 1992; March 15, 1993; June 3, 1994; August 29, 1995; *National Journal*, September 10, 1994, p. 2109.

97. Neal Rosenthal, U. S. Bureau of Labor Statistics, quoted in *Los Angeles Times*, March 16, 1996. Also see Sklar, *Chaos or Community?*, pp. 23–27.

98. See David Frum, "Welcome, Nouveaux Riches," *New York Times*, August 14, 1995.

99. For example, see Sylvia Nasar, "The 1980s: A Very Good Time for the Very Rich," *New York Times*, March 5, 1992; Benjamin Schwarz, "American Inequality: Its History and Scary Future," *New York Times*, December 19, 1995. Also see Phillips, *Boiling Point*, chap. 1 and pp. 170–171; Newman, *Declining Fortunes*; Lawrence Mishel and Jared Bernstein, *The State of Working America, 1994–95* (Washington, D.C.: Economic Policy Institute, 1994); Harrigan, *Empty Dreams;* "Death of the Middle Class," *Tri-State Defender*, October 21–25, 1995, p. 4A; *New York Times*, September 7, 1992; October 7, 1994. For a detailed application of this analysis to the specific circumstances of African Americans, see Carnoy, *Faded Dreams*, especially chap. 5.

100. *New York Times*, July 26, 1992. The low wage figure was actually $6.10 per hour in 1990 dollars, so I adjusted it up for inflation.

101 1995 *Statistical Abstracts*, pp. 469, 474.

102. For a good empirical depiction of this bimodality, see Greg Duncan, Timothy Smeeding, and Willard Rodgers, "W(h)ither the Middle Class? A Dynamic View," in Papadimitriou and Wolff, *Poverty and Prosperity*, chap. 7. Also see Sheldon Danziger and Peter Gottschalk, *America Unequal* (Cambridge, Mass.: Harvard University Press, 1995); *New York Times*, February 22, 1992; *Washington Post*, December 1, 1991.

103. Duncan, "W(h)ither the Middle Class?; Sylvia Nasar, "One Study's Rags to Riches Is Another's Rut of Poverty," *New York Times*, May 18, 1992.

104. Duncan, "W(h)ither the Middle Class?, p. 263; *New York Times*, December 16, 1990; January 12, 1992.

105. For example, see Uchitelle, "Moonlighting Plus;" Phillips, *Boiling Point*, pp. xxi-xxiii and 157–163; Newman, *Declining Fortunes*; Schor, *The Overworked American;* Sternleib and Hughes, *Income and Jobs*, chap. 5; *New York Times*, January 26,1988; February 15, 1990; Congressional Research Service, *Measures of Racial Earnings*; Levy, "Vanishing Middle Class."

   As for the special position of African Americans, see for example, *New York Times*, November 26, 1990, p. A11; Wade Nobles, "Public Policy and the African-American Family," in Van Horne, *Race*, p. 105.

106. For example, see Schor, *The Overworked American*; Phillips, *Boiling Point*, pp. 161–162.

107. Duncan, "W(h)ither the Middle Class?"; Levy, "Vanishing Middle Class."

108. In a related development, pension savings have declined as well (e.g., see *New York Times*, April 13, 1992).

109. For example, see Bob Herbert, "Bogeyman Economics," *New York Times*, April 4, 1997.

110. For example, see Phillips, *Boiling Point*, pp. 175–177.

111. Quoted in A. M. Rosenthal, "American Class Struggle," *New York Times*, March 22, 1995.

112. Duncan, "W(h)ither the Middle Class?", p. 248.

113. Hamilton, "Conduit Colonialism and Public Policy," pp. 42–43.

114. Sklar, *Chaos or Community?*, pp. 95–98.

115. Cited in Richard Morin, "Sociologist takes on the 'welfare myth,'" in the Memphis *Commercial Appeal*, April 29, 1994.

116. 1992 Yankelovich Clancy Shulman poll, reported in Memphis *Commercial Appeal*, April 29, 1994.

117. Quoted in Sklar, *Chaos or Community?*, p. 96.

118. Block, *The Mean Season*, pp. ix and 48; Martin Gilens, "Race Coding and White Opposition to Welfare," *American Political Science Review* 90 (September 1996), pp. 593–604.

119. See chapter 3 above.

120. *New York Times*, March 23, 1995. Also see Bane and Ellwood, *Welfare Realities*, chap. 2; *New York Times*, February 23,1987; Manning Marable, *How Capitalism Underdeveloped*

Black America (Boston: South End Press, 1983), pp. 43–44; Harrington, *New American Poverty*, p. 28.

According to Bane and Ellwood, the average welfare *spell* is one to two years, while the median is three years. Over the course of one's lifetime, the median total years on AFDC is four, with some one quarter of the recipients on ten years or more. On any given day, the majority have been on more than eight years, which provides some idea just how many go on and off all the time. Meanwhile, those on for long terms tend to be disabled, caring for a disabled child, undereducated, and/or lacking child care options. (See Sklar, *Chaos or Community?*, p. 97.)

121. For example, see *New York Times*, March 23, 1995; Sklar, *Chaos or Community?*, p. 95.
122. Bane and Ellwood, *Welfare Realities*, chap. 2.
123. Average benefit for 1993. See *New York Times*, March 23, 1995. This ranged from $923 in Alaska to $120 in Mississippi. See *National Journal* June 10, 1995, pp. 1385–1386; *New York Times*, July 5, 1992.
124. Report of the U.S. Department of Health and Human Services, October 1995.
125. *New York Times*, March 23, 1995; Sklar, *Chaos or Community?*, p. 94.
126. Sklar, *Chaos or Community?*, p. 99. also see Harrell Rodgers, *Poor Women, Poor Families: The Economic Plight of America's Female-Headed Households* (New York: Sharpe, 1990).
127. Michael Parenti, *Democracy for the Few* (New York: St. Martin's, 1995), pp. 101–102; *U.S. News and World Report*, April 3, 1972, p. 57.
128. For example, see Block,*The Mean Season*, chap. 2; Sklar, *Chaos or Community?*, p. 96.
129. See *New York Times*, March 3, 1994. Also see U.S. Congress, Joint Economic Committee, 93d Cong., 1st sess., "Issues in Welfare Administration," *Studies in Public Welfare*, Paper No. 51, pt. 2, March 12, 1973 (Washington, D.C.: GPO, 1973); *New York Times*, May 22, 1977.
130. *National Journal*, December 1, 1990, p. 2931.
131. For example, see Herbert Gans, *The War Against the Poor: The Underclass and Anti-Poverty Policy* (New York: Basic Books, 1995).
132. Donald Kaul, "Over the Coffee," *Des Moines Register*, January 18, 1977. Also see Leonard Goodwin, *Do the Poor Want to Work?* (Washington, D.C.: Brookings Institution, 1972); Harrington, *New American Poverty*, p. 28. For a more recent example, see Rachel Swarns, "4,000 Hearts Full of Hope Line Up for 700 Jobs," *New York Times*, March 19, 1997.
133. Bane and Ellwood, *Welfare Realities*, chap. 2; Julie Kosterlitz and Jonathan Rauch, "Working, but Still Poor," *National Journal*, June 18, 1988, pp. 1600–1604; Sar Levitan and Isaac Shapiro, *America's Contradictions* (Washington, D.C.: Johns Hopkins University, 1987); Sklar, *Chaos or Community?*, p. 95; Block, et al., *The Mean Season*, pp. 87–88.
134. Lou Harris poll, published May 19, 1989.
135. NORC poll, reported in the *New York Times*, January 4, 1993. For more on the character and values of the poor, see Charles Henry, "Understanding The Underclass: The Role of Culture and Economic Progress," in Jennings, *Race, Politics, and Economic Development*, chap. 4; Rhonda Williams, "Culture as Human Capital," Marilyn Lashley and Melanie Njeri Jackson (eds.), *African Americans and the New Policy Consensus* (Westport, Conn.: Greenwood, 1994), chap. 3; Michael Katz, *The Undeserving Poor: From the War on Poverty to the War on Welfare* (New York: Pantheon, 1989).
136. Sklar, *Chaos or Community?*, p. 95.
137. Christopher Jencks, *Rethinking Social Policy* (Cambridge, Mass.: Harvard University Press, 1992), p. 205. Jenck's 1988 figures have been converted to 1994 dollars.

138. Mike Royko column in Memphis *Commercial Appeal*, May 3, 1993, p. A9.
139. *New York Times*, July 10, 1992 (close).
140. For example, see Harrington, *New American Poverty*, chap. 3.
141. For some good examples of how such animosity crosses racial lines, see Harrington, *New American Poverty*, p. 30; Philip Au Claire, "Public Attitudes towards Social Welfare Expenditures," *Social Work* (March-April 1984), p. 143.
142. Gallup poll, November 1964.
143. *New York Times*, August 3,1977; June 28, 1978. Also see Block, *The Mean Season*; Sklar, *Chaos or Community?*, chaps. 5 and 8; Greenberg, *Capitalism*, pp. 159–160.

    At the federal level, for instance, AFDC amounted to less than 1 percent of the total national budget, and only cost the average tax payer roughly $150 per year. Such public aid was still less than 4 percent of that budget even after adding Medicaid. See 1995 *Statistical Abstracts*; *New York Times*, March 23, 1995; Sklar, *Chaos or Community?*, p. 96.
144. For example, see polling data presented in *National Journal*, March 5, 1994, pp. 516–520; Sklar, *Chaos or Community?*, p. 96. Also see Fay Lomax Cook and Edith Barrett, *Support for the American Welfare System: The Views of Congress and the Public* (New York: Columbia University, 1992).
145. *New York Times*, June 9, 1978.
146. *New York Times*, August 3, 1977; June 28, 1978. Also a Gallup poll in February 1979 found 54 percent of Americans in favor of cutting "welfare" programs in order to balance the federal budget, 29 percent for cutting "defense," and no other option attracting the approval of even 10 percent.
147. Gallup poll, December 1978.
148. Gallup poll, June 1977.
149. *New York Times*/CBS poll, reported in the *New York Times*, April 6, 1995.
150. Ibid., p. 95.
151. Ibid., p. 94.
152. Ibid., p. 95; *New York Times*, November 19, 1996.
153. See David Rosenbaum, "Unemployment Insurance Aiding Fewer Workers," *New York Times*, December 2, 1990.
154. See Robert Pear, "Low Medicaid Fees Seen As Depriving The Poor of Care," *New York Times*, April 2, 1991.
155. For a comprehensive overview of this extended attack on the American welfare state, see Mickey Kaus, *The End of Equality* (New York: Basic Books, 1992). Also see *New York Times*, December 30, 1997; January 21, 1998.
156. High-income cutoff point for the bottom 20 percent of American families was $17,535 in 1980 but had declined to $16,952 by 1993 (in 1993 dollars). See 1995 *Statistical Abstracts*. Also see *New York Times*, December 30, 1997; *National Journal*, January 17, 1998, pp. 112–115.
157. Starobin, "Unequal Shares," p. 2179.
158. Gallup Poll (July 1990), cited in Harrigan, *Empty Dreams*, p. 22. Also see Jennifer Hochschild, *Facing Up to the American Dream: Race, Class, and the Soul of a Nation* (Princeton: Princeton University, 1995); Harrington, *New American Poverty*, p. 148; Sklar, *Chaos or Community?* pp. 94–95.
159. *New York Times*, February 19, 1984.
160. Lester Thurow, *Generating Inequality* (New York: Basic Books, 1975), ch. 6.
161. Paul Menchik, Conference on Research in Income and Wealth (New York: National Bureau of Economic Research, 1979).
162. Thurow, *Generating Inequality*, esp. chaps. 5, 6.
163. Phillips, *Boiling Point*, pp. 191–192.

164. Nick Ravo, "A Windfall Nears In Inheritances From The Richest Generation," *New York Times*, July 22, 1990; Keith Bradsher, "For Most U. S. Households, Inheritances Hardly Count," *New York Times*, July 25, 1995.

165. Sylvia Nasar, "Those Born Wealthy or Poor Usually Stay So, Studies Say," *New York Times*, May 18, 1992. Also see Greg Duncan and James Morgan, "An Overview of Family Economic Mobility," in Greg Duncan, et al. (eds.), *Years of Poverty, Years of Plenty* (Ann Arbor, Mich.: University of Michigan, 1984).

166. For example, see Gary Orfield and Carole Ashkinaze, *The Closing Door: Conservative Policy and Black Opportunity* (Chicago: University of Chicago, 1991); Martin Kilson, "Black Social Classes and Intergenerational Poverty," *Public Interest* 64 (Summer 1981), pp. 58–78.

167. For example, see U.S. Department of Commerce, Bureau of the Census, *Current Population Surveys*; *Occupational Changes in a Generation Survey* (1973).

168. See *National Journal*, September 28, 1991, pp. 2321–2322; Richard Coleman and Lee Rainwater, *Social Standing in America*, 1978 (New York: Basic Books, 1978).

169. Oliver and Shapiro, *Black Wealth/White Wealth*, p. 196; Also see *New York Times*, December 13, 1993.

170. For example, see *New York Times*, June 17, 1996; Oliver and Shapiro, *Black Wealth/White Wealth*, pp. 152–153; U.S. Department of Commerce, Bureau of the Census, "School Enrollment—Social and Economic Characteristics: October 1993," *Current Population Reports* p. 20–479 (Washington, D.C.: GPO, 1994), p. 69.

171. For example, see Karen Arenson, "Cuts in Tuition Assistance Put College Beyond Reach of Poorest Students," *New York Times*, January 27, 1997.

172. See Department of Commerce, "School Enrollment."

173. For example, see DeMott, *The Imperial Middle*, pp. 139–140.

174. For example, see Phillips, *Boiling Point*, p. 12.

175. See Carnoy, *Faded Dreams*, p. 107.

176. For example, see Schor, *The Overworked American*, pp. 39–40.

177. For example, see Jones, "The Black Underclass," pp. 60–61; Lucius Barker and Mack Jones, *African Americans and the American Political System* (Englewood Cliffs, N.J.: Prentice-Hall, 1994), pp. 337–338; Alexander Astin, *The Myth of Equal Access to Higher Education* (Atlanta: Southern Education Foundation, 1975).

178. *New York Times*, April 23, 1978.

179. Sklar, *Chaos or Community?*, p. 107; *New York Times*, March 11, 1990; June 6, 1990; June 10, 1990; December 19, 1997.

180. Sklar, *Chaos or Community?*, pp. 106–109. Specifically for racial implications, see, for example, Hacker, *Two Nations*, p. 173; E.D. Hirsch, Jr., "Good Genes, Bad Schools," *New York Times*, October 29, 1994.

181. See Ronald Ferguson, "Paying for Public Education: Evidence on How and Why Money Matters," *Harvard Journal of Legislation* (Summer 1991).

182. For example, see DeMott, *The Imperial Middle*; Harrigan, *Empty Dreams*, pp. 6–24; Ostrander, "Upper Class Women," p. 79.

183. See Oliver and Shapiro, *Black Wealth/White Wealth*, pp. 152–170.

184. Monoghan, for instance, grew up in an orphanage, yet went on to found Domino Pizza and own the Detroit Tigers major league baseball team. See Harrigan, *Empty Dreams*, p. 9.

185. For a detailed discussion of the structural impediments to socioeconomic mobility for the black underclass in particular, see Wilson, *Truly Disadvantaged*; Glasgow, *The Black Underclass*.

PART THREE

BLACKS IN AMERICAN POLITICS

Chapter 6

The Judicial Arena

Inasmuch as the primary object of a government, beyond the mere repression of physical violence, is the making of the rules which determine property relations of members of society, the dominant classes whose rights are thus to be determined must perforce obtain from the government such rules as are consonant with the larger interests necessary to the continuance of the economic processes, or they must themselves control the organs of government.

Charles Beard[1]

The United States prides itself on being a nation ruled by laws and not by individuals. The country's written constitution is central in guaranteeing individual rights and the political process that will enforce them. In addition, such written rules of the game are beyond the immediate reach of the governing elites at any point in time. But what if the rules of the game, not to mention their interpreters and enforcers, are seriously biased from the outset?

This chapter will suggest that much of the American political system designed at the constitutional convention in Philadelphia was crafted and has functioned to protect an unequal distribution of property. Democracy was limited in part to protect certain rights and liberties for all citizens; however, a number of these limitations have also served to protect historic inequalities, which for African Americans are tremendous.

THE FOUNDING FATHERS

In analyzing the Constitution, scholars have tended to praise the democratic spirit and foresight of the Founding Fathers and to laud the brilliantly adaptable document and governmental system they devised. Indeed, many of the Founding Fathers may well have been brilliant and visionary men dedicated to at least an 18th-century vision of rights and democracy. And the document they designed has endured longer than any written constitution in the history of the world. It has also helped preserve an array of individual liberties. But that is not the whole story—nor was it supposed to be.

> We hold these truths to be self-evident: That all men are created equal; that they are endowed by their Creator with certain unalienable rights; that among these are life, liberty, and the pursuit of happiness; that, to secure these rights, governments are instituted among men, deriving their just powers from the consent of the governed.[2]

That, of course, was Thomas Jefferson, himself a slaveholder.[3] But his was not the only influential voice of the period. Many were much more concerned with protecting the existing distribution of property.[4]

Gouverneur Morris of Massachusetts, for example, wrote that "men don't unite for liberty or life, . . . they unite for the protection of property."[5] John Adams added, "The moment the idea is admitted into society that property is not as sacred as the laws of God, and that there is not force of law and public justice to protect (it), anarchy and tyranny commence."[6] Consider also the words of two of the best known of the Founding Fathers, Alexander Hamilton and James Madison.

> The difference of property is already great amongst us. Commerce and industry will icrease the disparity. . . . Your government must meet this state of things, or combinations will . . . undermine your system.
>   The people, sir, are a great beast. . . . The same state of the passions which fits the multitude, who have not a sufficient stock of reason and knowledge to guide them, . . . very naturally leads them to a contempt and disregard of all authority.[7]

> An increase of population will of necessity increase the proportion of those who will labor under all the hardships of life, and secretly sigh for a more equal distribution of its blessings. These may in time outnumber those who are placed above the feelings of indigence. According to the equal laws of suffrage, the power will slide into the hands of the former.
>   . . . Whenever the majority shall be without landed or other equivalent property and without the means or hope of acquiring it, what is to secure the rights of property against the danger from an equality and universality of suffrage, vesting complete power over property in hands without a share in it.
>   Landholders ought to have a share in the Government. . . . They ought to be so constituted as to protect the minority of the opulent against the majority.[8]

Such sentiment reflected the views of political philosopher John Locke, whose *Second Treatise on Civil Government* was very influential in shaping the outlooks of America's founders. Locke, for example, was so obsessed with the protection of property that his writings included provisions for rebelling against an unresponsive government but never against the sanctity of private property. If the latter were challenged, all rights were to be suspended until the threat to property had been effectively overcome.[9]

But to understand more fully the fears of Locke, and especially those of Madison and other Founding Fathers, it is important to put all of this into historical perspective.

The Founders were exclusively white men, most of whom held significant personal wealth.[10] Although a strong national government made sense for the purposes of regulating their interstate commerce and protecting their property from both foreign and domestic invaders, they were highly suspicious of what the lesser propertied majority might do if given a proportionate share of the political power. Such fears were fed by social movements beginning to surface in Massachusetts, Rhode Island, New Hampshire, and Pennsylvania. Small farmers, in particular, were beginning to physically resist foreclosures and to forcibly free debtors from prison, while pressing for voting rights and a shift to paper currency in order to help them overcome their extensive debts.[11]

Shays's Rebellion was one of the most frightening of these developments. In the winter of 1787, Daniel Shays led an armed group in a series of raids across the Massachusetts countryside, spreading to the very outskirts of Boston. Not only did they free prisoners, but also they attacked courts, lawyers, and legislators. Mired in debt and weary from years of seemingly futile peaceful protest, they were now violently demanding lower taxes, a repudiation of past debts, and other concessions. By the time they were finally subdued by the state militia, 11 people lay dead and dozens wounded.[12]

> All communities divide themselves into the few and the many. The first are the rich and well-born, the other the mass of the people. The voice of the people has been said to be the voice of God; and however generally this maxim has been quoted and believed, it is not true in fact. The people are turbulent and changing; they seldom judge or determine right. Give therefore to the first class a distinct permanent share in the government. . . . Can a democratic assembly who annually revolve in the mass of the people be supposed steadily to pursue the public good? Nothing but a permanent body can check the imprudence of democracy.
>
> Alexander Hamilton[13]

As they gathered in Philadelphia, then, the Founding Fathers had a good bit more on their minds then "life, liberty, and the pursuit of happiness" for all. A number of them also set out to protect their property interests—including their enslaved human property.[14]

THE CONSTITUTION OF THE UNITED STATES

> The Constitution is a law for rulers and people, equally in war and peace, and covers with the shield of its protection all classes of men at all times and under all circumstances.
>
> U.S. Supreme Court (1866)[15]

> The Constitution was a compromise between slaveholding interests of the South and moneyed interests of the North for the purpose of uniting the thirteen states into one great market. For commerce, the northern delegates wanted laws regulating interstate commerce, and urged that such laws require only a majority of Congress to pass. The South agreed to this, in return for allowing the trade of slaves to continue.
>
> Howard Zinn (1980)[16]

Did the elitists succeed in incorporating their views into the United States Constitution? To answer that question, we must first consider how their conservative political philosophy was included in the governmental system outlined in Articles 1 through 6 and then focus on the nature of the civil rights guaranteed in various other constitutional passages.

Chief Justice Charles Evans Hughes noted, "We are under a constitution, but the constitution is what the judges say it is."[17] The U.S. Supreme Court assumes the role of final constitutional interpreter by virtue of Article 3, which states, "The judicial power shall extend to all cases, in law and equity, arising under this constitution." And since the Court's decision in *Marbury v. Madison* (1803), it has also reviewed the constitutionality of laws passed by legislatures. So we must consider the conservative biases built into the Constitution not only by the Founding Fathers but also by the Supreme Court justices who have interpreted their words.

The Governmental System

First we shall examine the conservative devices built into the governing process (many of which will be discussed in greater detail in Chapters 7 and 8). Then we will note additional care taken to secure the sanctity of private property, particularly as it extends to contracts between individuals.

Governmental Process.   The governmental process set out in Articles 1 through 6 established numerous roadblocks to majority rule, for example, checks and balances within the Congress, among the three branches, and between the national and state governments. As a case in point, legislation had to pass both houses in identical form, was subject to a presidential veto, and would be reliant on executive- or state-level implementation. It was much easier to block laws than to pass them. Also, since there was no provision for national referenda, all legislation had to pass through that maze of governmental decision makers.

As James Madison put it:

> [If] you take in a greater varieties of parties and interests; you make it less probable that a majority of the whole will have a common motive to invade the rights of other citizens. . . . A rage for paper money, for an abolition of debts, for an equal division of property, or for any other improper or wicked project, will be less apt to pervade the whole body of the Union than a particular member of it.[18]

And who would pick the governmental decision makers? The ones with the longest terms of office, U.S. senators, were actually chosen by state legislatures until a constitutional amendment more than 125 years later. The chief executive was to be elected by an electoral college rather than directly by the people. And although the House of Representatives (like state legislatures) would be chosen directly by the people, it was half a century before "the people" came to include most nonpropertied white men, a century and a half for most white women, and two centuries for most African Americans.

Property-related Clauses.   To be doubly safe, a number of explicit property-related clauses were added, and although they never specifically mentioned slavery or race, the implications for most African Americans were quite clear. For example,

Article 1, Section 9, essentially granted legal sanction to the importation of slaves for the next 20 years. Article 4, Section 2, read, "No person held to service or labour in one state . . . escaping into another, shall . . . be discharged from such service or labour, but shall be delivered up on claim of the party to whom such service or labour may be due." And there was also the infamous *three-fifths compromise* in Article 1, Section 2, reducing enslaved human beings to the legal status of three-fifths of a noncitizen, merely to be counted for the purposes of determining a state's share of federal taxation and its congressional representation. Both provisions—the mandatory returning of runaway slaves and the three-fifths compromise—were in effect for nearly a century, ultimately requiring a civil war to undo.[19]

As for property in general, the Fifth Amendment guaranteed that "no person shall . . . be deprived of . . . property, without due process of law; nor shall private property be taken for public use, without just compensation." An army and a navy were established to defend the nation's territory—most of which was owned by a relatively small group of elites.[20] A militia was created to suppress insurrections. The Congress was empowered to regulate commerce. And state governments were explicitly barred from coining their own money, allowing the repayment of debts in paper currency, or otherwise "impairing the obligation of contracts."

This hyperconcern over property, debts, and contracts really ended up amounting to the following: The Constitution of the United States would protect one's right to make unlimited profits, far beyond the necessities of life, while at the other end of the spectrum, it would be illegal to refuse repayment of a debt, even if one was starving to death. Jefferson's "right to life" would not imply a right to eat.

Finally, the entire document was never placed before the American people for ratification. Instead, it was ratified by state legislatures, and those legislatures, like their counterpart in Washington, were composed almost exclusively of white males who possessed a significant amount of property, just like the people who were allowed to elect them. What is more, ratification was marked by rumors of bribery, misinformation, and economic coercion, including advertiser boycotts of antifederalist newspapers and the calling in of debts of Constitution opponents.[21]

When it came to interpretation of this document by the judicial elites the legislative elites had appointed, it was more of the same. In *Trustees of Dartmouth College v. Woodward* (1819), the Supreme Court judged that corporations were "persons" in the eyes of the law and thus eligible for constitutional protection. In *Pollock v. Farmers' Loan and Trust Co.* (1895), the Court invalidated the graduated federal income tax, leading a New York bank president to praise the court as the "guardian of the dollar, defender of private property, enemy of spoilation, [and] sheer anchor of the Republic."[22] The Court would also protect a national bank and other even more blatant monopolies, imprisonment of anticapitalist dissenters, deportation of immigrant radicals, violent strikebreaking, Ku Klux Klan actions, and Jim Crow laws. And until 1937, it found that the Constitution protected child labor, sweatshops, and 16-hour workdays, as the fifth and fourteenth Amendments were interpreted as forbidding the state and federal governments from depriving corporate owners of their property without appropriate "due process of law."

For African Americans, all of this simply promised to reinforce the legacies of slavery. The political system had been consciously designed to impede fundamental change, while the protection of existing property relations would further slow black efforts to overcome an inequality imposed on them by their many years of enslavement.[23]

Constitutional Rights

But what about the civil rights guaranteed to all residents of the country? To begin with, realize that there was no Bill of Rights until four years after the constitutional convention, when ratification appeared to be in some doubt, and that the first ten amendments involved negative and not positive rights: protecting people from governmental intrusion but not guaranteeing governmental protection.

These constitutional rights are clearly negative. Government is not to make laws that prohibit religious practice or free speech and assembly. Yet the Constitution does not guarantee a job at a livable wage, health care when one is desperately ill, or quality educational opportunities. Freedom of the press does not guarantee one an avenue for expression unless one owns a press. Government may not search one's house without a warrant, but there is no guarantee of a house to live in. These are but a few of many possible examples.

Also realize that the absence of positive guarantees inhibits full utilization of rights protected against governmental interference. For example, one may choose not to register and vote, if one's employer likes to employ only "good Negroes." Being dependent on governmentally determined eligibility for public housing and a welfare check may well chill one's willingness to be identified as an active protester against governmental policy.[24] Wealthy corporations and individuals can chill protests against their actions by threatening expensive harassment lawsuits against the protestors. A caseworker can make a warrantless search of a welfare recipient's home. A poor woman may well lose her constitutionally protected right to an abortion if she has no means to pay for it. And despite democratic "one person, one vote" rhetoric, the wealthy are the only ones in a position to influence elections and elected officials by virtue of large personal campaign contributions. The wealthy, by being able to afford the best advocates, are even far more likely to be successful before the nation's highest trial and appellate courts.[25]

One of the most glaring examples of wealth-related rights can be seen in the institutional barriers to bringing a lawsuit into the United States judicial arena. For example, in the context of the wealth and income inequalities described in Chapters 4 and 5, consider the fact that bringing a single employment discrimination suit can cost $100,000, exclusive of attorneys' fees.[26] The U.S. Supreme Court eased this burden somewhat in the 1960s by allowing successful plaintiffs to recover such costs from defendants (*Newman v. Piggie Park Enterprises*, 1968). Thereafter, however, at least two decisions seem to reduce the likelihood that the fee recovery principle will encourage indigent people to bring lawsuits (*Marek v. Chesny*, 1985; *Evans v. Jeff D.*, 1986).

On the face of it, at least some of these inequities would seem to run afoul of the Fourteenth Amendment's equal protection clause. Yet, on several occasions, the Supreme Court has made it clear that such is simply not the case. For example, the Fourteenth Amendment has not been read to guarantee equal funding of public schools,[27] free school bus service for the poor,[28] increased welfare benefits for larger families,[29] or public funding of abortions for indigent women.[30] For all intents and purposes, economic inequalities are to be taken as a given and are not to be subject to constitutional redress.[31]

Race and Civil Rights

> The rich inheritance of justice, liberty, prosperity and independence, bequeathed by your fathers, is shared by you, not by me. The sunlight that brought light and healing to you, has brought stripes and death to me. This Fourth of July is yours, not mine. You may rejoice, I must mourn.
>
> Frederick Douglass (July 4, 1852)[32]

For most African Americans, it took a civil war to gain recognition that even negative rights were applicable to them. But those rights have been applied and extended inconsistently. Both the emphasis on negative rights and their erratic enforcement have caused considerable uncertainty at any point in time—the kind of uncertainty that is supposed to be minimized in a constitutional system.

Prior to the Civil War, black rights were suppressed time and again. In *Prigg v. Pennsylvania* (1842), for example, the U.S. Supreme Court upheld the Fugitive Slave Act requiring slaveowners' human property to be returned. In *Jones v. Van Zandt* (1847), the Court even went so far as to describe slavery as "a sacred compromise" in the Constitution. Then, in *Dred Scott v. Sanford* (1857), the justices made quite clear where they placed the large majority of African Americans in the constitutional order of things. Nearly a century after the Revolutionary War, the Court declared that 4 million black slaves were chattel and not citizens. They had no constitutional rights at all, but their owners' possession of them was protected by the "due process" clause of the Fifth Amendment. In other words, such property could not be taken from slave owners without giving each of them full due process of law.

These kinds of developments led abolitionist William Lloyd Garrison to burn a copy of the U.S. Constitution before a large gathering of the New England Anti-Slavery Society, calling the document "a covenant with death and an agreement with hell." To which, the crowd responded with a resounding "Amen."[33]

Following the Civil War, three key constitutional amendments altered the ground rules. The Thirteenth Amendment, ratified in 1865, outlawed slavery. The Fourteenth, ratified three years later, required each state to recognize the citizenship of "all persons born or naturalized in the United States," as well as extend them due process and equal protection under state laws. The Fifteenth Amendment (1870) prohibited the federal and state governments from denying any (male) citizen the right to vote "on account of race, color, or previous condition of servitude." How the Supreme Court interpreted these amendments, however, is another story altogether.

Once Reconstruction ended and the federal troops were gone, former slaves had little other than the letter of the law to protect them. Faced with intense racial discrimination in the job market, as well as outright physical intimidation, most ended up in economic peonage hardly distinguishable from their previous legalized enslavement. Their right to vote was denied through a series of election laws that appeared racially neutral but turned out to be quite discriminatory in application. These included highly arbitrary tests of a voter's literacy (literacy tests) and special taxes that had to be paid at the polls in order to be allowed to vote (poll taxes)—a disenfranchisement upheld by the U.S. Supreme Court in decisions such as *Williams v. Mississippi* (1898). In addition, a host of segregationist Jim Crow laws emerged to circumvent Fourteenth Amendment guarantees. For example, a Louisiana law required that blacks ride on separate railroad cars, and the Supreme Court upheld such laws in its infamous *Plessy v. Ferguson* (1896) decision. Such segregation of the races was not seen as denying blacks "equal protection of the laws."[34]

Segregated, without the vote, reduced to near economic enslavement, and living in continual fear of white violence, little seemed to have changed for the large majority of African Americans. Nevertheless, in the face of all of this, there was increasing organized resistance. The NAACP, for example, was born out of the Niagara Movement and began to press for black rights on a number of fronts. Communities were organized. Information was disseminated. Protest marches were launched. Elected officials were lobbied. Probably most noteworthy of all, federal lawsuits were filed on behalf of those so blatantly being denied basic human rights.[35] The successes and failures in this last arena are the primary concern of this chapter.

Education.   In this area, successes were achieved in legally requiring more equal educational opportunities from elementary to graduate schools. The Supreme Court, however, now seems to have drawn the line on the extension of these rights, despite the continued existence of a largely segregated public school system and the serious discrepancies in educational quality discussed in Chapters 3 and 9.[36]

From the late 1930s to the late 1960s, some major strides were made in the legal battle to acquire truly equal educational opportunities for black children. In *Gaines v. Canada* (1938), for example, the Supreme Court ruled that true equality required that the state of Missouri provide equal law schools for its black students, rather than simply paying their way to attend in another state. Twelve years later, in *Sweatt v. Painter* (1950), the Court ruled that Texas's separate black law schools were not equal, in part because of their "isolation from the individuals and institutions with which the law interacts." And in *McLaurin v. Oklahoma* (1950), the Court judged that segregation within an integrated school impaired a black student's "ability to study, to engage in discussions and exchange views with other students, and, in general, learn his profession."

The landmark case, of course, was *Brown v. Board of Education* (1954). Legally segregated public schools were no longer to be tolerable under the "equal protection" clause of the United States Constitution. "Separate" governmental treatment would cease to be viewed as ever being "equal." However, when pressed for some immediate action to enforce that decision, the Supreme Court backed off a bit; in *Brown v. Board of Education* (1955), it simply required implementation "with all deliberate speed." Nevertheless, the Court did not stand idly by. It barred blatant evasions in *Cooper v. Aaron* (1958), *Watson v. Memphis* (1963), and *Griffen v. Prince Edward County* (1964), and it ultimately did call for speedier compliance in decisions such as *Green v. County School Board* (1968), *Alexander v. Holmes County* (1969), and *United States v. Montgomery County Board of Education* (1969). Then, in *Swann v. Charlotte* (1971), a unanimous Court upheld measures such as court-ordered busing in situations where local school authorities had failed to redress long histories of segregation; and in *Runyon v. McCrary* (1976), it even ruled that an all-white private school could not discriminate on the basis of race.

But as the composition of the Court changed, so did the thrust of its decisions. Members of the more liberal Warren Court were replaced by the more conservative appointees of Republican presidents such as Richard Nixon and Ronald Reagan. It was not long, then, before the brakes began to be applied. The newly constituted Supreme Court would not prove to be nearly as aggressive in attacking educational inequities like segregation. As a matter of fact, it would rein in some of the previous efforts.

In *Keyes v. School District No. 1* (1973), the Court ruled that a clear "intent to segregate" (not just statistical evidence) must now be demonstrated before desegregation was required. And in *Milliken v. Bradley* (1974), they also strictly limited busing across school district lines, further fueling white flight to the suburbs for the purposes of avoiding school integration. Then, in decisions such as *Oklahoma City v. Dowell* (1991) and *Missouri v. Jenkins* (1995), the justices absolved two large cities of further responsibility for desegregation efforts even though there was little evidence of success. Thus, most all of the considerable school segregation that has resulted from the nation's blatantly segregated residential patterns appears to be beyond court-ordered remedies.[37]

In *San Antonio v. Rodriguez* (1973), the Court upheld the funding of public schools by property tax formulas, despite the huge differences in school district resources that resulted. Although, in *U.S. v. Fordice* (1992), they did require that Mississippi's small traditionally black colleges receive proportionately equal funding from the state government.[38]

As for affirmative action, *California v. Bakke* (1978) allowed race-conscious affirmative action efforts in college admissions, but only if race was just one of several factors considered and no inflexible quotas were used. However, their refusal to overturn lower court decisions in *Kirwan v. Podberesky* (1995) and *Texas v. Hopwood* (1996) has now cast serious doubt about the future of race-based college scholarships specifically, and the entire application of state affirmative action programs in general.

The same sorts of ebbs and flows in Court protection are apparent in other areas as well. Let us look at six more: elections, jobs, housing, public facilities, criminal punishment, and the right to speak in protest.[39]

Elections.   In the realm of suffrage, it took a full century to begin to enforce the Fifteenth Amendment in recalcitrant states. The most basic right in a democratic system, the right to vote, was withheld from nearly half of America's black citizens for some 100 years after a civil war and a constitutional amendment had supposedly laid the question to rest. The delay resulted in large part from the Supreme Court's dogged reluctance to put the most fundamental right in a democracy above the conservative principle of federalism.

The United States Constitution leaves it up to the states to establish who is eligible to vote. According to Article 1, Section 4, "The times, places, and manner of holding elections for senators and representatives, shall be prescribed in each state by the legislatures thereof; but the Congress may at any time by law make or alter such regulations." Why the Congress for so long avoided its responsibility in this area will be explored in Chapters 7 and 8. For now, note that the Supreme Court of the United States essentially sat on its collective hands throughout the second half of the nineteenth century, refusing to intervene in such "state matters," particularly signifi-cant given the absence of forceful congressional efforts to right this blatant wrong.

The first half of the twentieth century was somewhat better, although in many ways it simply demonstrates the inconsistency with which the federal courts attacked the evasive maneuvers of these states. In *Guinn v. United States* (1915), the Court fi-nally put an end to the notorious "grandfather clauses," which had denied registra-tion preferences to all whose grandparents had not been registered to vote—virtually all southern blacks. Given the dominance of the Democratic party in the South, how-ever, southern representatives were essentially chosen in the Democratic party's pri-mary elections. Thus when the Court declared in *Newberry v. United States* (1921) that primary elections were "in no real sense" part of federal elections, registered blacks could simply be excluded from these southern primaries and in essence be stripped of any real control over who would ultimately be elected in the region. *Nixon v. Herndon* (1927) barred state governments from writing such restrictions into state law, but *Grovey v. Townsend* (1935) allowed such exclusion if done by the parties themselves.

The Court changed composition and orientation in the late 1930s. This time, the change was in a more liberal direction. In *United States v. Classic* (1941), the Court reversed *Newberry* and found primaries to be an essential step in the federal election process. In *Smith v. Allwright* (1944) they reversed *Grovey* and ruled that because states were so directly involved in regulating such primaries, these were not purely private activities. And when states tried to repeal all related statutes in order to make the primaries truly private affairs, such efforts were rejected by the Court in *Rice v. Elmore* (1947) and *Terry v. Adams* (1953). Primary elections had come to be seen as integral parts of the electoral process and thus subject to the provisions of the Fif-teenth Amendment.

Nevertheless, by the early 1960s, a number of other laws and practices still left the overwhelming majority of southern blacks either unregistered or underrepre-sented. To reverse these would require strong Court-supported action on the part of the federal government.

States like Louisiana, for example, drew their election districts in ways that would minimize the impact of registered black votes, and one of the most blatant of these plans was struck down by the Court in *Gomillion v. Lightfoot* (1960). Yet the real action was just beginning.

The Twenty-fourth Amendment was added to the United States Constitution, barring poll taxes in federal elections. Then, in *Harper v. Virginia Board of Elections* (1966), the U.S. Supreme Court finally struck down the poll tax in state voting as a vi-olation of "equal protection of the laws." A combination of the 1964 Civil Rights Act and the 1965 Voting Rights Act (both discussed further in Chapter 8) allowed consid-erable federal intervention in the "times, places, and manner of holding elections," previously a nearly exclusive state purview. For example, federal examiners were al-lowed to register voters under certain circumstances, and a number of states had to "preclear" new voting regulations with federal officials.[40] The U.S. Supreme Court, for its part, upheld the role of federal examiners in *South Carolina v. Katzenbach* (1966) and preclearance in *Allen v. State Board of Elections* (1969).

Enter the Burger Court, however, dominated by appointees of Richard Nixon. Once again it would be hesitant to intervene in "state matters" in the absence of clear "purposeful intent to discriminate." The issue was apportionment schemes that had the result of reducing black representation. For example, in *Whitcomb v. Chavis* (1971), *Beer v. United States* (1976), and *Mobile v. Bolden* (1980), the Court upheld the practice of multimember district at-large elections, despite their dilution of geographically concentrated black votes. And in *Richmond v. United States* (1975), it allowed urban annexations of white suburbs, which clearly served the purpose of diluting the black vote. In *Presley v. Etowah County* (1992), the court also allowed the white majority on a county commission to dilute individual commissioner authority when two African Americans finally were elected to that board.

Nevertheless, in *Rome v. Georgia* (1980), the justices finally blocked an annexation plan—though only because the subsequent apportionment did not "fairly reflect the strength of the black community after annexation," not because of the discriminatory effect of the annexation itself. And in *Thornburgh v. Gingles* (1986), the Court upheld the revised Voting Rights Act's "discriminatory results" standard (rather than requiring "purposeful intent to discriminate") in finally overturning a set of large multimember election districts as racially discriminatory.[41]

The latest point of contention, however, involves racial gerrymandering designed to redress past exclusion. In *Williamsburg v. Carey* (1977) and *Voinovich v. Quilter* (1993), for instance, the Court refused to block state efforts at race-conscious gerrymandering designed specifically to enhance black representation. And, in *Johnson v. DeGrandy* (1994) the Rehnquist court reiterated its support for the concept of such racially conscious "influence districts." Yet, in a series of decisions beginning with *Shaw v. Reno* (1993), the Court began to severely limit this remedy.[42]

Lastly, despite the ultimate bans on racially discriminatory grandfather clauses, white primaries, literacy tests, poll taxes, and some racial gerrymandering, there are still a variety of impediments to black suffrage. Economic and physical intimidation employed by individual whites against individual blacks, for instance, are forms of discrimination for which judicial remedy has proved much more difficult than when government is the offender.[43]

Jobs.   The 1964 Civil Rights Act banned racial discrimination in the workplace, and in *Griggs v. Duke Power Company* (1971), the Supreme Court rejected employment standards unrelated to job performance when the result was to exclude black workers. Thereafter, the 1991 Civil Rights Act placed the burden of proof directly on the employers, allowed jury trials, and also allowed for both compensatory and punitive damages to be awarded.[44] But regardless of discriminatory impact, the Court demanded discriminatory intent before it would overturn performance-related tests (*Washington v. Davis*, 1976) or existing seniority systems (*Teamsters v. United States*, 1977).

The federal government also established affirmative action requirements, following John Kennedy's first mention of the concept in his 1961 Executive Order

10925. Yet in terms of enforcement, the Supreme Court has drawn an important distinction. Affirmative action plans, even for the Burger Court, were acceptable as remedial efforts in job-training programs (*United Steelworkers v. Weber*, 1979), hiring when attempting to overcome past discrimination by that agent (*Sheet Metal Workers v. EEOC*, 1986; *Firefighters v. Cleveland*, 1986), and promotion when seeking to rectify such past discrimination (*United States v. Paradise*, 1987; *Johnson v. Transportation Agency*, 1987), but they were not constitutionally permissible in guiding layoffs, particularly where a legitimate seniority system was in place (*Memphis Firefighters v. Stotts*, 1984) or in the absence of a very clear and compelling state interest (*Wygant v. Jackson Board of Education*, 1986). Thus the last hired could continue to be the first fired, which significantly tempers training, hiring, and promotion assistance in an economy that regularly experiences both boom and slump periods. In addition, many existing government set-asides for black contractors would no longer be allowed (*Richmond v. Croson*, 1989 and *Adarand v. Pena*, 1995), significantly slowing recent gains by a number of black firms.[45]

Housing.   In 1917, Louisville, Kentucky, was forbidden from engaging in blatantly segregationist zoning (*Buchanan v. Warley*). In addition, state and local governments were barred from enforcing discriminatory "restrictive covenants" written into the deeds of houses (*Shelley v. Kramer*, 1948). Then *Reitman v. Mulkey* (1967) struck down California's attempt to place private real estate transactions outside of governmental review. *Jones v. Mayer* (1968) resurrected an 1866 civil rights act to guarantee blacks equal opportunity to "purchase, lease, sell, hold, and convey real and personal property." And *Hunger v. Erickson* (1969) would not allow the city of Akron to require popular referenda before any fair-housing ordinances could go into effect.

But having the right to acquire a home anywhere in town and having the means to do so are two quite separate things. Even when the government helps out with housing assistance, equal rights still get denied. For example, many blacks have been forced by economic necessity to rely on public housing; thus the location of public housing has also become a focus of attention in the battle to secure equal housing opportunities. Into the fray bounded the Burger Court, with its "purposeful intent to discriminate" standard. In *Arlington Heights v. Metropolitan Housing District* (1977), for example, the Court ruled that the segregating effects of the city's zoning laws, as they affected predominantly black public housing, were not enough to violate the equal-protection clause. There must be clear evidence of discriminatory intent. And even when sufficient intent was determined and desegregation was ordered, the U.S. Supreme Court, in 1991, chastised a federal judge for holding individual city council members in contempt and fining them when they failed to pass the legislation necessary to carry out his desegregation order.[46]

Public Facilities.   The 1875 Civil Rights Act barred racial discrimination in public accommodations; yet the U.S. Supreme Court struck down those provisions in 1883 (*Civil Rights Cases*), arguing that the segregationist practices of private hotels, theaters, railroads, and the like did not involve "state action" as required to justify such a law under the Fourteenth Amendment. Jim Crow became the order of the day in many such businesses until the 1960s. In *Burton v. Wilmington Parking Authority*

(1961), the Supreme Court ruled that a private restaurant with a lease in a state-owned building could not discriminate without violating the equal-protection clause. The Civil Rights Act of 1964 finally prohibited all such discrimination and was upheld by the Court in *Heart of Atlanta Motel v. United States* (1974) and *Katzenbach v. McClung* (1974).

Nevertheless, the battle was not over. In particular, a number of these facilities were converted to private clubs in order to restrict patronage. And although the Court disallowed such a dodge in *Daniel v. Paul* (1969), it ruled that no state action was involved when a Moose Lodge refused to serve blacks, even though it was operating under a state liquor license (*Moose Lodge No. 107 v. Irvis*, 1972). Beyond that, *Tonkins v. Greensboro* (1959) allowed public swimming pools to be sold to segregating private operators, and *Palmer v. Thompson* (1971) allowed Jackson, Mississippi, to close all of its city pools rather than integrate them.

Criminal Punishment.   It was not until 1935, in *Norris v. Alabama*, that the U.S. Supreme Court finally outlawed the systematic exclusion of blacks from juries, and not until 1986, in *Vasquez v. Hillery*, did it extend this to grand juries. Thus the Sixth Amendment guarantee of an "impartial jury," on the books for two centuries, was at last deemed applicable to African Americans. Yet in *Swain v. Alabama* (1965), the Court refused to bar a prosecutor's use of preemptory challenges to exclude blacks from juries unless there was a clear racial pattern in such exclusions. And although *Batson v. Kentucky* (1986) did not accept such preemptory challenges simply on the grounds that blacks are less likely to convict other blacks, one must realize that lawyers normally do not have to give their reasons for such exclusions. Thus *Swain* is still governing for all practical purposes, and blacks are still at times being convicted by all-white juries even in racially mixed communities. As Justice Scalia made clear in *Holland v. Illinois* (1990), the Sixth Amendment guarantees an impartial jury, but not a representative one.

Yet, long before such cases even go to trial, important political decisions are made concerning which types of crimes are to be most heavily punished and which types of criminals most aggressively pursued. In 1996, accusations of racial bias in such decision making led to the case of *U.S. v. Armstrong* (1996). There was no disputing the fact that sentences for possessing and/or selling crack cocaine were more severe than those applied in cases involving notably more expensive powder cocaine. The additional reality was that the overwhelming majority of crack cocaine defendants were inner-city blacks, while those accused of powder cocaine violations were more likely to be suburban whites. Nevertheless, the Court rejected allegations of unequal treatment, while the nation's jail populations have continued to become ever blacker in composition.[47]

Probably the most blatant example of continuing racism in this area, however, concerns the ultimate punishment: the death penalty. In *Furman v. Georgia* (1972), the Supreme Court halted further executions until the procedure for assigning the death penalty was reformed. In part, the Court felt that existing practice had allowed its application in an "arbitrary and capricious" way toward black defendants. Four years later, in *Gregg v. Georgia*, the Court seemed satisfied that additional safeguards such as separate sentencing hearings had alleviated the problem. Executions resumed, and by the spring of 1987, some 70 people had been executed, 42 of them black. Of the nearly 1,900 people on death row awaiting execution in the mid–1980s, 42 percent were black.

Enter University of Iowa researcher David Baldus. Controlling for 230 separate factors in 2,484 Georgia cases, Baldus concluded that killers of whites were 4.3 times more likely to receive a death sentence than killers of blacks.[48] Though it did not challenge the accuracy of those findings, the U.S. Supreme Court refused to allow such general statistical evidence to invalidate the procedure by which Georgia assigned the death penalty in this particular case (*McCleskey v. Kemp*, 1987). In dissent, Justice William Brennan lambasted his fellow justices by stating, "Since *Furman v. Georgia*, the court has been concerned with the risk of the imposition of an arbitrary sentence, rather than the proven fact of one." And he went on to warn, "We remain imprisoned by the past as long as we deny its influence in the present."

Yet, to further compound the dilemma, a string of Supreme Court decisions such as *McCleskey v. Zant* (1991), *Keeney v. Tamayo-Reyes* (1992), *Wright v. West* (1992), and *Herrera v. Collins* (1993) have made it significantly more difficult to appeal such decisions. Even when states choose to ignore new evidence of "actual innocence," there is no longer presumed to be a right to appeal such decisions in federal court as possible violations of provisons in the United States Constitution.

The Right to Speak in Protest. The First Amendment decrees that "Congress shall make no law . . . abridging the freedom of speech . . . or the right of the people, peaceably to assemble, and to petition the Government for a redress of grievances." In addition, as of *Gitlow v. New York* (1925), such restrictions were extended to state legislatures by means of the Fourteenth Amendment. Nevertheless, in practice, "no law" has come to mean "some laws." For example, *Schenck v. United States* (1919) allowed the suppression of protest if it created a "clear and present danger." Gitlow also made an exception if the speech was likely to create a "bad tendency" in its audience. *Cox v. New Hampshire* (1941) allowed governments to require a permit for all "parades and processions." And *Chaplinsky v. New Hampshire* (1942) found "the lewd and obscene, the profane, the libelous, and the insulting or 'fighting words' (words that would provoke others to fight)" similarly unprotected by the First Amendment.

For the black community, such concerns became particularly relevant in the 1950s and 1960s, as civil rights protests proliferated. Once again, the Supreme Court's signals were mixed. Irving Feiner, for example, gave an impromptu address on a street corner in a predominantly black area of Syracuse. Among other things, Feiner declared, "The Negroes don't have equal rights; they should rise up in arms and fight for their rights." In *Feiner v. New York* (1951), the United States Supreme Court upheld his conviction for "disorderly conduct," arguing that the First Amendment does not protect "incitement to riot." More than a decade later, however, the more liberal Warren Court found that large numbers of black protesters, even when confronting a larger number of angry whites, were protected by the First Amendment (*Edwards v. South Carolina*, 1963; *Cox v. Louisiana*, 1965). But even though the Court allowed such highly inflammatory protests on public streets and even in a public library (*Brown v. Louisiana*, 1965), it would not allow them at a jail (*Adderly v. Florida*, 1966).

If the Constitution is what the Supreme Court says it is, what rights does it guarantee for African Americans? Lewis Steele has referred to the United States Supreme Court as "nine men in black who think white."[49] That may be a little too simplistic, as the Court's posture on race-related issues has varied considerably depending on the political orientation of the Court. Another way to look at that, however, is that the United States really does not have a constitutional system in which basic human rights are etched clearly in stone for all time. Instead, it has a constitutional democracy in which majority opinion can affect both who sits on the federal bench and how those justices decide cases—particularly in light of the fact that judges must make decisions that have a realistic chance of being implemented effectively by more democratically vulnerable agents.

A classic case in point is the recently revived controversy over whether private institutions may discriminate on the basis of race. The Constitution clearly states that governments may not; but many of the victories (especially in the areas of jobs, housing, education, and public facilities) required nongovernmental agents to cease discriminating as well. The real legal foundation for a number of these decisions was a pair of relatively obscure post-Civil War laws (now codified as 42 USCS 1981 and 1982). In decisions such as *Jones v. Mayer* (1968) and *Runyon v. McCrary* (1976), these laws were resurrected by the Warren Court and extended by the Burger Court in order to bar discrimination by private agents. However, when confronted with a private-sector employee's discrimination suit in 1988, newly confirmed Justice Anthony Kennedy cast the swing vote as the even more conservative Rehnquist Court decided it was time to reconsider this entire principle (*Patterson v. McLean Credit Union*, 1984). Although later reversed by the 1991 Civil Rights Act, such Court activity only reconfirms the contingent nature of all such judicial "victories."

IMPLEMENTATION

There is one more piece in the judicial puzzle. Despite what the Founding Fathers said in the Constitution and unevenness in interpretation, even outright legal victories mean nothing until they are implemented.

First, the organization of the U.S. judicial process is a clear example of federalism at work. There are federal courts and there are state courts, both with their own unique jurisdictions. The federal system is composed of U.S. district courts (which hold the initial trials), U.S. courts of appeals, and finally, the U.S. Supreme Court. Their jurisdiction is limited to national matters, as spelled out in Article 3 of the U.S. Constitution, and they must ultimately rely on the federal marshals of the U.S. Justice Department to carry out their decisions. Parallel to that, the 50 state systems are organized in a similar manner. Although the names of the specific courts vary from state to state, each state has local trial courts, most have intermediate courts of appeals, and all have a state Supreme Court. Jurisdiction covers state laws, which include most familiar crimes, and enforcement falls on the shoulders of state and local police departments.

The Judicial Process

A society rent along racial lines, in an overheated atmosphere in which both sides lack confidence in the justice system, is a society headed for catastrophe.[50]

Courts of Appeals.   The ultimate arbiter in this entire process, of course, is the Supreme Court of the United States. It is that court's responsibility to determine whether challenged state or federal government actions have offended the dictates of the United States Constitution, the "supreme" law of the land. But given that the United States does have a formal written constitution that has been amended a mere 17 times in 200 years, how can Supreme Court interpretation of it vary as much as it has? Why are there no permanent victories?

The answer to such questions lies in both the nature of the document and the nature of the justices who must interpret it. To begin with, terms like "due process of law" are ambiguous; thus interpretation is required as different circumstances arise. Second, justices vary in the way they define their roles. At one extreme are those justices who decide primarily on the basis of what they feel the Founding Fathers meant, while at the other extreme are those who give equal weight to *social need* at any given point in time. Activist justices like Thurgood Marshall and William Brennan continually voted to declare the death penalty unconstitutional, for example, even though the Founding Fathers' generation did not consider even dismemberment in the course of execution to be "cruel and unusual punishment" for some offenses. Clearly, who sits on any interpreting court becomes extremely important.

And just who does sit on the U.S. Supreme Court—or any of the federal courts, for that matter? That is determined by a relatively simple process. The president of the United States chooses a nominee to replace a retiring or deceased justice. That nominee is reviewed for professional competence and integrity by the American Bar Association (ABA). Then, if the president is satisfied with the ABA's evaluation, the nominee is placed before the United States Senate for confirmation and—over the course of the twentieth century—has normally been confirmed.[51]

So who ends up with these life-long appointments? As Lewis Steele and others have indicated, they are generally white Anglo-Saxon men who come from relatively wealthy backgrounds.[52] Their demographic profile closely resembles that of the elites who own most of the nation's wealth. African Americans are noticeably underrepresented. Only two black justices have ever sat on the U.S. Supreme Court, while scarcely more than 5 percent of lower federal court justices are black, most of them appointed by Presidents Jimmy Carter and Bill Clinton.[53]

There are at least four obvious reasons for these results. First of all, justices are drawn from the ranks of the legal profession, and only 3 percent of United States lawyers are black. Second, the justices are appointed and confirmed by elected representatives whose collective profile is quite similar to their own (the reasons for the representatives' homogeneity will be discussed in Chapter 7). Third, the prestigious law schools that tend to supply nominees have long been bastions of wealthy white elites (a subject explored further in Chapter 9). Fourth, the ABA is a very conservative organization, prompting black lawyers to form their own bar association to try to counter that influence.[54] Once again, institutionalized racism is in plain view.[55]

In a speech in June 1986 during his brief campaign for the presidency, Pat Robertson declared that Supreme Court rulings "are not the law of the land."[56] Seemingly illogical at the time, Robertson's statement was essentially correct— though not necessarily for the reasons he had in mind. To understand the validity of his remark is to understand another very important lesson about the judicial arena in the United States.

Appellate court decisions do not automatically translate into enforced behavior for a number of reasons. Most importantly, such courts do not have their own administrative arms or police forces. They are reliant on the executive branches of government to carry out their decisions, and executive bureaucracies often have their own political agendas. The justices in these courts also lack the staff, budget, and time to keep an eye on how their decisions are being enforced. Thus, by default, laws actually come to mean what law enforcement agents say the courts said they meant. And if their interpretation is unsatisfactory, back to the beginning the challengers often must go, to the trial courts.

Trial Courts.   Only a tiny fraction of lower court decisions ever work their way up the appeals hierarchy. Consequently, trial courts' interpretations and judgments normally stand as the law of the land. Although the national government is supposed to look after the basic rights of all American citizens, no matter where they live, the reality is that local judges end up deciding just what the national government had in mind. And it is at this level that the judicial process is least insulated from political pressure. Litigants have recognizable faces and networks of associates. Decisions often have direct and immediate effects on the local community. State trial judges are often elected to their positions, serving limited terms, and even the life-tenured federal judges informally have to be approved by elected U.S. senators from their state. On top of that, very few trial judges are black. There was not one black trial judge in the South from the end of Reconstruction to 1965. Even two decades later, there were fewer than 350 black trial judges in the entire nation.[57]

The implications for enforcement of Supreme Court victories are obvious. Because blacks have not fared as well in lower courts,[58] victories at higher levels have been impeded. In Virginia, for example, state and local governments were allowed to delay school integration by abolishing compulsory school attendance policies and closing integrated schools—including all the public schools in one county.[59] In addition, all-white schools were at times integrated by busing in black students, but all-black schools generally remained all-black, as whites were seldom bused to black schools for the purpose of desegregation.[60]

Law Enforcement Agents.   The zeal with which law enforcement agents enforce court-interpreted federal law also varies, depending on the political inclinations of the particular agents and the elected officials who appointed them. Examples of such uncertainty-producing inconsistency can be found at the highest levels of the federal law enforcement bureaucracy. Contrast, for instance, the approaches of Attorneys General Nicholas Katzenbach and Ed Meese or Equal Employment Opportunity Commission (EEOC) Chair Eleanor Holmes Norton and Civil Rights Commission

(CRC) Chair Clarence Pendleton.[61] Ronald Reagan's assistant attorney general, William Bradford Reynolds, was even quoted as saying, "We are not going to compel children who don't choose to have an integrated education to have one."[62] And no sooner had the U.S. Supreme Court upheld the Voting Rights Act's results standard in its *Thornburgh* decision, than Reynolds was stating that the Justice Department did not intend to employ that standard when preclearing new state election laws.[63] Meanwhile, Jeffrey Zuckerman, nominated by Reagan to be the general counsel to the EEOC, argued at his confirmation hearing that blacks and women could best end discrimination in the workplace by simply working more cheaply than whites.[64] Such politicized administration at this level, where media scrutiny is most intense, would seem to be only the tip of a very large iceberg.

Specifically, consider what local practice can mean for enforcement of the rights of those accused of a crime. Given these realities, it is no wonder that the black poor constitute roughly half of the American prison population.

The Criminal Justice System

Both individual and institutionalized racism are readily apparent in the criminal justice system. From arrest to bail decisions to sentencing, African Americans can never be certain where and when such racism will appear. Although this discussion in no way seeks to make excuses for the behavior of criminals, it does raise serious questions about the equity of treatment in a system that intentionally allows a considerable degree of discretion at each stage.

To begin with, some nine in ten Americans do things in the course of their lives that could land them in prison.[65] Nevertheless, it is not a cross-section of the American population that ends up being arrested and convicted of such criminal behavior. Instead, America's prisons are overflowing with low-income individuals, roughly half of whom are black.[66]

Police.   At the street level, complaints of excessive and discriminatory uses of police force did not end in the 1960s.[67] Beneath such behavior on the part of white police officers lurk stereotyping, fears, and anger. In December 1986, for example, an all-white New Orleans suburb was experiencing an increasing number of burglaries. In response, its sheriff ordered that any black seen in the area be stopped and questioned.[68] Or, who can forget the graphic videotape of four Los Angeles police officers repeatedly beating black motorist Rodney King as he lay prone on the ground.[69] Within months of the King beating, Malice Green was bludgeoned to death by two flashlight-wielding Detroit officers.[70] In October 1995, black motorist Johnny Gammage was pulled over while driving his dark blue Jaguar through a predominantly white Pittsburgh suburb, only to be beaten and choked to death on the spot after allegedly attacking five white police officers.[71] Dead, too, is Anthony Baez, a 29-year-old Bronx man who was choked to death after his football accidentally hit a squad car.[72] While parked in front of his own house in April 1996, Lebert Folkes was pulled from behind the wheel of a car mistakenly reported to be stolen and shot in the face at point blank range.[73] In April 1997, Atlanta police were videotaped beating 27-year-old Timmie Sinclair repeatedly with their fists and a tactical baton as his wife and two children watched from the family car.[74] The nationwide doubling of black police officers since 1972 should help increase the equity of treatment by police,[75] but even if police treatment becomes more equitable, larger problems lurk elsewhere in the system.

Bail.   Once arrested and charged, there is the question of bail. Presumed innocent until proved guilty, the criminal suspect is not to be punished by imprisonment prior to conviction and sentencing. Therefore, the suspect normally should be released, with bail set high enough to ensure that he or she will appear at the subsequent proceedings but not so high as to be considered "excessive," which would violate the Eighth Amendment of the United States Constitution. In reality, of course, the poor are often unable to post bail and thus end up in jail for months awaiting trial.[76] Meanwhile, they are not as able to assist in their own defense, for example, by lining up witnesses; and if convicted, they will ultimately be less likely to get probation because they have not been working regularly.[77]

Legal Representation.   More than 90 percent of all criminal cases will end outside of court with a "plea bargain" whereby the charge is reduced in return for a guilty plea. Whether a case is settled in or out of court, the quality of legal representation is extremely important. Fully 90 percent of people in prison could not afford to hire a lawyer and thus had one appointed by the court.[78] What are such lawyers paid? The national average in 1985 was $196 per case,[79] far below the tens of thousands of dollars private firms routinely charge for similar defenses.[80] It should be no surprise, then, when stories like the following begin to surface:

> James Messer, a poor man, was charged with murder. The first lawyer appointed to defend him begged off, citing community outrage at the crime. So did the second. A third lawyer adopted a low-key strategy: He made no opening statement, called no witnesses, did not object to evidence and engaged in only cursory cross examination. At the sentencing hearing following conviction, he did not ask the jury to spare Mr. Messer's life, did not offer mitigating details inviting mercy and hinted that execution was appropriate. Mr. Messer soon found himself on Georgia's Death Row.
>
> Kevin Griffin's lawyer, a South Carolina public defender, had a hundred other clients. He was forced to begin Mr. Griffin's rape trial on short notice, with little chance to investigate and after working on another case until 11:30 the previous night. There was no time to prepare Mr. Griffin or anyone to testify. Mr. Griffin, convicted after a one-day trial, received 40 years.
>
> Peter Schwander was charged with robbery in Louisiana. His trial lawyer made no independent investigation of the facts, nor did he speak with Mr. Schwander before trial. After conviction, Mr. Schwander's appellate lawyer worked without critical parts of the trial record. Mr. Schwander was sentenced to 30 years in prison.[81]

Juries.   The juries that bring these sentences are hardly representative either. Normally chosen randomly from the list of enrolled voters, they exclude the disproportionate number of lower-income people who have not registered. Then, from the group that is chosen, hourly workers may be excused on the basis of "hardship." Thus the juries end up disproportionately populated by middle-class white business persons and professionals.[82]

Not surprisingly, then, a stockbroker gets a small fine for making $20 million in an illegal stock manipulation, whereas the same day a black man gets one year in prison for stealing a $100 television from the back of a truck.[83] There are indications that the poor are notably less likely to get suspended sentences or probation.[84] Even controlling for prior criminal records, blacks appear to get longer sentences than whites for the same crimes.[85] The race of the victim is significant as well. In the early 1980s, for instance, the average sentence for a black raping another black was four years, a white raping another white was five, a white raping a black was six, and a black raping a white was 16.[86]

Incarceration.   Despite an explicit constitutional prohibition of "cruel and unusual punishment," the United States harbors harsh realities in its prisons and mental hospitals for the criminally insane. The conditions inside many U.S. prisons have been widely publicized. Extortion, robbery, assault, and homosexual rape are commonplace in overcrowded and underfunded prisons, in which much of the policing is often left to the convicts themselves. Less publicized is the role mental hospitals have occasionally played in all of this. Perceived troublemakers, many of them black, have at times been subjected to mind-altering drugs, shock treatments, aversion therapies, and even lobotomies.[87] And, on top of all this, the poor are more likely to remain in prison, as their appeals are significantly less likely to be heard.[88]

Overall, then, even the limited negative rights guaranteed by the United States Constitution are inconsistently interpreted and enforced, creating very real uncertainty in the minds of African Americans.[89] This, the least political of the several government arenas, seems destined by design to ebb and flow in its judgments, to the point of reinforcing some of the most fundamental inequalities in the status quo by its lack of consistent action to the contrary.

Radicals and the Law

Despite the inherent limits of the rights expressed in the U.S. Constitution, as well as the uncertainty created by some obvious ebbs and flows in their interpretation and implementation, the judicial arena has proved relatively receptive to a number of black demands for equal opportunities within the present economic structure. But when radical voices that challenge the historical maldistribution of property are raised, the interpreters and implementers of the Constitution seem to revert to the original purpose of protecting property above and beyond all else. American history is replete with radical individuals and groups who were under the erroneous impression that such views were protected under the Bill of Rights. For the majority of African Americans, seemingly locked in the economic subordination that is slavery's legacy, this is not good news.

Radicals in General.   At the constitutional level, the signals are mixed. Consider advocates of communism as an alternative to capitalism. In *De Jonge v. Oregon* (1937), the U.S. Supreme Court decided that states must respect the First Amendment rights of communists to assemble, although in *Dennis v. United States* (1951) it reversed itself amid the anticommunist hysteria of the McCarthy period. Six years later, in *Yates v. United States* (1957), the Court reversed itself again. Now there was to be constitutional protection for communists' advocacy of an abstract doctrine that called for the overthrow of the existing political-economic system but not for direct advocacy of such an overthrow. And as late as 1961, in *Scales v. United States*, the Court upheld the conviction of a man for his active membership in a Communist party branch that the Court apparently felt had stepped over the boundary. Ironically, in *Brandenburg v. Ohio* (1969), the Court began requiring that advocacy be likely to incite lawlessness before it could be banned, and thus the Ku Klux Klan was not to be prosecuted under a more restrictive Ohio statute, while in *Haig v. Agee* (1981) the Court allowed the executive branch to renew and revoke passports selectively on political grounds. Thus socialist scholars like Regis De Bray and Ernest Mandel could be prevented from accepting lecturing invitations at American universities and ex-patriot Margaret Randell could be deported for her left-wing political advocacy.[90]

Historically, such constitutional waiverings have left the door open for considerable government harassment of radical groups. The federal government, for instance, has used the Internal Revenue Service to harass such groups.[91] It also has prosecuted under vague laws against conspiring to harm the United States, as when it jailed Eugene Debs and other socialist leaders during World War 1.[92] States used "criminal syndicalist" laws to repress the emergence of radical labor unions like the International Workers of the World (IWW), one of the few early union efforts that was both racially integrated and dedicated to socialism. Localities have often used "disorderly conduct" ordinances to arrest radical demonstrators. Tolerated were even more blatant and systematic repressions like the Red Raids of 1919 and the McCarthy hearings of the early 1950s, the latter leading to the practice of *blacklisting* radicals so that they could not work. Yet in 1978, when then United States ambassador to the United Nations Andrew Young spoke of "political prisoners" in the United States, he was resoundingly chastised by many elected officials and much of the mass media. Nevertheless, it is difficult to ignore the political trials of groups like the Chicago 8, the Panther 21, and the Wilmington 10 or those of individual dissidents like Dr. Benjamin Spock or Phillip and Daniel Berrigan. And, before ever getting to trial, there have been a number of contrived and often deadly police raids of radical groups, both black and white.[93]

Black Radicals.   The judicial process has been particularly harsh on blacks who were deemed to be delivering "dangerous" messages. Most were dealt with at levels well below the United States Supreme Court. They simply seemed to fall out of the protective reach of the United States Constitution.

Jamaican-born black nationalist Marcus Garvey, for example, was able to attract thousands of largely low-income blacks to his Universal Negro Improvement Association, an organization that, among other things, urged blacks to form and patronize separate, communally-owned black businesses. His success prompted federal authorities like William Burns and J. Edgar Hoover anxiously to discuss the need to deport such a "notorious Negro agitator." As Garvey began to build up a series of black businesses, often by soliciting investors through the mail, soon he and three other officers of one such firm were indicted for mail fraud. Although the sole witness could not even remember what the advertisement had said, Garvey alone was convicted and given the maximum sentence, which included five years in prison. Two years later, under political pressure, President Coolidge commuted his sentence but also ordered his deportation.

Actor Paul Robeson, an outspoken socialist, never even participated in a political protest march, let alone became involved in disruption or violence. Nevertheless, in 1949 he stated, "It is unthinkable that American Negroes will go to war on behalf of those who have oppressed us for generations against a country [the Soviet Union] which in one generation has raised our people to the full dignity of mankind."[94] Thereafter, he was effectively blacklisted, and his income fell from $100,000 in 1947 to $6,000 in 1952. Although never convicted of any crime, he would have to leave the United States in order to make a living.[95]

Radical minister Ben Chavis was arrested on numerous occasions in the course of political protests, only to be acquitted each time his cases ultimately got to trial. He was finally successfully jailed as one of the Wilmington 10. They were convicted of arson, although all three witnesses against them later recanted their testimony.[96]

Black activist Martin Sostre, an outspoken critic of heroin use in the ghetto, was arrested in New York and convicted of selling $15 worth of heroin to an informer. He was then sent to prison in 1967 even after the only witness against him, an informer, recanted his testimony. Sostre was finally granted amnesty in December 1975—after the political scene had quieted considerably.[97]

Socialist Frank Shuford, whom the prosecutor would label a "revolutionary troublemaker," was arrested for shooting two store clerks in Santa Ana, California. Although at home with family and friends at the time, he was convicted by an all-white jury and sentenced to 30 years in prison even though there was no physical evidence and neither clerk could identify him.[98]

In early 1970, scholar Angela Davis, an avowed communist, began to assist in the defense of the Soledad Brothers, three black prisoners accused of killing a prison guard. She also continued to speak out against both racism and capitalism. Soon she was fired from her teaching position at UCLA and shortly thereafter was sought for "conspiracy" in connection with a bungled prisoner escape plot. Even though she had no previous arrest record, she became only the third woman ever to be placed on the FBI's "Ten Most Wanted" list, which described her as "armed and dangerous," a classification that placed her life in jeopardy. Arrested in October 1970, she was held for days in solitary confinement while outside, the president of the United States publicly called her a "terrorist." Ultimately extradited to California for trial, the evidence was so thin that she was subsequently acquitted by an all-white jury.

Black Panther leader Huey Newton was convicted of felony assault with a knife in 1964 and manslaughter in 1968. Thus he was in jail during a key period from October 1967 through August 1970. Ultimately he got new trials, and all charges were dismissed. Nevertheless, in 1978 he was convicted of being in illegal possession of a gun, and while out awaiting final judicial action, he was rearrested in 1985 for embezzling government funds from a children's education and nutrition program and again for being a felon in possession of a gun. Subsequently, he was imprisoned and began serving 15 months to 3 years for the 1978 conviction.

In April 1969, some 21 members of the Black Panther party were indicted for conspiracy to kill a police officer and for placing dynamite in a large department store and on subways. They spent two years in jail awaiting trial and then another 15 months in court before a jury unanimously acquitted them after only two and one-half hours of deliberation.

Black Panther Johnny Spain was even less fortunate. He spent 21 years in prison as a result of two separate murder convictions—one for a 1966 killing and the other related to an aborted prison escape. In March 1988, his convictions were finally reversed, and he was released at the age of 38.

So when Andrew Young spoke out in 1978, there were indeed numerous black persons in prison at least in part as a result of their radical political activities, including 24 Black Panthers, 25 members of the Black Liberation Army, and 12 members of the Republic of New Africa organization.[99] The 1981 annual report of Amnesty International, for example, accused the FBI of fabricating evidence in order to convict members of the Black Panthers.[100]

Nevertheless, those are cases that at least got to a court of law, however unequal the justice applied. A number of outspoken black activists, many of them not even radicals, were less fortunate yet. They were dealt with directly by such agents as mobs, local police, or the FBI.

For decades following Reconstruction, black "troublemakers" were lynched, while state and local law enforcement agents stood idly by or occasionally even assisted. Meanwhile, the federal government deferred to "states' rights" and refused to intervene, as they had in the days of slavery. Such respect for federalism cost many blacks their lives, despite Fourteenth Amendment guarantees of due process and equal protection under the laws, not to mention Eighth Amendment prohibitions against cruel and unusual punishment.

A more recent example of this phenomenon occurred during the period of civil rights activism between 1957 and 1968. For the nearly 100 civil rights activists murdered during that period, there were few arrests and virtually no murder convictions.

The case of George Jackson is instructive. Serving an indeterminate sentence for a $70 robbery committed in his youth, after 10 years in prison he gradually became radicalized. He proceeded to write books and organize fellow inmates until he was shot to death in an alleged escape attempt in August 1971. An FBI agent later testified about a plot to kill Jackson by contriving what would look like an escape attempt.[101]

Local police often were not nearly as circuitous in their approach. For example, unarmed black students were gunned down during protests in Orangeburg, South Carolina, and Jackson, Mississippi, and more than 40 Black Panthers were shot and killed by police between 1968 and 1971. One of the most blatant incidents occurred in Chicago in December 1969. In a predawn raid, police claimed they met with armed resistance. In fact, Black Panther leaders Fred Hampton and Mark Clark were found shot to death in their beds, and later congressional investigations would implicate the FBI in a plot to assassinate them.[102]

FBI harassment of black activists is now well documented.[103] Its "Counterintelligence Program" (COINTELPRO), for example, was designed in Director J. Edgar Hoover's own words, "to expose, disrupt, misdirect, discredit, or otherwise neutralize" radical black groups.[104] Between 1956 and 1971, it carried out 295 actions against black groups and individuals. These included extraordinary efforts to undermine Rev. Martin Luther King, Jr., a political activist working for racial integration and black people's right to register and vote. Hoover publicly called King "the most notorious liar in the country," and internal FBI memos talked about the need "to destroy Doctor Martin Luther King." Just prior to his receiving the Nobel Peace Prize, for example, the FBI sent King and his wife separate packages. Coretta Scott King received cassette tape recordings of alleged sexual trysts involving her husband, while Martin received a letter that implicitly invited suicide:

> King, there is only one thing left for you to do. You know what it is. You have just 34 days in which to do it. The exact number has been selected for a specific reason. It has definite practical significance. You are done.[105]

Undaunted by such efforts, King continued his civil rights activities until assassinated in 1968. As chairperson of the U.S. House committee that investigated that assassination, Congressman Louis Stokes concluded that he was murdered because "he had begun to wake up poor people in this country, not only poor black people but also poor white people."[106]

OPTIONS FOR BLACK AMERICA

What are the overall potentials and limitations of the judicial arena in the search for racial justice in America? On the positive side, this arena is more insulated from majority rule and is thus a logical place for minorities seeking to force the majority to behave. Rights can be sought without the same need to compromise found in more political arenas, and it takes fewer people, connections, and political resources to enter the game. On the other hand, it does require a very important political resource—money—and it can be quite costly in terms of both legal fees and lost wages. It is a very slow process, with victories often coming years after the initial discriminatory behavior. Such victories can be stalled or reversed in implementation or by subsequent court decisions. It does not require the kind of mass mobilization and organization that can generate the political pressure necessary to sustain the victories. It is in many ways actually depoliticizing, for it is largely an elite-level activity that promotes passive spectatorship rather than activism at the grass-roots level. Finally, it is not nearly as neutral a process as it looks on paper, especially the more the demands challenge the distribution of wealth in the society.[107]

What, then, can be done in terms of reforming the judicial arena to allow it more effectively to protect the most basic rights of African Americans?

The U.S. Constitution

Positive Rights.   Within enforceable standards of individual responsibility, more positive rights must be written into the United States Constitution. These rights might include housing, health care, a quality education, a job at a livable wage, and an adequate guaranteed annual income for people unable to work.[108] Hardly an unprecedented notion, such propositions were included in Franklin Roosevelt's "Economic Bill of Rights," as well as the United Nations "Universal Declaration of Human Rights."[109] Of what value is the right to vote, for instance, if you are so destitute you will sell your vote, or so ignorant you do not understand your alternatives?

Political Reform.   In conjunction with that, the nation's political structures must be altered to make them more responsive and responsible. Only then will it be realistic to expect passage and effective implementation of the legislation "necessary and proper" to carry the positive rights into being. In particular, as will be considered at length in the next two chapters, it is time to discuss reductions in a number of the checks and balances built into the political system—especially in light of the major reason the Founding Fathers put them there in the first place.

Applying the Law

More Black Judges.   As for interpretation and adjudication, there is clearly a need for more black judges. Despite a few exceptions, there is mounting evidence that a judge's behavior on the bench will reflect his or her social and economic background.[110] Judge Bruce Wright put it this way:

> Black judges who have themselves escaped the gravitational pull of the ghetto, but who still bear the marks of their narrow escape, know the rough tensions of a two-culture existence. There is, therefore, a special insight of compassion which only a black judge can bring to the law.[111]

As the system's gatekeepers, it is critical that judges possess the necessary perspective, sensitivity, and openness to various legal issues and approaches.

Depoliticizing Judicial Appointments.   A new method of selecting judges should be considered in order to remove legal interpretation as far as possible from political influence. Judges at all levels could be appointed instead of elected. Such appointments could be done by random selection from a large list of candidates approved by their peers. The list could be weighted to ensure that blacks, women, and other previously excluded groups would have far more equal demographic representation on the bench. Such a process would help minimize the introduction of politics and racism into the judicial arena, while helping to maximize the rule of law.[112]

More Equitable Law Enforcement.   Finally, at the implementation stage, more black officers are needed at all ranks in federal, state, and local law enforcement agencies. In addition, some of these agencies could be placed in the judicial, rather than the executive, branch so as to limit politics in implementation as well. And as a constructive check, neighborhoods should be given a significant role in choosing, overseeing, and disciplining the police who regularly patrol them.[113]

NOTES

1. Charles Beard, quoted in Howard Zinn, *A People's History of the United States* (New York: Harper & Row, 1980), p. 89.
2. Declaration of Independence.
3. Jefferson, arguably the most progressive of the Founding Fathers, held any number of racially suspect opinions. Such views are recorded in his only book, *Notes on the State of*

Virginia. For excerpts, see David Shipler, "Jefferson Is America — And America is Jefferson," *New York Times,* April 12, 1993.

4. For example, see Jennifer Nedelsky, *Private Property and the Limits of American Constitutionalism: The Madisonian Framework and its Legacy* (Chicago: University of Chicago, 1990).

5. Quoted in Max Farrand (ed.), *The Records of the Federal Convention of 1787,* vol. 1 (New Haven, Conn.: Yale University Press, 1937), p. 536.

6. John Adams, *Works,* vol. 6 (New York: AMS Press, 1971), p. 9.

7. Alexander Hamilton quoted in Farrand, *Records of the Federal Convention,* pp. 424, 432; and in Mary Jo Kline (ed.), *Alexander Hamilton* (New York: Harper & Row, 1973), p. 45.

8. James Madison quoted in Farrand, *Records of the Federal Convention,* pp. 421, 422, 423; and in Marvin Meyers (ed.), *The Mind of the Founder* (Indianapolis: Bobbs-Merrill, 1973), pp. 504–505.

9. John Locke, "Second Treatise on Civil Government," in Maurice Cranston (ed.), *Locke on Politics, Religion, and Education* (New York: Collier, 1965).

10. Charles Beard, *An Economic Interpretation of the Constitution,* (New York: Macmillan, 1962).

11. Samuel Morrison, *The Oxford History of the American People* (New York: Oxford University Press, 1965), p. 274.

12. David Szatmary, *Shays's Rebellion: The Making of an Agrarian Insurrection* (Amherst: University of Massachusetts Press, 1980); Zinn, *A People's History,* chap. 3; Michael Parenti, *Democracy for the Few* (New York: St. Martin's, 1995), pp. 51–52.

13. Alexander Hamilton, quoted in Zinn, *People's History,* p. 95.

14. For example, see Donald Robinson, *Slavery and the Structure of American Politics* (New York: Harcourt Brace and Jovanovich, 1971).

15. *Ex parte Milligan* (1866).

16. Zinn, *People's History,* p. 97.

17. Quoted in Dexter Perkins, *Charles Evans Hughes* (Boston: Little, Brown, 1956), p. 16.

18. Clinton Rossiter (ed.), *The Federalist Papers* (New York: New American Library, 1961), pp. 83–84.

19. For further discussion of the pro-slavery aspects of the United States Constitution, see Donald Nieman, *Promises to Keep: African-Americans and the Constitutional Order, 1776 to the Present* (New York: Oxford, 1991), chap. 1.

20. See discussion in chapter 10 below.

21. Jackson Turner Main, *The Social Structure of Revolutionary America* (Princeton, N.J.: Princeton University Press, 1965).

22. Quoted in Ira Katznelson and Mark Kesselman, *The Politics of Power* (Orlando, Fla.: Harcourt Brace Jovanovich, 1987), p. 190.

23. For example, see Howard Zinn, *Declarations of Independence: Cross-Examining American Ideology* (New York: Harper Collins, 1990), chap. 9; Mervyn Dymally, ed., *The Black Politician: His Struggle for Power* (Belmont, Cal.: Wadsworth, 1971); Derrick Bell, "The Elusive Quest for Racial Justice: The Chronicle of the Constitutional Contradiction," in Paulette Robinson and Billy Tidwell, eds., *The State of Black America, 1995* (New York: National Urban League, 1995), pp. 225–239; Opoku Agyeman, "The United States Supreme Court and the Enforcement of African-American Rights: Myth and Reality," *PS: Political Science and Politics* (December 1991), pp. 679–684; Leslie Carr, *Color-Blind Racism* (Beverly Hills, Calif: Sage, 1997).

24. See Frances Fox Piven and Richard Cloward, *Regulating the Poor* (New York: Vintage, 1971), pp. 299–300.

25. For example, see Kevin McGuire, *The Supreme Court Bar: Legal Elites in the Washington Community* (Charlottesville: University of Virginia, 1993).

26. Steven Holmes, "Workers Find It Tough Going Filing Lawsuits Over Job Bias," *New York Times*, July 24, 1991; Julius Chambers, "The Law and Black Americans: Retreat from Civil Rights," in National Urban League, *The State of Black America, 1987* (New York: National Urban League, 1987), pp. 26–27.

27. *San Antonio Independent School District v. Rodriquez* 411 US 1 (1973).

28. *Kadrmas v. Dickinson* 487 US 450 (1988).

29. *Dandridge v. Williams* 397 US 471 (1970).

30. *Harris v. McRae* 448 US 297 (1980).

31. The one narrow exception is state provision of counsel for indigent clients accused of a crime, discussed at greater length below.

32. Quoted in Zinn, *Declarations of Independence*, pp. 231–232.

33. Ibid., p. 231.

34. See W. E. B. Du Bois, *Black Reconstruction* (New York: Russell, 1935).

35. For example, see Jack Greenburg, *Crusaders in the Courts: How A Dedicated Band of Lawyers Fought For The Civil Rights Revolution* (New York: Basic Books, 1994).

36. See Meyer Weinberg, *A Chance to Learn: A History of Race and Education in the United States* (New York: Cambridge University Press, 1977), chaps. 1–3, 7.

37. For example, see *New York Times*, December 14, 1993; May 18, 1994.

38. Also see *Academe* (May-June 1994), pp. 7–17; Rochelle Stanfield, "Reform by the Book," *National Journal*, December 4, 1993, pp. 2885–2887.

39. For example, see Abraham Davis and Barbara Graham, *The Supreme Court, Race, and Civil Rights* (Thousand Oaks, Cal.: Sage, 1995), pp. 355–359; Robert Carter, "Thirty-Five Years Later: New Perspectives on *Brown*," in Herbert Hill and James Jones, eds., *Race In America: The Struggle for Equality* (Madison: University of Wisconsin, 1993), chap. 4; Michael Combs, "The Supreme Court, African Americans, and Public Policy: Changes and Transformations," in Huey Perry and Wayne Parent, eds., *Blacks and the American Political System* (Gainesville: University of Florida, 1995), chap. 8; Julius Chambers, "Black Americans and the Courts: Has the Clock Been Turned Back Permanently?," in Robinson and Tidwell, *The State of Black America, 1995*, pp. 241–255.

40. Full preclearance has been required in Alabama, Alaska, Arizona, Georgia, Louisiana, Mississippi, South Carolina, Texas, and Virginia. Partial preclearance also has been required in California, Florida, Michigan, New Hampshire, New York, North Carolina, and South Dakota.

41. For example, see Sonia Jarvis, "Historical Overview: African Americans and the Evolution of Voting Rights," in Linda Faye Williams (ed.), *From Exclusion to Inclusion* (Westport, Conn.: Greenwood, 1992), pp. 17–33.

42. Such decisions included *Shaw v. Reno* (1993), *Council V. Sundquist* (1995), *Miller v. Johnson* (1995), *Bush v. Vera* (1996), *Shaw v. Hunt* (1996), and *Reno v. Bossier Parish* (1997). For an interesting symposium on this entire matter, see "The Voting Rights Act After Shaw v. Reno," *PS: Political Science and Politics* (March 1995), pp. 24–56. Also see Charles Cameron, David Epstein, and Sharyn O'Halloran, "Do Majority-Minority Districts Maximize Substantive Black Representation in Congress?" *American Political Science Review* 90 (December 1996), pp. 794–812.

43. For example, see Charles V. Hamilton, *The Bench and the Ballot: Southern Federal Judges and Black Votes* (New York: Oxford University Press, 1973), chap. 8.

44. Although upholding the act in principle, the U.S. Supreme Court declared key provisions not to be applicable retroactively. For example, see *Landgraf v. USI Film Productions* (1994) and *Rivers v. Roadway Express* (1994).

45. For example, see Michael deCourcy Hinds, "Minority Business Set Back Sharply By Courts' Rulings," *New York Times*, December 23, 1991.

46. See *Spallone v. U.S.* (1990).

47. For example, see Jeffrey Abramson, "Making the Law Colorblind," *New York Times*, October 16, 1995.

48. David Baldus et al.,"Comparative Review of Death Sentences: An Empirical Study of the Georgia Experience," *Journal of Criminal Law and Criminology* (June 1983).

49. Lewis M. Steele, "Nine Men in Black Who Think White," *New York Times*, October 13, 1968.

50. Robert Herbert, "Madness, Not Justice," *New York Times*, October 6, 1995.

51. Of the first 132 nominees, 103 were confirmed by the U.S. Senate—roughly 78%.

52. Steele, "Nine Men." Also see Herman Schwartz, *Packing the Courts: The Conservative Campaign to Rewrite the Constitution* (New York: Scribner, 1988); Thomas Dye and Harmon Ziegler, *The Irony of Democracy* (Belmont, Cal.: Wadsworth, 1993), pp. 334–335; Gerry Spence, *With Justice For None: Destroying An American Myth* (New York: Penguin Books, 1989), p. 93.
    In 1997, for example, six of the nine U.S. Supreme Court justices appeared to have assets that exceeded one million dollars. See *New York Times*, May 22, 1997.

53. As of 1994, 42 of 837 federal judges were black—roughly 5 percent. Meanwhile, African Americans comprised only 3% of all the nation's judges. See Linn Washington, *Black Judges on Justice: Perspectives from the Bench* (New York: New Press, 1994), p. xi; *New York Times*, July 12, 1989; A. Leon Higginbotham, "The Case of the Missing Black Judges," *New York Times*, July 29, 1992; Sheldon Goldman, "The Bush Imprint on the Judiciary: Carrying on a Tradition," *Judicature* 44 (April-May 1991); David Savage and Ronald Ostrow, "More Women, Minorities Named Judges by Clinton," Memphis *Commercial Appeal*, January 18, 1994.

54. Joel Grossman, *Lawyers and Judges: The ABA and the Politics of Judicial Selection* (New York: Wiley, 1965); Joseph C. Howard, "Why We Organize," *Journal of Public Law*, vol. 20 (1971), pp. 381–382.

55. For example, see Helen Edwards, *Black Faces in High Places* (Orlando, Fla.: Harcourt Brace Jovanovich 1971).

56. *New York Times*, June 28,1988.

57. Linn Washington estimates that of the nation's 30,000 judges at all levels, roughly 1,000 were black in the early 1990s. See Washington, *Black Judges on Justice*, p xi.

58. Kenneth Vines, "Federal District Judges and Race Relations Cases in the South,"*Journal of Politics* (May 1964), pp. 337–357; Washington, *Black Judges on Justice*.

59. Bob Smith, *They Closed Our Schools*, (Chapel Hill: University of North Carolina Press, 1965).

60. Willis Hawley, *Strategy for Effective Desegregation: A Synthesis of Findings* (Nashville, Tenn.: Center for Education and Human Development Policy, 1987); Charles V. Willie, "The Future of School Desegregation," in *National Urban League, State of Black America, 1987*.

61. For a brief description of the defunding of the Civil Rights Commission over the course of the Reagan and Bush years, see "Agency in Decline," *New York Times*, October 13, 1991.

62. *New York Times*, November 20, 1981.

63. *Washington Post*, August 30,1986, p. A1.

64. See Chambers, "Law and Black Americans," for this and other examples of enforcement laxity and policy reversals during the Reagan presidency.

65. Katznelson and Kesselman, *Politics of Power*, p. 207. Also see Robert Bohm, "Crime, Criminal and Crime Control Policy Myths," *Justice Quarterly* 3 (1986), p. 201.

66. For example, see Holly Sklar, *Chaos or Community?* (Boston: South end, 1995), chap. 7. Also see Evan Stark, "The Myth of Black Violence," *New York Times*, July 18, 1990; U.S.

Department of Justice, Bureau of Justice Statistics, *Correctional Populations in the United States, 1993*, NCJ–156241 (Washington, D.C.: GPO, 1995).

67. Robert Smith, *Racism In The Post-Civil Rights Era: Now You See It, Now You Don't* (Albany: State University of New York, 1995), pp. 46–47; Christopher E. Smith, *Courts and the Poor* (Chicago: Nelson-Hall, 1991), pp. 19–23; John Harrigan, *Empty Dreams, Empty Pockets* (New York: Macmillan, 1993), p. 270; Michael Parenti, *Democracy for the Few* (New York: St. Martin's, 1995), chap. 9; Samuel Yette, *The Choice: The Issue of Black Survival In America* (Silver Spring, Md.: Cottage Books, 1971), chap. 6; *New York Times*, March 2, 1975; April 15, 1979; March 21, 1991; August 5, 1993; *Nation*, July 29/August 5, 1991; August 24, 1993; *Newsweek*, July 4, 1977; Joan Walsh, "Police Brutality Divides Milwaukee," *In These Times* (September 9, 1981), p. 6; Howard Smead, *Blood Justice* (New York: Oxford University, 1986); Douglas A. Smith and Christy Visher, "Street-Level Justice: Situational Determinants of Police Arrest Decisions," *Social Problems* 29 (1981); Theodore Becker and Vernon Murray, *Government Lawlessness in America* (New York: Oxford University Press, 1971).

68. *New York Times*, December 23, 1986.

69. For details, see Davis and Graham, *The Supreme Court, Race, and Civil Rights*, pp. 397–403.

70. For very abbreviated lists of other recorded examples of such police brutality, not to mention all of the incidences never recorded, see Alphonso Pinkney, *The Myth of Black Progress* (New York: Cambridge University, 1984), pp. 76–78; Michael Parenti, *Democracy for the Few* (New York: St. Martin's, 1995), pp. 134–135; Davis and Graham, *The Supreme Court, Race, and Civil Rights*, pp. 403–406.

71. *New York Times*, October 18, 1996.

72. See Bob Herbert, "A Brutal Epidemic," *New York Times*, April 28, 1997.

73. Ibid.

74. See Kevin Sack, "Police Chief Says Officers at Fault in Beating," *New York Times*, May 13, 1997.

75. However, it also should be noted that this trend seems to have reached a plateau. See *New York Times*, April 8, 1996. They are still nowhere near proportionate to the black proportion of large city populations. See Andrew Hacker, *Two Nations: Black and White, Separate, Hostile, Unequal* (New York: Scribner's, 1992), p. 236. And, these black officers continue to lag behind their white counterparts in assignments, promotions, and respect. For example, see *Wall Street Journal*, September 7, 1995, p. A1.

76. Smith, *Courts and the Poor*, pp. 23–26; Stuart Nagel, "Disparities in Criminal Procedure," *UCLA Law Review* (August 1967), pp. 1272–1305; Herbert Jacob, *Urban Justice* (Englewood Cliffs, N.J.: Prentice-Hall, 1973), p. 103.

77. For example, see Harrigan, *Empty Dreams, Empty Pockets*, p. 271; Smith, *Courts and the Poor*, pp. 24–25.

78. For a description of this process, see Smith, *Courts and the Poor*, pp. 31–33.

79. *New York Times*, February 28, 1986. Also see "Criminal Defense for the Poor, 1986,: *Bureau of Justice Statistics Bulletin* (Washington, D.C.: GPO. 1986), p. 6; Smith, *Courts and the Poor*, pp. 29–33.
    Average expenditures ranged from $63 in Arkansas to $540 in New Jersey.

80. Smith, *Courts and the Poor*, p. 30. Smith notes that assigned counsel are paid as little as $25 per hour, with absolute case maximums of $1,500; contrasted to private firms who routinely charge anywhere from $10,000 to more than $100,000 for comparable legal services.

81. *New York Times*, February 28, 1986. For more examples, see Anthony Lewis's columns in *New York Times*, August 16, 1991; January 4, 1993.

82. Michael Parenti, *Democracy for the Few* (New York: St. Martin's, 1995), p. 125; Valerie Hans and Neil Vidmar, *Judging the Jury* (New York Plenum Press, 1986); Herbert Jacob, *Justice in America* (Boston: Little, Brown, 1972), p. 104.

83. Leonard Downie, Jr., *Justice Denied* (New York: Praeger, 1971).

84. Jeffrey Reiman, *The Rich Get Richer and the Poor Get Prison* (New York: Macmillan, 1990); Michael Parenti, *Democracy for the Few* (New York: St. Martin's, 1995), chap. 8; Smith, *Courts and the Poor*, pp. 35–36; Nagel, "Disparities in Criminal Procedure."

85. For example, see U.S. Sentencing Commission, *Special Report to the Congress: Mandatory Minimal Penalties in the Federal Criminal Justice System* (Washington, D.C.: GPO, 1991); Holly Sklar, "Young and Guilty by Stereotype," *Z Magazine*, July/August 1993, pp. 52–61; Memphis *Commercial Appeal*, September 25, 1995; *Dallas Times Herald,* August 19, 1990; *Denver Post*, May 1,1977.

86. Calvin Larson, *Crime, Justice, and Society* (Dix Hills, N.Y.: General Hall, 1984), p. 225.

87. Michael Parenti, *Democracy for the Few* (New York: St. Martin's Press, 1983), pp. 175–181; Michael Parenti, *Democracy for the Few* (New York: St. Martin's Press, 1995), pp. 127–128, 146.

88. For example, criminal defendants who could pay the filing fee were twice as likely to have their appeals heard by the U.S. Supreme Court. See Janis Judson, *The Hidden Agenda* (University of Maryland Ph.D. thesis, 1986).

89. For example, nearly two-thirds of African Americans and only one-quarter of whites perceive the U.S. criminal justice system as "biased against blacks." See CBS News polls cited in *National Journal*, June 24, 1995. Also see ABC News-*Washington Post* poll (May 1992); *Time*-CNN poll (May 1992); various polls cited in Janet Elder, "Racial Divide on Simpson," *New York Times*, October 2, 1995.

90. *New York Times*, June 4, 1982; November 16, 1986. And after Congress attempted to prohibit the use of ideological criteria in the granting of such visas, the State Department continued to maintain what were called "lookout lists" that accomplished much the same thing. See Michael Parenti, *Democracy for the Few* (New York: St. Martin's, 1995), p. 141.

91. For example, see ibid., p. 140.

92. Ibid., p. 141.

93. For example, see ibid., chap. 9; Yette, *The Choice*, chap. 6.

94. Quoted in Edward Greenberg, *The American Political System* (Boston: Little, Brown, 1983), p. 75.

95. Ibid., pp. 73–75. See Martin Doberman, *Paul Robeson* (New York: Knopf, 1989).

96. For example, see Michael Parenti, *Democracy for the Few* (New York: St. Martin's, 1995), p. 144.

97. Ibid., p. 144; *New York Times*, December 25, 1975; Zinn, *People's History*, p. 508.

98. Michael Parenti, *Democracy for the Few* (New York: St. Martin's, 1995), p. 145.

99. Michael Parenti, *Democracy for the Few* (New York: St. Martin's, 1983), p. 164. And for an updated list, see Michael Parenti, *Democracy for the Few* (New York: St. Martin's, 1983), pp. 167–148.

100. *New York Times*, September 11, 1981.

101. Eric Mann, *Comrade George* (New York: Harper & Row, 1974); Zinn, *People's History*, pp. 509–510; *Guardian*, April 21, 1976.

102. *Chicago Tribune*, April 20, 1976; June 12, 1976; Zinn, *People's History*, pp. 455, 542–543.

103. For example, see Michael Parenti, *Democracy for the Few* (New York: St. Martin's, 1995), pp. 150–151.

104. *Village Voice*, September 9, 1981, p. 25.

105. Zinn, *People's History*, p. 453. Letter quoted from David Wise, "The Campaign to Destroy Martin Luther King," *New York Review of Books*, November 11, 1976, pp. 40–41.

106. Emily Rovetch (ed.), *Like It Is* (New York: Dutton, 1981), p. 42.

107. See Gerald Rosenberg, *The Hollow Hope: Can Courts Bring About Social Change?* (Chicago: University of Chicago, 1991); Derrick Bell, *And We Are Still Not Saved: The Elusive Quest for Racial Reform* (New York: Basic Books, 1987); Harold Cruse, *Plural but Equal: Blacks and Minorities in America's Plural Society* (New York: Morrow, 1987).

108. In 1996, for instance, a group of progressive labor leaders called for a constitutional amendment that would guarantee a livable minimum wage and a 32-hour work week. See *National Journal*, June 15, 1996, p. 1295. For more detailed proposals, see Julius Chambers, *"Brown v. Board of Education,"* in Hill and Jones, *Race In America*, chap. 8; Charles V. Hamilton, "Social Policy and the Welfare of Black Americans: From Rights to Resources," *Political Science Quarterly* (Summer 1986), pp. 239–255. Also see Leslie Dunbar, "Government For All the People," in Leslie Dunbar, ed., *Minority Report* (New York: Pantheon, 1984), pp. 191–221.

109. For examples drawn from the texts of these documents, see Sklar, *Chaos or Community?*, p. 170.

110. Randall Black, *Private Pressure on Public Law: The Legal Career of Justice Thurgood Marshall* (New York: Kennikat, 1973); Michael D. Smith, "Social Background and Role Perception of Black Judges," paper presented at the annual meeting of the American Political Science Association, New Orleans, September 4–8, 1973; Gilbert Ware (ed.), *From The Black Bar: Voices for Equal Justice* (New York: Putnam, 1976); Bruce Fein, *Significant Decisions of the Supreme Court, 1978–1979 Term* (Washington, D.C.: American Enterprise Institute, 1980), pp. 22–23; George W. Crockett, Jr., "The Role of the Black Judge," *Journal of Public Law* 20 (1971), pp. 398–399.

111. Quoted in Lucius Barker and Jesse McCorry, *Black Americans and the Political System* (Cambridge, Mass.: Winthrop, 1976), p. 158.

112. For a similar proposal, see Spence, *With Justice for None*, chap. 13.

113. For example, see Neal Peirce, "Community Policing That Works," *National Journal*, October 12, 1996, p. 2190.

Chapter 7

The Electoral Arena

The vote has become a fetish with many Negroes, but there is little evidence that social problems anywhere in the world are solved by fetishism.

Ralph Bunche, 1944[1]

For nearly a century after the abrupt end of Reconstruction, the majority of African Americans were effectively denied their constitutionally guaranteed right to vote. With the assistance of civil rights and voting rights acts in the 1960s and 1970s, however, blacks finally were able to register and vote much more freely. The results were dramatic. For example, whereas there were fewer than 500 black elected officials in the entire country in 1965, that number grew to more than 8,000 in the subsequent 30 years. Nevertheless, the impact on public policy and subsequently on the life conditions of many of these newly enfranchised citizens has not been comparably dramatic. To begin making some sense of that, serious questions must be raised about America's democratic system. This chapter will examine the nature and functions of the electoral process; the next one will consider the response of legislative and executive officials.

ELECTIONS AND DEMOCRACY IN AMERICA

Just what are the prerequisites of self-government? If there was only one person around, the question would be purely academic. The sole citizen would relate to his or her environment by making all the decisions that governed that person's own actions within it. But once that individual joins a *community*, a procedure is needed for determining the community's interests in matters of social concern. Now, if these

160

communal decisions remain in the hands of "the people" rather than in the hands of one person or an exclusive few, this arrangement can be loosely labeled a democracy. And a common way for a democracy to reach decisions is by majority rule. In a small town, a town meeting might be called every Friday night, where the residents could come together for the purpose of making these decisions by majority preference. But if the population is large and the issues many and complex, some division of labor becomes necessary. Thus a representative democracy is born, whereby politicians are elected to make the decisions, and they must be chosen and reviewed in a manner that will enable them to know and represent the interests of the people (or at least a majority of the people) in matters of public policy.

Political theorist Joseph Schumpeter addressed the prerequisites of a representative democracy, concluding that the essential element is citizen opportunity to vote for either the politicians in office or a set of competing politicians wishing to get into office. Thus the role of the voter becomes somewhat analogous to that of the consumer in the market economy, choosing freely from among a limited number of competing candidates.[2]

Elections thus allow the general public to set the broad outlines of governmental policy by virtue of whom they elect or reject. To facilitate that, political parties arise to help clarify electoral choices, as well as to allow the subsequent government to organize itself in a more efficient manner. In the United States, however, both the election process and political party process are inherently biased against fundamental redistributive change.

From the founding of the country, the electoral process was not designed to empower the masses; suffrage was limited largely to propertied white males,[3] and the United States Senate was to be elected by state legislators. Those restrictions have since been modified, but a number of others continue to institutionalize race and class inequities. For example, registration and campaign finance procedures are prejudiced against working- and lower-class people, and a two-party system guarantees that the major parties are virtually incapable of educating and leading the public in any direction that would fundamentally challenge the socioeconomic status quo.

For African Americans, these realities are becoming increasingly obvious. Wherever blacks have been enfranchised, they have nearly always followed prescribed electoral strategy. They have often been geographically concentrated in areas of strategic importance to the two major parties. They turn out to vote at nearly the same rate as whites. And they have voted as a relatively cohesive bloc for the dominant party in nearly every election since the Emancipation Proclamation. Unfortunately, for reasons such as those alluded to already, the electoral system is severely limited in its capacity to allow serious challenge to the worst of the legacies of slavery.

That is not to say that success in the long battle to gain suffrage has been a hollow victory. Electoral mobilization has led to control over some institutional levers of political power, enabling a number of blacks to improve their life situations. It has also provided an organizational structure for sustaining the vigilance and pressure needed to perpetuate those gains. In addition, the right to vote—regardless of the political-economic system—is a necessary condition for advancing the causes of equality and self-determination. In the American context, however, the electoral process alone would not appear to be a sufficient mechanism for achieving those results. Acquiring and exercising the right to vote may well be more than "fetishism," but it presently leaves African Americans a far cry from self-determination in a racially just America.

THE BLACK ELECTORAL EXPERIENCE

> Once dubbed "the greatest Democratic ward in the country" by President Franklin Delano Roosevelt, [Chicago's] 24th ward . . . has always been good about delivering the vote. It was the first West Side ward to elect a black alderman, a black committeeman and a black state representative. For Mayor Harold Washington, the ward delivered a resounding 99.5 percent of its vote. . . . Walter Mondale won 98 percent.
>
> Yet for a community that has had such an impact at the polls, it shows few signs of benefiting in return.[4]

In the 1960s, nearly three and one-half centuries after blacks first arrived on the American continent, large legal impediments to their self-governance remained. Nevertheless, the majority of southern blacks were finally able to register and vote for the first time since Reconstruction, and the number of black elected officials increased dramatically. Still, pockets of resistance remain to this day, and electoral gains have been tempered by, among other things, the limits of the electoral process itself.

The Battle for Suffrage

Enslaved blacks had no political rights whatsoever. The *Dred Scott* decision made that point quite emphatically. In addition, Staughton Lynd and others emphasize that even so-called free blacks faced considerable racial discrimination, including discrimination in their efforts to cast a ballot.[5] The struggle for an unimpeded right to vote would be a long and arduous one, and many people would give their lives to the endeavor, both figuratively and literally.

The first major victories were marked by the Emancipation Proclamation and the Civil War amendments to the United States Constitution. Slavery was terminated, and the Constitution was amended to state that "the right of citizens of the United States to vote shall not be denied or abridged by the United States or any State on account of race, color, or previous condition of servitude." In addition, "No State shall make or enforce any law which shall abridge the privileges or immunities of citizens of the United States; nor shall any State deprive any person of life, liberty, or property without due process of law; nor deny to any person within its jurisdiction the equal protection of the laws."

For the overwhelming majority of African Americans, most of whom would reside in the South for at least another half century, these legal pronouncements had meaning as long as northern troops were around to enforce them. When the Republican party abandoned Reconstruction in order to gain the presidency in 1876, all of that changed rapidly. In terms of suffrage, legal impediments like poll taxes, literacy tests, and all-white primaries, as well as both physical and economic intimidation, quickly disenfranchised nearly all southern blacks.[6]

Even after many migrated North, discrimination remained the rule of the day. In urban political machines, for example, blacks were recruited but often confined to parallel party organizations. These organizational appendages would turn out the black vote for white Democratic candidates and in return would receive limited amounts of patronage and sometimes a few black seats in party and governmental decision-making bodies. The relationship of the black community to the Chicago political machine is one well-analyzed example, while the New York City machine and its parallel Union of Colored Democrats is an even more extreme case in point.[7]

At the state level, practices such as racial gerrymandering have been commonplace. In this arrangement, election district lines are drawn to distribute the black vote in such a way as either to maximize the electoral chances of white Democratic candidates or to dilute the impact of the black vote altogether. In terms of the latter, for example, the black community would be divided so that no voting district would have a black majority; and then to be doubly certain, a runoff provision might also be added to require a second election between the top two candidates if no one attained a majority in the first round of voting.[8]

Chapter 6 documents how over time the federal courts struck down a number of the discriminatory practices just mentioned. Between 1957 and 1970, the Congress added vigor to the enforcement of such constitutional rights by passage of a series of civil rights and voting rights acts. In particular, new voting laws and regulations in suspect election districts had to be precleared by the federal courts, registration records had to be kept much more systematically, and penalties were increased for the violation of voting rights. Federal judges could appoint referees to review the qualifications of rejected applicants, the Commission on Civil Rights was created to investigate abuses, and the attorney general of the United States was authorized to bring lawsuits where necessary. A second reconstruction was under way.[9]

Political Participation

Millions of previously disenfranchised black Southerners stepped forward to claim the right so long denied them. In the 11 southern states from Virginia to Texas, the surge was quite apparent. Whereas 1.5 million blacks voted in 1960, that figure jumped to 2.2 million by 1964, 3.1 million by 1968, 3.6 million by 1972, and 4 million by 1976. Mississippi saw its black turnout rate increase from 6 percent to 59 percent over this period, meaning that nearly three out of five eligible black voters were at last registered and voting. Alabama's increased from 14 percent to 55 percent. Arkansas witnessed an increase from 38 percent to 81 percent.

With the legal barriers all but eliminated, blacks' political participation soon approached that of their white counterparts. Although their overall voting rate has continued to lag at least 5 percentage points behind that of whites, blacks tend to be just as active in other forms of electoral participation, such as campaigning.[10] Nevertheless, participation rates of both groups are quite low by international standards, and participation has been declining steadily since 1960.

To begin with, both black and white Americans vote at lower rates than voters in virtually every other democracy in the world. Turnout rates in other Western democracies, for example, almost always exceed 75 percent, and in a number of countries they regularly exceed 90 percent. In this country, less than one-half of all eligible voters chose to vote in the most recent presidential election, with turnout much lower

yet in nonpresidential years. African-American voting, like white voting, has been declining rather steadily since the mid–1960s, despite the sizable addition of previously
disenfranchised southern blacks. Where black turnout was nearly 60 percent in the
presidential elections of 1964 and 1968, it is now less than 50 percent in presidential
years and lower than that otherwise.[11]

Why are a large number of African Americans choosing not to exercise their
franchise? Despite the limited data available on the black electorate,[12] political analysts have suggested a number of tentative explanations. Some of them are true for
whites as well, while others are unique to the black experience.

The most commonly heard explanation for black nonparticipation is that African
Americans fall disproportionately into lower socioeconomic groups that have traditionally participated less often. That obviously explains some of the variation between
black and white voting rates.[13]

It also has been pointed out that the growing number of African-American males
in prison, combined with the disenfranchisement of many convicted felons, has had a
significant impact on the black vote. Roughly one in seven black men are ineligible to
vote either because they are in prison or have a felony conviction. And combined
with the fact that one in three black males in their twenties is currently either in
prison, jail, on probation, or on parole, this phenomenon poses serious long-term
consequences for black electoral clout.[14]

In addition, physical intimidation did not cease with the passage of the civil
rights and voting rights acts, and the kind of economic dependence discussed in
Chapter 4 has continued to leave the black community particularly vulnerable to economic intimidation, such as threats of being fired or losing credit.[15] Studies of registration procedures in the South also found a number of registration offices to be located in intentionally remote places; only open during unusual hours; and
administered by hostile political appointees.[16]

Yet well before that, a major politicizing agent was disappearing at precisely the
wrong time. The urban political machine was being dismantled just as large numbers of blacks began to migrate into the nation's large cities, placing them in a position to assume their turn at the helm. In particular, a reform movement was stripping the machines of the kinds of patronage that had proved so useful in the process
of politically mobilizing earlier immigrant groups.[17] This had at least three significant
consequences.

First, many in the black community came instead to be galvanized around charismatic individuals like Marcus Garvey, Martin Luther King, Jr., and Malcolm X. The
problem there was that when the charismatic leaders were gone, it was much more
difficult to transfer their power to others and thereby hold the organizations together.

Second, there was more of a tendency to mobilize around large and highly
charged issues like police brutality and desegregation. Yet, as the machine had
quickly discovered, it is usually much easier to politicize large numbers of people and
sustain their political energies over the long term by using divisible and more tangible patronage benefits like jobs, food, and personal help. Not only that, but determining the correct policy for addressing communitywide issues can polarize the
group, while divisible benefits can be widely dispersed, providing a little something
for everybody and thus keeping the organization together.

Finally, local machine patronage was being displaced in part by national programs with national eligibility standards and a large national bureaucracy to administer them. No longer would recipients have to "deliver the vote" in order to qualify for governmental assistance. And even more depoliticizing would be the fact that the bureaucrats on whom many now relied were far removed from electoral control. There was simply less reason for low-income ghetto residents to register and vote. In addition, there was certainly less incentive to undertake the very tedious work of finding and funding candidates, registering voters, and getting out the votes on election day.[18]

Beyond the decline of the politicizing party machine is the comparably depoliticizing litigation orientation discussed in Chapter 6. Instead of requiring grass-roots political activism, heavy early reliance on the judicial arena promoted passive spectatorship among many potential activists in the black community.[19]

Before reaching conclusions from these problematic trends, however, it is also useful to note the tremendous variation in black turnout from one election to the next; witness the outpourings of support for black candidates like Mayor Harold Washington in Chicago (1983), Mayor W. W. Herenton in Memphis (1991), and Democratic presidential candidate Jesse Jackson (1984 and 1988). Walton and others ... ...out appears to be very responsive to specific race-relevant combinations of candidates and campaigns, as well as organizational efforts.[20]

The Voters' Choice

Once registered and voting, how have African Americans cast their ballots? Despite popular misconceptions to the contrary, blacks have not voted as a monolith. Nonetheless, they have voted more cohesively for a longer period of time than virtually any other racial or ethnic group in American history. Before tracing that electoral behavior, however, first consider some of the dominant voting strategies advocated over time.

Alternative Voting Strategies. As the 1984 presidential election approached, prominent black leaders such as Andrew Young, Richard Hatcher, and Mickey Leland formed groups like the 1984 Election Strategy Group and the Black Leadership Family.[21] There was considerable debate over whether the time was ripe for Jesse Jackson to seek the presidency and, even if he did, whether black leaders should support him or Democratic front-runner Walter Mondale. The debate reflected two important currents that had run through black electoral strategy for more than half a century. The following discussion will briefly touch on both of those (major party and black candidate strategies) and others.[22]

Major-Party Strategy. This approach accepts the premise that in a two-party system like the one in the United States, one of the two major parties will always hold the power. Thus the wisest approach is to try to maximize influence over those parties. That can be done in one of two ways.

Black elected officials such as Walter Fauntroy, Andrew Young, and others have long advocated working within the dominant political party most predisposed to black interests at any particular point in time. That has come to be the Democratic party over the course of the past half century.

Meanwhile, newspaper editor and author Chuck Stone called for "political oscillation" between the two major parties, essentially delivering the black vote to the highest bidder. As Vernon Jordan put it, "The black vote must be earned with iron-clad commitments to the programs and policies black people need."[23] With such a thought in mind, CORE's Floyd McKissick talked about creating an "apparatus, not a party . . . [to] develop an independent platform which it will attempt to sell to the Democrats and Republicans."[24]

Third-Party Strategy.   Another general approach advocates stepping away from the two relatively unresponsive major parties and supporting one of four basic types of minor parties: (1) multiracial protest parties that form to rally people around a particular cause, like the Liberty party in its opposition to slavery; (2) multiracial ideological parties that in each election run candidates dedicated to their world view, such as the Communist party of the United States; (3) black independent parties, like the Lowndes County Freedom Organization in Alabama; or (4) black parallel parties operating as black branches of one of the major parties, such as the Mississippi Freedom branch of the Democratic party.[25]

Black Candidate Strategy.   One of the best articulations of this position was presented by the Organization of Afro-American Unity in 1964. Stressing the need for racial solidarity behind race-conscious African-American candidates, it argued that a primary goal must be to

> organize the Afro-American community block by block to make the community aware of its power and potential; we will start immediately a voter-registration drive to make every unregistered voter in the Afro-American community an independent voter; we propose to support and/or organize political clubs, to run independent candidates for office and to support any Afro-American already in office who answers to and is responsive to the Afro-American community.[26]

Besides many well known mayoral-level examples, Jesse Jackson's success at rallying the large majority of the black vote in his 1984 and 1988 bids for the Democratic Party's presidential nomination provides another highly visible instance of this type of unity.[27]

Nonelectoral Strategy.   Finally, there are those like black studies professor Robert Allen who argue against participating in the electoral process at all. Allen states, "Dabbling in elections on the pretext of 'organizing and educating' is an unnecessary waste of scarce resources. This activity may inflate egos, but it does little to build a mass-based organization."[28] Instead, forms of organized resistance and "direct action" are advocated. A less radical variation of this theme is presented by Edward Brown, Director of the Voter Education Project. According to Brown, "The view is that Blacks have nowhere else to go but Blacks always have somewhere to go:

they can go fishing."[29] Essentially this is a call for strategic nonparticipation at select times.[30] Such options will be discussed further in Chapter 10.

Major-Party Support.   Ever since Emancipation and the Civil War amendments, the black vote in elections for national office has gone largely to one of the two major parties of the day. For approximately the first 70 years it was the Republicans, and since then it has been the Democrats.

Although polling data was not generated until quite recently, there are indicators of this early partisan loyalty. In the House of Representatives, for example, all black representatives were Republicans prior to 1932, while virtually all have been Democrats since then. Polling, begun in the latter period, has consistently shown that the majority of blacks identify with the Democratic party and side with that party on most prominent political issues.[31]

The Republican Era (1865–1912).   It is not difficult to understand why early allegiance went to the party of Lincoln, the Republicans, and not the southern-based and blatantly racist Democrats. Not only had the Republicans led the "good fight" during the Civil War, but also they subsequently produced the Civil War amendments, Radical Reconstruction of the South, and the 1866 Civil Rights Act. Yet the honeymoon was over when Rutherford B. Hayes sold out Reconstruction in 1876. Soon the southern Republican party actually began to divide along racial lines, culminating in the Lily White Republicans and the Black and Tan Republicans. This split at the state and local levels helped the southern Democrats push through the notorious black codes and Jim Crow laws that would quickly reduce most of the nation's blacks to a degrading and physically perilous "second-class citizenship."

Era of Transition (1912–1936).   The Great Migration landed many blacks in large cities accessible by rail. There they normally were recruited by the local Democratic machines, and their votes often could be bartered for small amounts of patronage. At the national level, this new relationship was nearly cemented by President Woodrow Wilson. He had courted black voters, at least in very general language, despite his party's powerful southern wing. Nevertheless, after being elected with the help of a number of defecting black votes, he rather quickly took steps that essentially eliminated black opportunities for federal appointments, and he even promoted the segregation of the federal bureaucracy. The Republicans, for their part, were so cavalier about their black support that presidential candidate Herbert Hoover even endorsed the South's Lily White faction in 1928—helping him do better in that region than any other Republican had up until that time.[32] Despite continued reticence on the part of the Democrats, black loyalty to the national Republican party began to waiver in the 1928 and 1932 presidential elections.

The Democratic Era (1936–present).   The national Democratic party did not seat a black as even an alternate convention delegate until 1924, and four times it ran a presidential candidate (Franklin Delano Roosevelt) who had served in the Wilson administration; had openly avoided direct appeals to black voters; and had even been deafeningly silent on relevant issues such as fair employment opportunities, the right to vote, and lynching (with southern Democrats actively opposing antilynching legislation). Nevertheless, the party's implementation of a social welfare state seems to have been warmly received in the economically depressed black community. Thus the presidential election of 1936 marks a major watershed of sorts. Even though the electoral transition would not really be complete until 1944[33] and the shift in party identification would take until 1964,[34] the switch from Republican to Democratic voting in national-level elections was nearly revolutionary.[35]

Under the increasing pressure of a growing civil rights movement, the Democrats made moves that would cement their gain. Besides continuing to press forward with their social welfare agenda, the 1940 Democratic platform contained a very moderate plank endorsing enforcement of the Fourteenth Amendment and nondiscrimination in government service. President Roosevelt created the Fair Employment Practices Commission in 1941. The 1944 party platform contained clear support for enforcement of the Fifteenth Amendment. The 1948 convention adopted a civil rights plank even though it created a serious regional split within the party. President Harry Truman desegregated the military and presented civil rights legislation to the Congress. And then came the civil rights and voting rights acts, Lyndon Johnson's War on Poverty, a host of other Great Society programs, the appointment of Thurgood Marshall as the first African American to sit on the United States Supreme Court, support for busing and affirmative action, a system for guaranteeing black representation at the party's presidential conventions, and the 1989 election of Ron Brown as the first black to head a major political party in U.S. history.

In the meantime, the Republicans were sending mixed signals. Sensing an opening in the previously solid Democratic South, the Republicans sought to capitalize on the serious split within the Democratic party over the issue of black rights. For example, President Eisenhower was quite slow in protecting the civil rights movement in the South, and Richard Nixon adopted an overt "southern strategy," with his law-and-order and antibusing positions as well as his unsuccessful nominations of two allegedly racist justices to the U. S. Supreme Court.[36] Nevertheless, the Republicans also created Heritage Groups within the party to reach out to various racial and ethnic constituencies, and this soon led to the development of Republican Black Nationality Clubs. In addition, there was a call for "positive action" to secure more black representation at the 1976 Republican national convention. Yet, beginning with the Reagan era, the party's position became essentially that blacks would be better off without special treatment or much of the social welfare state, benefiting along with everyone else from the national economic growth Republicans claimed to be providing.

Consequently, African Americans have become significantly more attached to the Democratic Party. In 1996, for instance, there were 88 African Americans on the Democratic National Committee, but only one on the Republican. Blacks comprised 21 percent of the delegates to the Democratic national convention, while fewer than 3 percent of the Republican delegates were black. There were 539 black Democratic state legislators, compared to 11 on the Republican side.[37] There have been only four black Republicans to sit in the U. S. Congress since Reconstruction, while all the rest have been Democrats. The only black governor was a Democrat. In addition, African

Americans have normally been casting over 85 percent of their votes for Democratic presidential candidates, and in the process they have come to comprise a full one-quarter of those electoral constituencies.[38]

Having traced these general, national-level trends, however, it should be noted that some definite qualifications are in order. After the great national-level switch of 1936, for instance, plenty of black Republican votes were still cast at the state and local levels, against the established Democratic machines in the North and against racist Democratic candidates in the South. At this subnational level, blacks have been very issue oriented, often voting against the individual candidates who seem to pose the greatest threat to perceived black interests.[39] In addition, the black community has had its share of internal splits; for example, Marcus Garvey appealed to disenchanted lower-income blacks who had not been well received by many of their more established black counterparts upon the migrants' turn-of-the-century arrival in northern cities.

Minor-Party Support.   A number of blacks have also moved away from the two major parties altogether. Black experience with third parties predates the Civil

of less tangible benefits: mobilization, consciousness raising, education, and hope being among them.

Multiracial Protest Parties.   Three of the best-known examples are the Liberty, Populist, and Progressive parties. Free blacks were an important component of the antislavery Liberty party during the 1840s and 1850s. Blacks were also significant contributors to the Populist party's efforts in the 1890s, although they came to be treated rather shabbily in that allegedly progressive organization as race became a major issue dividing its crucial southern constituency. They were also courted to a limited extent by the reformist Progressive party a couple of decades later, although specific black grievances were essentially avoided.

Multiracial Ideological Parties.   From rather early on, the American Communist party made overt appeals to the black community. That was also true, to a lesser degree, of a variety of socialist parties. Historians differ as to reasons, but blacks have never been attracted to such parties in sizable numbers. At the very least, the parties' primary focus on class conflict did not seem to leave enough room for addressing racism as an independent phenomenon.[40]

Black Political Parties.   On a number of occasions, blacks have chosen to step outside predominantly white major and minor parties to form creative political organizations of their own. Independent parties have provided aggregation and articulation of distinctly black perspectives, and parallel black parties have allowed black members of the two major parties to challenge their dominant white factions, especially at the state and local levels. Examples of the former in the nineteenth century were the Colored Independent party (Pennsylvania) and the Negro Protective party (Ohio). More recent examples have included the Lowndes County Freedom Organization (Alabama), the United Citizens party of South Carolina, and the national Freedom Now party. Recent examples of parallel parties are the Mississippi Freedom Democratic party and the National Democratic party of Alabama.[41]

Black Independents.   One final phenomenon requires close scrutiny: the drift of many black voters, particularly young blacks, away from strong partisan attachment altogether. Available data indicate that the number of black "independents" increased markedly in the 1970s, much as it did in the nation as a whole.[42] Even more specifically, the number of blacks identifying themselves as strong partisans dropped from a peak of nearly 60 percent in 1968 to roughly 40 percent or less thereafter.[43] Hanes Walton estimates that one-third of the black electorate is no longer closely affiliated with either of the two major parties but instead floats back and forth between their candidates, depending on the particular issues and personalities involved.[44] Of greatest significance is the fact that this phenomenon is most apparent among blacks under 30 years of age. In 1986, for example, more than half of all blacks over 30 years of age expressed a "strong" commitment to the Democratic party, while that was true for just one-third of those under 30. In addition, strong partisanship was declining considerably faster in the black community than in the nation as a whole.[45] Thus the black vote may well be increasingly less predictable as time goes on.

Electoral Gains

> No white candidate is likely to feel and express, as a black could, the ache and anger of black communities ravaged by joblessness and the snatching away of even those rickety ladders that offered some promise of a way up and out of hopelessness for poor blacks.[46]

Black Elected Officials.   Thousands of African Americans presently hold elective office, but achieving that has been a very long battle, with untold black representation lost in the interim. To begin with, poll taxes, literacy tests, racial gerrymandering, outright intimidation, and other tactics deprived blacks of input during some pivotal years. In 1880, for example, blacks held majorities in some 311 counties but were almost completely disenfranchised. By 1970, when basic voting rights were finally being protected, blacks held majorities in only 102 counties.[47] The state of Mississippi, where blacks have comprised more than 40 percent of the population since slavery, did not elect a black member of Congress from the end of Reconstruction until choosing Mike Espy in 1986. Statewide malapportionment, prior to the 1962 *Baker v. Carr* decision, deprived black voters of proportional representation for crucial decades in which they had heavy concentrations in large northern cities. In addition, disposable income has often been in short supply, forcing many black candidates to run underfunded campaigns.

Nonetheless, most of these obstacles are finally beginning to be overcome. As a result, black elected officials have proliferated. That increase has been most dramatic in the South. Whereas only 72 blacks held elective office there in 1965, for example, that figure had jumped to 2,128 by 1976. Meanwhile, at the state and local levels across the country, although Douglas Wilder of Virginia is the only post-Reconstruction black to have been elected to a governorship,[48] a number of African Americans have served as mayors of large cities, including Atlanta, Baltimore, Birmingham, Charlotte, Chicago, Denver, Detroit, Gary, Houston, Kansas City, Jackson, Los Angeles, Memphis, Newark, New Orleans, New York City, Philadelphia, San Francisco, Seattle, St. Louis, and Washington, D. C.

Nationally, there have been at least 15 black members in the House of Representatives at any point since 1972. Edward Brooke of Massachusetts and then Carol Moseley-Braun of Illinois have sat in the United States Senate. And even though no black has held the office of president or vice president, nor even been the presidential or vice presidential candidate of a major party, blacks have been the nominees of third parties for over a century. In addition, Congresswoman Shirley Chisholm was a bona fide candidate for the Democratic nomination in 1972, winning more than 150 delegates to the Democratic national convention. Jesse Jackson then broke through a number of the major party barriers. In 1984, he garnered 16 percent of the Democratic primary vote (more than 3 million votes) and gained nearly 400 convention delegates. In 1988, he did far better yet, winning more than 29 percent of the primary vote (nearly 7 million votes) and gaining over 1,000 convention delegates.

The tangible gains resulting from these electoral victories are a bit more difficult to calculate. There now exist a Congressional Black Caucus and a Caucus of Black State Legislators, both of which are in a position to press for black causes (see Chapter 8). And although there is little empirical evidence to suggest that major governmental priorities are much different when blacks hold public office, having institutional power over revenue raising, budgets, staffs, and statutes has still made some difference. In terms of tangible rewards at the local level, for example, there have been more black appointments, more governmental contracts extended to black-owned businesses, and fewer reported incidences of police brutality. Intangible gains include more role models, hope, pride, politicization, articulation of black demands, and opportunities to break down white stereotypes.[49] At very least, having Wilson Goode in the Philadelphia mayor's office once held by Frank Rizzo and Richard Arrington as mayor of the city that previously employed Sheriff Bull Connor almost certainly increased governmental sensitivity to black perspectives.

But there have been some serious limitations as well. It is true that there are now more than 8,000 black elected officials, but that is still less than 2 percent of all the elected representatives nationwide, while African Americans appear to comprise an even smaller proportion of appointed governmental officials.[50] As Neal Peirce put it, "A rule of thumb is that it's the exceptional black who can win in a constituency that's less than 65 percent black."[51] Or, where they are elected with a significant number of white votes, black candidates often have had to seriously moderate their racial agendas.[52]

One of the most visible prizes has been winning the office of mayor, but some of the specific limitations faced by black mayors are also instructive. The large majority are weak mayors in council-manager forms of government, and approximately one-half represent towns of less than 2,000 people—towns like Cotton Plant, Arkansas; Waterproof, Louisiana; and Mount Bayou, Louisiana.[53] The roughly two dozen black mayors of cities larger than 100,000 people face other limitations. The reform movement has stripped them of most of the patronage their predecessors employed to hold together a governing coalition. Their cities are generally so desperately poor that Paul Friesema has called black control of them a "hollow prize."[54] And a primary reason why most of these black mayors have been able to win is that there are now black majorities or near majorities in most of these cities—primarily because many of the more affluent whites have fled to the suburbs. The fact that those whites have taken their tax base with them may be even more of a problem than the further racial polarization that their flight represents.[55]

White Elected Officials.   Contrary to a popular misconception, blacks do not automatically vote for black over white candidates when the choice is available. In the 1967 mayoral race in Philadelphia, or the 1984 and 1985 Democratic primaries in New York City, for example, the majority of black voters opted for white candidates over black alternatives. Nor is the black community destined to be indefinitely pleased with the performance of a black representative. The black mayor of West Memphis, Arkansas, for example, lost much of his black base and was replaced by a white man. In the overwhelming majority of electoral situations, however, African Americans find themselves facing only white choices. It is in this circumstance that the electoral process seems to have proved especially deficient.

Although a minority group, black voters have generally followed the standard prescription for electoral success. They tend to live in strategically important areas and to deliver their vote as a bloc.[56] It is generally assumed that the Democratic party requires clear victories in large northern cities and at least a few southern states. For the past half century, blacks in these strategic locations have cast their ballots for Democratic candidates, forming the party's most cohesive and identifiable voting bloc. Yet this loyalty has not translated into comparable political rewards. What is more, white Democrats' concern for black problems seems to be declining at a time when national Democratic party reliance on the black vote has never been higher: Blacks now cast some 25 percent of the votes for Democratic presidential candidates, while white America has given a majority of its votes for the Democratic presidential candidate only once since World War II, in the Democratic landslide election of 1964.

The 1976 presidential election and its aftermath are a classic case in point. Jimmy Carter received 50.1 percent of the popular vote and only 297 (out of 538) electoral votes. He won 47 percent of the white vote and 95 percent of the black vote. In addition, black votes for Carter exceeded his margin of victory in 13 states, with a total of 216 electoral votes. Yet, as his term expired, only one in three blacks approved of the president's job performance, and not even one in four was satisfied with what he had tried to do for the black community.[57] Part of the reason can be found in limits inherent in the American electoral process (discussed next) and in the American legislative process (discussed in Chapter 8).

A CONSERVATIVE ELECTORAL PROCESS

The American electoral process, as presently structured, is simply incapable of empowering most Americans. Instead, it has evolved into an effective mechanism for helping to conserve the unequal distribution of wealth and power in the society—impeding, rather than facilitating, fundamental change. We shall touch on several examples of this conservative nature.

The Electoral Process

To begin with, as indicated at the outset of this chapter, there is little opportunity for direct popular rule. Rather, the American electorate is left to pursue national demands through elected representatives. There are, however, a number of impediments even to indirect popular input. The registration and campaign finance procedures discriminate against those in the lower socioeconomic classes. Viable electoral choices are severely limited. It is difficult for government to respond to the issue preferences expressed at election time, even if those preferences are clear. In addition, a host of major decisions fall beyond the reach of elected officials altogether.

Initiatives.   The one exception to the lack of direct democracy is the initiative process available in roughly half the American states. Citizens at the state and local levels can draft their own legislation, and if enough compatriots sign their petition, the issue can be brought to the electorate for a direct vote. In a number of states, the proposal becomes statutory law if approved by a majority of the voters, just as if it had been passed by the state legislature. Nevertheless, the petitioning process normally requires an intimidating amount of time and energy. This option was not available at state and local levels until the turn of the twentieth century, and there is no comparable provision at the national level.

Registration Laws.   In nearly every state, a citizen must be registered to vote by a specified date, generally a few weeks prior to election day. Some states also demand reregistration if the person has not voted in the last four years, while virtually all states require reregistration if one moves to a new election district. The result is that roughly one-third of the electorate has remained unregistered at any point in time.[58] The United States is the only Western democracy that requires this much of a registration hurdle.[59]

"Politics is the world's second oldest profession." (political adage)

Campaign Finance.   As campaign costs have proliferated in the era of television advertising, large campaign contributors have come to play an ever more critical role. It now costs more than $1 million to run a typical large-city mayoral or statewide campaign and thousands of dollars to run for many lower offices—sums beyond the means of most potential candidates and very difficult to raise in small contributions. Thus wealthy individuals and organizations must often be wooed. And as Sheila Collins notes:

> What was not fully appreciated was that by the time blacks entered electoral politics as a significant national voting bloc, the rules of power had changed. It was not the ability to deliver votes to a candidate that counted, but the ability to deliver money.[60]

The Congress, in fact, saw this developing and passed the 1974 Campaign Finance Act in the wake of the Watergate scandal. Among other things, it set limits on the amount of money an individual could give to a particular campaign, as well as the total amount of money presidential campaigns could receive and spend. The U. S. Supreme Court, however, seriously weakened the act by declaring key parts of it to be violations of First Amendment freedom of expression. Specifically, in *Buckley v. Valeo*, the Court disallowed limits on the amount of money one could contribute to one's own campaign, unless one agreed to such limits by accepting public financing. It also disallowed limits on the amount of money an individual or group could spend independently on a candidate's behalf.[61] Then, in 1996, they also removed limits on the amount of money political parties could receive and spend on behalf of candidates.[62]

Money spent on a candidate's behalf has come to be called "soft money," and there are essentially no governmental limits on what individuals, groups, or parties can spend in this way so long as they do not coordinate their efforts with a particular campaign. A popular soft money device has been the "issue advertisement," whereby specific candidates are chastised or praised for their votes on particular issues, without directly endorsing or opposing their individual candidacies.[63]

Another glaring loophole was the allowance for Political Action Committees (PACs). Although a single donor can give a maximum of only $5,000 to any particular federal PAC and each federal PAC cannot contribute more than $5,000 to any individual candidate, there are no limits on the number of PACs that can form nor the number of them to which any person can contribute. There are also no federal limits whatsoever on state-level PACs. As a result, thousands of PACs give millions of dollars to congressional candidates each election—largely to incumbents, especially conservative Republican incumbents.[64] And although presidential campaigns now are financed primarily out of the federal treasury—with each major-party candidate allowed $62 million in 1996 for example—PACs still spend additional millions on behalf of those candidates, as do political parties.[65]

By the time all was said and done in 1996, a total of some $800 million had been spent on the presidential election alone, while major-party congressional candidates spent over $660 million, and that does not include the millions of additional dollars spent on their behalf.[66] Not only that, but such campaign contributions do seem to influence subsequent behavior on the part of elected governmental officials. It is hard to imagine that the millions of dollars Archer-Daniels-Midland has donated to candidates of both parties over the years has in no way contributed to the multimillion dollar federal tax break allowed for ethanol, one of the company's primary products.[67] As Congressman Barney Frank put it, "We are the only people in the world required by law to take large amounts of money from strangers and then act as if it has no effect on our behavior."[68] Retired Congresswoman Pat Schroeder characterized Congress as a "coin-operated legislative machine."[69] Where does all this money come from?

To begin with, people in the upper socioeconomic classes simply have more money to give and know more people who have money. Thus it should come as no surprise that the bulk of all campaign funds are generated by the owning class.[70] With blacks essentially excluded from those socioeconomic circles, the reality of most campaign funding effectively shuts out black America.

Weak Political Parties.   After studying the functions of political parties, Walter Burnham concluded that "critical elections" are a dynamic mechanism that helps political systems adapt to fundamental changes in their environment. In the course of these, parties respond by organizing themselves around the new, most polarizing issues in the society. This shift enables them to represent the spectrum of interests generated by the change. For example, the Civil War divided the nation, and the party system responded with the northern Republicans opposing the southern Democrats on ensuing issues such as reconstruction policies. Burnham argues, however, that the American party system failed to respond adequately to the issues and interests that stemmed from the industrial revolution. Instead of capitalist and socialist parties emerging to reflect paramount opposing interests within an industrial economy—as was the case in virtually every multiparty democracy on earth—both major American parties accepted capitalism as a given.[71]

> We don't have a two-party system in this country. We have Demopublicans. It's one party of the corporate class, with two wings—the Democrats and the Republicans. They both say the other can't do the job for the working people, and they're both right.[72]

But even had historical events caused the parties to polarize around the issue of how capital was to be owned and operated, it is doubtful whether the structure of America's party system would have allowed a conversion of these positions into meaningful electoral choices over an extended period. After a lifetime of studying America's political parties, E. E. Schattschneider concluded that "decentralization of power is by all odds the most important single characteristic of the American major party."[73] How does decentralization normally affect meaningful electoral input?

Lack of Unity.   Under a model parliamentary system, a national party's platform has real meaning, for candidates elected under that party's banner will be held to voting the party line. Their allegiance is guaranteed by the fact that they will have been nominated to run by the party's national committee, and thus their loyalties are secured by both the party's screening process and their own desires to run for office again someday. Consequently, the party (or the working coalition of parties) that wins a majority of the legislative seats not only gets to choose the country's chief executive (or prime minister), but also can be counted on to carry out the policies promised in the party platform.

In the United States, by contrast, chief executives and legislatures are elected separately, and there is no guarantee that the executive and both branches of the legislature will be controlled by the same political party. In fact, in only one-third of the governments since 1956 have the president and both houses of Congress been of the same party. A similar number of state governments have likewise fallen under mixed-party control.

Beyond that, each of the two major parties is composed of a national organization, 50 state branches, and thousands of local ones—many of which have little in common other than name. This is true because the national committee is weak, without any significant sanctions for disciplining either state and local organizations or the candidates who often independently seek their nominations. Even the party's presidential candidate has been chosen in a series of statewide primaries and caucuses, with the national party normally convening simply to ratify that choice. Thus the national party platform, often little more than a compromise document designed to appease the various core constituencies in the party, is far from binding on candidates elected under the party label.

Unsurprisingly, party unity in the halls of the nation's legislatures is limited, for the elected representatives rarely owe anything to a national party organization. Using 90 percent loyalty as a standard for determining party voting cohesiveness on any particular bill, Julius Turner found that from 1921 to 1948, only 17 percent of the roll calls in the U.S. House of Representatives met that criterion. These figures have since declined further yet, despite some recent growth in party cohesiveness.[74]

In the absence of party discipline, the positions taken by the candidates of the two major parties overlap considerably. And, once elected, some Republicans vote more liberally than some members of the generally more liberal Democratic party, while some Democrats vote more conservatively than members of the generally more conservative Republican party. Thus party label is not a highly reliable indicator of a politician's policy inclinations and is therefore a less than reliable voting cue.

Political parties also appear to be losing their ability to influence voter choices. Nationwide, for example, the proportion of self-identifying independents rose from less than 10 percent of registered voters in the 1920s to more than one in three voters since the early 1970s. Also, a sizable number of people now split their ticket, meaning that they vote for members of different parties on the same ballot.[75]

Democratic Implications.   Party weakness reduces the ability of elected officials to overcome impeding checks and balances established by the Founding Fathers. Without party discipline, it becomes extremely difficult for hundreds of independently elected representatives to pass and implement comprehensive legislation through the policymaking maze (described at length in Chapter 8). That is no doubt why a number of the more conservative Founding Fathers so adamantly opposed the very formation of political parties.[76]

The absence of meaningful party platforms and the party discipline necessary to enforce them also contributes to a lack of accountability. Candidates can and do say one thing in the campaign and do another once in office.[77] This would be significantly less likely if candidates were more effectively bound to a national party platform.

Political parties stand to serve four primary functions: (1) to educate voters about policy matters, (2) to lead voters toward the policies the party has formulated, (3) to organize elections, and (4) to organize government after the elections. As it turns out, America's weak parties perform well on only half of these. The major parties generally do a respectable job of conducting elections and providing a structure whereby subsequent legislatures can choose their leaders and committees. They are far less successful in the other two areas. Campaigns are increasingly being left to hired campaign consultants, the most sophisticated of whom take continuous tracking polls to determine what the voter wants to hear at any point in time. The candidate then carefully tailors his or her image and statements accordingly; and more polls are used to determine whether the candidate's messages are satisfying those public wishes, however uninformed. In addition, a disproportionate number of these messages end up as 15- and 30-second advertisements that attack the opposition in an increasingly vituperative manner while saying little of what the messenger intends to do.[78] Not much leadership or education is likely to come from that process. As a matter of fact, such campaigning actually appears to be increasing cynicism and alienation, while depressing voter turnout.[79]

The vapidity of contemporary media-oriented campaigns will be discussed further in Chapter 9, as will the growth of mass media as an independent political force in its own right. Meanwhile, one other agent has grown in political strength as parties have slipped even further into insignificance. That agent is the interest group.

Interest groups tend to fill the void left by declining political parties. The United States, with likely the weakest political parties among existing democracies, has the broadest array of active interest groups. That development poses a serious problem. It leaves individual representatives more vulnerable to lobbying pressure than in a stronger party system. Therefore, almost every vote must be carefully cast so as to avoid offending a resource-rich special-interest group.[80]

Even if the United States had a strong-party parliamentary system, another potent arrangement would continue to make it difficult for the electoral process to provide viable alternatives that challenge the underlying socioeconomic structure. That arrangement is the two-party system.

The Two-Party System

As Sheila Collins puts it, "One of the most carefully guarded preserves of United States class rule [is] the two-party system."[81]

Figure 7.1 is designed to help clarify the inherently conservative logic of a two-party arrangement. This is true in particular because the two major parties are free to take their more ideologically extreme supporters for granted and do battle over the moderates in the middle. Those at the ideological extremes really have no place else to go if they wish to vote for a viable candidate, and for a major party to move too far in order to appease them is to risk abandoning the center to the other party. Thus party platforms and policies must be moderated to appeal to the middle and normally do not provide alternatives sharply different from the status quo.[82] The Democratic party, for example, requires a minimum of 15 percent showing in its primaries in order to gain any convention delegates. In the process, it can avoid the potential embarrassment of smaller groups raising controversial issues at the televised national convention.

From the voters' perspective, this leaves many of them dissatisfied with both major parties and often voting against the more offensive of two moderates rather than having the chance to vote for a viable candidate who is strongly advocating positions in line with their own predilections.[83] In the Fall of 1995, for instance, a CNN-*Time* magazine poll found 56 percent of Americans wishing there was a viable third party to compete with the Democrats and Republicans.[84] Even the 1980 presidential election between well-known "conservative" Ronald Reagan and "liberal" incumbent Jimmy Carter was still a classic case in point. The campaign came to revolve around which social programs to cut and which defense programs to increase. Neither candidate suggested fundamental alterations in either the existing welfare or warfare states. Polls found more than half the voters unable to distinguish any "important differences" between the candidates, less than one-third perceiving any such differences between the parties, and more than one-third of the Reagan voters claiming to have voted against Carter rather than for Reagan.[85]

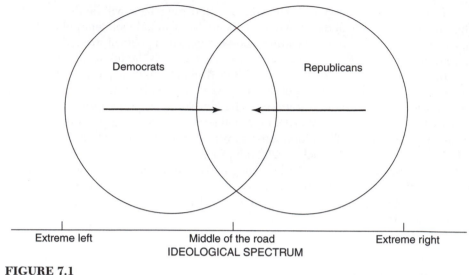

FIGURE 7.1
The Conservative Two-Party System

So why has a multiparty system not developed? The answer cannot be found in the absence of powerful cleavages in the society. No other Western nation has nearly as many interest groups nor a history of more violent interest clashes in areas such as labor and race relations. More significant are the following seven factors.

Single-Member Districts.   Under this arrangement, a single representative is chosen from each election district. Finishing first is all that counts; thus voting for anyone other than one of the two most viable candidates is essentially wasting one's vote (the electoral college system for electing the president is a classic example of this winner-take-all arrangement). And the two most viable candidates are almost invariably those put forward by the two major parties.

In a multimember district where public officials are selected by proportional representation, there is much more incentive for third-party voting. Although there are numerous forms of proportional voting, a general example should still be instructive. If the district is to choose three members of Congress, for example, the top three vote-getters would then go to the House of Representatives, with a third-place finish just as good as a first. The voter is less likely to be wasting a vote by casting it for a third-party candidate, as that person will not need nearly as many votes to acquire a seat. If such a system had been in place in northern Mississippi, for instance, and if the white votes were split at all, black voters could have concentrated their votes on a single black candidate and would most likely have had a black representative well before 1986.

In fact, there have been a few experiments with proportional representation at the local level in the United States. In the case of New York City, however, it was dropped shortly after two Communists were elected to the city council in 1947.

Plurality Elections.   Not only is just one person chosen from each district in most cases, but also that person normally needs only a plurality of the votes. In other words, the person who gets the most votes wins, even if he or she does not get an electoral majority. Once again, this encourages people to concentrate their attention on the top two candidates, as a second- or third-place finish is meaningless. Were a majority to be required, as it sometimes is in nonpartisan general elections at the local level, finishing other than first can still land one in a run-off election between the top finishers. In such a case, there would be more incentive for the voter to consider third-party candidates.

Getting on the Ballot.   Besides the disincentives to vote for third-party candidates when they appear on the ballot, it is often quite difficult for them to get on the ballot in the first place. Most states require some sort of petitioning process, although some actually waive this requirement if a party received a certain percentage of the vote in the previous election—obviously favoring the two major parties. Otherwise, the petitioning process can be difficult. States often require thousands of signatures collected across a number of districts within a relatively brief period of time. In addition, the signee often must not have signed any other petition or voted in another party's primary, and some states throw out an entire petition if it contains even one illegal name.[86]

The results? In 1968, George Wallace made one of the best third-party showings for president in the history of the United States. Yet he had been able to get his name on the ballots of only a little over half the states. Ross Perot, on the other hand, did not face nearly as many impediments a quarter of a century later, in large part thanks to the efforts of two men. In the 1980 presidential election, independent John Anderson and Libertarian Ed Clark mounted successful court challenges against many of the most restrictive state election laws, and each was finally able to have his name on all 50 state ballots. Nevertheless, the *New York Times* estimated that it still took 1.2 million signatures and $750,000 to accomplish that feat.[87]

Public Financing Formulas.   As mentioned earlier, the 1974 Campaign Finance Act provided for public financing of presidential campaigns. In 1996, for instance, major party candidates Bill Clinton and Bob Dole each received $62 million of taxpayers' money with which to fund his campaign. A third-party candidate can qualify for public monies only after gaining at least 5 percent of the national vote. In 1980, John Anderson polled 6.6 percent and became the first third-party candidate to qualify, making him eligible to receive roughly $4 million in the next election had he chosen to run again. Ross Perot waived public financing in 1992 so that he could spend $64 million of his own money in that race. In 1996, however, he opted to take his roughly $30 million in public financing, with the various campaign limitations that resulted.

Equal Time on the Airwaves.   The 1934 Communications Act specifies that stations that provide free airtime to one candidate must provide "equal time" to opponents. In practice, however, that has seldom applied to third-party challengers.

Most significantly, that provision can be legally waived for interviews, documentaries, coverage in newscasts, and even candidate debates. In 1980, for example, John Anderson was excluded from the Carter-Reagan debates on national television, as was Ross Perot when Bill Clinton and Bob Dole debated in 1996.[88] And, beyond the formats just mentioned, television and radio stations simply are not likely to be voluntarily extending free airtime to any candidate. Thus financially strapped third parties must purchase advertising time if they wish to receive any significant media exposure at all.

Police Harassment.   As the Watergate hearings revealed, federal law enforcement agents had been using legally dubious procedures to monitor the activities of certain "suspicious" third parties, mostly socialists. Phones were tapped, offices were broken into, mail was read, and so on.[89] Of course, this was nothing new in American history. Socialist parties have mounted about the only serious nationwide threat to two-party hegemony. In 1918, Socialists held 1,200 offices in 340 cities, including 79 mayors in 24 states, 32 state legislators, and one member of Congress. Shortly thereafter, the police raids began. Meetings were disrupted, and leaders were deported or jailed, often on trumped-up charges.[90]

Miscellaneous Obstructions.   There are other impediments to serious third-party challenges. At one point, the United States Postal Service provided reduced-rate postage only to the two major parties.[91] In their long-standing positions of domination, representatives of the two major parties have continually been able to gerrymander voting districts to help secure their own seats. The U.S. Supreme Court has ruled that states are not required to allow candidate names to appear on more than one party's ballot line, making *fusion* candidacies more difficult—where a major and minor party, for example, might endorse the same candidate.[92] In addition, as will be discussed further in Chapter 9, the ratings-conscious mass media have definite inclinations to reduce all campaigns to a two-person "horse race" of sorts, meaning that third-party candidates are simply ignored for the most part.[93]

For all these reasons, American third parties have been inconsequential—especially by international comparison. At the national level, third-party representatives in Congress have been extremely rare, and only once did a minor party presidential candidate receive more than one vote in four, when defecting Republican and former president Theodore Roosevelt polled 27.4 percent of the 1912 popular vote.[94]

Governmental Limitations.

Governmental leeway is being seriously circumvented by the economic realities of the postindustrial economy. Increasingly desperate for capital investment, government must contour public policy ever more closely to the needs of those who own highly mobile corporate capital. Therefore, the two major parties can be expected to become even more economically conservative in their overall policy orientations.[95]

Beyond that, in an economic system like the one in the United States, the majority of decisions that affect people's lives are made in the private sector anyway; and there is little reason to expect either of today's two dominant political parties to challenge that arrangement. As Robert Allen put it:

Political power in America is dependent upon those who control valued resources and critical institutions, not vice versa. And those who have this power cannot be voted out of their positions by the public at large, because the base of their power lies outside the formal political sphere. Their base of power lies in the corporations and the large public institutions which are interdependent, but largely removed from the sway of public pressure.[96]

Electoral Aftermath

Whether they are black or white, the ability to cast a vote every four years to help determine which millionaire will represent them does not bring poor people flocking to the polls. Since their votes are ineffective, their real political power is not increased by voting, and consequently their motivation to continue voting is lowered still further.[97]

Is C. T. Vivian, quoted here, correct about the nature of the electoral choices available? To what degree has the American electorate demonstrated disinclination to participate in this very conservative electoral process? And how does this arrangement function to preserve the political-economic status quo?

Elite Candidates.   The large majority of America's public officials and candidates for those positions tend to be wealthy, middle-aged, white Anglo-Saxon Protestant males.[98] Richard Hamilton, among others, has found that because they live, work, and play separately:

The white Protestant upper-middle class (and also the equivalent upper class) form an "isolated mass." They are separated and cut off from the rest of the society and as a result have their own separate consciousness and understandings about what is going on elsewhere in the society.[99]

This raises questions as to whether these men can effectively represent many of the interests of nonelites. For example, why suppose that they can be sensitive to the psychological devastation a breadwinner feels when even temporarily unemployed? Why expect them to feel concern for the plight of junkies or prison inmates when such people are so far removed from their daily lives? Why be surprised when they put abstract principles such as "maintaining the international balance of power" ahead of concern for tenants' rights to heat and hot water 24 hours a day, cockroach extermination, and the like?

Turnout Decline.   Table 7. 1 shows that the turnout rate for Americans in general closely parallels the turnout in the black community. Most Americans normally do not vote, even in national elections. Beyond that, more than two-thirds do not belong to any organization that takes stands on political issues, and only a very small minority contributes in any way to the campaign process.[100] It is also a fact that even fewer tend to turn out for state and local balloting. In addition, whereas presidential voting turnout exceeded 60 percent of the eligible voters in all but the period immediately following the extension of women's suffrage (doubling the electorate) and the period of disruption during World War II, such participation has been decreasing rather markedly since the early 1960s and now hovers around 50 percent. In relation to

TABLE 7.1

ELECTORAL TURNOUT IN NATIONAL ELECTION YEARS, 1960–1996 (PERCENTAGE OF ELIGIBLE VOTERS)

Presidential Years		Off-Year Elections	
1960	63	1962	45
1964	62	1966	45
1968	61	1970	44
1972	55	1974	36
1976	54	1978	35
1980	53	1982	38
1984	53	1886	34
1988	50	1990	33
1992	55	1994	36
1996	49		

Source: U.S. Department of Commerce Bureau of the Census. Staistical Abstracts of the United States (Washington D.C.: GPO).

other representative democracies, the United States has one of the lowest levels of electoral involvement on earth.[101]

Just who are the tens of millions of nonvoters, and why are they not participating? Increasingly less is learned by looking for indications in their demographic characteristics. Voting studies have demonstrated that the nonparticipant is more likely to be under 25 years of age and have a relatively low level of education and income; but as the number of nonvoters increases to the point of becoming a majority, the nonvoting population begins to look demographically similar to the population as a whole. Of more help are direct surveys. Such surveys indicate that mistrust and alienation have soared since the 1960s, accompanied by a precipitous decline in people's regard for the two major political parties.[102] That dissatisfaction is also reflected in political *tune-out*.

As an indication of their *tuning out* politics, most Americans do not know which party controls the Congress and cannot name their representative in the U.S. House of Representatives, let alone recall that person's party affiliation. As a matter of fact, a majority do not even know that they have two senators, let alone know the senators' names and parties. Thus it should not be surprising that less than 20 percent can identify how their senator or representative voted on any piece of legislation.[103]

Political scientists William Flanigan and Nancy Zingale conclude:

> Most candidates in most elections are unknown quantities for the average voter. Typically, voters will be aware of the candidate's party affiliation and whether or not he is an incumbent, but not much more. Furthermore, [even] these elements of information may come to the attention of the voter only if they are indicated on the ballot.[104]

As a consequence, competition for national office has diminished, and the reelection of incumbents is virtually assured.

Less Competition.   In 1956, for instance, only 41 percent of the members of the U.S. House of Representatives had won their seats by gaining 60 percent or more of the vote in their districts. By the mid–1980s, more than three out of every four representatives had won by such a margin. Or, to look at it another way, consider the number of races that were generally classified as *competitive*—meaning that the winner won by no more than 55 percent of the vote. In 1936, about one-third of the races fit that classification. By the 1990s, the figure had declined to roughly one in five House contests.[105]

Secure Incumbents.   Not only are the races becoming less competitive, but also the same people often are running away with these contests election year after election year. For example, 25 incumbent presidents have sought reelection, and nearly three-quarters of them have been successful. No sitting president has been denied his party's renomination since the direct primary was added in 1912. On Capitol Hill, members of the U.S. House of Representatives have come to be successful in 90 to 98 percent of their reelection bids, while the norm for U.S. Senators has come to exceed 80 percent.[106] On the state and local level, it appears to be more of the same. In New York City, for example, 95 percent of state senate, 92 percent of state assembly, and 93 percent of city council incumbents were successful when challenged in their bids for reelection.[107]

Incumbents are able to secure their positions in part by the process of gerrymandering. At least if they are in the majority party, they are normally in a position to have significant input in the decisions as to where to draw the district lines, allowing them to enhance their own possibilities of reelection. Such secure seats explain in large measure why nearly 90 percent of all PAC money goes to incumbents.[108]

Systemic Preservation.   In the end, instead of being ruled by the many, America finds itself ruled by the few. Elections do not serve to guarantee that the elected politicians will know and represent the interests of all the people. Instead, a minority of poorly informed voters turns out to choose between wealthy white men who run with the help of large campaign contributors and relatively meaningless party labels. These men then take capitalism as a given and are predisposed toward policies that help preserve present economic arrangements.

Yet it becomes more than a matter of insensitivity to popular needs. The electoral process itself, at least for those who participate in it, also helps to deflect pressure to change the socioeconomic structure described in Chapters 3–5. Frustrations are channeled through what normally amount to nonthreatening exercises in democratic futility. Limited political energies are exhausted. Finally, as Murray Edelman puts it, elections are "rituals of symbolic reassurance which serve to quiet resentments and doubts about particular political acts" and to "reaffirm belief in the fundamental rationality and democratic character of the system."[109]

OPTIONS FOR BLACK AMERICA

> The Voting Rights Act reflects . . . America's "instrumentalist bias," its preoccupation with the formal, outward trappings of democratic government, . . . and its neglect of the substantive underpinnings of real democracy.[110]

If the American electoral process is to be converted into a mechanism whereby black citizens can have meaningful input into the political decisions that affect their lives, there is a definite need to accomplish and then move beyond what Lester Salamon has referred to as "instrumentalist" solutions. As with the judicial process, structural changes also must be pursued if and when the opportunity presents itself.

Toward Equal Input

Increasing Voter Turnout.   To begin with, a variety of alternatives have been suggested for increasing participation, some of which have proved successful where they have been tried. These range from making the registration and voting procedures more flexible to automatic registration and compulsory voting.

Approximately three in ten eligible voters are currently unregistered, and political scientists Raymond Wolfinger and Steven Rosenstone have estimated that at least one-third of those unregistered individuals could be added to the rolls by simply making all states' registration laws as liberal as those in the most permissive state.[111] Examples of such permissiveness include presenting a registration application to every high school senior, registration by mail, and election-day registration at the polls. Congress did pass the 1993 Motor Voter Act, which requires states to register people when they renew their driver's licenses; but the more extreme position would be to call for automatically registering people when they attain the age of eligibility, as is done in all the other Western democracies.[112]

But even if one can register at a variety of places, one must still vote at a specific place, on a specific day, during a limited number of hours. There is the option of an absentee ballot, but that normally requires thinking of the election in advance, picking up the ballot, and then having the completed ballot notarized before submitting it. Proposals for change range from making voting hours more flexible (say, 6 A.M. to 7 P.M. over a five-day period), to not drawing jurists from the list of registered voters (a practice that seems to intimidate some potential registrants), to allowing voting by mail as Oregon has attempted,[113] to the creation of either tax incentives to encourage voting or fines to discourage nonparticipation. Even the latter two, the most extreme of these suggestions, have been administered successfully in a number of other democracies.

National Initiatives.   Once enfranchised, the general public obviously cannot be expected to study and vote on every issue that faces all three basic levels of government. The nation has simply become too large and complex for the town-meeting principle to apply much anymore. Nevertheless, there are still individual issues that could well be decided by the electorate as a whole. Initiatives have been used at the state and local levels for decades, without the dire consequences that some theorists fear must accompany mass decision making.[114] As a matter of fact, it is hard to argue that even the most controversial of successful public initiatives, such as Proposition 13 in California, is any more bizarre than some of the legislation that elected representatives have concocted over the years, such as the internment of Japanese Americans during World War II.

Since the mid–1970s, a number of national initiative proposals have been considered on Capitol Hill. In 1977, for example, Senator James Abourezk proposed to allow a national initiative if the corresponding petitions were signed by at least 3 percent of the number of voters that had voted in the previous presidential election—2 to 3 million signees by recent standards. The signatures would have to be obtained in at least ten different states, and three issue areas would be excluded from consideration by this method: constitutional amendments, declarations of war, and calling out federal troops.

A decade later, Senator Mark Hatfield introduced virtually the same legislation, arguing that a national initiative option would

> be an exercise of the sovereign power of the American people to govern themselves . . . (provide) a concrete means for citizens' participation in the policymaking function of our Government . . . lessen the sense of alienation from their Government felt by millions of Americans . . . enhance the accountability of Government . . . [and] produce an open, educational debate on issues which otherwise might have been inadequately addressed.[115]

Community Control.   A variety of proposals emerged in the 1960s suggesting that more political decisions directly affecting neighborhoods needed to be made at the neighborhood level. For example, residents in the affected neighborhoods could be authorized to hire and fire certain police officers or to award certain public contracts.[116]

Deprivatizing Decisions.   Corporate owners and managers have always made major decisions that had implications not only for large numbers of their own workers but also for their surrounding communities as well. Decisions to move a production operation or have more of the work done elsewhere and shipped back for final assembly (*contracting out*) are two of the most common of such judgments in postindustrial America. To date, almost all of these have been seen to fall outside the purview of democratic control, and that needs to change—either through more public control of corporate decisions or more community input by way of local workers owning the corporations in the first place.

In the interest of public control, Oregon's Employment Stability Act, proposed in 1981 and discussed again in Chapter 10 below, would have required departing businesses with more than 50 employees to (1) provide one year's notice even before any significant layoffs could occur, (2) compensate an abandoned community by paying 85 percent of any "adjustment costs," (3) pay for the relocation of all workers, (4) pay employee benefits for a full year after closing, and (5) give the Oregon Bureau of Labor and Industry the first option to buy the abandoned business. Similar legislation has been proposed in nearly two dozen states, while congressmen Perry Bullard, William Ford, Donald Riegle, and Peter Kostmayer and senators Howard Metzenbaum and Harrison Williams introduced national variants. Then, in 1988, the federal government did succeed in passing a bill that at least requires businesses employing more than 100 people to give 60 days' notice to their employees before closing.[117]

Beyond public input into the decisions of large companies whose stock is held by the small owning class, there is also the alternative of broadening ownership to include far more residents of the local community. In 1983, for example, 10,000 steelworkers in Weirton, West Virginia, spent nearly $200 million to buy the failing steel plant where they worked. Far more sweeping was a proposal considered in Sweden.

It would have taxed individual income and corporate profits in order to establish a fund that labor unions could use to buy up the nation's corporate stock—a gradual approach to socialism.

Election Rules.   Section 5 of the 1965 Voting Rights Act needs to be extended, not phased out. Every new election law in the country should be precleared to guarantee that it will not result in racial discrimination. At the very least, this could help put an end to racially discriminatory gerrymandering. Courts have recently been requiring a showing of "discriminatory intent" at the time the lines were drawn before they will strike such lines as illegal. Preclearance, by contrast, would shift the burden of proof to those drawing the lines. They would have to prove that discrimination would not result.[118]

Another area for reform is the parties' nomination procedures. Short of centralizing the entire process, certain changes would improve representation in the present procedure. The Democratic party needs to abandon its "15 percent rule," which requires a candidate to get at least 15 percent of a state's primary votes in order to be awarded any convention delegates. Elimination of that rule would give fairer representation to citizens voting for a less dominant candidate. In addition, both parties should be encouraged to extend, not narrow, their affirmative action efforts. Not only should there be race and sex quotas for delegations to the national nominating conventions, but there should be class quotas as well. More people from the middle, working, and lower classes need to participate directly in whatever decisions occur, and the national parties should develop a formula that would allow them to use party funds to subsidize the convention expenses of those who need such assistance.

Campaign Financing.   Private money needs to be as far removed from the electoral process as possible. People with large personal fortunes should not have added influence over elections or elected officials by means of campaign contributions. One way would be to extend the Campaign Finance Act to further limit the amount of private money individuals can contribute to candidates and political parties. States such as Minnesota and cities such as Los Angeles and New York have already moved forward in this area.[119]

Yet, to more fully accomplish the goal of divorcing money from politics, the nation needs to work toward complete public financing of all political campaigns. A more equitable version of the existing presidential model could be adopted at all levels, and states such as Maine have already begun to adopt this type of system.[120] Meanwhile, if current congressional representatives remain resistant to providing such funds to their challengers, a constitutional amendment may be in order, requiring public financing as a necessary extension of the fundamental right to vote. In addition, the cost could be reduced by requiring radio and television stations to provide a set amount of free airtime to all candidates, with no purchases of additional time allowed. That practice already exists to a degree in countries as diverse as Great Britain and Japan; and the basic principle was endorsed by both President Bill Clinton and FCC Chairman Reed Hundt.[121]

It appears that a constitutional amendment also will be necessary to reverse the U.S. Supreme Court's *Buckley v. Valeo* ruling of 1976. Once public financing is in place, candidates must not be free to spend their own fortunes in their campaigns, even if they would rather do that than accept public financing. In addition, there should be no private spending on a candidate's behalf. If the Court feels that the First Amendment presently precludes such a rule, democracy would seem to require that the constitution be altered to allow for this change.

Toward Real Choices

Multiparty System. American voters, despite their current level of alienation, seem quite capable of casting rational ballots when presented with clear and substantial choices.[122] Therefore, once voter input becomes more equalized, a viable multiparty system seems essential if real choices are to be available on a regular basis. To achieve that will require serious alterations in the various rules that presently reinforce the inherently conservative two-party arrangement. For example, multimember districts could be used, with representatives chosen by proportional representation and cumulative voting.[123] Lenient national standards should govern the petitioning process, so that small parties can more easily find their way onto general election ballots. The Federal Election Commission must be reconstituted to include minor-party representatives, and this newly constituted body must find a formula for public financing that funds all established parties in the same way that the two major parties are presently funded. In addition, the equal-time provision must be rewritten to guarantee that all parties certified by the FEC receive their fair share of free time on the airwaves.

Stronger Political Parties. Besides opening the door to a larger number of political parties, those parties must be strong enough to lead, educate, and govern once they come through that door. If they are to be expected to propose meaningful platforms and execute those policies if elected, existing rules and practices must be altered.[124] Most importantly, the nation needs to move toward a parliamentary system. Party nominees should be chosen by party members in caucus settings, not by the more ephemeral primary process. In addition, this caucus system must be centralized enough so that each party speaks with one voice across the various states, and disloyal elected officials can be summarily denied nomination the next time around. Public financing and television airtime should be channeled through the party organizations, not given directly to candidates. Finally, top members of the executive branch should be chosen from the ranks of the elected legislature. In point of fact, a bona fide multiparty system could lead to this even under current arrangements, as the President of the United States would most likely be chosen in the House of Representatives when no candidate achieved the electoral college majority required.[125] Both this last proposal and the strengthening of party control over representatives elected under party banners would go a long way toward overcoming the almost unbelievable American "legislative maze" discussed next.

NOTES

1. Ralph Bunche in Dewey Grantham (ed.), *The Political Status of the Negro in the Age of FDR* (Chicago: University of Chicago Press, 1973), p. 88.
2. Joseph Schumpeter, *Capitalism, Socialism, and Democracy* (New York: Harper & Row, 1950), pp. 273–283.

3. In the original states, for instance, only Pennsylvania allowed the nonpropertied to vote.

4. Chicago Tribune Staff, *The American Millstone: An Examination of the Nation's Permanent Underclass* (Chicago: Contemporary Books, 1986), pp. 34–35.

5. Staughton Lynd, "Slavery and the Founding Fathers," in Melvin Drimmer (ed.), *Black History: A Reappraisal* (Garden City, N.Y.: Anchor/Doubleday, 1969). Also see Hanes Walton, Jr., *Black Political Parties* (New York: Free Press, 1972), pp. 20–23.

6. For example, see Jack Bass, "Election Laws and their Manipulation to Exclude Minority Voters," in *The Right to Vote: A Rockefeller Foundation Conference* (New York: Rockefeller Foundation, 1981), pp. 1–32; J. Morgan Kousser, "The Undermining of the First Reconstruction: Lessons for the Second," in Chandler Davidson, ed., *Minority Vote Dilution* (Washington, D.C.: Howard University Press, 1984), pp. 27–46; Steven Lawson, *Black Ballots: Voting Rights in the South, 1944–1969* (New York: Columbia University Press, 1976), pp. 6–8.

7. Harold Gosnell, *Machine Politics: Chicago Model* (Chicago: University of Chicago Press, 1934,1968); James Q. Wilson, *Negro Politics* (New York: Free Press, 1965).

8. For example, see Bernard Grofman, et al., *Minority Representation and the Quest for Voting Equality* (New York: Cambridge University Press, 1992); John O'Loughlin, "Racial Gerrymandering: Its Potential Impact on Black Politics in the 1980s," in Michael Preston, et al., eds., *The New Black Politics: The Search For Political Power* (New York: Longman, 1982), chap. 11; Eddie Williams and Milton Morris, "Is the Electoral Process Stacked against Minorities?" in A. James Reichley, ed., *Elections American Style* (Washington, D.C.: Brookings Institute, 1987), pp. 141–145; John Bennett and Peter Brown, "U.S. sues Georgia over runoff law; dilution of black vote claimed," Memphis *Commercial Appeal*, August 10, 1990, p. A9; James Barnes, "Minority Mapmaking," *National Journal*, April 7, 1990, pp. 837–839; James Barnes, "Minority Poker," *National Journal*, May 4, 1991, pp. 1034–1039.

9. For example, see Bernard Grofman and Chandler Davidson, eds., *Controversies in Minority Voting: The Voting Rights Act in Perspective* (Washington, D.C.: Brookings Institute, 1992), especially part I.

10. See Robert Smith and Richard Seltzer, *Race, Class, and Culture: A Study in Afro-American Mass Opinion* (Albany, N.Y.: SUNY Press, 1992), pp. 35–36, 62–63; Michael Preston, "The 1984 Presidential Primary: Who Voted for Jesse Jackson and Why?" in Lucius Barker and Ronald Walters, eds., *Jesse Jackson's 1984 Presidential Campaign* (Urbana: University Of Illinois Press, 1989).

11. For example, see Hanes Walton, Jr., *Invisible Politics: Black Political Behavior* (Albany, N.Y.: State University of New York Press, 1985), pp. 108–109; *National Journal*, July 20, 1991, p. 1802; U.S. Department of Commerce, Bureau of the Census, *Statistical Abstracts of the United States, 1995* (Washington, D.C.: GPO, 1995), Tables 459, 461.

12. It is important to note that the data on the causes of black political behavior are severely limited. As Hanes Walton, Jr., so aptly points out, nearly all that is known has been drawn from national samples of fewer than 400 blacks, even though a sample of 1,500 is normally required in order to reduce the sampling error to 3 percent. The black population was not systematically sampled as a separate entity but simply as one of the many facets of the American electorate. That significant limitation must be kept in mind when reviewing explanations in the text. See Walton, *Invisible Politics*, pp. 78–82.

13. Katherine Tate, *From Protest to Politics: The New Black Voters in American Elections* (Cambridge, Mass.: Harvard University Press, 1994), chap. 4; Walton, *Invisible Politics*, chap. 5; Cathy Cohen and Micahel Dawson, "Neighborhood Poverty and African-American Politics," *American Political Science Review* 87 (June 1993), pp. 286–302.

14. It should be noted that 13 states permanently bar convicted felons from voting, while 46 states deny the franchise to those presently in prison. See Sentencing Project, *Intended*

and Unintended Consequences: State Racial Disparities in Imprisonment (Washington, D.C.: Sentencing Project, 1997); *New York Times*, January 30, 1997; *Washington Post*, January 30, 1997, p. A3.

15. See Lester Salamon and Stephen Van Evera, "Fear, Apathy, and Discrimination," *American Political Science Review* (December 1973), pp. 1288–1306; Douglas St. Angelo and Paul Puryear, "Fear, Apathy, and Other Dimensions of Black Voting,"in Preston, *The New Black Politics*; Charles V. Hamilton, *The Bench and the Ballot: Southern Federal Judges and Black Votes* (New York: Oxford University Press, 1973), chap. 8; Don Edwards, "The Voting Rights Act of 1965, As Amended," in Lorn Foster, ed., *The Voting Rights Act: Consequences and Implications* (New York: Praeger, 1985), p. 7; *New York Times*, November 10, 1988; *Nation*, April 9, 1988, p. 486; Richard Cloward and Frances Fox Piven, *Why Americans Don't Vote* (New York: Pantheon, 1988).

16. For example, see the work of the Atlanta-based Voter Education Project. Also *Vote Fraud Trials Threaten Democracy* (Alabama Blackbelt Defense Committee, Gainesville, Ala.: February, 1986).

17. For example, see Charles V. Hamilton, "Political Access, Minority Participation, and the New Normalcy," in Leslie Dunbar, ed., *Minority Report: What Has Happened to Blacks, Hispanics, American Indians, and Other Minorities in the Eighties* (New York: Pantheon Books, 1984).

18. For example, see Theodore Lowi's Preface to the Second Edition of Gosnell, *Machine Politics*; Marilyn Lashley, "Reclaiming the State: Representative Government and Public Policy Access," in Marilyn Lashley and Melanie Njeri Jackson, eds., *African Americans and the New Policy Consensus* (Westport, Conn.: Greenwood Press, 1994).

19. For example, see Hamilton, "Political Access, Minority Participation, and the New Normalcy."

20. Walton, *Invisible Politics*, chap. 5; Marcus Pohlmann and Michael Kirby, *Racial Politics at the Crossroads: Memphis Elects Dr. W. W. Herenton* (Knoxville: University of Tennessee, 1996); St. Angelo and Puryear, "Fear, Apathy, and Other Dimensions."

21. *Washington Post*, March 6, 1983, p. A2; also see *New York Times*, November 16, 1987.

22. For a general discussion of such strategies as applied over time, see Ronald Walters, *Black Presidential Politics in America: A Strategic Approach* (Albany, N.Y.: SUNY Press, 1988).

23. Chuck Stone, *Black Political Power in America* (Indianapolis: Bobbs-Merrill, 1964); quoted in *New York Times*, July 23, 1979.

24. Quoted in Robert Allen, *Black Awakening in Capitalist America: An Analytical History* (Garden City, N.Y.: Anchor/Doubleday, 1969), p. 143.

25. A rationale for the latter two strategies can be found in Kwame Toure and Charles V. Hamilton, *Black Power* (New York: Random House, 1967), chaps. 4–5.

26. Quoted in George Breitman (ed.), *The Last Year of Malcolm X* (New York: Merit, 1967), p. 109

27. According to CBS/New York Times exit polls, Jackson managed 77 percent of the black vote in 1984 and 92 percent in 1988. For a fuller discussion, see Tate, *From Protest to Politics*; Michael Dawson, *Behind the Mule: Race and Class In African-American Politics* (Princeton, N.J.: Princeton University Press, 1994), pp. 137–142; Walters, *Black Presidential Politics in America*.

28. Allen, *Black Awakening*, p. 273.

29. Quoted in Tate, *From Protest to Politics*, p. ix.

30. For a fuller discussion of this strategy, see ibid.

31. For example, see R. W. Apple, "G.O.P. Tries Hard to Win Black Votes, but Recent History Works Against It," *New York Times*, September 19, 1996.

32. See Paul Lewinsohn, *Race, Class, and Party* (New York: Grosset & Dunlap, 1965), pp. 173–174.

33. Following the switch that occurred from 1936 to 1944, blacks could normally be counted on to cast at least 80 to 90 percent of their votes for the Democratic presidential candidate, a nearly complete reversal of what could be found prior to 1936.

34. Democratic party registration and identification jumped abruptly from roughly 50 percent prior to 1964 to more than three-quarters of all black partisans thereafter. A sizable number of black independents did appear beginning in the 1970s, however, and they will be discussed later in this chapter.

35. For a general summary, see Tate, *From Protest to Politics*, chap. 3; Dawson, *Behind the Mule*, pp. 127–135.

36. For example, see Dan Carter, *From George Wallace to Newt Gingrich: Race in the Conservative Revolution* (Baton Rouge, La.: Louisiana State University Press, 1996).

37. Apple, "G.O.P. Tries Hard . . . "

38. The presidential exceptions have been: 1956, when 36% of the black vote was cast for incumbent President Eisenhower; 1960, when the Democrat's nominated a northern Catholic candidate (Kennedy) who managed only 71 percent of the black vote; and 1992, when Ross Perot siphoned off 7 percent of the black vote, leaving the Democratic candidate, Bill Clinton, with 82 percent.

   Also, Oscar DePriest (Ill.), Gary Franks (Conn.), and J.C. Watts (Okla.) are black Republicans who served in the U.S. House; while Ed Brooke (Mass.) was a black U.S senator.

   See Lucius Barker and Mack Jones, *African Americans and the American Political System* (Englewood Cliffs, N.J.: Prentice Hall, 1994), p. 230; Louis Bolce, Gerald DeMaio, and Douglas Muzzio, "Blacks and the Republican Party: The 20% Solution," *Political Science Quarterly* 107 (Spring 1992), pp. 63–80; Dawson, *Behind the Mule*; Tate, *From Protest to Politics*, chap. 2; Franklin Gilliam and Kenny Whitby, "Race, Class, and Attitudes toward Social Welfare Spending: An Ethclass Intrepretation, *Social Science Quarterly* 70 (March 1989), pp. 88–100.

39. See Walton, *Invisible Politics*, pp. 140–146.

40. See Wilson Record, *Race and Radicalism* (Ithaca, N.Y.: Cornell University Press, 1964); Wilson Record, *The Negro and the Communist Party* (New York: Atheneum, 1971); Henry Williams, *Black Response to the American Left*, 1917–1920 (Princeton, N.J.: Princeton University Press, 1973); Harold Cruse, "Revolutionary Nationalism and the Afro-American," *Studies on the Left* (1962).

41. See Walton, *Black Political Parties*.

42. Gallup polls found that figure to be 15 percent in 1950 and 24 percent by 1993.

43. Warren Miller and Santa Traugott, *American National Election Studies Data Sourcebook, 1952–1986* (Cambridge, Mass.: Harvard University Press, 1989); Everett Carll Ladd, *Transformations of the American Party System* (New York: Norton, 1978).

44. Walton, *Invisible Politics*, pp. 120–124. Other important analyses of the contemporary black electorate include Rod Bush (ed.), *The New Black Vote* (San Francisco: Synthesis Publications, 1984); James Jennings and Melvin King, *From Access to Power: Black Politics in Boston* (Cambridge, Mass.: Schenkman, 1986).

45. Gallup/Joint Center for Policy Studies poll, Summer 1986, reported in the Memphis *Commercial Appeal*, August 5, 1987, p. A9. Also see *New York Times*, October 27, 1988.

46. M. Carl Holman, president of the National Urban Coalition, quoted in *New York Times*, April 20, 1983.

47. Walton, *Invisible Politics*, p. 83.

48. Actually, the first black governor was P.B.S. Pinchback of Louisiana (1872–1873).

49. For example, see Lucius Barker, ed., *Black Electoral Politics* (New Brunswick, N.J.: Transaction, 1990); Lawrence Bobo and Franklin Gilliam, "Race, Sociopolitical Participation, and Black Empowerment," *American Political Science Review* 84 (June 1990), pp.

377–393; *New York Times*, June 5, 1991; Leonard Cole, *Blacks in Power* (Princeton, N.J.: Princeton University Press, 1976); Sharon Watson, "Do Mayors Matter?" paper presented at the annual meeting of the American Political Science Association, Washington, D.C., August 1980; Edmund Keller, "The Impact of Black Mayors on Urban Policy," *Annals of the American Academy of Political and Social Science* (September 1978); William Keech, *The Impact of Negro Voting* (Chicago: Rand McNally, 1968).

50. Harold Stanley and Richard Niemi, *Vital Statistics on American Politics* (Washington, D.C.: CQ Press, 1992), pp. 395–397; Smith and Seltzer, *Race, Class, and Culture*, pp. 16–17.

51. Neal Peirce, "Minorities Slowly Gain State Offices," *National Journal*, January 5, 1991, p. 33. Also see Frank Parker, *Black Votes Count* (Chapel Hill: University of North Carolina Press, 1990).

52. For example, see James Barnes, "Into the Mainstream," *National Journal*, February 3, 1990, pp. 262–266.

53. For example, see Sheila Collins, *The Rainbow Challenge: The Jackson Campaign and the Future of American Politics*, (New York: Monthly Review Press, 1986), p. 90.

54. Paul Friesema, "Black Control of Central Cities: The Hollow Prize," *Journal of the American Institute of Planners* (March 1969).

55. For example, see Marcus Pohlmann, *Governing the Postindustrial City* (New York: Longman, 1993), chap. 9.

56. For example, see Diane Pinderhughes, "The Black Vote—The Sleeping Giant," in National Urban League, *The State of Black America, 1984* (New York: National Urban League, 1984), pp. 69–93.

57. See Marcus Pohlmann, *Political Power in the Postindustrial City* (Millwood, N.Y.: Associated Faculties Press, 1986, pp. 128–129; *New York Times*, January 18, 1980; March 28, 1978. For a more general discussion of this subject, see George Sinkler, *The Racial Attitudes of American Presidents* (Garden City, N.Y.: Doubleday, 1972).

58. Bureau of the Census, *Statistical Abstracts of the United States, 1995*, Table 459.

59. For example, see G. Bingham Powell, Jr., "American Voter Turnout in Comparative Perspective," *American Political Science Review* 80 (March 1986), pp. 20–21, 36.

60. Collins, *Rainbow Challenge*, p. 89.

61. *Buckley v. Valeo* 424 U.S. 1 (1976).

62. *Colorado Republican Federal Campaign Committee v. FEC* (1996). As of 1996, then, federal law limited individual contributions to $1,000 per presidential candidate, $2,000 per congressional candidate, $5,000 per Political Action Committees (PAC), and $20,000 per party for "hard money" purposes (defined below). PACs were only allowed to give $15,000 per party. Corporations (since 1907) and labor unions (since 1943) may not give any money directly to candidates, but they were now allowed to give unlimited amounts to political parties for "soft money" purposes (defined below). For example, see Eliza Newlin Carney, "Party Time," *National Journal*, October 19, 1996, pp. 2214–2218; *New York Times*, December 26, 1996.

63. For examples, see James Barnes, "The Great 'Soft'-Money Flood of '96," *National Journal*, June 1, 1996, p. 1219; Eliza Newlin Carney, "Air Strikes," *National Journal*, June 15, 1996, p. 1313; James Barnes, "The Old Soft-Money Shoe," *National Journal*, September 30, 1995, p. 2446; Robin Toner, "Interest Groups Take New Route To Congressional Election Arena," *New York Times*, August 20, 1996.

64. Eliza Newlin Carney, "Backdoor PACs," *National Journal*, March 2, 1996, pp. 468–473; Dan Clawson, Alan Neustadtl, and Denise Scott, *Money Talks* (New York: Basic Books, 1992); Joan Lowry, "Taking Congress Off The Block," Memphis *Commercial Appeal*, March 14, 1993, p. B3; Maxwell Glen, "Republicans and Democrats Battling to Raise Big

Bucks for Vote Drives," *National Journal* (September 1, 1984), p. 1618; Thomas Edsall, *The New Politics of Inequality* (New York: Norton, 1984); *Public Citizen* (May-June 1988), p. 14.

65. *New York Times*, October 18, 1996; December 26, 1996; Neil Lewis, "Limits on Donating to Candidates Aren't Deterring the Big Spenders," *New York Times*, May 16, 1992; Elizabeth Drew, *Politics and Money* (New York: Macmillan, 1983), p. 107.

66. See *New York Times*, October 18, 1996; December 26, 1996; January 3, 1997; Peter Stone, "Labyrinth of Loopholes," *National Journal*, November 25, 1995, pp. 2912–2917.

67. For example, see *New York Times*, December 26, 1996; Richard Hall and Frank Wayman, "Buying Time," *American Political Science Review* 84 (September 1990), pp. 797–820.

68. Quoted in *New York Times*, December 26, 1996.

69. Interview on NBC Nightly News, October 23, 1996.

70. See *New York Times*, October 18, 1996; December 26, 1996; James Barnes, "Greener Acres," *National Journal*, April 23, 1994, pp. 950–953; Jean Cobb, et al., "All The President's Donors," *Common Cause Magazine*, March/April 1990, pp. 21–40; David Adamany, "Money, Politics, and Democracy: A Review Essay," *American Political Science Review* (March 1977), p. 291; Edsall, *New Politics of Inequality*.

71. Walter Burnham, *Critical Elections and the Mainsprings of American Politics* (New York: Norton, 1970). More recently, see Kevin Phillips, *The Politics of Rich and Poor* (New York: Harper Collins, 1990), pp. 47–51.

72. William Winpinsinger, president of the International Association of Machinists, *Guardian* (Fall 1981).

73. E. E. Schattschneider, *Party Government* (New York: Holt, Rinehart and Winston, 1942), p. 129.

74. Julius Turner, *Party and Constituency: Pressures on Congress* (Baltimore: Johns Hopkins Press, 1970), pp. 16–17; *Congressional Quarterly Almanacs* (Washington, D.C.: Congressional Quarterly, various years).

75. See Norman Ornstein, Thomas Mann, and Michael Malbin, *Vital Statistics on Congress, 1993–1994* (Washington, D.C.: CQ Press, 1994); Harold Stanley and Richard Niemi,*Vital Statistics on American Politics* (Washington, D.C.: CQ Press, 1990), p. 132; Everett Carll Ladd, Jr., "On Mandates, Realignments, and the 1984 Presidential Election," *Political Science Quarterly* 100 (Spring 1985), p. 23.

76. See Richard Hofstadter, *The Idea of a Party System* (Berkeley: University of California Press, 1969); Henry Jones Ford, *The Rise and Growth of American Politics* (New York: Macmillan, 1898).

77. For example, see William Greider, *Who Will Tell The People: The Betrayal of American Democracy* (New York: Simon and Schuster, 1992); Charles O. Jones, "The Role of the Campaign in Congressional Politics,"in M. Kent Jennings and Harmon Ziegler (eds.), *The Electoral Process* (Englewood Cliffs, N.J.: Prentice-Hall, 1966); Warren Miller and Donald Stokes, "Constituency Influence in Congress," *American Political Science Review* (March 1963), pp. 45–56.

78. For example, see Jerry Hagstrom, "Ad Attack," *National Journal*, April 4, 1992, pp. 810–815; Joel Swerdlow, "The Decline of The Boys On the Bus," *Washington Journalism Review* (January/February 1981), pp. 15–19; A. James Reichley, *The Life of the Parties* (New York: Free Press, 1992).

79. See Stephen Ansolabehere and Shanto Iyengar, *Going Negative: How Attack Ads Shrink and Polarize The Electorate* (New York: Free Press, 1995); Jack Germond and Jules Witcover, "Why Americans Don't Go To The Polls," *National Journal*, November 23, 1996, p. 2562; Randall Rothenberg, "Voters Complain Negative Campaigns Are Driving Them Away," *New York Times*, November 3, 1990; David Broder, "Massive Survey Finds Polit-

ical Gridlock of Growing Cynicism," *Washington Post*, September 19, 1990; Greider, *Who Will Tell The People*.

80. For example, see Jonathan Rauch, *Demosclerosis* (New York: Times Books, 1994).
81. Collins, *Rainbow Challenge*, p. 228. Also see Bernard Sanders, "This Country Needs a Third Political Party," *New York Times*, January 3, 1989.
82. For further discussion of the moderating influence of the American political party system, see Thomas Dye and Harmon Ziegler, *The Irony of Democracy* (Belmont, Cal.: Wadsworth, 1993), pp. 167–168; Clinton Rossiter, *Parties and Politics in America* (Ithaca, N.Y.: Cornell University Press, 1960); Austin Ranney, *Curing the Mischief of Faction* (Berkeley: University of California Press, 1975); Burnham, *Critical Elections*, p. 90.
83. For example, see Morris Fiorina, *Retrospective Voting in America* (New Haven, Conn.: Yale University Press, 1981); *Business Week*, June 11, 1984; *Washington Post*, May 27, 1988.
84. Cited in *National Journal*, December 7, 1996, p. 2667. Also see *Times Mirror* survey data presented in the *New York Times*, September 21, 1994.
85. *New York Times*, November 16,1980; Gallup Opinion Index (December 1980), p. 30; Everett Carll Ladd, "The Brittle Mandate," *Political Science Quarterly* (Spring 1981).
86. For an outline of each state's petitioning requirements and deadlines as they applied to the 1996 presidential election, see *New York Times*, September 28, 1995. And for a detailed case study of how the petitioning process protects incumbents, see Larry Rockefeller, "Primaries Are a Protection Racket," *New York Times*, September 15, 1992. Also see Michael Specter, "New York's Arcane Election Laws May keep Tsongas Off Primary Ballot," *New York Times*, February 28, 1992.
87. *New York Times*, April 1, 1980.
88. The sponsoring League of Women voters has designed its own qualifying criteria, based almost exclusively on the minor party candidate's standing in national public opinion polls. Thus, they did allow Ross Perot to participate in 1992, but not in 1996. For a full listing of the criteria applied in the 1996 decision, see *New York Times*, September 19, 1996. Also see James Barnes, "The Debate Over The Debates," *National Journal*, September 28, 1996, p. 2084.
89. For example, see Howard Zinn, *A People's History of the United States* (New York: Harper & Row, 1980), pp. 542–543; Edward Greenberg, *The American Political System* (Boston: Little, Brown, 1983), pp. 290–293.
90. James Weinstein, *The Decline of American Socialism* (New York: Monthly Review Press, 1967).
91. See Richard Walton, "Two-Party Monopoly," *Nation*, August 30-September 6, 1980.
92. *Timmons v. Twin Cities Area New Party* (1997). Also see Linda Greenhouse, "High Court Deals Setback to Minor Parties," *New York Times*, April 29, 1997; Jack Germond and Jules Witcover, "The Court Toasts The Two-Party System," *National Journal*, May 3, 1997, p. 890.
93. For example, see Robert Lichter and Richard Noyes, *Good Intentions Make Bad News: Why Americans Hate Campaign Journalism* (Boston: Rowland and Littlefield, 1995).
94. Roosevelt garnered 88 electoral votes in 1912 as well, also the most by a third-party presidential candidate in U.S. history. After Roosevelt, the next best third-party presidential showings in this century have been Ross Perot's 18.9 percent (0 electoral votes) in 1992, Robert LaFollette's 16.6 percent (13 electoral votes) in 1924, and George Wallace's 13.5 percent (46 electoral votes) in 1968.
95. For example, see Pohlmann, *Governing the Postindustrial City*.
96. Allen, *Black Awakening*, p. 187.
97. C. T. Vivian, *Black Power and the American Myth* (Philadelphia: Fortress, 1970), p. 98.

98. For example, see Thomas Dye, *Who's Running America?* (Englewood Cliffs, N.J.: Prentice-Hall, 1995), chap. 3.

99. Richard Hamilton, *Class and Politics in the United States* (New York: Wiley, 1972), p. 507. Also see Lewis Lipsitz, "On Political Belief: The Grievances of the Poor," in Phillip Green and Sanford Levinson (eds.), *Power and Community* (New York: Pantheon, 1970); Kenneth Dolbeare and Murray Edelman, *American Politics* (Lexington, Mass.: Heath, 1981), pp. 260–268.

100. Roper Organization, *Roper Report* 93–8 (August 7–14, 1993); Center for Political Studies, University of Michigan, *National Election Studies*, 1956–1996; Sidney Verba, et al., "Citizen Activity: Who Participates? What Do They Say?" *American Political Science Review* 87 (June 1993); Lester Milbraith and M. L. Goel, *Political Participation* (Chicago: Rand McNally, 1977).

101. For example, see Powell, "American Voter Turnout in Comparative Perspective;"*The Economist* (December 1978).

102. For example, see Verba, et al., "Citizen Activity . . . "; Ruy Teixeira, *The Disappearing American Voter* (Washington, D.C.: Brookings Institution, 1992); Cloward and Piven, *Why Americans Don't Vote*; Ruy Teixeira, *Why Americans Don't Vote: Turnout Decline in the United States, 1960–1984* (New York: Greenwood Press, 1987); Greider, *Who Will Tell The People*; Eliza Newlin Carney, "Opting Out of Politics," *National Journal,* January 17, 1998, pp. 106–111.

103. Robert Erickson and Norman Luttbeg, *American Public Opinion* (New York: Wiley, 1973), p. 25; Subcommittee on Intergovernmental Relations, Confidence and Concern (Washington, D.C.: GPO, 1973), p. 215; *New York Times*, May 28, 1989; May 6, 1990; June 12, 1990.

104. William Flanigan and Nancy Zingale, *Political Behavior of the American Electorate* (Boston: Allyn & Bacon, 1978), p. 130.

105. *Congressional Quarterly Weekly Report;* Alan Abramowitz, "Incumbency, Campaign Spending, and the Decline of Competition in U.S. House Elections," *Journal of Politics* 53 (February 1991), pp. 34–56; David Brady, *Critical Elections and Congressional Policy Making* (Stanford: Stanford University Press, 1988); *New York Times*, June 15, 1987. Also see John Bibby, Thomas Mann, and Norman Ornstein, *Vital Statistics on Congress* (Washington, D.C.: American Enterprise Institute, 1980), pp. 53–54.

106. Bureau of the Census, *Statistical Abstracts of the United States, 1995*, Table 443. These numbers seem to be overstated by the fact that incumbents may choose to retire rather than face impending defeat; however, they also understate incumbent success by failing to delineate those incumbent defeats attributable to unfavorable redistricting. Overall, then, they remain a relatively reliable indicator.

107. Marcus Pohlmann, "The Electoral Impact of Partisanship and Incumbency Reconsidered," *Urban Affairs Quarterly* (June 1978), p. 500.

108. Abramowitz, "Incumbency, . . . "; *New York Times*, June 15, 1987; Federal Election Commission, *Reports on Financial Activity* (Washington, D.C.: GPO, various years).

109. Murray Edelman, *The Symbolic Uses of Politics* (Urbana: University of Illinois Press, 1964), p. 17.

110. Lester Salamon, "Protest, Politics, and Modernization in the American South," Ph.D. dissertation, Harvard University, 1971, pp. 627–628.

111. Raymond Wolfinger and Steven Rosenstone, "Effect of Registration Laws on Voter Turnout," *American Political Science Review* 72 (March 1978).

112. Concerned about increasing the number of voters likely to vote for Democratic candidates, congressional Republicans succeeded in eliminating the provision that also would have allowed registration at welfare offices. Nevertheless, "motor-voter" laws do appear to have increased registration in the states where they have been employed. For example,

see Richard Cloward and Frances Fox Piven, "Democracy on Wheels," *New York Times*, June 17, 1992.

For other proposals as well as a fuller rationale for increasing voter participation, see Arend Lijphart, "Unequal Participation: Democracy's Unresolved Dilemma, *American Political Science Review* 91 (March 1997), pp. 1–14.

113. See *New York Times*, November 17, 1995.

114. For a classic example, see William Kornhauser, *The Politics of Mass Society* (New York: Free Press, 1959).

115. *Congressional Record*, vol. 125, no. 11 (February 5, 1979).

116. For example, see Toure and Hamilton, *Black Power*, pp. 166–172; Jacqueline Pope, "The Colonizing Impact of Public Service Bureaucracies in Black Communities," in James Jennings, ed., *Race, Politics, and Economic Development* (New York: Verso, 1992).

117. See Bennett Harrison and Barry Bluestone, "The Incidence and Regulation of Plant Closings," in Larry Sawers and William Tabb (eds.), *Sunbelt/Snowbelt* (New York: Oxford University Press, 1984), pp. 368–402; William Tabb, "A Pro-people Urban Policy," in William Tabb and Larry Sawers (eds.), *Marxism and the Metropolis* (New York: Oxford University Press, 1984), p. 371; *Public Citizen* (May–June 1988), pp. 15–17.

118. John O'Loughlin, "Racial Gerrymandering," in Preston, *The New Black Politics*.

119. For example, see Richard Berke, "Campaign-Fund Limits: Congress Blushes, States Act," *New York Times*, June 24, 1990.

120. For example, see Eliza Newlin Carney, "Taking On the Fat Cats," *National Journal*, January 18, 1997, pp. 110–114.

121. *New York Times*, March 12, 1997; David Broder, "Where Money Goes," Memphis *Commercial Appeal*, February 12, 1997. For a compilation of more skeptical responses, see Eliza Newlin Carney, "Tuning Out Free TV," *National Journal*, April 12, 1997. Meanwhile, both PBS and Fox have voluntarily toyed with the idea. For example, see Michael Oreskes, "PBS Plans More Time for Candidates," *New York Times*, June 17, 1990; Lawrence Mifflin, "Fox To Give Free TV Time To Candidates For President," *New York Times*, February 27, 1996.

122. For example, see Benjamin Page and Robert Shapiro, *The Rational Public* (Chicago: University of Chicago Press, 1992).

123. In a "multimember" arrangement, besides determining the percentage of the vote each winner must attain, there are also a variety of ways of conducting the voting. For example:

(1) Candidates run for the seats available; the voter casts one vote for his or her most preferred candidate; and the top vote getters win the seats up for election that time.

(2) Canndidates run for the seats available; however, under this scheme the voter may cast the number of votes that corresponds to the number of positions up for election, and the top vote getters win the seats. Detroit and San Francisco select their entirely at-large city councils by this method. One slight variation, however, is that some such systems permit the voter to cast one or more of these votes for a particular candidate ("cumulative voting"). Cumulative voting was used to choose members of the Illinois legislature from 1870 to 1980. It also was employed in Pennsylvania. A theoretical justification is carefully presented in Lani Guinier, "The Triumph of Tokenism: The Voting Rights Act And The Theory Of Black Electoral Success," *Michigan Law Review* 89 (March 1991), pp. 1077–1154; and Lani Guinier, "No Two Seats: The Elusive Quest For Political Equality," *Virginia Law Review* 77 (November 1991), pp. 1414–1514. Also see Peter Applebome, "Where Ideas That Hurt Guinier Thrive," *New York Times*, June 5, 1993. For examples of how it has been used in Alabama localities to increase the number of black elected officials, see Edward Still, "Cumulative Voting and Limited Voting in Alabama," in Wilma Rule and Joseph Zimmerman, eds., *United States Electoral Systems* (New York: Praeger, 1992); *New York Times*, June 5, 1993.

(3) Candidates run for the seats available, and the voter may cast votes for as many of the candidates as he or she approves of ("approval voting"). Again, the top vote-getters win the seats. This is about the most consensual system available, with those ultimately chosen having the broadest bases of popular support.

(4) Candidates run for the seats available, and the voter orders his or her preferences as 1,2,3, etc. for the total number of positions to be filled. Thereafter, a formula is used to determine how many of these "weighted votes" are needed to be elected (the "Hare system"). A tremendous variety of such "proportional representation" schemes are employed throughout the world, but most are designed to be used in highly partisan elections (normally in parliamentary systems), or at least in elections where people cast their ballots for a particular group rather than particular candidates. Under the "list plan" for instance, each party or group presents an ordered slate, wins a number of seats proportionate to their party/group percentage of the total vote, and then particular winners are assigned beginning at the top of their slate. See Douglas Amy, *Real Choices/New Voices: The Case for Proportional Representation Elections in the United States* (New York: Columbia University Press, 1993); E. Lakeman, *How Democracies Vote: A Study of Majority and Proportional Electoral Systems* (London: Faber and Faber, 1974). A few proportional representation arrangements have been tried in the United States (e.g., Boulder [1918–1950], Cleveland [1924–1934], Cincinnati [1926–1957], Toledo [1936–1952], New York (1937–1945), and Worcester [1950–1960]). Some remnants are left in the Cambridge and New York City school board election systems. However, these are rare exceptions and the system in virtually nonexistent in U.S. cities today. For a discussion of the New York City experience, see Martin Gottlieb, "The 'Golden Age' of the City Council," *New York Times*, August 11, 1991.

(5) Candidates run for a particular at-large seat of their choice; the voter casts one vote in each race; and the top vote-getter in each race wins that particular seat ("winner-take-all"). Cities such as Memphis, Jacksonville, Houston, and Indianapolis have used this system for selecting their at-large councilpersons, filling each seat every election. An alternative is to stagger the terms of those elected from multimember districts such as these, as is done in the United States Senate.

124. For example, see Paul Starobin, "Dare to Bicker!" *National Journal*, March 22, 1997, pp. 558–563.

125. For example, see Theodore Lowi, "The Party Crasher," *New York Times Magazine*, August 23, 1992, pp. 28–33.

Chapter 8

The Legislative Arena

The Congress, the presidency, and the bureaucracy are intricately intertwined in the process of writing, passing, and executing the federal laws of the land. Thus they combine to form the legislative arena. Like its judicial and electoral counterparts, this arena is conservative by design. Beyond the unrepresentative demographics of its members, its rules and procedures make fundamental change extremely difficult to accomplish.

Legislation is initiated by either the president or the Congress. It must then often command majorities at more than 40 separate congressional junctures. It can be stalled at any one of those junctures and can even be checked by the threat of a filibuster in the Senate. Once the legislation survives this procedure, the president can veto it, and it will take two-thirds majorities on both house floors to override. And even if that succeeds, the executive bureaucracy may be slow to enforce the law after it is enacted. Clearly, legislated change, especially if at all controversial, is much easier to stop than to pass. The system is normally inclined toward small incremental changes at most rather than major comprehensive ones.

As a consequence, the legislative apparatus has been very difficult to move in the struggle to secure basic civil rights for African Americans. Although blacks have achieved passage of some major pieces of legislation, those gains have come sporadically, at a very high cost, and have proved difficult to sustain.

In the twentieth century, for example, despite a half century of formal lobbying, clear allegiance to the dominant party of the day, and decades of mounting organized protest, the Congress and the president continually failed to respond to black interests in a meaningful way. Finally, between 1957 and 1970, three civil rights acts, two voting rights acts, and a constitutional amendment to ban the poll tax became law.

The cost of gaining that legislation was high. Violent racial unrest stirred in more than 150 cities, leaving more than 100 people dead and thousands injured. Massive demonstrations and nonviolent civil disobedience also occurred across the nation. Although by no means a supporter of violence, even Martin Luther King, Jr., argued that at times you have to create a crisis in order to force a dialogue. In a political system so closely wedded to the status quo, that should not be surprising.

The battle does not end with the passage of legislation, however, as the laws then have to be implemented if change is actually to occur. Given the system of federalism, for example, much of that implementation is left to local white bureaucrats, many of whom come from the very areas that denied the rights in the first place.

But even more important is the fact that the federal government can take back what it gives out. This became quite obvious during the Reagan years, for instance, when social programs were cut back and enforcement of some major civil rights laws was relaxed. Without independent control over certain levers of power, blacks end up dependent both on white-created legislation and white administration of those laws.

Nevertheless, there have been a few hopeful signs. The growth of the Congressional Black Caucus has been a significant development, as has the increasing black presence at the top and bottom levels of the executive bureaucracy. Nevertheless, the legislative arena remains very resistant to change.

THE CONSERVATIVE DANCE OF LEGISLATION

> There's a breakdown in the . . . machinery. There are 100 gauntlets and 1,000 vetoes. . . . You simply can't sustain any kind of policy through that process.[1]

The "dance of legislation"[2] now often begins in the White House. After being advised by various members of the executive bureaucracy, the president sends a legislative proposal to the Congress. That proposal must wend its way through a veritable maze on Capitol Hill in order to gain passage. If passed, it returns to the president's desk to be signed—assuming that its final form is still acceptable. Then it must be implemented, at which point the executive bureaucracy returns to center stage.

The following discussion will consider each of these primary actors separately: the president, the Congress, and the bureaucracy. What results is a portrait of a massive and lumbering legislative machine, biased against fundamental change, except in times of crisis.

The Presidency

The president has come to be the single most important actor in the legislative process. But before beginning, it is worth noting that the president has really become the presidency. In the late 1920s, Herbert Hoover performed his executive functions with the help of one secretary and two assistants. Today, presidents are assisted by the Executive Office of the President, which employs more than 5,000 specialized staff persons. The risk inherent in relying on such a corps and the much larger federal bureaucracy for information and advice is that the president can at times become a veritable captive of these advisers.

Presidential Power.   In many ways, the growth and bureaucratization of the presidency reflect its expanded responsibilities and power. A good bit of this expansion can be attributed to both the march of events and technological developments.

Crises such as the Civil War and the Great Depression presented opportunities for unprecedented extensions of "emergency" presidential powers. During the Civil War, Abraham Lincoln assembled troops, drew money from the United States Treasury, and suspended a number of constitutional rights—all while the Congress was not even in session. To reduce panic during the Great Depression, Franklin Delano Roosevelt declared a "bank holiday"—closing the banks for 100 days simply by executive decree. In addition, since the United States has become increasingly involved in world politics, the president's role has grown even greater. As the single spokesperson for the nation as a whole, the president comes to be delegated considerable power in international affairs, especially if the public can be convinced that the country faces a serious foreign threat. Presidents also have nearly 500 pieces of legislation that extend them "emergency powers" under various circumstances, not to mention the precedents set by Lincoln, Roosevelt, and others. And all of that is true despite efforts to limit such accumulated powers with legislation such as the 1973 War Powers Act and the 1976 National Emergency Act.

The growth and development of the mass media has added potent tools to the arsenal of presidential power. Presidents can now speak directly to the nation, and they seem capable of commandeering media access virtually whenever they wish. Theodore Roosevelt pioneered strategic use of the press, and Franklin Roosevelt made comparably good use of the radio airwaves. John Kennedy and Ronald Reagan became masters of the most invasive medium of all, television. There is simply no way 535 members of the U.S. Congress, for instance, can speak singularly enough to compete with most presidents in the mass media.

Besides the opportunities afforded by perceived emergencies and media access, two constitutionally defined entities, the veto and the executive budget, have also evolved into potent weapons.

Since the days of Andrew Jackson, presidents have been vetoing legislation purely on policy grounds. Presidents originally felt this should be done only if they deemed the Constitution to have been violated by the legislation; nowadays, presidents feel free to veto simply because they do not like the policy. Even the threat of such a veto can normally force the Congress either to a compromise or to abandon the legislation altogether. The Congress needs to marshal two-thirds majorities in both houses if the veto is to be overridden, and that has proven to be difficult. Less than 4 percent of the approximately 2,500 presidential vetoes have ever been overridden by the Congress, and that figure does not include presidential "pocket vetoes" or the many situations in which the mere threat of a veto was enough to scuttle the legislation.[3] On top of all that, Congress handed the president a line-item veto as well.[4]

Even more important is the fact that much successful legislation has come to originate from the White House. Armed with the authority cited in Article 2, Section 3, of the Constitution ("[The president] shall from time to time give to the Congress information of the state of the Union, and recommend to their consideration such measures as he shall judge necessary and expedient"), the president is often setting the Congress's agenda, swaying both what will be discussed and the range of alternatives that will be considered. Of particular significance is the practice of introducing a full executive budget, a prerogative first formalized by President Harry S. Truman.[5]

Note the significance of the presidency in the process that results. Information is generated from a 3 million-person bureaucracy and compiled by the Office of Management and Budget—which happens to have some 600 staff members of its own. The president then sends the proposed legislation to the Congress, draws on the Congressional Liaison Office to help lobby it through, and sends top administrators to testify at committee hearings. In addition, accommodative legislators realize that come reelection time, the president can introduce additional legislation targeted to their constituents—a military base here, a water or highway project there. Once these rarely controversial rewards skip through the legislative process, those members of Congress are then invited to the White House for a photo session when the bill is signed, producing impressive pictures that will be beamed back home to appear in the local media.

Finally, the president not only has the first word but also one of the last. In particular, through appointments and personal leadership, the president can affect the enthusiasm with which the federal bureaucracy will implement any congressionally passed legislation.

Presidential Bias.   Just how close to the people is this increasingly powerful president? One can get a sense of that by looking both at the demographics of the individuals who have held that office and how one gets access to them.

To begin with, all but one of the American presidents has been a white Protestant man, and the exception was a white Catholic man. In addition to the narrowness of perspective likely to stem from such backgrounds, virtually all of them have been relatively wealthy professionals. Beyond that, most of the people they come to appoint to high office reflect the same elite characteristics.[6]

How does one get to speak to a president to make one's views known? Unless called on for advice, one of the only certain avenues is to buy one's way in. The Watergate hearings revealed that one could speak to Richard Nixon for a $50,000 campaign contribution.[7] During the Iran-contra investigation it came to light that a $300,000 private contribution to the Nicaraguan contras warranted a conversation with President Ronald Reagan.[8] George Bush doled out middle-level advisorial positions to large contributors.[9] And wealthy individuals could speak with President Clinton and even sleep in the Lincoln bedroom of the White House in return for sizable contributions to the Democratic Party.[10]

Nevertheless, even if one of these increasingly powerful presidents had the inclination to redistribute wealth and power from elites to nonelites, he or she would still encounter plenty of obstacles.

The Congress

Once legislation has emerged from the White House and been introduced on Capitol Hill, the dance becomes incredibly convoluted. Senator David Pryor (D-Ark.) characterized it as a "slow-motion system of inefficiency and procedural imprisonment." According to Senator Paul Trible (R-Va.), "the whole policymaking process stands at the brink of incoherence." Retiring Senator Thomas Eagleton (D-Mo.), exhausted and disillusioned, referred to it as an "unmanageable circus." Senator David Evans (R-Wash.) concluded, "There's a feeling of lack of accomplishment, or maybe more accurately a sense that the whole system is breaking down."[11] And Representative Richard Bolling (D-Mo.) wrote:

> In the many years I have been a member of Congress, [it] has revealed itself to me as ineffective in its role as a coordinate branch of the Federal Government, negative in its approach to national tasks, generally unresponsive to any but parochial economic interests. Its procedures, time-consuming and unwieldy, mask anonymous centers of irresponsible powers. Its legislation is often a travesty of what the national welfare requires.[12]

The Legislative Maze.   The most basic steps in this process were designed by the Founding Fathers, and the rest have emerged over time as the Congress has grown in size and responsibilities. Consider a typical piece of contested budgetary legislation as it successfully wends its way through this tangled maze.

1. Bill is introduced in the House.
2. Speaker refers the bill to committee.
3. Committee chair refers the bill to subcommittee.
4. Subcommittee approves its version of the bill.
5. Full committee approves its version of the bill.
6. Speaker places the bill on the House calendar.
7. Rules committee sets rules for the bill's debate.
8. Full House approves the rules.
9. Full House passes its version of the bill.
10. Senate leader refers the House bill to committee.
11. Committee chair refers the bill to subcommittee.
12. Subcommittee approves its version of the bill.
13. Full committee approves its version of the bill.
14. Leadership places the bill on the Senate calendar.
15. Full Senate passes its version of the bill.
16. House rejects changes, calls for a conference.
17. Senate agrees to join in a conference committee.
18. Conference committee passes a compromise version.
19. Full Senate accepts the compromise bill.
20. Full House accepts the compromise bill.
21. President signs the bill into law.[13]

Now the spending has been authorized. Repeat the entire process when it comes time for the spending to be appropriated (that is, when the checks are actually to be written). Since the Budget Act of 1974, the Congress has been striving to initiate its own budget rather than being so dependent on the president's agenda. In this newest budgetary process, the maze must be traversed in order to set targets and then negotiated again when time comes for official authorization in the Fall. Also, a bill may be referred to more than one committee each time around if its subject matter spills over into other committees' jurisdictions.

This is a highly conservative process. An opponent of a bill need only muster majority support at one of the many discretionary junctures and the bill may well die. In addition, if all else fails, the opposition may be able to launch a filibuster in the Senate, or the president may be persuaded to veto the legislation, increasing the steps necessary for passage.

Because the Senate allows unlimited debate on most legislation, a member can simply hold the floor for days and thus prevent any other debate or votes from taking place.[14] Rule 22 was added to allow the full Senate to halt any such filibuster. As the rule presently reads, 16 colleagues must be willing to incur the wrath of the filibustering member by signing a cloture petition. Once that is done, a vote can be taken, and 60 votes ends the debate. Even under the revised rules, only about 40 percent of cloture votes have been successful, besides the fact that many cloture efforts fail for lack of 16 signatures in the first place.[15] And since the mid–1970s, even the traditional filibuster has become somewhat obsolete.

There are now new and improved methods of filibustering that are impervious to the cloture rule. One involves the presentation of an endless stream of amendments, calling for a roll-call vote on each. Another is even more inventive. In the spring of 1987, for example, a group of Senate Republicans sought to forestall a vote on a military appropriations bill. John Warner (R-Va.) refused to vote on the routine motion of approving the previous day's journal. As the full Senate must vote to excuse a fellow senator from voting, a roll call was ordered on Warner's refusal. Dan Quayle (R-Ind.) then refused to vote on that motion, and a roll call was taken on Quayle's refusal. On and on it went.[16] Also in the Senate, individual members have traditionally been allowed to place a temporary *hold* on a nomination or piece of legislation. Today, such holds are often placed anonymously, indefinitely, and at very least serve notice that a filibuster is possible if the matter is pressed anyway.[17]

A presidential veto is always a possibility as well. And as we have seen, overrides of presidential vetoes have been relatively rare.

Thus if a proponent of a bill suspects defeat at any of the multiple legislative steps or can reasonably anticipate a filibuster or a presidential veto, the legislation is in serious trouble. Either the bill will never be introduced, a huge majority will have to be mustered to overcome the opposition, or a compromise will have to be struck with the bill's opponents. Even a single opponent can create havoc for virtually any proposed piece of legislation. Little wonder that it seems to take a national crisis before anything approaching fundamental comprehensive change can be steered through this incredible maze.[18]

Institutional Bias.   In addition to the heavy inclination toward stasis created by the formal procedures of the Congress, a number of informal realities shape the legislative dance. Bureaucratization and the increasing role of interest groups are readily apparent, as are various coping mechanisms. But even free of all the pressure, there is little reason to believe the typical congressperson is going to be inclined toward fundamental change.

The bureaucratization of the Congress is difficult to overlook. There are now roughly 300 specialized committees and subcommittees on Capitol Hill at any point in time, and their actions or inactions determine the fate of virtually all legislation.

For example, nearly two-thirds of strong committee recommendations survive on the floors of both houses of Congress. Not only do the individual congresspersons serving on these various committees play enhanced roles, but staff people are also proliferating in both numbers and importance. As recently as 1947, there were approximately 500 committee staff persons and another 2,000 working directly for individual representatives. A half century later, those numbers had increased more than fivefold, to more than 3,000 committee staffers and more than 11,500 direct employees. Given the volume of legislation to be addressed and the resultant pace at which most representatives are forced to operate, there is little time for study or reflection. Instead, legislative detail and even much agenda setting are left to these unelected staffers. As Representative Michael Harrington put it before retiring, "The country has no goal, no sense of direction, no vision. Congress is a bureaucracy. We have government by managers and engineers."[19]

In addition, as the process has become decentralized, the role of the special-interest groups has been enhanced. As best as can be estimated, roughly 7,000 groups have some 15,000 representatives in Washington at any given time today. More than half are corporations, another quarter are professional or trade associations, and less than 2 percent represent civil rights or minority groups.[20] Possessing a far greater wealth of information than the average representative, these groups regularly appear at committee hearings to fill the record with facts and figures that support their particular position. They also arm friendly representatives with information as those congresspersons press the position outside committee chambers. Beyond that, interest-group activity on the Hill is only minimally regulated, and modern electronic technology allows them to communicate to a representative's constituents almost instantaneously to try either to reward or to punish the elected official for each action or inaction.[21]

Faced with a 1,300-page procedural manual, interest-group pressure, and an absence of strong party organizations to insulate them (see Chapter 7), it begins to become obvious why the Congress has developed a number of coping mechanisms that allow its members to protect their seats without challenging the existing maldistribution of wealth and power. For example, the majority of bills are introduced largely as political gestures, designed to appease constituents with the appearance of active support for their causes. Most never reemerge from committee, and thus "the Congress" as a body can be blamed for their deaths. Serious legislation also gets bogged down; consequently, much of it ends up getting lumped together into huge "continuing resolutions"—massive budgetary laws that simply continue existing levels of spending when changes have not been able to find their way through the maze. These allow the status quo to be maintained by including something that virtually every representative wants continued. Thus "pork barrel" legislation lives on, as each district continues to get its pet highway or water project, military base, or whatever. Little wonder that the Reagan administration's Grace Commission on government waste found huge inefficiencies—for example, it found that 2,700 of the nation's then 3,000 military bases could be shut down without doing any damage whatsoever to national security.

As a result, the Congress has tended to become a rather cozy and stagnant club in which members graciously trade favors in order to stay in office.[22] Rather than risk

engendering controversy, it is far easier to keep a low profile, leave the existing priorities of the Congress essentially as they are, and tend to constituent service. Such service is enhanced by going along with one's colleagues in order to gain their support—
support in getting seats on committees and subcommittees particularly relevant to
one's home district, not to mention ultimate passage of legislation that will benefit individuals in the district. Then, as seniority accumulates, a representative can become
a chairperson, a position that will allow more protection of these constituent tidbits
by virtue of the chair's agenda-setting discretion.

Even if every member of Congress had a safe seat and none of the obstructions
or lobbyist pressures existed, there are still good reasons to believe that these representatives would not be inclined to alter the present distribution of wealth and power
in the United States. These are largely middle-aged, upper-class, professional, white
males—unusually homogeneous by international standards.[23] Their congressional
compensation puts them in the top 1 percent of the population, with a combined income and benefit package exceeding $150,000 per year. They are asked to address
problems in the factory environment having never worked in one and to write med-
ical-care legislation without having ever had to stand in line at a public hospital. A
number have had financial interests in the very corporations with which they were
dealing.[24] Representative Ron Dellums (D-Cal.) concluded that they tend to be
"mediocre prima donnas who don't understand the level of human misery in this
country."[25]

Nonetheless, members of Congress must stand for reelection periodically. The
bureaucrats who populate the next tier in the process are almost completely insulated from popular pressure, have certain institutional agendas of their own, and are
regularly influenced by lobbyists as well.

The Bureaucracy

> Contrary to what civics textbooks might suggest, passing legislation today is just the very
> first step. After that, you have to run through a veritable gauntlet of administrative
> processes and procedures to get the law carried out.
>
> Rep. Ron Wyden (D-Ore.)[26]

It is no secret that the Founding Fathers set out to create a federal government that
would be dominated by the legislative branch. The experience with England's King
George III had not left most of them yearning for another dominant executive. Yet,
there is clear evidence today that the executive branch has grown much larger than
its legislative counterpart. The current United States Government Manual, for instance, contains approximately 40 pages devoted to the Congress and more than 600
pages describing the executive branch. It has not always been that way.

When George Washington took the oath of office in 1789, he was to administer a
federal bureaucracy of approximately 780 people. By the time Andrew Jackson assumed the office of president nearly a half century later, there were still fewer than
2,000 federal bureaucrats. Over the course of the next 100 years, the federal bureaucracy would grow significantly. By 1930, for example, Herbert Hoover was overseeing an executive branch that numbered 600,000. As the federal government has assumed more responsibilities, particularly with the emergence of Franklin Roosevelt's

New Deal, the figure has grown to nearly 3 million. That means the federal bureaucracy has increased almost fivefold since the early 1930s.

Besides the proliferation of federal responsibilities, however, there is another important explanation for this bureaucratic expansion. It appears to be far easier to create a new agency than to eliminate an existing one. For example, Common Cause studied this phenomenon over a 15-year period and found 236 agencies were created and only 21 were dissolved.[27] Once programs develop constituencies, it is very difficult to steer cuts past the members of Congress who represent the programs' constituents. Recall that the process of Congress is quite sensitive to the reelection needs of its members. In addition, the bureaucrats themselves become some of their own best lobbyists.

Bureaucratic Power.   Not only have bureaucracies developed a resilience to the congressional ax, but these unelected public officials have also accumulated a sizable amount of independent policy-making power. Harry Truman once confessed, "I thought I was president, but when it comes to these bureaucracies, I can't make them do a damn thing."[28]

Application Discretion.   When the Congress passes a law, it will almost always contain at least some ambiguous language. This allows flexibility as the law is applied by the bureaucracy. Among other things, this practice saves the Congress from having continually to rewrite its legislation to fit each new situation that arises. So while the Congress passes some 600 laws per year, the federal bureaucracy issues 10 times that many regulations. The Federal Register, which records all such administrative laws, often ends up containing more than 60,000 pages of fine print.

Besides filling in the gaps between the lines of congressionally passed laws, the bureaucracy also has ample opportunity to shape those laws in the course of enforcement. Each day bureaucrats must make decisions such as who meets federal guidelines and thus qualifies for federal monies or who is out of compliance with a federal regulation and thus faces penalties. This power is enhanced by the fact that most of these decisions are seldom visible by either the Congress, top-level administrators, or the public.[29] To keep ever more decisions out of the public eye, the executive branch has increased penalties for leaking information and has often been harsh in its punishment of *whistleblowers*—insiders who choose to go public with embarrassing revelations about internal bureaucratic matters.[30]

Agenda Setting.   Besides application discretion, bureaucrats are crucial sources of information and advice. They generally possess some of the most extensive expertise in their fields of specialization, and they also tend to be the ones asked to compile relevant data describing what is occurring in those areas. More and more of them even have their own public relations staffs. Consequently, they have ample opportunity to set the legislative agenda in the course of evaluating what has worked in the past and proposing what needs to be done in the future. As a case in point, when the air force asks for a new bomber, few people are in a position to second-guess those bureaucrats' assessment of the situation—especially since the size and complexity of government have left elected officials further and further removed from what is actually going on in the various fields. At the very least, short of major complaints or scandals, such bureaucrats are in a strong position to have their current budget and practices reapproved.[31]

Job Security.   A combination of civil-service status and unionization further insulates the bureaucracy. The overwhelming majority have attained their positions through civil-service procedures. They listed their qualifications, took a test, were ranked, and were later appointed by the Civil Service Commission primarily on the basis of that ranking. Not only are elected officials normally limited to a very marginal role in their hiring, but the bureaucrats thereafter can only be fired for serious cause, such as dereliction of duty. When they choose subtly to drag their feet rather than enthusiastically enforce a law they oppose, elected officials can do little about it. The tiny percentage of top-level administrators, appointed rather than hired through civil service, can be pressured and fired, but those appointed administrators are not in the position to do much more than persuade and cajole the bureaucrats beneath them. Career civil servants, a number of whom are also unionized, normally cannot be effectively commanded to do much of anything. They ultimately proceed pretty much as they deem best.

Institutional Bias.

A variety of bureaucratic realities mitigate against having this extensive power turned against the status quo. Close relationships tend to form between bureaucrats and the groups of people they serve or regulate. Meanwhile, regulation itself is often obstructed by a fragmentation of authority.

Clientelism.   For a variety of reasons, bureaucrats develop close affinities with their clients. To begin with, clients are valuable allies in each agency's standard quest to retain current levels of funding, if not increase them. As the Federal Communications Commission (FCC) fought the development of cable television, for example, the major networks became even closer political allies. Such affinity is also enhanced by the fact that individuals often move back and forth between the bureaucracy and their clientele group, a practice called the *revolving door* syndrome. As a case in point, Edward Herman found 21 of 33 FCC commissioners returning to the communications industry once they left the commission; most of the others retired.[32] More than one-half of all regulatory appointees previously served in the industry they are to regulate.[33]

A significant result of these trends have at times been variations of what are termed *iron triangles*. These are tight, mutually accommodative relationships among the client, the administrative agency, and the related congressional committee responsible for oversight. A classic example is the close working relationship between the oil industry, the Department of the Interior, and congressional committees that oversee commerce, the environment, energy, and natural resources. Because committee power increases with seniority, there is much time for the ranking members of these congressional committees to grow close to the clients and bureaucrats in the triangle, not to mention the *revolving door* syndrome discussed above.[34]

Regulatory Limitations.   Government agencies appear adept at retaining services for clients. They have more difficulty when it comes to punishing people in the course of law enactment. Besides protecting clientele groups, such regulatory bodies are often understaffed. In addition, authority is often fragmented across a whole host of departments, agencies, and subagencies. In the area of civil rights enforcement, for example, that duty is spread across the likes of the Civil Rights Division of the Justice Department, the Department of Education, the Department of Health and Human Services, the Civil Service Commission, the Office of Federal Contract Compliance in the Department of Labor, the Equal Employment Opportunity Commission, the Civil Rights Commission, the Federal Housing Authority, and the Department of Housing and Urban Development. In such a tangle of overlapping, fragmented authority, it is often difficult to determine precisely who has failed when a law goes underenforced.[35]

BLACKS IN THE LEGISLATIVE ARENA

> Although the Congressional Black Caucus has taken strong, progressive positions over the years, . . . it has been a voice crying in the wilderness. The legislation black congresspersons would need to pass in order to demonstrate that there was real hope for the majority of black Americans . . . suggests changes the United States political system is incapable of making. As a result, the Congressional Black Caucus and other black leadership forums have increasingly functioned to enhance the individual careers of the black middle class—those who can profit from the incremental benefits the system is capable of granting, rather than the distributive justice it will not concede.[36]

Over the course of United States history, the interests of African Americans have been particularly affected by decisions or nondecisions in the federal legislative arena—which has just been shown to be practically impervious to fundamental change. Although the federal government has delivered some helpful major pieces of legislation at times,[37] that has normally occurred only when accompanied by both considerable social turmoil and the leadership of a strong and congenial president.[38]

The Presidency

Given the increasing nationalization of American politics over time, as well as the resistance to racial justice often confronting African Americans at the state and local levels, it is not surprising that black political attention soon turned to Washington. Besides looking to the United States Supreme Court, African Americans often have turned to the one official elected nationwide and least likely to be beholden to any single state or local constituency: the president of the United States.

We shall focus in this section on only part of the presidential response: the appointments, orders, and general postures of key presidents. In our discussion of the Congress, we shall take up major pieces of legislation often initiated by presidents and steered through under their leadership.

Presidential appointments and other actions reflect real ebbs and flows in presidential commitment to black interests. A few presidents, usually with a crisis at hand, cautiously bucked the racist attitudes prevalent in the nation and provided the leadership necessary to pass and implement landmark civil rights legislation. More commonly, the most that even friendly presidents delivered were things like patronage for a small number of blacks, highly visible token appointments, high-level meetings with carefully selected black leaders, and a sizable amount of rhetoric. Most of the time, however, presidents have contributed far less or acted in ways widely considered to be contrary to black interests.[39]

The Slavery Period.   Prior to the end of the Civil War, such presidential actions tended to be almost completely antithetical to the interests of African Americans. George Washington, for instance, sought restitution for several thousand slaves taken by British troops toward the end of the Revolutionary War. John Adams pressed Great Britain and Mexico for formal agreements that would guarantee the return of runaway slaves. During the Civil War, President Abraham Lincoln only selectively emancipated the slaves, allowing the institution to continue in slave states that were fighting under the Union banner. Meanwhile, most presidents from Washington through Lincoln pressed for active enforcement of domestic fugitive slave laws but minimally enforced the 1808 ban against further importation of slaves.

The Civil War Era.   Nonetheless, Lincoln did wage the Civil War, at least in part because of the escalating turmoil over the issue of slavery. He negotiated a treaty with Great Britain to suppress the African slave trade, and he eventually announced the emancipation of all slaves held in the United States. Yet his successor, Andrew Johnson, was nearly impeached fighting the imposition of Reconstruction on the South. Then, after Ulysses S. Grant made some reasonable attempts to extend black rights, Rutherford B. Hayes ultimately abandoned Reconstruction altogether in order to win the presidential election of 1876.

The 1876 electoral vote was so close between Hayes and Democrat Samuel Tilden that it hung on disputed results in South Carolina, Louisiana, and Florida. When, among other things, the Republican candidate agreed to press for official termination of Reconstruction by withdrawing federal troops from the South, that seemed to break the impasse. The House of Representatives resolved the dispute in Hayes's favor, Hayes became president of the United States, and soon the troops were gone.

The Jim Crow Period.   What followed was a period that ranged from presidential indifference to outright hostility. Republican presidents generally could be counted on to continue delivering small amounts of patronage, but that was about the best of it. Amid legal resegregation, black disenfranchisement, and increasing numbers of lynchings, presidents were doing little to protect African Americans. Nevertheless, as blacks attempted to escape some of the worst of this by migrating to the North, a small number of token gestures would be forthcoming.

Other than some legislative efforts on the part of Benjamin Harrison, Woodrow Wilson appeared to be offering some of the first direct presidential overtures in a very long time. What he proceeded to deliver was quite another thing, however. Although he appointed Robert H. Terrell as a municipal judge in Washington, D.C., he also phased out virtually all blacks from the civil service and instituted segregated dining and rest room facilities for federal employees. President William Howard Taft had appointed William H. Lewis assistant attorney general, but such tokenism generally marked the extent of presidential concern.

Gains amid Turmoil.   As the Great Depression drove national unemployment rates to some 25 percent and food riots occurred in the streets, something had to be done. In response, President Franklin Roosevelt initiated the New Deal. Beyond pressing for the establishment of a social welfare state, however, he offered little that directly addressed the discrimination and violence plaguing blacks in both the North and the South at the time.

Virtually nothing was forthcoming until blacks began to rebel violently in cities such as New York and Detroit. A. Philip Randolph also threatened to lead a massive march on Washington just as United States involvement in World War II was beginning. Roosevelt finally responded by appointing a number of blacks to advisory positions in various federal departments, comprising what came to be called his Negro Cabinet. He also issued Executive Order 8802 prohibiting racial discrimination in defense-related industries and in government. Then, as an enforcement vehicle, he created the Fair Employment Practices Commission to investigate discrimination in industries servicing the federal government. However, the commission had no authority to punish the companies when such discrimination was encountered, and it was reluctant to cancel government contracts with discriminating companies in the middle of a war effort. Therefore, besides embarrassing a few such firms into compliance, job discrimination continued pretty much unabated.

As the Congress of Racial Equality (CORE) began to escalate civil rights activities with marches, "freedom rides," and the like, Harry S Truman became the first president openly to advocate full equal rights for African Americans. He created a civil rights committee to provide advice and a more effective committee to battle discrimination in businesses under government contract. In 1948, he issued Executive Order 9981, which finally desegregated the military, and he introduced various pieces of civil rights legislation in the Congress. He also continued the practice of appointing blacks to significant positions, including the federal bench. Nevertheless, it was not until after he had chosen not to seek reelection that he called for a national civil rights policy backed by the "full force and power of the Federal Government."[40]

Dwight Eisenhower favored military segregation as late as 1948, although once elected he continued federal pressure to eliminate discrimination among government contractors. Meanwhile, he never formally announced his support of the 1954 *Brown v. Board of Education* decision, was slow to send federal troops to Little Rock to enforce court-ordered school desegregation, and was silent when Martin Luther King, Jr., was sentenced to four months at hard labor in Georgia's Reidsville State Prison.

John F. Kennedy made a very timely phone call to the jailed Dr. King at a crucial point late in the 1960 presidential campaign, but he was far slower to respond once he took the oath of office. He avoided the entire subject of race in his inaugural address, did not include racial issues as a topic for any of his initial task forces, was slow to press for Civil Rights Commission hearings, and appointed racist judges to the federal bench in the South. It took two years before he finally pressed for desegregation of public housing, and even then, only about one unit in five was affected. He settled for a watered-down effort at desegregating military residential units, and he did not cut federal aid to states that continued to discriminate in public employment.

Nonetheless, the civil rights movement was gathering force across the South, and the atmosphere was becoming even more highly charged. Reverend Theodore Hesburgh served on the Civil Rights Commission during this period, and he concluded that the civil rights issue imposed itself on the Kennedy administration, rather than the other way around. "The time schedule was not guided from the White House, but it was guided by the march of events and the White House had to react to it."[41]

Besides appointing a number of black administrators, judges, and advisers—appointments now obligatory for Democratic presidents—Kennedy finally was forced more directly to join the battle against discrimination in voter registration. At first, he simply endorsed the private Voter Education Project but did not commit the Justice Department to active assistance. Yet as images from Birmingham and elsewhere seared the public consciousness in the spring of 1963, and as plans for a huge march on Washington went forward, Kennedy moved. He agreed to send temporary voting referees wherever less than 15 percent of a local black population was registered and the attorney general of the United States filed a formal complaint. He appointed the Equal Employment Opportunity Commission, as well as a Committee on Equal Opportunity in Housing to enforce nondiscrimination in federally assisted housing. He also issued Executive Order 10925, which included the first federal mention of affirmative action as a requisite for federal contractors.

As Lyndon Johnson took office, racial unrest was reaching its peak. Massive demonstrations swept the South, and more than 100 urban ghettos went up in flames. In that volatile setting, Johnson moved quickly. Besides major appointments—Robert Weaver as the first black head of a cabinet department (Housing and Urban Development), Andrew Brimmer to the Federal Reserve Board, Thurgood Marshall as solicitor general and later first black justice on the U.S. Supreme Court—the Johnson presidency would be marked by the greatest legislative gains in African-American history. Nevertheless, even though a combination of events and presidential leadership had succeeded in overcoming the conservative legislative maze, implementation would be another story. The institution of federalism would impede strong enforcement of many of these long-awaited gains. Like Eisenhower and Kennedy before him, President Johnson would be hesitant to introduce federal observers, examiners, and troops. On paper, a second reconstruction was under way, but this one would be implemented much more cautiously than the first.

Despite some initial hesitancy, however, the Johnson administration did finally begin to enforce the laws. Soon, much legal discrimination had been successfully eliminated. Major legal impediments to voting, employment, and housing opportunities had been swept aside, and black advancement in each area slowly began to become apparent. Yet as the unrest dissipated, the pendulum began to swing back the other way. Race would become a divisive issue imbedded in many policy debates, and negative white reaction to the forementioned gains would be successfully pandered to for political advantage.[42]

A Return to Reticence.   In 1968, while numerous public opinion polls indicated that white America felt that government had gone too far in its assistance of blacks, Richard M. Nixon won the presidency on a platform that had clear racial undertones. If elected, he would work to end school busing and would bring "law and order" back to the country—the latter being a thinly veiled promise, in part, to crush inner-city rebellions. Although ghetto unrest had been put down rather effectively by the time he was inaugurated, once in office Nixon proceeded to implement a number of regressive policies. Despite signing a revised version of Executive Order 11245 adding further details to federal affirmative action policy, his administration would be relatively lax in its enforcement of the civil rights legislation on the books,[43] and it would quite openly work to reduce enforcement of court-ordered school busing. Probably its most significant legacies, however, were the appointments of four relatively conservative justices to the Supreme Court and the development of amorphous block grants to replace many of the much more narrowly targeted and redistributive project grants that had emerged as part of Lyndon Johnson's Great Society efforts.

Eight years of Ronald Reagan would mean even more of the same. Between 1981 and 1989, not only would the Justice Department all but cease to enforce busing orders and affirmative action laws, but the solicitor general would argue against the constitutionality of such policies when they came before the Supreme Court. Beyond that, hostile federal judges were appointed, and the Equal Employment Opportunity and Civil Rights commissions were stacked with persons who opposed many existing civil rights laws and practices. Social welfare efforts would be reduced, and aside from the appointment of Samuel Pierce as secretary of the Department of Housing and Urban Development (HUD) and of Colin Powell to finish a term as national security adviser, about all that the Reagan administration offered to blacks was a promised share in the economic growth Reagan claimed was resulting from his laissez-faire economic policies—a share that never materialized for most blacks.[44]

Ronald Reagan's successor, George Bush, like Richard Nixon's successor, Gerald Ford, entered office with a more conciliatory posture than his predecessor. One of Bush's first acts was to appoint Louis Sullivan as secretary of the Department of Health and Human Services. However, where the domestic policies of the Ford administration diverged only minimally from the conservative Nixon approach, the Bush administration would not deviate much from the Reagan domestic agenda either, despite his promise of a "kinder and gentler America."[45]

Jimmy Carter and Bill Clinton provided brief interludes, but even they failed to deliver what many blacks had expected. The executive appointments were indeed forthcoming, a record number of blacks were appointed to the federal bench, there were fewer cuts in social spending, and regulatory enforcement of civil rights was increased, including the addition of a civil rights office in the powerful Office of Management and Budget. Nevertheless, a policy of fiscal restraint thwarted hopes of any major federal efforts to reinvigorate the Great Society, and relations between African Americans and the White House soon became strained. Jimmy Carter, for example, was not even invited to the 1979 legislative weekend of the Congressional Black Caucus, while Bill Clinton was chastised for actions such as withdrawing the nomination of Lani Guinier to become assistant attorney for civil rights, scaling back federal affirmative action efforts, and signing the 1996 Welfare Reform Act—essentially ending the federal government's long-standing guarantee of a social safety net for every citizen.[46]

The Congress

Legislation.   Mired in its own incredibly convoluted procedures, the Congress has generally been even less responsive to black interests than the presidency. In the absence of forceful demands propelled by serious social turmoil and strong presidential leadership, it has done little to attack the individual and institutionalized racism that has so long plagued black America.

The Slavery Period.   Not only was slavery tolerated in the nation and its territories, but it was legal even in the nation's capital until the outbreak of the Civil War. The Fugitive Slave Act, passed in 1793, mandated the return of runaway slaves, and it was fortified by provisions included in the Compromise of 1850. This was hardly the extent of legalized discrimination. Even free blacks were barred from the militia, navy, marines, and postal service. They were also all but barred from obtaining a passport, and they were denied preemption rights to public lands.

The Civil War Era.   In the aftermath of the Civil War, the Congress (devoid of much southern opposition) moved boldly to strike down the legal vestiges of slavery. This "reconstructive" effort included the Wade-Davis bill, the Reconstruction Act of 1867, creation of the Freedmen's Bureau, three proposed amendments to the U.S. Constitution, and the Civil Rights Act of 1875.

The Wade-Davis bill marked the Congress's effort to be harsher on ex-Confederates than President Lincoln was being. In particular, it sought to preclude a much larger number from voting, and it demanded more guaranteed loyalty from newly reconstructed southern states. However, when the president refused to sign the bill, the Congress was not capable of overriding his veto.

Following Lincoln's death, however, Congress became more responsive to black interests, and its majority Republican party courted newly enfranchised black voters who faced racist violence, intimidation, and emerging black codes in the postwar South. Of particular significance, Congress proceeded to adopt the Reconstruction Act over President Andrew Johnson's veto. The act divided the old Confederacy into five military districts and imposed martial law. For readmission into the Union, each state had to implement universal (male) suffrage to those swearing allegiance to the Union, write new state constitutions acceptable to the Congress, and ratify the Fourteenth Amendment to the United States Constitution.

The Freedmen's Bureau was established to deliver a number of badly needed services to dislocated southern blacks, as well as some southern whites. It was to provide food, health care, education, and resettlement assistance. It also was empowered to intervene on behalf of black workers to help establish workable contracts with their new employers; and it was to provide its own courts when local courts were deemed to be unreliable.

The Civil War amendments to the U.S. Constitution were each passed by the Congress and then ratified by the states between 1865 and 1870. The Thirteenth Amendment banned slavery and involuntary servitude in the United States and its territories, unless the involuntary servitude was part of a legitimate punishment for a crime. The Fourteenth prohibited states from abridging federal "privileges and immunities"; denying life, liberty, or property without "due process of law"; and denying "equal protection of the laws." The Fifteenth declared that the right to vote was "not to be denied or abridged by the United States or by any State on account of race, color, or previous condition of servitude."

At the very end of this period, the Congress passed the Civil Rights Act of 1875. It outlawed the exclusion of blacks from public accommodations, including privately owned hotels, theaters, boats, and railroads. Yet, that law would be struck down by the Supreme Court eight years later, and it would be nearly another century before those rights would be restored.

The Jim Crow Period.   In the lull from the Hayes compromise in 1876 until the turmoil of the Great Depression period of the 1930s, the Congress proved incapable of doing much to protect southern blacks from increasing oppression. Legalized segregation and disenfranchisement were tolerated, as was outright violence. In fact, the Congress actually contributed to some of this. For example, in 1878 it prohibited the use of federal troops in elections and 16 years later cut all appropriations for election marshals. This, of course, left black voters to fend for themselves. Final amnesty was granted to the remainder of the previously "disloyal" southern Confederates in 1898. Probably most alarming of all was the fact that an antilynching bill never did emerge from the legislative maze. Nonetheless, the period was not devoid of progress. The 1883 Pendleton Act, for instance, created a merit system for hiring federal bureaucrats. That change inadvertently helped blacks by limiting opportunity for discriminatory federal hiring.

Gain Amid Turmoil.   As social unrest rocked the nation throughout much of the period between 1930 and 1968, some direct aid and protection finally began to emerge from Washington in response to black demands. Domestic crises once again would provide the catalyst necessary to overcome the inherent stasis of the legislative process.

As early as 1930, under intense pressure from the NAACP in particular, the U.S. Senate blocked the nomination of John J. Parker to serve on the Supreme Court. Parker was alleged to have once stated that "participation of the Negro in politics is a source of evil and danger to both races."[47] As discussed earlier, the Congress is much better equipped to stop proposals than it is to pass them. But the level of crisis was about to allow even the latter.

New Deal legislation in the 1930s was designed to address many of the violent and nonviolent biracial demands arising out of the Great Depression. Emergency relief was provided. Social welfare programs such as Aid to Families with Dependent Children (AFDC) were created. Unemployment compensation was established, as was a minimum wage and a 40-hour workweek. Collective bargaining was protected, legalizing unionization. A variety of federal jobs were created to put unemployed people back to work. Child labor was prohibited. And the Social Security system was brought into being.

Following World War II, violent and nonviolent protest would gather momentum. This time, however, the rebels were predominantly African Americans demanding the enforcement of rights they had gained nearly a century earlier. Once again, the Congress found ways to respond.

The Civil Rights Act of 1957 was the first major piece of civil rights legislation to find its way through Congress since 1875. It established the Civil Rights Commission to investigate violations of the Fourteenth and Fifteenth Amendments. It authorized the attorney general of the United States to protect federal voting rights, including criminal prosecution of judges. And nondiscriminatory criteria were established for the selection of federal jurors.

The Civil Rights Act of 1960 mandated that stricter voting records be kept, and if a "pattern or practice of discrimination" could be demonstrated, federal judges were authorized to adjudicate voter registration disputes, or the attorney general could appoint federal referees to resolve them. It also made it a federal crime to use interstate commerce to threaten or carry out a bombing and added much stiffer penalties for people convicted of violent acts such as this.

The Civil Rights Act of 1964 (see case study below) was the most sweeping piece of legislation to date, and it passed by virtue of the fact that the Senate was able to invoke cloture over a filibuster for the first time since 1917. The act mandated the desegregation of public schools and accommodations and set forth provisions for equal employment. Federal aid was to be withheld from discriminatory state and local governments. It extended and broadened the role of the Civil Rights Commission and created the Equal Employment Opportunity Commission (EEOC). A Community Relations Services division was created in the Commerce Department to mediate race-related social disputes. In the area of suffrage, it required even stricter record keeping, authorized the Commerce Department to compile registration and voting statistics in areas suggested by the Civil Rights Commission, prohibited disenfranchisement due to minor errors, tightened limitations on literacy tests, and provided a process whereby either the prospective registrant or the attorney general could appeal voter application denials to an independent three-person federal panel.

The Congress also addressed the issue of poll taxes. Even though a congressional ban could not get past filibusters in the Senate, a constitutional amendment did survive all the way to ratification in February 1964. Thus the Twenty-fourth Amendment was added to the Constitution barring "any poll tax or other tax" from precluding a person from voting in a primary or general election for federal office.

The capstone to the suffrage fight was the Voting Rights Act of 1965. It directed the attorney general to bring suit challenging the constitutionality of poll taxes in state elections and provided authority to bring suit against other practices even if there was only statistical evidence of discrimination. When a federal suit was pending, federal courts were authorized to temporarily ban the discriminatory practice in question. In addition, all literacy tests and other suspect practices were suspended in states where less than half of their eligible voters turned out in the 1964 presidential election. Those states were Alabama, Alaska, Georgia, Louisiana, Mississippi, South Carolina, Virginia, and North Carolina. Finally, designated election districts were required to submit all new voting qualifications to federal judges for preclearance.

Meanwhile, President Johnson was steering his Great Society programs through a Congress that had two-thirds Democratic majorities in both houses—enough to overcome a "conservative coalition" of Republicans and southern Democrats. This round of social legislation included food stamps, Medicaid, Head Start, Legal Aid, community mental health centers, Model Cities projects, and other programs.

Three final legislative actions warrant mention. The 1968 Civil Rights Act prohibited racial discrimination in the rental or sale of housing, unless a private owner chose to make the transaction without the use of a real estate broker. The Supreme Court nominations of two alleged racists, Clement Haynesworth and G. Harrold Carswell, were rejected by the Senate.[48] And the Voting Rights Act of 1970 banned any new literacy tests.

A *Return to Reticence*.   With those legislative gains in place and racial turmoil finally abating, a political backlash loomed on the horizon.[49] From Richard M. Nixon's inauguration in 1969 through the end of George Bush's term in 1992, conservative Republicans held the White House for all but four years, with Republicans even controlling the Senate for six. In the one brief four-year interlude, little in the way of redistributive policies emerged from the legislative arena under moderate Democrat Jimmy Carter. Then, when another moderate Democrat, Bill Clinton, succeeded Bush, he became saddled with a conservative Republican majority in both houses of congress only two years into his first term.[50] Thus the legislative maze was back intact, and no new major civil rights legislation would be forthcoming. As a matter of fact, the real battles would be over efforts to reduce black gains from the previous era.

As examples of this assault on previous gains, one must consider the following. There were serious efforts to pass antibusing legislation and to reduce the federal courts' jurisdiction over school desegregation and affirmative action. A fair-housing bill was defeated in 1981. And the renewal of the 1965 Voting Rights Act faced some stiff opposition. The resulting reality even led Ronald Reagan's conservative EEOC chairman Clarence Thomas to lament that "there are greater penalties for breaking into a mailbox than there are for violating someone's basic civil rights."[51]

Nevertheless, the period was not all bleak. The Voting Rights Act was ultimately renewed; additional enforcement provisions were amended to the Fair Housing Act; and both the 1988 and 1991 Civil Rights Acts combined to nullify the negative effects of a handful of narrow U. S. Supreme Court interpretations of previous federal laws.[52]

Blacks in Congress

Augustus Hawkins (D-Calif.) observed:

> Twenty years ago, black members couldn't even eat in the House dining room. It was an unwritten rule. They were made to feel unwelcome. Now I'm chairman of the committee that has jurisdiction over that dining room.[53]

By contrast, Manning Marable argues:

> There is something essentially absurd about a Negro politician in racist/capitalist America.[54]

Black interest groups face certain rather formidable disadvantages in their efforts to lobby bills through the federal legislative maze. In particular, their primary constituency is relatively small—roughly 13 percent of the national population. In addition, it is relatively poor, making it difficult to fund large lobbying offices in Washington or to endow cooperative politicians with sizable campaign contributions. Political scientists Harold Wolman and Norman Thomas concluded that "few blacks are actively consulted by the White House, the agencies, or the key congressional leaders."[55] Unfortunately, that appears to be just about as true today as it was when they wrote in 1970. Thus, short of crisis situations, attaining fundamental change through the legislative process will be very difficult indeed. Nonetheless, there are still important things to be gained by having at least small amounts of clout in the corridors of the Congress, even if those gains do not add up to fundamental change. In particular, blacks can gain their share of patronage from the congressional pork barrel, while the inherent conservatism of the Congress can be used by crafty insiders to help stave off assaults on gains won during periods of unrest.

Black Representatives.   Lobbying white elected officials is one way to proceed. However, well-placed black congresspersons can provide other important inroads. Parren Mitchell (D-Md.) describes one approach:

> During a recent lame duck session [of Congress], when few people expected much to happen, I introduced an amendment to the Surface Transportation Act of 1982, which represents a $71 billion expenditure over four years. My amendment provided a 10 percent set-aside for minority businesses—that represents $7 billion over four years. Now, that's using the system. I would also point out that, in 1975, under the Public Works Act, I introduced an amendment to create a 10 percent set-aside. From that, we received $400 million of a $4 billion expenditure. In reality it amounted to over $625 million that flowed into minority businesses.[56]

From the founding of the nation until 1869, not one African American served in the United States Congress. From 1869 until 1901, only 20 blacks served in the House of Representatives and 2 in the Senate, all representing "reconstructed" southern states. First to be elected were Jefferson Long (R-Ga.) and Joseph Rainey (R-S.C.). Thereafter, the majority of representatives came from the Carolinas, and both senators (Hiram Revels and Blanche Bruce) came from Mississippi. Nevertheless, the number of black legislators diminished rapidly following the Hayes compromise of 1876, and the last one, George White (R-N.C.), scarcely made it into the twentieth century.

Black congresspersons would reappear on Capitol Hill in 1929, however, and their numbers would grow steadily beginning in the 1940s. Chicago sent the only blacks to Congress in the period from 1929 to 1944. One of them, Oscar De Priest, was a black Republican, holding office from 1929 until 1934. He was then succeeded by Democrat Arthur Mitchell, who gave way to William Dawson in 1942. Dawson was joined by Harlem's Adam Clayton Powell two years later, and the black contingent gradually grew to nine members by 1969. That number reached a peak of 40 in the early 1990s, in part due to the short-lived creation of the "black-influence districts" discussed in Chapter 6.

Most black congresspersons, in Reconstruction and thereafter, have represented heavily black districts. Only three African Americans have been elected to a major statewide office in this century, those being U. S. Senators Edward Brooke (R-Mass.) and Carol Moseley-Braun (D-Ill.), and Democratic Governor L. Douglas Wilder of Virginia. Whites still appear uncomfortable voting for blacks; and until those attitudes change, the number of black representatives in Washington is not likely to grow much larger.[57]

Despite their relatively small numbers, many of the contemporary black representatives have held important positions in the U. S. House of Representatives, positions that have provided opportunities to effect change. William Gray was majority whip, while he, Harold Ford, and Melvin Watt served on their party's Steering and Policy Committee. Adam Clayton Powell was chairman of the Health, Education, and Welfare Committee. Other chairs have included Robert Nix, head of the Post Office and Civil Service Committee; Ron Dellums, Committee on the District of Columbia and later the Armed Services Committee; Parren Mitchell, Small Business; Augustus Hawkins, Education and Labor; William Gray, Budget; William Dawson and later John Conyers, Government Operations. As for key subcommittees, Charles Diggs headed the Foreign Affairs Subcommittee on Africa; John Conyers, the Judiciary Subcommittee on Criminal Justice; Julian Dixon, the Appropriations Subcommittee on the District of Columbia; and Charles Rangel, the Ways and Means Subcommittee on Select Revenue Measures.[58] Besides insider opportunities to gain black patronage and block unfriendly bills, such positions provide occasions to research and publicize issues. As Ron Dellums put it, "It does give me the opportunity to set the agenda, explore issues, [and] bring witnesses' that have never been presented."[59] In addition, such positions provide opportunities to travel and speak, not to mention the Committee on the District of Columbia's jurisdiction over a predominantly black constituency.[60]

> The Congressional Black Caucus remains committed to the position that government must be an active force for the enhancement of social justice and human dignity. We have had to become leaders and fight aggressively to protect constitutional freedoms and social justice for not just minorities but for all Americans.[61]

The Congressional Black Caucus. In an effort to maximize what little black presence existed on Capitol Hill, Charles Diggs made an overt attempt to unite with Adam Clayton Powell and William Dawson in the mid–1950s. By 1969, their numbers had grown to nine, and Powell would become the first chairperson of a more formal organization called the Democratic Select Committee. They then renamed themselves the Congressional Black Caucus (CBC) in 1971, and within a decade their ranks would more than double.

Besides organizing legislative efforts in the Congress, the primary functions of the Caucus include collecting data, formulating budgetary proposals, and initiating investigations—for example, investigating the 1971 police killings of Chicago Black Panthers Mark Clark and Fred Hampton. They have also lobbied presidents on both domestic and foreign policy matters—for example, pressing for aggressive civil rights enforcement at home and justice for predominantly black populations in nations such as Haiti and South Africa.[62] In addition, the Caucus began orienting new black congresspersons prior to their arrival on Capitol Hill.[63]

Unfortunately for the Caucus, its formation has coincided with a marked decline in social unrest and a string of less than cooperative presidencies. Consequently, the group has often found itself on the defensive, fighting simply to protect existing programs. Even its source of funds was challenged by a 1981 change of rules that prohibited caucuses from using public space and funds if they received outside monies. In response, the Caucus officially formed three separate branches designed to operate away from Capitol Hill: a foundation to raise money, a legislative service organization to do research, and a political action committee for channeling campaign funds to critical campaigns. Thereafter, when foundation income exceeded spending for items such as internships and scholarships, the CBC even purchased its own building in the nation's capital.[64]

Although no longer an official congressional caucus, after 1995 rule changes further limited use of governmental resources, the Congressional Black Caucus Foundation continues to function in order to accomplish at least two stated purposes. It seeks both to provide a black perspective in the Congress and to press for equal opportunities.

First, it intends to lend a black perspective to legislative deliberations. To maintain the uniqueness of that input, in 1975 it rejected the membership of Fortney Stark, Jr., a white California Democrat who represented a district that happened to be 30 percent minority. After a month of careful consideration, they concluded that for symbolic reasons as well as a substantive unity of perspective, they would remain an exclusively black organization. As stated by Charles Rangel, it is important that they " . . . share the common social, cultural, and political experience of being black in America."[65] Subsequently, white "associate members" have been allowed, but they do not participate in the group's closed-door meetings.

Second, the organization is committed to equal opportunity in America. Given that its members tend to represent the major black ghettos across the country, its general policy goals were not difficult to define. As then CBC chairman Charles Rangel put it, "We have no permanent friends, no permanent enemies, just permanent interests of black and minority constituents."[66] But charting approaches to serve those interests has not always been easy. In 1972, for example, the Caucus split over the presidential candidacy of its own member Shirley Chisholm, and it also could not reach consensus about whether to send representatives to the National Black Political Convention being held in Gary, Indiana, that year. In addition, as its numbers have grown, so has the diversity of its constituencies. Nevertheless, there has been a remarkable amount of unity overall, especially in the resolve to battle attacks on major legislative gains won in previous periods.[67]

The Bureaucracy

> To say that we will pursue vigorous enforcement of civil rights laws does not mean that we accept—uncritically and unthinkingly—present approaches and assumptions.[68]

As stated earlier, laws ultimately mean whatever the people assigned to enforce them define them to mean. Those same administrators also filter the information generated by their agencies as they set the nation's legislative agenda. They can facilitate the policy orientations of the elected representatives. They can also obstruct and undermine.

In the Reagan administration, for example, the solicitor general was normally in court arguing against federal civil rights extensions. The Civil Rights Division of the Justice Department was on record as being opposed to affirmative action laws, and the entire administration simply did not actively enforce them. Neither Justice nor the Education Department pressed school desegregation; Assistant Attorney General William Bradford Reynolds declared, "We are not going to compel children who don't choose to have an integrated education to have one."[69] In addition, the Internal Revenue Service was not inclined to challenge the tax-exempt status of private schools that discriminated by race.

Top-level presidential appointees are not alone in shaping the implementation of federal legislation. Lower-level federal administrators and state and local law enforcement officials—both groups normally drawn from the local area—are ultimately left the responsibility of enforcing many of these laws. Local officials, for example, ended up monitoring many of the desegregation efforts mandated by the 1964 Civil Rights Act. The attorney general and his or her Washington staff simply could not observe every hotel registration, school admission, and hiring decision. That, of course, created certain problems when the implementing officials were the same type of people whose failure to protect blacks had led to this legislation in the first place.

Of some consolation to black America, however, is the fact that a sizable portion of lower-level federal bureaucrats are now black. For example, whereas there were only 620 blacks in the entire federal bureaucracy in 1883, that figure had grown to more than 2,300 within 10 years after the creation of the federal civil service system, and has now grown to more than 400,000—a percentage exceeding the proportion of blacks in the population as a whole.[70] In addition, agencies such as EEOC have begun to gradually regroup and reassert themselves since the end of the Reagan-Bush era.[71]

Overall, then, at the planning and implementation stages, a combination of presidential influence, bureaucratic realities, and federalism can have a significant impact on the shape federal legislation will ultimately take. Escaping the legislative maze is only part of the task.

Case Study: The 1964 Civil Rights Act

The 1964 Civil Rights Act came into being in the midst of the most extensive and intense black unrest in the history of the United States. Its route to passage provides a good example of how all the pieces fit together. It also indicates just how tortuous this procedure can be, even in the most optimal of times.

President John F. Kennedy submitted the bill to the Congress in June 1963 as what he called the "fires of frustration and discord" were sweeping the nation.[72] He then made speeches in support of the legislation, lobbied key congresspersons, and sent his cabinet members up to the Hill to testify on its behalf.

Emanuel Cellar (D-N.Y.), chair of the House Judiciary Committee, received the bill from the speaker and referred it to his Subcommittee No. 5. Public hearings then proceeded for months. Ultimately, an even stronger bill emerged out of subcommittee and was passed by the full Judiciary Committee.

Sailing in the Senate was not as smooth. Mississippi Democrat James O. Eastland, chair of the Senate Judiciary Committee, did all he could to scuttle the bill.

Only one witness was heard over an 11-day period, and then the bill was tabled. It was quite clear to proponents that it would be extremely difficult to dislodge the civil rights bill from Eastland's committee.

Meanwhile, back in the House, problems were building as well. Howard Smith (D-Va.), who chaired the House Rules Committee, was refusing even to call the committee together. With no rule, the bill could not go to the House floor, where passage actually looked likely. At that critical juncture, however, John Kennedy was assassinated and Lyndon Johnson assumed the office of president. Johnson, former majority leader in the Senate and a very skillful legislator, moved quickly to dislodge the bill from the House Rules Committee. He organized enough support to force the rules consideration to the House floor if necessary. Smith finally conceded the inevitable, and the House soon had its rules—rules that did not favor quick and simple passage, however.

More than eight months from its introduction, the civil rights bill had finally reached the House floor. There, under relatively loose rules, 122 amendments were offered, and nine full days of debate ensued. Nonetheless, the marginally amended bill was finally passed by a vote of 290–130.

There had been no movement in the Senate Judiciary Committee. Consequently, majority leader Mike Mansfield took a calculated gamble. He would circumvent Senator Eastland, despite the political risks of alienating the chair of such a powerful committee. In an extremely rare move, he took the House bill directly to the Senate floor by way of a parliamentary maneuver that was approved by a vote of 54–37. Those 54 senators were taking a considerable political risk, for any one of them might someday need timely and friendly consideration in the Senate Judiciary Committee. Nevertheless, the process moved forward, despite the risks.

The next obstruction was a Senate filibuster. Southern senators, led by the likes of Richard Russell (D-Ga.), began to exercise their procedural right to unlimited debate. Needing 67 votes to invoke cloture at that time, undecided votes had to be corralled. Proponents reached compromises with the waverers that narrowed the bill's scope and significantly weakened its enforcement components. Nonetheless, cloture was finally imposed by a 71–29 vote, another relatively rare occurrence. The 71 senators seemed to be willing to risk ill will and subsequent retaliations.

Despite 99 separate attempts at amendment, the bill came to a final vote on the Senate floor, where it passed 73–27. Because the bill differed from the original House version, however, more delay loomed.

Prodded by the all-out lobbying effort of one of the most politically astute presidents in the history of the nation, there was enough support in the House to avoid a conference committee and take the matter directly to the House floor. This time the once-defeated chair of the Rules Committee proved more cooperative, and there was a full House vote within one month. The civil rights bill, as amended by the Senate, passed the House by a vote of 289–126 slightly over a year after it had first been introduced.

The bill was then signed into law by President Johnson, and the friendly Warren Court rather quickly upheld the constitutionality of key passages. Nevertheless, the battle was far from won. Short of sending legions of federal observers and law enforcement officials, implementation of the 1964 Civil Rights Act would be left to state and local judges and administrators. Enactment would be slow, arduous, and, as recent developments indicate, never final.[73]

OPTIONS FOR BLACK AMERICA

> The Congressional Black Caucus, in order to be effective within the electoral context, would have to understand and directly attack the structural conditions of black subordination. Otherwise, structural constraints will continue to undermine seeming advances won through electoral politics and incremental strategies.[74]

A variety of these "structural constraints" need to be addressed not only by the CBC but also by all groups and individuals who acquire power and hope to facilitate the institutionalization of a more open and just system. Among other ways, change can be facilitated by significantly reducing the number of checks and balances that presently comprise the legislative maze, by institutionalizing more direct popular control at the bureaucratic level, and by both increasing the number of black officials in the legislative arena and using those positions to educate and mobilize mass constituencies.

Reducing Checks and Balances

A Parliamentary System. One of the most sweeping changes would involve amending the U.S. Constitution so as to convert from a presidential to a parliamentary arrangement similar to those used in virtually every other representative democracy in the world. Instead of electing the president and the Congress separately, the electorate would simply choose the entire Congress at once. When a majority of the elected legislators agreed to work together, that majority would pick the president and cabinet from their own ranks, forming a government. That government would be far more united in its initiation, passage, and implementation of a legislative program, and when it could no longer hold together for this purpose, new elections would be called. When the public expressed its general will at election time, the legislative process would be much more capable of responding.

Fewer Specific Checks. Among the specific checks that need to go are unlimited debate in the Senate—the procedure that has given rise to the filibuster. Also needed are standing rules in both houses of Congress that would automatically limit debate and amendments unless majorities vote to alter them for a given bill. In addition, both houses must design rules that make it easier for majorities to extract bills from committee. And even though it poses less of a problem under a parliamentary arrangement, the presidential veto also should be eliminated.

In order to protect minority groups from having their interests ignored by this now more majoritarian legislative process, however, it may be appropriate to adapt and then implement propositions set forth by Lani Guinier. Guinier argues for a series of procedures designed to contribute to what she terms "proportional interest representation." These include requiring supermajorities on certain critical types of legislation (effectively creating a "minority veto"), rotation of key legislative offices, and a cumulative voting process to allow minorities to effectively pool their votes for issues they deem particularly essential.[75] In addition, much of this "democratization"—whether in the form of national referenda or streamlining the regular legislative process—may well need to follow, rather than proceed, the kinds of consciousness raising discussed in Chapter 9 below.

Less Federalism.   Besides streamlining the federal legislative process, state and local checks need to be reduced as well. Public policy must be more centralized. More federal laws must be formed and implemented by federal bureaucrats who have not been chosen from the areas they serve. This could be accomplished by first classifying all federal jobs as either involving policy-related discretion or not involving such discretion. For example, most nonclerical employees involved in implementing the nation's justice system would be included in the first category, while most postal employees would be in the latter one. Then, those in the first category would be recruited under the Civil Service System from across the nation, and thereafter as many as possible would be randomly assigned outside the region from which they applied. They would also be rotated periodically from one region to another (similar to much of the foreign service). In addition, the Justice Department needs to be expanded and given a freer rein to observe and intervene locally in the implementation of federal law.

Institutionalizing Popular Control

A number of agencies are needed to empower the general public in its relationships with both the governmental bureaucracy and the private sector. Ombudsmen, as are prevalent in Europe, could serve as liaisons between service recipients and the agencies assigned to deliver those services.[76] To provide citizens with assistance in the private sector as well, a Consumer Protection Agency could aid them in challenging questionable practices of private corporations, much as the Environmental Protection Agency is designed to protect the environment. Lastly, a much larger and stronger Legal Aid program would enable all citizens, regardless of income, to use the courts to redress grievances arising in either the public or private arena.

Affirmative Action

It continues to be important to broaden all searches in order to find a greater number of highly qualified African Americans to appoint to executive, staff, and bureaucratic positions throughout the legislative arena. Besides lending black perspectives to governmental agenda setting and policymaking, as well as providing hope, role models, and other more symbolic advantages, the presence of blacks in these positions may cause other blacks to be less hesitant about approaching various governmental entities in active pursuit of their interests.[77] In addition, such affirmative action efforts will give blacks opportunities to amass the kind of experience and contacts necessary to penetrate the higher levels of executive decision making in the federal government.[78]

Educating and Mobilizing

These types of streamlining and institutionalization facilitate change. Even after the system becomes more open, however, public demand for specific policy changes must continue. Several black members of Congress have suggested ways of enhancing that probability by using the full scope of existing governmental positions.

In an interview with Jeffrey Elliot, Representative Major Owens (D-N.Y.) indicated that one of his primary goals was "to push prerogatives of a congressperson to the limit." As he put it, "Congress gives me a platform. . . . And I intend to use that platform to offer leadership."[79]

In more specific terms, Congressman Gus Savage (D-Ill.) concluded:

> Being a legislator is only one side of the coin. But there's another side—namely, the ability to serve as an informal mass educator, a mobilizer, and an agitator when necessary. As I see it, my job is to galvanize people, to energize people . . . For example, I think I was better able to contribute to the Nuclear Freeze campaign outside Congress than I was as a member. I led 200,000 people in a Nuclear Freeze demonstration in Lisbon, Portugal.[80]

Individual leaders can do only so much. Of far more importance is institutionalizing this consciousness-raising process, and it is to that end that the discussion now turns.

NOTES

1. David Stockman, former director of the Office of Management and Budget, *New York Times*, April 12, 1984.
2. Coined by Eric Redman in *The Dance of Legislation* (New York: Simon & Schuster, 1973).
3. Harold Stanley and Richard Niemi, *Vital Statistics on American Politics* (Washington, D.C.: CQ Press, 1994), p. 278.
4. See *New York Times*, April 10, 1996.
5. For a fuller description of this evolution, see Lawrence Chamberlain, *The President, Congress, and Legislation* (New York: Columbia University Press, 1946), pp. 450–464.
6. For example, see Thomas Dye, *Who's Running America?* (Englewood Cliffs, N.J.: Prentice Hall, 1995), chap. 3.
7. Howard Zinn, *A People's History of the United States* (New York: Harper & Row, 1980), 535.
8. Testimony before the Select Committees on the Iran-Contra Investigation, 100th Cong., 1st sess., May 21, 1987 (Washington, D.C.: Government Printing Office, 1987).
9. See *New York Times*, February 20, 1989.
10. For example, see *New York Times*, February 15, 1997. See Chapter 7 for a more detailed discussion of the influence of money in contemporary electoral campaigns.
11. Quoted in Jim Fain, "The Nation Is the Loser," Memphis *Commercial Appeal*, May 23, 1988. More recently, see David Boren, "Why I Am Leaving the Senate," *New York Times*, May 13, 1994; Eliza Newlin Carney, "Exodus," *National Journal*, January 20, 1996, pp. 108–113.
12. Richard Bolling, *House Out of Order* (New York: Dutton, 1965), p. 17.
13. For an excellent visual depiction of this process, see Marjorie Hunter and Tom Bloom, "The Longest-Running Game in Town," *New York Times*, June 24, 1985.

14. Over time, senators have surrendered their right to formally filibuster certain types of legislation, (e.g., significant budget and trade matters). See Sarah Binder, "The Senate Strangles Itself," *New York Times*, July 13, 1996.

15. For examples of recent uses of the filibuster, see Anthony Lewis, "Destructive Abuse of Filibuster in Effect Violates Constitution," *New York Times*, October 22, 1994; Arthur Flemming and Ray Marshall, "Tyranny of the Minority," *New York Times*, May 30, 1994.

16. *New York Times*, May 21, 1987.

17. For example, see Norman Ornstein, "Prima Donna Senate, "*New York Times*, September 4, 1997; Robert Pear, "Senator X Kills Measure on Anonymity," *New York Times*, November 10, 1997.

18. See Walter Oleszek, *Congressional Procedures and the Policy Process* (Washington, D.C.: CQ Press, 1989); Aaron Wildavsky, *The Politics of the Budgetary Process* (Boston: Little, Brown, 1974); Charles Lindbloom, "The Science of Muddling Through," *Public Administration Review* (Spring 1959).

19. Quoted in Marguerite Michaels, "Why Congressmen Want Out," *Parade* (November 5, 1978). Also see Lawrence Haas, "Behind the Times," *National Journal*, March 30, 1991, pp. 722–726.

20. Kay Lehman Schlozman and John Tierney, *Organized Interests and American Democracy* (New York: Harper & Row, 1986); Mark Petracca, "The Rediscovery of Interest Group Politics," in Mark Petracca, ed., *The Politics of Interests: Interest Groups Transformed* (Boulder Colo.: Westview Press, 1992), p. 14.

21. For example, see Jonathan Rauch, *Demosclerosis* (New York: Times Books, 1994); Allan Cigler and Burdett Loomis, eds., *Interest Group Politics* (Washington, D.C.: CQ Press, 1994); Petracca, *The Politics of Interests*; Peter Stone, "Lobbyists on a Leash?" *National Journal*, February 3, 1996, pp. 242–245.

22. Roger Davidson and Walter Oleszek, *Congress Against Itself* (Bloomington: Indiana University Press, 1977); Jeffrey Birnbaum, "Rep. Armey, Texas Firebrand, Changes Tactics and Starts Accomplishing Things in the House," *Wall Street Journal*, June 2, 1988, p. 1.

23. Dye, *Who's Running America?* chap. 3; *Congressional Quarterly Weekly Report* 49 (January 16, 1993), pp. 12–13; Norman Ornstein, et al., *Vital Statistics on Congress* (Washington, D.C.: CQ Press, various years).

24. Congressional Quarterly, *Weekly Reports* (September 1,1979), p. 1823. Also see John Berg, *Unequal Struggle: Class, Gender, Race, and Power in the U. S. Congress* (Boulder, Colo.: Westview Press, 1994).

25. Quoted by Alex Poinsett, *Ebony* (June 1973), p. 64.

26. Quoted in *New York Times*, March 31, 1991.

27. Common Cause, *Sunset* (Washington, D.C.: Common Cause, 1976).

28. Quoted in Thomas Cronin, *The State of the Presidency* (Boston: Little, Brown, 1975), p. 19.

29. For example, see Graeme Browning, "Getting the Last Word," *National Journal*, September 14, 1991, pp. 2194–2199.

30. John Hayes, *Lonely Fighter* (Secaucus, N.J.: Lyle Stuart, 1979); Helen Dudar, "The Price of Blowing the Whistle," *New York Times Magazine* (October 30, 1977); *New York Times*, April 14, 1982; *Washington Post*, October 3, 1982; Bob Cohn, "New Help for Whistle Blowers," *Newsweek*, June 27, 1988, p. 43.

 The 1989 Whistleblower Protection Act (previously vetoed by President Reagan) grants various types of protection to any direct or indirect government employee who can link his or her firing to whistle blowing; although it has seldom been invoked to date. For continuing examples, see *Washington Post*, July 16, 1990; March 6, 1992.

31. For example, see Lawrence Haas, "Programs That Never Say Die," *National Journal*, March 2, 1991, p. 537; Lawrence Haas, "Never Say Die," *National Journal*, March 28, 1992, pp. 755–757.

32. Edward S. Herman, *Corporate Control, Corporate Power* (New York: Cambridge University Press, 1981), p. 179.

33. *New York Times*, October 3, 1976. For numerous high profile examples, see Thomas Dye and Harmon Ziegler, *The Irony of Democracy* (Belmont, Calif.: Wadsworth, 1993), pp. 93–96. Also see William Greider, *Who Will Tell The People: The Betrayal of American Democracy* (New York: Simon & Schuster, 1992), chap. 4.

   Subsequent efforts, such as 1978 and 1989 acts of Congress, and a 1993 executive order, have attempted to regulate this practice by, among other things, restricting lobbying efforts until a year or more out of office. Nevertheless, virtually nothing stops industry people from being appointed to the regulatory positions in the first place, and Congress places no such limits on its own members. For example, see Peter Stone, "Big Bucks For Former Members," *National Journal*, October 12, 1996, p. 2177.

34. For example, see Douglas Cater, *Power In Washington* (New York: Random House, 1964), pp. 26–50; Roger Davidson, "Breaking Up Those 'Cozy Triangles': An Impossible Dream," In Susan Welch and J. G. Peters, eds., *Legislative Reform and Public Policy* (New York: Praeger, 1977); Jeffrey Berry, "Subgovernments, Issue Networks, and Political Conflict," in Richard Harris and Sidney Milkis, eds., *Remaking American Politics* (Boulder, Colo.: Westview Press, 1989), pp. 239–260; Daniel McCool, "Subgovernments as Determinants of Political Viability," *Political Science Quarterly* 105 (Summer 1990), pp. 269–293.

35. For a case study of how the FAA failed to adequately regulate ValuJet, contributing to the fateful 1996 jetliner crash in the Florida Everglades, see Jeff Shear, "Potentially Dangerous Liaisons," *National Journal*, July 13, 1996, p. 1552.

36. Sheila Collins, *The Rainbow Challenge: The Jackson Campaign and the Future of American Politics* (New York: Monthly Review Press, 1986), p. 92.

37. For an overview of the positive economic effects of federal intevention, as an example, see Robert Smith and Richard Seltzer, *Race, Class, and Culture: A Study in Afro-American Mass Opinion* (Albany, N.Y.: State University of New York Press, 1992), pp. 39–43.

38. For example, see Hugh Davis Graham, *Civil Rights and the Presidency: Race and Gender in American Politics, 1960–1972* (New York: Oxford University Press, 1992).

39. For example, see Steven Shull, *The President and Civil Rights Policy: Leadership and Change* (New York: Greenwood, 1989); James Riddlesperger and Donald Jackson, eds., *Presidential Leadership and Civil Rights Policy* (Westport, Conn.: Greenwood, 1995); Kenneth O'Reilly, *Nixon's Piano: Presidents and Racial Politics from Washington to Clinton* (New York: Free Press, 1995); Desmond King, *Separate and Unequal: Black Americans and the United States Federal Government* (New York: Oxford University Press, 1995).

40. Quoted in John Hope Franklin, *From Slavery to Freedom: A History of Negro Americans* (New York: Knopf, 1980), p. 451.

41. Interview by Joseph O'Connor, March 27, 1966, John F. Kennedy Library.

42. For example, see Thomas Edsall and Mary Edsall, *Chain Reaction: The Impact of Race, Rights, and Taxes on American Politics* (New York: Norton, 1992); Dan Carter, *From George Wallace to Newt Gingrich: Race in the Conservative Revolution* (Baton Rouge, La.: Louisiana State University Press, 1996).

43. Gary Orfield, *Congressional Power* (Orlando, Fla.: Harcourt Brace Jovanovich, 1975), p. 73.

44. See Steven Shull, *A Kinder, Gentler Racism? The Reagan-Bush Civil Rights Legacy* (Armonk, N.Y.: M.E. Sharpe, 1993); Kenneth Jordan and Modibo Kadalie, "Black Politics During the Era of Presidents Reagan and Bush," in Hanes Walton, Jr., ed., *Black Politics and Black Political Behavior: A Linkage Analysis* (New York: Praeger, 1994); Alphonso Pinkney, *The Myth of Black Progress* (New York: Cambridge University, 1984), chaps. 2

and 10; Steven Holmes, "With Glory of Past Only a Memory, Rights Panel Searches for New Role," *New York Times*, October 10, 1991; Peter Kilborn, "Backlog of Cases Is Overwhelming Jobs-Bias Agency," *New York Times*, November 26, 1994; Kevin Phillips, "Reagan's America: A Capital Offense," *New York Times Magazine*, June 17, 1990.

45. See Shull, *A Kinder, Gentler Racism?* Jordan and Kadalie, "Black Politics During the Era of Presidents Reagan and Bush;" Holmes, "With Glory of Past Only a Memory . . . ;" Kilborn, "Backlog of Cases Is Overwhelming Jobs-Bias Agency."

46. For a good overview, see Henry Sirgo, "Blacks and Presidential Politics," in Huey Perry and Wayne Parent, *Blacks and the American Political System* (Gainesville: University of Florida Press, 1995). And for a strong critique of presidential inaction, see Earl Ofari Hutchinson, *Betrayed: A History of Presidential Failure to Protect Black Lives* (Boulder, Colo.: Westview, 1996).

47. Quoted in Franklin, *From Slavery to Freedom*, p. 385. Also see Kenneth Goings, "The NAACP Comes of Age: The Defeat of Judge John J. Parker," in Winfred Moore et al. (eds.), *Developing Dixie: Modernization in a Traditional Society* (Westport, Conn.: Greenwood Press, 1988).

48. Joel Grossman and Stephen Wasby, "The Senate and Supreme Court Nominations: Some Reflections," *Duke Law Journal* (August 1972).

49. In addition to the assassination of national civil rights leader Martin Luther King, Jr., and the police repression discussed in Chapter 6, explanations for the demise of the turmoil can be found in Peter Goldman, *Report from Black America* (New York: Simon & Schuster, 1970), pp. 113–132.

50. As an example, note the battle over African American Dr. David Satcher's nomination to become surgeon general of the United States. See Richard Berke and Steven Holmes, "In Confirmation Delays, A New G.O.P. Strategy," *New York Times*, November 11, 1997.

51. Interview in Jeffrey Elliot (ed.), *Black Voices in American Politics* (Orlando, Fla.: Harcourt Brace Jovanovich, 1986), p. 150.

52. For an empirical overview, see Kenny Whitby, *The Color of Representation: Congressional Behavior and Black Interests* (Ann Arbor, Mich.: University of Michigan Press, 1997).

53. Quoted in *New York Times*, March 11, 1983.

54. Manning Marable, *How Capitalism Underdeveloped Black America* (Boston: South End Press, 1983), p. 170.

55. Harold Wolman and Norman Thomas, "Black Interests, Black Groups and Black Influence in the Federal Political Process," *Journal of Politics* (November 1970), p. 875.

56. Interview in Elliot, *Black Voices*, p. 37.

57. For example, see Carol Swain, *Black Faces, Black Interests: The Representation of African Americans in Congress* (Cambridge, Mass.: Harvard University Press, 1993); Linda Williams, "White-Black Perceptions on the Electability of Black Political Candidates," *National Political Science Review* 2 (1990), pp. 45–64.

58. For further examples of black committee and subcommittee chairs, see Hanes Walton, Jr., *Invisible Politics: Black Political Behavior* (Albany: State University of New York Press, 1985), pp. 198–200.

59. *New York Times*, March 11,1983.

60. For a good overview of the history of black representatives in Congress, see Berg, *Unequal Struggle* chap. 6; And for more on the specific advantages of having such black representatives, see Swain, *Black Faces, Black Interests*, pp. 217–222.

61. Interview in Elliot, *Black Voices*, p. 46.

62. For an example of foreign policy influence, see Steven Holmes, "With Persuasion and Muscle, Black Caucus Reshapes Haiti Policy," *New York Times*, July 14, 1994. Also see the Anti-Apartheid Act of 1986.

63. For example, see *National Journal*, November 28, 1992, pp. 2732–2733.
64. For example, see William Welch, "Congressional Blacks Have $2 Million Chest," *New York Times*, September 15, 1989.
65. Quoted in the CBC press release dated June 19, 1975.
66. *New York Times*, March 18, 1974.
67. For further discussion see Marguerite Ross Barnett, "The Congressional Black Caucus," in Michael Preston et al. (eds.), *The New Black Politics* (White Plains, N.Y.: Longman, 1982); Lionel Barrow, Jr., "Blacks in Congress," *Crisis*, June-July, 1992; Graeme Browning, "Flex Time," *National Journal*, July 31, 1993, pp. 1921–1925; Berg, *Unequal Struggle*, pp. 121–136; Richard Champagne and Leroy Rieselbach, "The Evolving Congressional Black Caucus: The Reagan-Bush Years," in Perry and Parent, *Blacks and the American Political System*; David Bositis, *The Congressional Black Caucus in the 103rd Congress* (Lanham, Md.: University Press of America, 1994).

    Recent chairpersons have included Kweisi Mfume (D-Md.), Donald Payne (D-N.J.), and Maxine Waters (D-Cal.).
68. Clarence Thomas, EEOC chairman in the Reagan administration, in Elliot, *Black Voices*, p. 153.
69. Quoted by Louis Stokes in Elliot, *Black Voices*, p. 48.
70. Blacks made up roughly 17 percent of the federal bureaucracy by the mid–1990s. United States Civil Service Commission, *Minority Group Employment in the Federal Government* (Washington, D.C.: GPO, various years); Harold Stanley and Richard Niemi, *Vital Statistics on American Politics* (Washington, D.C.: CQ Press, 1993), p. 406.
71. For example, see K.C. Swanson, "How The EEOC Is Trying To Right Itself," *National Journal*, May 18, 1996, pp. 1104–1105.
72. *Vital Speeches*, July 1, 1963, pp. 546–547.
73. For a more complete discussion of this legislative journey, see Milton Morris, *The Politics of Black America* (New York: Harper & Row, 1975), pp. 267–276. For an even more detailed analysis of a comparable example, the 1965 Voting Rights Act, see Stephen Lawson, *In Pursuit of Power* (New York: Columbia University Press, 1985). For an example of an important bill that did not emerge from the legislative maze this unscathed, see Mary Eisner Eccles, "Backers Defend Revised Humphrey-Hawkins Bill," Congressional Quarterly, *Weekly Reports* (November 26, 1977), pp. 2475–2476.
74. Barnett, "Congressional Black Caucus," p. 52.
75. Lani Guinier, "Voting Rights and Democratic Theory," in Bernard Grofman and Chandler Davidson, eds., *Controversies in Minority Voting* (Washington, D.C.: Brookings Institute, 1992), pp. 283–292.
76. For example, see Stanley Anderson, *Ombudsmen for American Government* (Englewood Cliffs, N.J.: Prentice-Hall, 1968).
77. For example, see John Hindera, "Representative Bureaucracies: Imprimis Evidence of Active Representation in the EEOC District Offices," *Social Science Quarterly* 74 (March 1993), pp. 95–108; Kenneth Meier and Joseph Stewart, Jr., "The Impact of Representative Bureaucracies: Education Systems and Public Policies," *American Review of Public Administration* 22 (September 1992), pp. 157–171; Gregory Thielemann and Joseph Stewart, Jr., "A Demand-Side Perspective on the Importance of Representative Bureaucracy," *Public Administration Review* 56 (March/April 1996), pp. 168–173.
78. For example, see Dean E. Mann, "The Selection of Federal Political Executives," *American Political Science Review* (March 1964).
79. Interview in Elliott, *Black Voices*, p. 68.
80. Elliot, *Black Voices*, p. 9.

Chapter 9

The Information Arena

R ecent public opinion polls provide ample evidence of growing political alienation and mistrust across the American citizenry. These feelings are not, however, accompanied by large-scale challenges to either the race and class structures described earlier or the political system that reinforces them. To the contrary, public opinion polls have actually found, for example, that a clear majority of Americans favored federal aid to help Chrysler Corporation out of its economic difficulties,[1] a reduction in social welfare programs designed to help individual indigents out of their economic predicaments,[2] and a regressive rather than progressive tax arrangement to pay the governmental tab.[3] Although the American public appears generally frustrated by basic political-economic outcomes, it nevertheless tends to support structures and policies that reinforce the status quo. As long as that remains so, democratizing the political process will only make it easier for the majority to help perpetuate the inequities in that status quo.

To understand such a mind-set requires looking beyond Easton's input, output, and conversion processes and focusing on the feedback mechanisms and political environment (see Chapter 2). Thus our analysis now turns from the conservative natures of the judicial, legislative, and electoral processes to two important conservative influences on the knowledge and opinions that underlie popular demands or the lack thereof: schools and the mass media.

EDUCATION

A primary role of the educational system in virtually every nation is to engender faith in the country's basic institutions. The United States is certainly no exception. In both subtle and not so subtle ways, the American educational system as a whole functions to generate support for the political-economic system. We shall consider examples ranging from the overt pledge of unquestioning allegiance to the national flag to the more covert "hidden curriculum" built into behavioral expectations such as "Obeys promptly and willingly" on elementary school report cards. We shall conclude with specific examples of how such institutionalized bias has affected the black community.

Overt Indoctrination

> In the political sphere, the child is taught he is free, a democrat with a free will and a free mind, lives in a free country, makes his own decisions. At the same time he is a prisoner of the assumptions and dogmas of his time, which he does not question because he has never been told they exist.[4]

Patriotic Rituals.   Schools are responsible for imparting both knowledge (cognitive learning) and appropriate emotional attachments (affective learning). The pledge of allegiance at the beginning of each school day and the playing of the national anthem before each interscholastic athletic event are examples of the latter and the most obvious of the educational system's efforts to indoctrinate its students. As a matter of fact, comparing political indoctrination in the United States and the former Soviet Union in the heat of the Cold War, American scholars George Bereday and B. B. Stretch found more elementary school time being devoted to overt political indoctrination in the United States.[5]

The Curriculum.   Only slightly more subtle are the ways in which such reinforcing mechanisms are built into the school curriculum. Beginning in the elementary school, students are taught that the Congress and elections are the essence of the American political process, while structural biases are ignored.[6] For example, by arbitrarily separating the study of government and economics, the interrelationship between money and politics can be more easily overlooked. The focus tends to be on the fairness of the procedures and not structural biases—for example, "Is everyone eligible to vote?" as opposed to "Does the maldistribution of wealth give the wealthy clear advantages in terms of electoral input?" From such myopia comes the conclusion that the nation is a model representative democracy, open to a wide array of individuals and interest groups.

People who have assumed positions of power over the course of American history are glorified. Christopher Columbus is exalted as a courageous and skillful seaman; his brutal treatment of the Arawak Indians, however, is seldom mentioned.[7] The genocide inflicted on Native Americans, the inhumanity of slavery, the second-class citizenship women and blacks endured for more than a century after the American Revolution—all of these are mentioned but played down.[8] Instead, curricula overflow with heroics during the Revolutionary War against Britain, the brilliance of the Constitution, and the honesty of Abraham Lincoln.

How has this come to be? For one thing, many of the teachers do not know any better themselves; their own educational experiences, even through graduate school, are often just as devoid of critical analysis.[9] As Jonathan Kozol puts it:

It is a clever North American deception to allow professor, scholar, editor alike to say what they please when we know well what they please is what we like. When wishes, ideas and dreams themselves can be confined like this, words can be free. The bulls, once surgically restrained, receive all barnyard privileges.[10]

In addition, like any other institution that provides a product, schools require money to operate. Where does that money come from? For the public schools, most of it is drawn from government tax revenues. However, especially at the university level, more and more of this money comes from wealthy people in the private sector—often arriving with at least implicit ideological strings attached.

The owning class has long had a vested interest in the information, training, behavioral moderation, and other services schools provide. For instance, owners benefit from the development of a pliant and productive work force and from a citizenry that will not seek to upset the political-economic apple cart. Schools generate information and new technologies that can improve corporate efficiency and international competitiveness. They provide reliable child care while parents work, child care that might otherwise have to be provided by employers. For those and many other reasons, it has made sense for the owning class to contribute its way into the cores of the schools.

Corporations donate books and audiovisual materials that both outline their perspective on the free enterprise system and provide a corporate view of contemporary policy issues such as health and environmental policies that pose threats to their profits. They also sponsor contests that reward schools and students for demonstrating traits they desire. In 1989, for instance, they spent an estimated $400 million on some 140,000 "business-school partnerships" with elementary and secondary public schools.[11] At the college level, they fund research institutes, faculty positions, and even entire departments in areas of interest to them,[12] and they sponsor faculty-business seminars and "executives on campus"—both of which allow the virtues of free enterprise to be extolled.[13] Wealthy conservatives have even formed the National Alumni Forum to help target their donations to college programs that support their views. As chairwoman Lynne Cheney put it, "It comes down to the question of who owns the university."[14]

Separate "think tanks," created by corporations, grind out research reports. Such reports are often available for classroom use free of charge, or the research findings end up as building blocks for authors writing school textbooks. Top scholars are lured by attractive salaries to work within the research agendas established by the particular organization. Examples of think tanks whose research has reinforced the existing political-economic system include the American Enterprise Institute, the Brookings Institution, the Hoover Institute, the Heritage Foundation, the Institute for Contemporary Studies, the International Institute for Economic Research, the Cato Institute, and the Institute for Educational Affairs.[15]

Meanwhile, at the elementary and secondary levels, corporations have a long history of providing both overt and covert commercial advertising during the school day. In the 1930s, for instance, the National Association of Manufacturers distributed a free weekly entitled the *Young American Magazine*, including articles such as "Your Neighborhood Bank." More recent examples include school buses bearing corporate logos, hallways dotted with advertising billboards, Channel One television with its news and commercials, and donated computer software imbedded with corporate insignias. The latter is an example of what has come to be called "sponsored educational material." Teachers are increasingly being bombarded with such items. Hershey's "The Chocolate Dream Machine" is a classic case-in-point. A video and curriculum guide, it incorporates a few vocabulary, geography, math, and science lessons into its depiction of the chocolate production process, and proceeds to describe "chocolate's place in a balanced diet."[16]

Besides purchasing opportunities to influence faculty and students, direct monetary contributions to a school also can affect internal school decisions as to resource allocation, curriculum, and even the hiring and firing of faculty members and administrators. In the spring of 1978, for example, liberal activist Jane Fonda spoke at Central Michigan University. In protest, Dow Chemical Company subsequently cut its substantial funding to that university. Such decisions are bound to have a chilling effect on the types of speakers many schools will dare bring to campus. Beyond that, governing boards of trustees are generally dominated by members of the owning class, often by those who have given the largest amount of money to the particular school. These boards have final say over a school's resource allocation, curriculum changes, and hiring and firing decisions.[17]

Therefore, even when teachers have been exposed to more critical perspectives, they are often treading on thin ice if they try to introduce such perspectives into elementary, secondary, and at times even collegiate classrooms.[18] Teachers, librarians, school administrators, and even school board members can be intimidated by powerful wealthy patrons and by reactionary groups and individuals as well. Often acting for what they see as patriotic or moral reasons, the reactionaries inadvertently do much of the censoring for the owning class. For example, especially at the elementary and secondary levels, they monitor library holdings, textbook selections, the hiring of teachers, invitations to speakers, selection of field trips, and the like, to watch for "dangerous" deviations from the status quo. Should they disagree with the educators' decisions, those responsible can at times be brought to their knees by negative publicity campaigns.[19]

Treatment of Alternative Views

> [An] important mission of the school is ... teaching [children] to think that whatever country they live in is the best country in the world; that its ways of thought and life are better than anyone else's.[20]

Students are often taught to limit criticism of the nation's institutions and practices unless they can demonstrate a superior alternative. Yet, at the same time, there are overt biases against conflicting ideas and alternative arrangements. In response to the Cold War, for instance, the state of Ohio required schools to teach "capitalism" before students could be exposed to "socialism." Similarly, the state of Florida required a course entitled "Americanism and Communism," with state law explicitly stating:

> No teacher or textual material assigned to this course shall present Communism as preferable to the system of constitutional government and the free enterprise, competitive economy indigenous to the United States.[21]

Outside the classroom, the federal government has at times placed restrictions on printed materials that can be imported, foreign speakers that can be heard, and even countries that can be visited. For example, American citizens are not free to visit socialist Cuba at their own discretion, and visas have been denied to foreign radicals invited to speak in American schools, churches, and even the United Nations.

Covert Indoctrination

It is [the teacher's] duty and responsibility to control the raw energies and desires of his charges and replace them with calmer, more moderate ideals. What would many happy citizens and trustworthy officials have become but unruly, stormy innovators and dreamers of useless dreams, if not for the efforts of their schools . . . Thus it is the school's task to subdue and control man with force and make him a useful member of society.[22]

Not only does the educational system overtly function to build system support and suppress serious contemplation of radical alternatives, but it also quietly socializes students into behavioral patterns that will make them both pliant citizens and pliant workers. From early on, they are taught to obey, memorize, and carry out tasks designed by others rather than to think for themselves, innovate, and challenge existing arrangements.

This should not be surprising in light of the genesis of mandatory public education. The early stirring of industrialization created upheaval across the economic, social, and political landscapes. Urbanization and wage labor would replace the intimacy and relative independence of small-farm existence, requiring the cultivation of a different set of skills and behavioral patterns. Government was called on to help facilitate this transition. The "teeming masses" would need to be trained and stabilized at the same time. Thus public education was born and expanded.

In 1881, for example, the business-oriented Citizens' Association of Chicago issued a report criticizing existing public schools for failing to provide "practical training, that training of hand and eye which would enable those leaving our schools to be useful and productive members of society almost immediately after leaving school."[23] Frustrated industrialists even began to create their own schools. At that point, however, public education finally adapted itself—at least in part to conform more closely to corporate needs. Innovations like polytechnical high schools were created, and work-related training began receiving considerably more attention across the entire educational scene.[24] Today this orientation has become so ingrained that it is hardly ever given a second thought.

Consider the following form letter, written by a Michigan public school principal:[25]

Dear Mr. and Mrs. Smith:

It gives me a great deal of pleasure to inform you that Mary has completed the . . . school year with perfect attendance. This is an outstanding achievement, especially in this day and age when industry and schools are finding much abuse in this area.

Regular attendance, whether it be at school or on the job, doesn't just happen. It takes much self-discipline, and is a great habit to form.

Sincerely,
Richard Jones
Principal

The Hidden Curriculum.   Open virtually any elementary school report card, and on one side there are spaces for placing grades achieved in the various academic subjects. On the other side is a behavioral checklist, and the items in that list are very telling. Besides recording the number of absences and number of times the student was tardy, many of the following behavioral traits are typically included and evaluated: accepts and respects authority, obeys promptly and willingly, follows directions, finishes work on time, respects the property of others, practices self-control, and is generally well mannered. By high school, Samuel Bowles and Herbert Gintis found subordinate and well-disciplined students rewarded, while the following traits were actually penalized: creativity, aggressiveness, independence, outspokenness, skepticism, helpfulness, emotion, and individuality.[26] And then there is competition:

> Set into mean-spirited competition against other children, he learns that every man is the natural enemy of every other man. Life, as the strategists say, is a zero-sum game: what one wins, another must lose, for every winner there must be a loser. . . . He may be allowed to work on "committees" with other children, but always for some trivial purpose. When important work is being done—important to the school—then to help anyone else or get help is called "cheating."[27]

Grades are given, and class rank is noted. Standardized tests are administered, and rankings again take center stage. Honors students are given special privileges in the school building. As a capstone to the entire experience, top students receive special note at the graduation ceremonies. Although students are not encouraged to be free-thinking individuals, they are expected to be self-centered and competitive—ideal traits for their future roles as cogs in the large corporate machine. They can then be motivated by individual material incentives and are less likely to band together for their mutual protection and empowerment.

In addition, as John Holt puts it:

> The schools, as they separate and label children, a few winners and a great many losers, must convince them, first, that there must always be a few winners and many losers, that no other human arrangement is possible, and secondly that whether winner or loser they deserve what comes to them. Only thus can we be sure that the winners will defend the system and the losers accept it without rancor. . . . The successful students are trained to think that being superior they have a right to more of life's goodies, a right to order other people around. The losers are trained to like what they get.[28]

Not only is the educational system training an appropriately skilled and manageable work force, but it is in fact preparing future workers by replicating many aspects of their future workplace. Students get used to a 40-hour workweek, work as drudgery done for external as opposed to intrinsic rewards, and acceptance of hierarchical authority and competition. On top of that, through mechanisms like tracking, students are introduced to structural inequality—advantages and limitations that shape the results of the larger competition before the race ever begins.

The resulting reality is all too predictable, as recounted by a third grade teacher:

> The first rule of education for me was discipline. Discipline is the keynote to learning. Discipline has been the great factor in my life. I disciplined myself to do everything—getting up in the morning, walking, dancing, exercise. If you won't have discipline, you won't have a nation. We can't have permissiveness. When someone comes in and says, "Oh, your room is so quiet," I know I've been successful.[29]

. . . by a welder at a Ford plant:

> How would you like to go up to someone and say, "I would like to go to the bathroom?" If
> the foreman doesn't like you he'll make you hold it, just ignore you. Should l leave this job
> to go to the bathroom I risk being fired. The line moves all the time.[30]

. . . and by authors Bowles and Gintis:

> Let your school system go hand in hand with the employment of your people; you may be
> quite certain that the adaption of these systems at once will aid each other.[31]

The Equalizer Myth.   Besides training the nation's work force, universal public
education was to level the playing field so that all children would have a relatively
equal opportunity to develop their talents and succeed in the economic marketplace.
As Samuel Bowles puts it, "The ideological defense of capitalism rests strongly on the
assertion that the equalizing effects of education can counter the disequalizing forces
inherent in the free market system."[32] Some of those disequalized effects were outlined in Chapters 3–5. In reality, however, the educational system quietly tends to
reinforce existing inequalities.

Both unemployment and income correlate rather well with years of education,
meaning that the more education one has, the less likely one is to be unemployed
and the more income one is likely to make. Thus, on the face of it, publicly provided
educational opportunities would seem to offer a springboard to economic prosperity.
According to a popular public-service advertisement, "To get a good job, you need a
good education."

Unfortunately, as discussed in Chapter 5 above, the employment status and income of a child's parents correlate with the number of school years completed,
meaning that the children of better-off parents generally finish more school years. In
addition, parental economic position often affects the quality of the school attended.
Lower-income areas have less of a property tax base from which to fund their public
schools, those schools are less attractive places to teach, and so on. In 1988, for instance, Princeton, New Jersey spent $7,015 per pupil and 93 percent of their stu-
dents passed standardized proficiency tests; while Camden spent $4,500 per pupil,
and 77 percent of their students failed.[33] In addition, elite private schools offer educational opportunities and prestige beyond the financial reach of most parents, not to
mention the additional job contacts these schools and more affluent parents can provide after graduation.[34]

Overall, then, education can affect one's economic position in life, but the economic class into which one is born has a significant impact on one's education. Thus
one's ultimate class position is more a function of the class into which one was born.
Once again, the race is fixed from the outset. All of which led Christopher Jencks and
his Harvard colleagues to conclude that the only realistic way to redistribute wealth
and thus alter the American class structure is to have government use its taxing and
spending powers to redistribute directly. As they saw it, the educational system provides only an illusion of equal opportunity; to expect it to lead the way toward more
societal equality is little more than wishful thinking.[35]

Of course, such illusions and wishful thinking can prove to be quite useful.
Everett Reimer, in his book *School Is Dead*, puts it this way:

Schools have held out unprecedented hope of social justice. To the elite they have been an unparalleled instrument, appearing to give what they do not, while convincing all that they get what they deserve.[36]

The Black Educational Experience

The state of New Jersey provided schooling for black residents as early as 1777, and religious and humanitarian groups set up private schools for free blacks in several other states. But black slaves were systematically denied most types of education. In many places, it was actually illegal to teach a slave to read. As a result, W. E. B. Du Bois estimated that only about 5 percent of former slaves were literate as of 1865.[37] Much of that was to change following the Civil War.

Freedmen's Bureaus were instrumental in helping pave the way for the creation of elementary, secondary, and college-level schools for former slaves, including assistance in the establishment of such well-known institutions as Howard, Fisk, and Atlanta universities and the Hampton Institute. By 1870, some 247,333 black students were attending 4,329 schools, and the cost to the Freedmen's Bureaus exceeded $5 million.[38]

The Freedmen's Bureaus were not the only organizations helping to expand black educational opportunities. Various black and white religious denominations, as well as private foundations like the Peabody Educational Fund, also became involved. Thus black schools continued to expand, and a few colleges like Oberlin and Berea were racially integrated despite strong social pressure to the contrary.

The school doors were opened even further with the series of Supreme Court decisions culminating in *Brown v. Board of Education* (1954). Thereafter, a combination of the growing civil rights and black power movements, not to mention riots in the streets, paved the way for even more racially equal educational opportunities. Busing and affirmative action plans were implemented, and curricula began to include more black perspectives; black history was taught in increasing numbers of high schools, and black studies programs emerged on a number of college campuses. In addition, whereas there was only one predominantly black college in 1854, there were more than 100 such schools by the early 1970s.

Once established, however, the black educational experience often included all of the previously mentioned conservative influences. There has been more than an ample amount of overt and covert indoctrination, as well as clear evidence that educational opportunities are far from equal.[39]

As an example of overt indoctrination, it is now becoming increasingly acceptable to study the political thought of Martin Luther King, Jr., a staunch Christian and an avowed pacifist. However, pity the poor elementary or secondary school teacher who tries to give equal time to the writings of black militants and socialists such as Malcolm X, Langston Hughes, Angela Davis, or Manning Marable, even in many predominantly black school settings.

After being fired for reading a poem by Langston Hughes to a class of black students in a Boston public school, Jonathan Kozol recalls what he was told:

> No literature . . . which is not in the course of study can ever be read by a Boston teacher without permission from someone higher up. When I asked her about this in more detail, she said further that no poem anyway by any Negro author can be considered permissible if it involves suffering.[40]

In his book *Death at an Early Age*, Kozol also retells the story of a teacher speaking to third- and fourth-grade black students in a ghetto school where "the books are junk, the paint peels, the cellar stinks, the teachers call you nigger, and the windows fall on your head." With fervent sincerity, the teacher tells them:

> You children should thank God and feel blessed with good luck for all you've got. There are so many little children in the world who have been given so much less. Thank God you don't live in Russia or Africa.[41]

Covert indoctrination is, of course, much more subtle. Black education has been replete with examples. Besides behavioral modification, for years most all elementary and secondary schools and even many colleges encouraged blacks to have what Lucius Barker and Jesse McCorry term a "subject orientation"—remaining passive and detached politically.[42] In addition, black pride, identity, and self-esteem were repressed by ignoring virtually all black history and culture.[43] African-American students also were advised to keep their expectations low. Malcolm X, for instance, recalls being encouraged to pursue carpentry, as his preference for the study of law was described by his high school counsellor as "no realistic goal for a nigger."[44] Even after the civil rights and black power movements forced some of that to change, problems remain. Particularly disturbing is evidence that a large number of black students are being prematurely tracked into nonacademic vocational programs, further reinforcing the legacy of slavery.[45]

Most blatant of all are the inequities in school funding and quality, shown here as they have related specifically to blacks. As indicated in Chapter 5, public school spending varies considerably in relation to the property values in the given school districts. With blacks found disproportionately in poorer neighborhoods, the implications of such class bias in school funding are clear. The situation may be getting even worse as middle-class whites flock to private schools and exhibit less willingness to increase funding for public education.[46] In the South, for instance, predominantly white schools outspent their predominantly black counterparts by a 3 to 2 ratio during the Jim Crow days at the turn of the century; the differential soon grew to 3 to 1 and is often even greater than that today.[47] Rather than serving as an equalizing influence, such an educational arrangement actually seems to increase both inequality of opportunity and inequality of results.

MASS MEDIA

Consciously or not, the mass media exert considerable influence in American politics. In the course of both public affairs and entertainment presentations, the media do much to generate support for the existing American political-economic system.

Evolution

From the limited-circulation party presses of the eighteenth century, we now have thousands of media sources reaching millions of individuals from all walks of life.

In 1789, John Fenno established the *Gazette of the United States* "to endear the general government to the people."[48] In reality, it was an occasional press designed to propagate the views of the Federalist party, and the Republicans subsequently started the *National Gazette* in order to convey their own messages. Soon a limited network of these "party presses" began to develop at various localities around the country, approximately 200 by the turn of the century. By 1835, there were some 1,200 of them, and as many as 65 published on a daily basis.[49]

As urbanization dawned in the mid-eighteenth century, independent newspapers began to emerge, targeting themselves to a mass audience rather than just the party faithful. The number of newspapers reached 3,500 in 1870 and 12,000 by 1890. This proliferation also was stimulated by technological developments such as the rotary press, the telegraph, and the railroads, all of which lowered the costs of news gathering, publication, and circulation. Soon, schools of journalism developed, and news reporting actually became a full-blown profession. Today there are approximately 1,500 dailies and 7,000 weekly newspapers, with circulation figures for the largest national newspapers exceeding 1 million each.[50]

Over the same period, a variety of national magazines began to appear. *Nation, Atlantic,* and *Harper's* emerged in the mid-nineteenth century, with *Scribner's, Mc-Clure's,* and *Cosmopolitan* appearing a few decades later. These often included articles by "muckrakers" such as Lincoln Steffens. Commercial magazines number in the thousands today.

Over the airwaves, the first commercial radio stations began operating in 1922. There are now approximately 12,000 such stations, including the recent addition of satellite radio broadcasting. Television appeared in the 1940s and has grown to include some 1,400 local stations. The 1970s brought cable television, and there soon were thousands of cable television systems, with even more options available via the satellite dish. The Cable News Network (CNN) and C-Span offer an exclusive around-the-clock focus on public affairs. Government entered the media business in the 1960s when Congress created the public radio and television systems. Lastly, we are just beginning to see the informational impact of the computer internet system. [51]

"Mass media," then, has come to include everything from television to radio, film, books, newspapers, magazines, and the internet. For the purposes of this chapter, however, we will focus primarily on television, radio, and the press.

Sources of Influence

Just what political power resources do the media possess? At the most fundamental level, they have explicit constitutionally protected prerogatives. In practice, they have evolved to the point that many are large, well-financed entities with access to very sizable audiences. Their power is further enhanced by the fact that the ownership of these media sources tends to be concentrated in the hands of a small number of wealthy elites.

The First Amendment.   The nation's early leaders felt strongly that a free flow of information was absolutely essential to a free society and a healthy democracy. Consequently, the First Amendment to the U.S. Constitution states: "Congress shall make no law . . abridging the freedom of . . . the press." But the U.S. Congress was not the only institution that would have to respect the media's liberty. In 1931, the U.S. Supreme Court concluded that "it is no longer open to doubt that the liberty of the press . . . is within the liberty safeguarded by the due process clause of the Four-teenth Amendment from invasion by state action."[52] States, and by extension local governments, were not to interfere with the "freedom of the press."

In 1971 the Supreme Court outlined more clearly what it meant by noninter-ference. The Court concluded that government bore the "heavy burden of showing justification for the imposition of . . . [prior] restraint on publication." Such re-straint would be allowed only when it was certain that a particular news story "would surely result in direct, immediate and irreparable damage to our nation or its people."[53] For all practical purposes, there was to be no direct governmental censorship.

The mass media can be held legally responsible for libel after the fact; however, a high standard has been established for proof. If the person claiming libel can rea-sonably be categorized as a "public figure,"[54] the burden is on that person to show not only that the story was untrue,[55] but also that the news agents presented the story "with knowledge that it was false or with reckless disregard of whether it was false or not."[56]

When operating in the realm of politics, then, mass media have extensive protec-tion. Government is precluded from halting the release of any particular story except in the most extremely perilous of circumstances. Even if the public figure covered can prove that the story was both false and damaging, the medium cannot be pun-ished unless the victimized public figure also can prove that the news agency either knew it was false or proceeded in "reckless disregard" of its authenticity.[57]

In essence, the print media have great latitude to publish whatever they want about public events and public figures without fear of governmental interference be-fore, during, or after the publication. This protection is generally true for electronic media transmissions as well, although some of them are subject to a few more gov-ernmental regulations than print media.[58]

Such freedom would mean little if these media sources could not afford to gather important information, no one was listening, or they could not decide what to do with the stories once they gathered them. The way in which media have evolved, however, has all but guaranteed that none of these apply. Not only are they excep-tionally free to pursue and present stories on any topic they choose, but they have ac-cumulated considerable capacity to do so.

Agenda-Setting.   Given the variety of actual and potential events unfolding hourly, as well as at least some limits on their own capacities, media must decide which stories to pursue and how to display what they find. By necessity, they are far more than a mirror that simply reflects everything that happens in society. They often have considerable discretion over what to cover, the placement, slant and tone of the story, and the headlines and pictures that will accompany it. They also choose whether to pursue it with follow-up stories or let it disappear from public view. In addition, they have the option of editorial comment.[59]

Events clearly will dictate coverage in a number of cases. A major presidential address, a natural disaster, or the crash of a jetliner will require extensive and promi-nent presentation. On the other hand, the media will use far more discretion in de-ciding whether or how to portray the thousands of less dramatic events occurring across the nation every day.

In exercising this discretion, mass media have become integral in the determination of the public policy agenda (the issues to be discussed and the alternative solutions to be considered). Regardless of whether they can control what people think, they clearly have considerable influence over what the public will think about. Many problems and alternatives are not discussed seriously until they are emphasized by the media. Therefore, what the media choose to discuss not only will be a reflection of what is on the minds of government officials and the nation's populace, but also can raise issues to a level of attention that will almost guarantee that they will become political agenda items.[60]

Audience.   The importance of that agenda-setting role is amplified by the size of the audiences. Television is the most dramatic example. More than 98 percent of American homes currently have at least one television set, and it is turned on an average of 6 to 7 hours each day. The average 16-year-old has spent more time in front of the television than at school. Roughly one-half of the American population can be found in front of their television screens during peak winter viewing hours, with more than 50 million people tuning into the nation's favorite individual programs. Not surprisingly, *TV Guide* is the top-selling magazine in the country.[61]

Other media sources have sizable audiences as well. More than 99 percent of American households own a radio, and the average person listens to radio more than 3 hours per day.[62] A majority of all adults regularly read one daily newspaper,[63] and considerably more read at least one magazine each month.[64]

Because of such numbers, advertisers are willing to pay handsomely for the opportunity to present messages via these channels. Thus sizable budgets have become available, allowing media to present an enormous amount of information to these huge audiences. In news coverage, for example, technological advances and financial resources allow them to make broad, often instantaneous news presentations. The development of computers, satellites, fax machines, and videotape have enhanced worldwide coverage and reduced news deadlines significantly. And, hand-held video cameras allow instantaneous presentation of television images from the immediate scene of the action.[65]

Ownership Concentration.   This power is enhanced further by the monopolization of media ownership. Such monopolies allow a relatively small number of individual elites to exercise much discretion. Let us consider the concentration of ownership in the two dominant media, television and newspapers.

From the inception of television in the 1940s until well into the 1970s, CBS, NBC, and eventually ABC had almost a complete monopoly. Between the national networks and their local affiliates, they essentially owned the airwaves. More recently, however, the Fox Network has emerged; and the number of independent stations has boomed, thanks in large part to viewer subscription cable and satellite television. Nevertheless, the major networks and their affiliates still attract a large majority of the television audience; a good many of the independents end up running and rerunning shows produced by the major networks; and the Federal Communications Commission (FCC) now permits the networks to purchase local cable units.[66]

In the press, monopolization is also considerable and has been steadily increasing. Press chains (single companies that own a variety of newspapers) controlled nearly one-half of all papers in 1970, and that figure grew to some three-quarters by the end of the decade, at which point 12 chains controlled more than one-third of all the nation's newspapers.[67] Then came the merger mania of the 1980s.

In one 3 month period, for instance, the Tribune chain purchased the *Newport News* for $130 million (104,000 circulation), Media News Group purchased the *Dallas Times Herald* for $110 million (244,629 circulation), Ingersoll purchased the *New Haven Register* and *New Haven Journal-Courier* for $170 million (218,519 circulation), Times Mirror purchased the *Baltimore Sun* for $400 million (356,927 circulation), and Gannett purchased the *Louisville Courier-Journal* and the *Louisville Times* for $300 million (295,965 circulation). Over a four-year span, Gannett purchased the two Louisville papers just mentioned as well as the *Jackson Clarion-Ledger*, the *Jackson Daily News*, the *Des Moines Register*, and the *Detroit News*—spending $705 million and adding 1.3 million readers. On top of that, chains have even begun to buy up other chains; in one instance, Samuel Newhouse purchased Booth Newspapers for $305 million.[68]

The largest of the chains are Gannett, Knight-Ridder, Newhouse, Times Mirror, Tribune, and Dow Jones, who combined currently own nearly 200 daily newspapers and sell approximately one-third of all the individual papers purchased each day. This process has left only about 400 daily newspapers in the entire country that are not part of a press chain, and those tend to be in small markets and to draw all but their local stories from a handful of national and international wire services. By the early 1990s, only 12 American communities still had fully competing newspapers under separate ownership.[69]

Not only is ownership concentrated within each medium, but ownership concentration across media is growing as well. At last count, Gannett, for example, owned 91 dailies, 38 nondailies, 10 television stations, and 16 radio stations. An individual newspaper, the *Washington Post* (part of the Times-Mirror chain), owned a television station, a radio station, a newsmagazine, and a news wire service. Or, consider the 1989 merger of Time, Inc. and Warner Communications, creating a $12 billion conglomerate with multiple television and cable stations, as well as film, book, and magazine interests. Thereafter, Time Warner also subsumed the $7 billion Turner Broadcasting System. Other major multimedia mergers have included Westinghouse, CBS, and Infinity Broadcasting; Viacom and Paramount; Capital Cities, ABC, and Disney; as well as the many acquired subsidiaries of Rupert Murdoch's News Corporation.[70]

The FCC has placed some limits on such conglomeration; for example, an individual company has not been allowed to own more than 12 television stations or 35 percent of a television viewing market.[71] Nevertheless, the FCC has been considering the elimination of all such regulations; such rulings scarcely make a dent in the overall monopolization of the nation's media anyway; and because the rulings generally are not applied retroactively, they affect only new acquisitions.[72]

The end result is that a handful of media giants have a powerful hold on what is known in the United States. Who actually owns these entities? In the mid–1980s, for example, as few as 10 business and financial corporations held the controlling shares of stock in CBS, NBC, ABC, 34 subsidiary television stations, 201 cable television systems, 62 radio stations, 59 magazines (including *Time* and *Newsweek*), and 58 newspapers (including the *New York Times*, *Los Angeles Times*, *Washington Post*, and *Wall Street Journal*).[73] Then came even more mergers. Meanwhile, WNET, the flagship channel in the Public Broadcasting System (PBS), has been heavily reliant on the Ford Foundation. Chapter 4 made it clear who controls these banks, financial corporations, and foundations, and do not forget that the owning and non-owning directors of these organizations sit on each other's boards, even within the media business.[74]

In Pursuit of Profit

> A monopoly enterprise typically uses its political clout, not to challenge authority, but to protect its monopoly.[75]

What drives the decisions of this highly monopolized industry so integral to the political-economic system? Conservatives for years have accused the media of having a "liberal bias," at least in part because a disproportionate number of their reporters are more ideologically liberal than the nation as a whole.[76] Nevertheless, more than one in ten radio and television stations are now controlled by religious fundamentalists.[77] In addition, as virtually the entire mass media industry is privately owned and operated for a profit, it normally must first serve the investment interests of its primary stockholders. As it turns out, this pursuit of profit has generally resulted in news and entertainment presentations that reinforce the existing distribution of wealth and power.

Serving Investors.   Focusing on television, Fred Friendly draws the following conclusion from his experiences as president of CBS News:

> By default we have permitted the investor's equity to control what is basically a public-service industry.[78]

As evidence, he ranks the top priorities guiding television's choice of what shows would appear:

1. Nielsen ratings.
2. Effect of those ratings on advertisers.
3. Effect of those ratings on expected earnings and thus stock market position.
4. The company's corporate image in the press, among the community leaders, and at the FCC.
5. Public service and good taste.[79]

To see just how effective television and radio networks are at following these criteria, consider their economic success. Advertisers were paying them some $79 billion a year by 1992. One-quarter of television air time, for example, came to be devoted to commercials and promotions.[80] Meanwhile, profit rates were markedly higher than in most business operations in the country.[81] So lucrative is such access to the airwaves that local television stations sell for millions of dollars, and even individual radio stations are regularly approaching $1 million in market value.[82]

Highly profitable, although on a somewhat smaller scale, newspapers also rely heavily on attracting advertisers. All newspapers combined draw nearly one-third of the nation's advertising revenue.[83] The resulting dependence is reflected in the allocation of newspaper space. Only 40 percent of space in the press is devoted to news while the other 60 percent is filled with advertisements. Calling them "news" papers actually seems to be a misnomer.[84]

Most of all the mass media are private corporations whose primary reason for being is to return profits for their stockholders. The above figures indicate that they take their job seriously and are quite good at it.[85] But besides leading them to sell advertisers a sizable share of the nation's means of mass communication,[86] their profit orientation also appears to have had a noticeable impact on the content of the news and entertainment that appears the rest of the time. This reality has definite political consequences.

Programming Impact.   Media critic John Leonard concludes that "the history of the United States [is being brought to us] not by the Senate and the House, but by Occidental Bank and Weed Eater."[87] He is implying that what the public knows and considers important may well be heavily affected by what large advertisers will and will not sponsor. What shapes those advertising decisions? The primary concern of corporations that spend thousands upon thousands of dollars for these opportunities to circulate information about their products almost always has to be reaching the largest buying audience possible. To attract advertisers, mass media companies must be able to attract and hold large audiences with the content of what they present.[88]

> The most serious threat to television and its claim to First Amendment freedoms is not the Federal Communications Commission or the Supreme Court, or an Imperial Presidency, but the runaway television ratings process. The current obsession with surveying the "habits" and "pulse" of television sets, rather than the response of and impact on human beings, has resulted in an industry preoccupied with short-term indicators and profits.[89]

What Friendly found true for television, Gannett's Al Neuharth and others also have found true for newspapers.[90] But it is not enough simply to attract the audience by serving them something that will catch their attention and conform to dominant values and attitudes. It is also essential to hold them. Thus once they have been attracted, it is much safer to anesthetize than to provoke or offend.

Television news gives highest priority to sensational stories that can be captured on film, such as airplane crashes, three-alarm fires, and multiple homicides. Thus the airwaves come to be dominated by what media critic Ben Bagdikian calls "fires, sex, and freaks"[91] or Dan Rather refers to as "bodies, mayhem, and lurid tales."[92] In between such stories, local stations serve up a hefty portion of "happy talk" banter between the various on-camera personalities.[93] On the national level, ABC plucked Roone Arledge from the *Wide World of Sports* to head up its news division in order to "liven up" the network's news programming. Absent, even at most newspapers, is probing in-depth investigative reporting, especially on subjects like workplace safety, poverty, and declining unionization rates.[94] As Edward R. Murrow noted early on, ". . . television in the main insulates us from the realities of the world in which we live."[95]

Empirically, Columbia University's Project for Excellence in Journalism studied all news reports on the 3 nightly network news programs in major newspapers and weekly news magazines. Over the past 20 years, they found the number of "straight news" stories to have shrunk to fewer than one third of all stories covered. Meanwhile, the number of "Features" on subjects such as celebrity lives and human interest have increased to 43 percent, nearly tripling over the same time period.[96]

Even election coverage, essential to the functioning of a healthy democracy, tends often to be narrow, superficial, and sensational. Unable to attract and hold large audiences with extensive discussion of issues, the focus shifts to cliches and candidate images. Is he "tough on crime"? Does she believe in "family values"? What passes for investigative reporting is often voyeurism into candidates' personal lives for the sensationalism that entails. Come election day, the results are reported as if it were a horse race. In a crowded primary, for example, a winner must be declared and crowned, even if that person received only 15 or 20 percent of the vote.[97]

Actually, radio and television stations are required by the FCC to devote at least 5 percent of their broadcasting time to "public affairs." If it were not for that rule, there might be even less news-related programming on the airwaves. Documentaries, for example, tend to be expensive to produce and tend not to draw large audiences. Even controversial documentaries have tended to do poorly in the Neilsen ratings. And as the major networks have gradually lost some of their monopoly status to cable television, increased competition seems to have led to even less inclination to absorb the financial losses entailed in documentaries. Instead, the viewer is given "newsmagazines" and early-morning "wake-up shows."[98]

Media critic John O'Connor described public affairs programming as follows:

> It is something the FCC likes to find in the program log of stations at license renewal time as an indication, however meaningless, that the customary quest for profits was tempered by an occasional gesture toward the real world beyond old movies and sitcoms."[99]

Entertainment, on the other hand, tends to be even more mind-numbing. As Norman Lear put it, "With painful predictability, the networks putter with the same tired formats, adding more sex here and more violence there—more mindlessness . . . "[100] Even on most cable stations, there is still the steady parade of game shows, soap operas, mindless situation comedies, and police dramas.[101] Serving up bland and minimally offensive programming is done at least in part to appease advertisers who want the largest possible audiences and normally do not want to be associated with unpopular issue positions.[102]

It is not completely mindless, however. As our means of mass communication are subsumed by giant multiheaded conglomerates, for example, it should come as no surprise when these conglomerates start talking about "synergy" in this context, "the dedication of an entire, far-flung media empire to selling its products with every means at its disposal."[103] In March of 1996, as a case-in-point, the "consumer editor" for ABC's Good Morning America "heaped 8 minutes of undiluted praise on the Disney Institute, a new resort, invoking the Disney name or Mickey Mouse's face 16 times."[104] Of course, ABC just happens to be owned by Disney. Conversely, how much news space can we expect to be devoted to probing the political and economic implications of such multimedia mergers?[105]

The flip side of this coin is omission. Time Warner, for example, delayed production of "Strange Justice," a made-for-television film about the Clarence Thomas hearings. This apparently was done at least in part to keep from offending Justice Thomas as the U. S. Supreme Court deliberated a cable-regulation case in which Time Warner had millions of dollars at stake.[106]

Profit-seeking media corporations and their advertisers also have a vested interest in defending a profit-based economic system. Thus the world view underlying most public affairs and entertainment programming is not difficult to identify.

The Dominant Values

> The United States, so strongly individualist in temper and so bourgeois in appetite, has never wholly mastered the art of collective solutions, or of readily accepting the idea of a public interest, as against private gain.[107]

Conferring Values.   Like the educational process, the mass media are an important part of American socialization. Faith in welfare-state capitalism must be reinforced, as must the illusion that the limited political system guarantees adequate democratic control. This is accomplished by omission and commission in both public affairs and entertainment programming.[108]

By omission, challenging perspectives often fall out of public affairs presentations. For example, newspapers run regular syndicated editorials by a number of spokespersons for the extreme conservative position, such as Cal Thomas or James Kilpatrick. However, absent are regular columns by socialists such as Noam Chomsky or Manning Marable. Talk radio has been dominated by ultraconservative voices such as Rush Limbaugh and Ken Hamblin. In the electoral arena, third-party candidates with potentially threatening views are ignored almost completely. And, even in their heyday, documentaries tended to concentrate on subjects like divorce, youth crime, and incest, rather than topics where analysis could threaten the political-economic status quo, such as labor unions, the military-industrial complex, or the positive side of life in countries where many basic industries are socialized.[109]

News coverage often bears the stamp of the same underlying values. Political scientist Michael Parenti notes, for instance, that labor issues get twisted to make the workers look irresponsible and greedy.[110] He also notes that the mass media both downplayed and apparently underestimated the size of two of the largest demonstrations in the nation's history—a half million people marching on Washington to protest Ronald Reagan's policies in September 1981 and a full million marching in New York City to oppose nuclear weapons in June 1982.[111] Meanwhile, the savaging of governmental figures through sensationalized scandal mongering feeds a conservative political culture that is already suspicious of those with political power, while at the same time weakening government's capacity to counterbalance private economic power.[112] The flip side of this form of slant is local media's inclination to inflate positives and play down problems in their immediate communities in order to "boost" the community's image in the eyes of potential investors. As a local business themselves, these media outlets have much at stake in the overall economic climate of their host community.[113]

Similar things can be found on the entertainment side. As Erik Barnouw put it, "Television entertainment is propaganda for the status quo."[114] For example, no television series has had a black militant or a courageous socialist as a hero. Quite the contrary, black militants and socialists, when they do appear, are normally portrayed as dangerous caricatures. Meanwhile, police shows condition the audience to accept police repression of such dissenters; and almost all series suggest at least implicitly that one can and will advance in the United States if one simply works hard enough at it.[115]

Contributing Factors. At least four forces contribute directly to this ideological posture. Media personnel and their standard operating procedures, advertisers, and government all contribute to the fostering of what Ralph Miliband has termed "a climate of conformity."[116]

To begin with, the primary decision makers in the media business are demographically homogeneous. Once again, they tend to be relatively well-to-do white men. In addition, all of the employees are ultimately answerable to members of the owning class who hold the controlling shares of stock in their particular company. Both realities contribute to the media's functionally conservative content.[117]

On top of that are a set of operational parameters that further encourage conformity. Television news broadcasts, for example, favor stories accompanied by compelling pictures and ones that can be presented in less than 2 minutes. Time and money constraints also prompt news journalists to feed off one another's stories.[118]

Then, besides these internal factors, the mass media face external influences as well. As Leonard Matthews, president of the American Association of Advertising Agencies, put it,

> To expect private companies to go on supporting a medium that is attacking them is like taking up a collection for money among the Christians to buy more lions.[119]

Although they are ultimately guided by the desire to maximize audience exposure and thus profits, advertisers will occasionally use their advertising money for overtly political purposes when they feel circumstances require it. At the national level, the thrust of the *Lou Grant* show came to be seen as too ideologically liberal, incurring the wrath of various right-wing organizations. Kimberly-Clark then pulled its advertising money, and the show was soon dropped.[120] Meanwhile, another advertiser refused to sponsor any program associated with liberal producer Norman Lear.[121] General Electric withdrew its sponsorship from an interview Barbara Walters conducted with Jane Fonda. Coming at the time of her popular film *The China Syndrome*, GE feared that it would contain "material that could cause undue public concern about nuclear power."[122] Gulf and Western pulled the plug on public television station WNET when that station ran a documentary entitled "Hunger for Profit," documenting multinational companies buying up large tracts of land in the Third World.[123] Similarly, General Motors threatened to pull its advertising from any magazine or television show that interviewed Michael Moore. Moore had recently done a scathing documentary about the auto giant, entitled "Roger and Me."[124]

At the local level, Brooklyn's Williamsburgh Savings Bank pulled its advertising from a local newspaper that had run a story on the practice of bank redlining (designating certain neighborhoods as too risky for investment). The tobacco industry's mere threat of withdrawing such money seems capable of censoring media coverage of that industry in Winston-Salem, North Carolina.[125] As a matter of fact, a 1992 survey found nine out of ten newspaper editors cognizant of such advertiser pressure, and more than one third aware of incidents in which such pressure had been successful in altering news coverage.[126] As a matter of fact, many advertisers have come to expect "early warning" notification of stories they could conceivably find unacceptable.[127]

Advertisers also draw on their stock of wealth in other ways to make certain that their own perspectives are presented on important political issues of the day. For example, they buy media time and space so that they can present their political points of view directly. Such "advocacy advertising" (or "advertorials") proliferated in the late 1970s and soon involved well over $1 million a year.[128] Texaco and Mobil, for instance, have both run numerous ads extolling "corporate perspectives" on various issues.[129] In addition, much of their regular commercial advertising is replete with conservative values as well, such as conditioning people to accept the virtues of profit-driven capitalism.[130] These same values permeate many public-service ads, most of which are delegated to the Advertising Council, a body comprised largely of corporate owners and executives.[131] On top of that, many of these corporations sponsor journalism prizes for what they deem to be outstanding work, fund trips to lavish conferences at which journalists can discuss issues of interest to the corporations, and even pay honoraria to journalists for speaking engagements.[132] Meanwhile, individual conservative philanthropists such as Richard Mellon Scaife use their untold millions to bankroll conservative advertisements as well as conservative magazines and media-monitoring organizations.[133]

Finally, government plays a role as well. The United States Information Agency, for example, has put out pamphlets like *The Problems with Communism*. Even more blatant is the fact that the "fairness doctrine," established in the Federal Communications Act, required all broadcasting stations to provide "balanced" coverage of controversial issues but explicitly stated that this did not include the "Communist perspective."[134] Then, in 1987, the FCC abolished the fairness doctrine altogether.[135]

The Black Experience

> Black people find themselves in a country with the legal and constitutional guarantee of freedom of the press but lacking the actual power to exercise that right because there is not freedom in the press. As a result, all Americans, but especially black people, suffer through distortion and deletion. Journalism has used its power of appraisal to mentally disenfranchise us.[136]

The legacies of slavery have been reinforced in numerous ways by the mainstream mass communications system in the United States. Not only have blacks suffered from the general reinforcement of the political-economic status quo, but also the dominant media have tended either to ignore African Americans or to caricature them, often brutally and destructively. In response, blacks have opted to found their own mass communications networks, not to mention the political component of a number of black churches.

Blacks and the White Media.   In terms of race, one need only look at the dearth of black stockholders, executives, and employees in the major national media to begin to understand why blacks have long been portrayed as caricatures and why black issues emerge so slowly in the public consciousness. But the problem runs far deeper than the general impact on society as a whole, for black consciousness itself also has been affected by these practices.

Underrepresentation.   As Hanes Walton, Jr., put it, "The perennial problem confronting black political opinion is that it cannot stop one sphere of society from creating its picture of reality, but it must constantly reshape the distortions it creates to fit its own perceptions."[137] One of the primary reasons for such misrepresentation would seem to be the disproportionately small number of blacks in the decision-making ranks of the mass media.

Blacks are underrepresented at all levels of the media business. Even after significant efforts by the FCC, beginning in 1978, African Americans still own fewer than 2 percent of the nation's radio and television stations.[138] Virtually none of the top network executives are black. Very few daily newspapers have blacks in executive management positions. In the entire national press corps, there are only a handful of syndicated black columnists and approximately 30 black editorial writers, while fewer than 6 percent of all print journalists are black and a nearly half of all daily newspapers have no minority journalists.[139] What is more, the modest gains blacks have been making seem to have leveled off in recent years,[140] and media executives have even began to talk openly about scaling back their diversity efforts.[141]

On the entertainment side, the situation is slowly improving. As late as the early 1980s, there were almost no blacks in decision-making positions here either. Even the much acclaimed television series *Roots*, for example, had no black producers, no black assistant producers, no black writers, and no black directors. Yet, following the commercial success of *The Cosby Show*, the number of black-oriented programs expanded, many of them under black direction. For example, executive producers of such programs have included Bill Cosby and Debbie Allen (*A Different World*), Keenan Ivory Wayans (*In Living Color*), and Quincy Jones (*Fresh Prince of Bel Air*).[142]

Overall, however, the dearth of blacks in discretionary positions has a number of implications. It no doubt leads to some inequity of treatment within the media ranks. On *Roots*, for example, two white actors earned more money for their performances than did all of the black cast combined.[143] More significant yet is the impact of what ends up being presented in the press and over the airwaves.

> One of the ways [in which] institutionalized racism is manifest is that the news media do not consider the condition of the black community to be newsworthy. The income gap between whites and blacks has widened. Segregation is greater in the North now than it was 25 years ago. Police brutality is still one of the major sources of irritation in the black community. Black teenage unemployment never fell below 35 percent . . . . Yet, little media attention was focused on these forms of racism.[144]

Invisibility.   As Jesse Jackson suggests, there is little coverage of chronic problems African Americans face. Court-ordered school busing is a classic case-in-point. Governmentally required busing of black students to inferior segregated schools received virtually no media coverage prior to the 1950s, whereas court-ordered busing of blacks to white schools filled the newspapers and the airwaves.[145] Syndicated black columnists William Raspberry and Carl Rowan both cite numerous examples of this phenomenon. In the midst of the 1967 Watts unrest, for example, Raspberry recalls searching the back issues of the *Los Angeles Times* without finding a single story on that predominantly black community.[146]

> Television programming still reflects stereotypes and prejudices that perpetuate feelings of inferiority in blacks and superiority in whites. Until minorities gain access in policy-making positions in programming, in both radio and television shows alike, . . . [television shows] will continue to poison the minds of viewers.[147]

Black Images.   While blacks have tended to be ignored in public affairs programming, when black faces do appear they are often the faces of poverty, crime, and other social pathologies.[148] In addition, African Americans often have been blatantly caricatured on the entertainment side. One need not watch many episodes of *Good Times, Sanford and Son, The Jeffersons,* or even *Martin, The Wayans Brothers,* and *Homeboys in Outer Space,* to harken back to the bad old days of Amos and Andy, Aunt Jemima, and Rochester. And although change has been occurring gradually, with the development of series such as *The Cosby Show, Moesha, Living Single,* and *Sister, Sister,* there are still a number of shows in which black characters continue to be presented as lightweight buffoons, mammies, superstuds, or criminals; only fueling the stereotypes held by much of white America.[149]

As Jesse Jackson summarized, "Television's major violation of us is a consistent combination of distortion and deletion which projects us as less intelligent, more violent, less hard-working, and less universal than we are." He goes on to conclude that "television's projection of us almost makes welfare, poverty, unemployment, and blacks synonymous.[150]

Such stereotyping does not stop with television. Harvard's Jeanne Chall, for instance, found blacks badly underrepresented and stereotyped in children's books as well.[151]

> It cannot be denied that by adding a few black faces on television, the medium which probably has the greatest impact on the black population, the white cultural rulers have taken a major step toward co-opting, distorting, and essentially nullifying [black America].[152]

Impact.   Feeding both white stereotypes and white indifference to black problems are only the most obvious results of such distortions. Just as devastating is the apparent impact on blacks' self-perceptions and political world views.

Blacks watch more television than whites, and they listen to considerably more radio than they watch television.[153] They also have been a more reliable newspaper market of late.[154] Consequently, they are exposed to the full gamut of mass media messages. This may well help explain why blacks exhibit the same inclination as whites to distrust political and economic leaders, leaders increasingly pilloried in the media. Like whites, blacks also demonstrate relatively low levels of political satisfaction. At the same time, both blacks and whites strongly support the rarely attacked political-economic system itself. Also, quite similar to whites, nearly three-quarters of all blacks identify themselves as moderate or conservative, only 17 percent conceive of themselves even as liberal, and very few as radical.[155] Meanwhile, in contrast to whites, African Americans as a group tend to have lower feelings of political efficacy and greater deference to authority.[156]

The end result is a black population that tends to mistrust the officials who operate the system they feel they have little control over, yet they remain loyal to that system and deferent to its leaders' authority. The degree to which any of this can be linked to the content of the media is uncertain; but, at very least, the media are reinforcing such perceptions by their failure to expose and attack the underlying structures themselves, and African Americans appear increasingly suspicious of the mainstream media. Jesse Jackson reached this conclusion:

> To the degree . . . journalism accurately and fairly informs and educates the public, to that same degree will it retain its moral authority and believability. Right now, as far as black people are concerned, it has been weighed and found wanting.[157]

It is in part out of such dissatisfaction with the white media that the black media have arisen, proliferated, and become important in the black community. In addition, the deficiencies of the white media contributed to the sizable role of the black church as a forum for political communication.

The Black Media

> The forces that operated on the Negro population for three centuries and more were of such nature as to create a distinctly separate Negro world within the American community.[158]

Beyond a strong informal network, or "grapevine," of information transference,[159] black-oriented media are quite important as well. Although often constrained by relatively small budgets, attributable in large part to a difficulty in attracting white advertisers, black media such as newspapers and radio stations can at least function without some of the shortcomings exhibited by their white counterparts. Black people are normally in the key decision-making positions, lending more of a black perspective to public affairs coverage and what entertainment is provided. Black-related issues are covered far more regularly, and black images are not as apt to be tarnished by the ignorance or prejudices of whites. Consequently, these media allow African Americans a less obstructed forum for political communication among themselves and for analyzing events from a black perspective, even if the larger American population remains reliant on the dominant sources.

> Negro newspapers of the twentieth century took up the cudgel in behalf of the underprivileged. They became the medium through which the yearnings of the race were expressed, the platform from which the Negro leaders could speak, the coordinator of mass action which Negroes felt compelled to take, and a major instrument by which many Negroes were educated with respect to public affairs.[160]

Black media emerged in the nineteenth century, with the first black newspaper appearing in 1827. One of the earliest and best known was the *North Star*, produced by Frederick Douglass primarily for the purpose of articulating antislavery points of view. Since those early days, some 2,700 different black papers have appeared, reaching peak proliferation in the 1950s. They grew in circulation with the advent of the Great Migration northward. As blacks became concentrated in central cities, several papers had circulations exceeding 100,000 by 1920 and twice that 20 years later.[161]

In recent years, approximately 200 black-owned newspapers have existed at any point in time, and most have been weeklies.[162] New York City has featured weeklies as well as the *Daily Challenge* (a daily) and the *New York Page* (a monthly). In political outlook, again using New York City examples, they have ranged from more racially separatist and politically radical papers like the *Big Red* and the *City Sun* to more integrationist and politically moderate papers like the *New York Voice* and the *Amsterdam News*. In between have been a variety of newspapers in other cities, such as Longworth Quinn's *Michigan Chronicle* (Detroit), John Sergstracke's long-standing *Chicago Defender*, Carlton Goodlett's *San Francisco Sun Reporter*, and Charles Tisdale's *Jackson Advocate*. Meanwhile, the National Association of Black Journalists has become well organized and increasingly assertive.[163]

As for magazines, John Johnson's personal empire includes *Ebony, Jet, and EM,* with a combined circulation of roughly 3 million. By 1990, the Johnson Publishing Company, the second largest black-owned business in the nation, also included a nationally syndicated television series and three radio stations.[164]

Over the airwaves, minorities own roughly 3 percent of the commercial radio and television stations across the United States,[165] and two black-oriented radio networks, the National Black Network and the Mutual Black Network. In addition, Bob Law's *Night Talk* has been a syndicated radio show, and it is part of the growth in black talk radio—a new and important medium for intracommunity communication and mobilization.[166] On television, *Tony Brown's Journal, Soul Train, Black Journal,* and the *Ebony/Jet Showcase* are among the nationally syndicated black programs, while cable television offers the Black Entertainment Network.

As far as common content, black radio stations, for example, focus far more on the work of black entertainers and types of music and humor traditionally popular in the black community. On the public affairs side, Alan Morrison concluded that these stations have "continued to voice the aspirations, articulate the demands and protests, and mirror the progress and problems of . . . Negro Americans."[167] Most of these sources have been restrained in their criticism of black elected officials and leaders. Instead, they have normally opted to discuss and critically analyze political issues of the day, without much of the general media's emphasis on "fires, sex, and freaks," and they spend a fair amount of time countering myths and attacks propounded in the white media.[168] In addition, they provide a forum for black leaders that for a long time tended to be limited to the black church.

THE BLACK CHURCH

The foundations of modern black politics are found within the black church.[169]

The black church has often served as an important network for political communication over the course of black history in the United States. The visibility and the extent of the church's political role is a phenomenon relatively unique to the experience of African Americans.

Independent black churches first began to appear in significant numbers during the period of the American Revolution, and they really flourished after the Civil War. The African Methodist Episcopal Church, for example, grew from 20,000 members in 1856 to more than 200,000 members by 1876. Black Baptists grew from 150,000 in 1850 to 500,000 by 1870.[170] Thereafter, these church memberships soared again. Reaching a membership peak around 1910, their numbers have fallen some since.[171]

Somewhat by default, the churches became central black institutions in the realm of politics. As John Hope Franklin explained it, "The lack of opportunities for Negroes to participate fully in the affairs of other institutions caused many to concentrate their energies and attention on the church."[172] Among other things, they recruited and provided a training ground for black political leaders as well as offering a forum for political communication and organization—especially during the darkest days of Jim Crow exclusion.[173] Ministers actually held positions at state constitutional conventions, on school boards, and in other public organizations during Reconstruction, and ministers like Martin Luther King, Jr. and Ralph Abernathy were at the forefront of the civil rights movement that would finally sweep away the Jim Crow laws. A number of black ministers have continued to hold elected public office, and black churches continue to play important supporting roles in black politics.[174]

Not confined by the economic necessity to turn a profit, as are most mass media, the black church has been in a relatively unique position to facilitate a truly free-wheeling discussion of political and economic alternatives. Nevertheless, black churches have been accused by some critics of having significant limitations as well.

The church, for example, has been accused of often directing attention primarily to spiritual well-being and life after death and at times seeming to downplay the impacts of U.S. history and the American political-economic system on the plight of many African Americans.[175] These, among other factors, are said to have led a number of black churches to be painfully apolitical at crucial times in black history. For example, Manning Marable and others have noted an almost deafening silence during lynchings, postReconstruction disenfranchisement, unabated economic exploitation, and attacks on black radicals.[176] Gary Marx even went so far as to speak of the churches' "opiate" effect in the political arena, implying that they often stifle political energies rather than promoting aggressive political activism.[177] In addition, a sizable number of black ministers have at times even taken up the conservative banner, as in fighting to retain segregation.[178]

To be fair, it is important not to lump all black churches and religious leaders together. There has been considerable variation in both the level of political activism and political-economic ideology, with considerable evolution evident over time. From reactionary Christian fundamentalism to radical Black Muslims to the liberalism exhibited by many members of the Southern Christian Leadership Council to the advocates of *liberation theology*, black churches and leaders have supported a tremendous range of political orientations.[179]

OPTIONS FOR BLACK AMERICA

Consider the efforts of Emma Bowen. Her Black Citizens for Fair Media had as many as 200 organizational members, including churches and professional associations. At its strongest, it met regularly with network-owned television stations in New York City to discuss black grievances, including the need for more training and hiring of black broadcasters and more documentaries on black problems.[180]

Another example is *The Chicago Reporter*, published monthly since 1972 and directed particularly at civic leaders, politicians, and mainstream media editors. Funded in large part by private foundations, this well-regarded newsletter has long provided honest and hard-hitting accounts of race and poverty issues in the city. For example, the *Reporter* undertook a statistical analysis of how a proposed redistricting plan would effect the racial balance of the city council. Their findings prompted the U. S. Justice Department to file a federal lawsuit that ultimately led to a less discriminatory plan.[181]

Besides similar private efforts to broaden the distribution of political-economic power, what else needs to be done to alter the conservative socialization process? Focus here will be placed on the two secular components of the information arena: education and the mass media.

Education

What all this boils down to is, are we trying to raise sheep—timid, docile, easily driven or led—or free men? If what we want is sheep, our schools are perfect as they are. If what we want is free men, we'd better start making some big changes.[182]

School Governing Boards.   One of these changes needs to be in the composition of the school boards and trustees who make the ultimate decisions concerning curricula, speakers, field trips, hirings, firings, and the like. To reduce the influence of the owning class, these positions could be filled randomly, leaving each person whose name is drawn the option to decline. But this would nevertheless involve filling these slots with people who are products of the existing educational system; thus the specific changes in that system must be discussed.

School Curricula.   Certainly children must learn skills and habits that ultimately allow them to support themselves; however, this can be done without leaving them so oblivious to their own exploitation in the current work place. To accomplish this, school curricula will require fundamental alterations, and teachers and administrators must be protected from political pressures during this implementation—as through the random selection of their highest superiors. Curriculum reform could begin with unification of the study of politics and economics; their interrelationships must be analyzed as a regular part of the curriculum. Alternative ideologies and political-economic systems must be studied at the same time that the dominant ones are taught. The histories of an increasingly diverse nation must be more broadly studied as well, and studied from more than the white Eurocentric perspective. Additionally, the people and events in American history must be evaluated critically rather than perfunctorily glorified. Overall, the schools must perform their socialization role by teaching even the youngest students to think and choose rather than simply to believe.[183]

Behavioral Instruction.   The emphasis in behavioral lessons must shift as well. Classroom order must be maintained if learning is to occur, but the schools have to move away from training robotlike individuals who are motivated primarily by individual incentives and competition. Instead of class rankings on the basis of rote knowledge and social conformity, emphasis should be on traits like creativity, innovation, independent thought, critical analysis, outspokenness, cooperation, and other-orientation. When those behavioral characteristics begin to dominate the elementary school checklists, progress will have been made.

School Funding.   Inequities in school funding have become so extreme that state courts have begun requiring more redistributive funding formulas.[184] Nonetheless, if we are serious about equal opportunity, schools need to be funded in an even more equitable fashion. No public school should have to operate on less than 90 percent of what the wealthiest public or private school has to spend. One way to raise the additional money necessary so as continually to elevate a number of the public schools to that level would be to set up a progressive school-funding arrangement on a national basis. Employers and employees could each be required to contribute a percentage of their incomes, in proportion to what they are making. These federal revenues would then be set aside exclusively for equalizing school funding. This would not only help guarantee more equal educational opportunities, but also tax most heavily many of the people who have gained the most from the educational system. In addition, given the demands of the postindustrial job market, it may well be time to consider extending publicly funded education beyond high school to at least two years of postsecondary study.

Mass Media

> For the press, . . . freedom is not simply a right and a privilege, it is a duty. [The press], more than any other institution, are trustees of the nation, because no one else gives their opinion so openly and so regularly.[185]

In terms of content, more freedom-restricting governmental censorship is not the answer. Instead, a variety of structural changes seem more appropriate to the goal of fundamentally altering certain media practices.

Black Perspectives.   Black presence needs to be increased in existing media and regulatory bodies. Virtually as true now as when the post-riot Kerner Commission concluded it in 1968, "Along with the country as a whole, the press has too long basked in a white world, looking out of it, if at all, with white men's eyes and a white perspective. That is no longer good enough."[186]

To begin with, the FCC needs one or more black commissioners, and it in turn needs to promote the hiring of more African Americans by radio and television stations. In addition, talented blacks must be located and then placed in managerial positions throughout the Public Broadcasting System (PBS). And, public funds should be made available to assist the starting of black media companies. The latter could involve setting aside portions of PBS monies for black public broadcasting stations and providing low-cost financing for black entrepreneurs seeking to start stations in the commercial sector.

Less Elite Control.   It seems appropriate to think of media as one of the nation's most "strategic industries," and one that requires a very strict standard for avoiding monopolization given the nature of the enterprise. The larger mass-media corporations should be subject to stiff antitrust laws. No investor, for example, should be allowed to hold stock directly or indirectly in more than one media company, to control more than 5 percent of that company's stock, or to have that share in a market in which he or she has other investments, creating possibilities for conflicts of interest. Then, within those less monopolized firms, media decision making should be insulated as much as possible from the profit concerns of stockholders and advertisers in order to reduce influence on media content. For example, the FCC could require that all advertisements be randomly assigned across the various media companies and slots that offer the audience size and demographics desired. Or, the U.S. Supreme Court could extend the logic of *DeSoto County Board of Supervisors v. North Mississippi Communications, Inc.*[187] Instead of finding only government to be in violation of the First Amendment when it pulls advertising money from unflattering media sources, this same principal could be applied to private companies that do the same thing.

Nonprofit Media.   Nonprofit public channels should be expanded and further freed from political pressure. One need only compare the quality of public affairs broadcasting on PBS and C-Span, in contrast to most commercial stations, to note the value of having healthy publicly funded alternatives. Beyond what already exists, a public wire service and public newspaper chain could be established, structured like PBS and National Public Radio (NPR). However, PBS, NPR, and the new Public Newspaper Network (PNN) need to receive the large majority of their operating revenues from the federal government, and that funding should be insulated from the direct control of elected officials. The latter could be accomplished by imposing a small operating tax on commercial radio and television stations, placing these funds in an entitlement budgetary category, and then putting them in a blind trust for 25 years at a time. In addition, the management of these public media could be chosen by professional journalists' associations.[188]

Direct Public Access.   Funding for public-service spots and public-service newspaper advertisements needs to be granted to the widest possible array of interest groups on a random basis. Commercial broadcasters should be obliged to carry them at various times across the entire broadcasting schedule. And, their messages should not be censored, except on the basis of nationally established obscenity guidelines. In addition, the advent of cable television has substantially increased possibilities for popular access. As low-frequency channels proliferate, these should be assigned randomly so that all interest groups have equal opportunities to communicate over these less expensive airwaves.[189]

More extreme would be a constitutional amendment to extend rights of free expression. Assuming that freedom of speech is essentially useless if no one else can be reached, First Amendment protection could be expanded to include a positive right to media access. It would then be up to government and the various media to determine how to comply before being compelled to do so by the courts.

NOTES

1. ABC New-Louis Harris poll, conducted September 1–5, 1979.
2. *New York Times*, August 3, 1977; June 28, 1978.
3. Benjamin I. Page, "Taxes and Inequality: Do the Voters Get What They Want?" unpublished manuscript.
4. Doris Lessing, *The Golden Notebook* (New York: Simon & Schuster, 1962), pp. xvi-xvii.
5. George Bereday and B. B. Stretch, "Political Education in the USA and the USSR," *Comparative Education Review* (June 1963).
6. Michael Parenti, *Democracy for the Few* (New York: St. Martin's, 1995), p. 35; Betty Bacon, ed., *How Much Truth Do We Tell Our Children?* (Minneapolis: MEP Publications, 1988); David Hess and Judith Tomey, *The Development of Political Attitudes in Children* (Garden City, N.Y.: Doubleday, 1968), p. 41; *New York Times*, September 23, 1970.
7. Howard Zinn, *A People's History of the United States* (New York: Harper & Row, 1980), chap. 1.
8. Formal exceptions include the state of New York requiring that all public school students be taught about the Irish potato famine, slavery, and the Holocaust; New Jersey adding the Armenian genocide at the hands of the Turks; and Montana including the "cultural integrity" of Native Americans.
9. John Harrigan, *Empty Dreams, Empty Pockets: Class and Bias in American Politics* (New York: Macmillan, 1993), pp. 96–97; Hess and Torney, *Development of Political Attitudes*; *New York Times*, September 23, 1970.
10. Jonathan Kozol, *The Night Is Dark and I Am Far from Home* (Boston: Houghton Mifflin, 1975), p. 177.
11. See Karen DeWitt, "Brought to You by Exxon—School Reform," *New York Times*, July 21, 1991.
12. For examples, see Parenti, *Democracy for the Few*, pp. 33–34; Clyde Barrow, *Universities and the Capitalist State* (Madison: University of Wisconsin, 1990), chap. 3; Aaron Johnson, "Corporate Takeover of Higher Education." *Democratic Left*, Issue 7/8, 1997, pp. 14–16. Kathleen Hart, "Is Academic Freedom Bad for Business?" *Bulletin of Atomic Scientists* (April 1989), pp. 28–34; Harvard Watch, *Scholars, Inc.: Harvard Academics in Service of Industry and Government* (Cambridge, Mass.: Harvard Watch, 1988); David Vogel, "Business's New Class Struggle," *The Nation* (December 15, 1979).

   In March of 1995, as an exception to the rule, Texas Oil magnate Lee Bass offered Yale University a $20 million grant if it would establish a Western Civilization program and allow him to oversee faculty hiring in that area. After considerable debate, Yale took the nearly unprecedented step of refusing such a donation. For example, see Jacques Steinberg, "Yale Returns $20 Million to an Unhappy Patron," *New York Times*, March 15, 1995; Jonathan Lear, "The $20 Million Question," *New York Times*, March 22, 1995.
13. For examples, see Barrow, *Universities and the Capitalist State*, chap. 3; Parenti, *Democracy for the Few*, pp. 33–34; *New York Times*, October 9, 1981; Sheila Harty, *Hucksters in the Classroom* (Washington, D.C.: Center for Study of Responsive Law, 1979); Betty Medsger, "The Free Propaganda That Floods the Schools," *Progressive* (December 1976).
14. See Memphis *Commercial Appeal*, March 18, 1995, p. A2.
15. For more on this trend, see Memphis *Commercial Appeal*, June 9, 1991, p. A5.
16. For example, see Alex Molnar, *Giving Kids the Business: The Commercialization of America's Schools* (Boulder, Colo.: Westview Press, 1996); Stewart Ewen, *PR! A Social History of Hype* (New York: Basic, 1996); Sheila Harty, *Hucksters in the Classroom*; William Honan, "Scholars Attack Public School TV Program," *New York Times*, January

22, 1997; Deborah Stead, "Cash-poor schools open doors to commercialism," *Memphis Commercial Appeal*, January 5, 1997, p. A6.

17. For examples, see Barrow, *Universities and the Capitalist State*, chaps. 2–3; Rodney Harrett, *College and University Trustees* (Princeton, N.J.: Educational Testing Service, 1969), p. 65.

18. For some specific examples at the college level, see Phillip Meranto et al., *Guarding the Ivory Tower* (Denver: Lucha, 1985); Barrow, *Universities and the Capitalist State*, chap. 7.

19. Examples are numerous and varied. Besides the ones detailed in ibid., Accuracy in Academia formed to secretly monitor the "truthfulness" of what was being taught in American classrooms. Marxist Bertell Ollman was denied the chairmanship of the University of Maryland's Department of Political Science after reactionary members of the state legislature rallied to force school officials to change their minds. Small reactionary groups have acquired virtual censorship power over government textbooks in Texas and English texts in East Tennessee. The list goes on. For example, see Rochelle Stanfield, "Pure Library Shelves, Pure Minds?" *National Journal*, September 19, 1992, p. 2153.

20. John Holt, *Freedom and Beyond* (New York: Dutton, 1972), p. 251.

21. *New York Times*, May 4, 1983. For an earlier analysis of how high school social studies texts treated communism and capitalism during the Cold War, see C. Benjamin Cox and Byron Massialas, *Social Studies in the United States* (New York: Harcourt, Brace, and World, 1967). Also see William Appleman Williams, *The Great Evasion* (Chicago: Quadrangle Books, 1964); Sidney Fine, *Laissez-Faire and the General-Welfare State* (Ann Arbor: University of Michigan, 1964).

22. Herman Hesse, *Beneath the Wheel* (New York: Farrar, Strauss & Giroux, 1968), p. 54.

23. Quoted in David Hagan, *Capitalism and Schooling*, dissertation, University of Chicago, 1978, p. 251.

24. For example, see San Francisco Board of Education, *Report of the Commission on Manual Training* (San Francisco, March 14, 1894); Joel Spring, "From Study Hall to Hiring Hall," *The Progressive* (April 1984), p. 31. For more detailed discussion of this entire subject, see Ira Katznelson and Margaret Weir, *Schooling for All: Race, Class, and the Decline of the Democratic Ideal* (New York: Basic Books, 1985); Barrow, *Universities and the Capitalist State*, chaps. 2–4.

25. Names have been changed.

26. Samuel Bowles and Herbert Gintis, *Schooling in Capitalist America* (New York: Basic Books, 1976), pp. 135–137; David Gordon, *Problems in Political Economy: An Urban Perspective* (Lexington, Mass.: Heath, 1977), p. 213; Daniel Bell, *The Cultural Contradictions of Capitalism* (New York: Basic Books, 1976).

27. John Holt, *The Underachieving School* (New York: Pitman, 1969), pp. 19–20.

28. Holt, *Freedom and Beyond*, p. 255.

29. Rose Hoffman, third-grade teacher, quoted in Studs Terkel, *Working* (New York: Avon, 1974), p. 635.

30. Phil Stallings, welder, quoted in Terkel, *Working*, p. 222.

31. Bowles and Gintis, *Schooling in Capitalist America*, p. 174.

32. Samuel Bowles, "Unequal Education and the Reproduction of the Hierarchical Division of Labor," in Richard Edwards (ed.), *The Capitalist System* (Englewood Cliffs, N.J.: Prentice-Hall, 1972), p. 219.

33. Benjamin DeMott, *The Imperial Middle: Why Americans Can't Think Straight about Class* (New York: William Morrow, 1990)

34. See Chapter 5. Also see Christopher Jencks, *Inequality: A Reassessment of the Effect of Family and Schools in America* (New York: Basic Books, 1972); Richard De Lone, *Small*

Futures: Children, Inequality, and the Limits of Liberal Reform (Orlando, Fla.: Harcourt Brace Jovanovich, 1979); Carnegie Council on Children Report, *Behavior Today* (September 10, 1979); Edgar Litt, " Civic Education, Community Norms, and Political Indoctrination," *American Sociological Review* 28–1 (February 1963), pp. 69–75.

35. Jencks, *Inequality*.
36. Everett Reimer, *School Is Dead* (Garden City, N.Y.: Doubleday, 1971), p. 19. For a more recent discussion of this point, see DeMott, *The Imperial Middle*.
37. W. E. B. Du Bois, *Black Reconstruction in America, 1860–1880* (New York: Atheneum, 1971), p. 638. Also see Carter Woodson, *The Education of the Negro prior to 1861* (Washington, D.C.: Associated Publishers, 1919).
38. John Hope Franklin, *From Slavery to Freedom: A History of Negro Americans* (New York: Knopf, 1980), p. 237.
39. For example, see James Comen and Norris Haynes, "Meeting the Needs of Black Children in Public Schools," in Charles Willie, Antoine Garibaldi, and Wornie Reed, eds., *The Education of African-Americans* (New York: Auburn House, 1991), chap. 5. And as for evidence of school succeeding in the political indoctrination of black children, see New York Times, July 4, 1990.
40. Jonathan Kozol, *Savage Inequalities: Children In America's Schools* (New York: Crown Publishers, 1991), p. 2.; Jonathan Kozol, *Death at an Early Age* (Boston: Houghton Mifflin, 1967), p. 147.
41. Kozol, *Death at an Early Age*, p. 33.
42. Lucius Barker and Jesse McCorry, *Black Americans and the Political System* (Cambridge, Mass.: Winthrop, 1976), p. 97.
43. For examples, see Kozol, *Death at an Early Age*; Bel Kaufman, *Up the Down Staircase* (Englewood Cliffs, N.J.: Prentice-Hall, 1964); Robert Coles, *Teachers and the Children of Poverty* (Washington, D.C.: Potomac Institute, 1970); Herbert Kohl, *36 Children* (New York: New American Library, 1967).
44. Malcolm X, *The Autobiography of Malcolm X* (New York: Grove Press, 1965), p. 36. For a more general discussion of the phenomenon, see Ray Rist, "Student Social Class and Teacher Expectations: The Self-Fulfilling Prophecy in Ghetto Education," *Harvard Educational Review* 40 (1970), pp. 411–451.
45. Kozol, *Savage Inequalities*, chaps. 2–3; *New York Times*, December 12, 1988; February 18, 1990; September 20, 1990; February 14, 1995; Memphis *Commercial Appeal*, November 25, 1988; Robert Green, *The Urban Challenge: Poverty and Race* (Chicago: Follett, 1977), pp. 217–221.
46. For a discussion of the "educational apartheid" that seems to be developing, see Neil Peirce, "'Governor Guts' Takes A Tough Stand," *National Journal*, February 27, 1993, p. 531.
47. Franklin, *From Slavery to Freedom*, p. 403. For a more detailed discussion of black educational opportunities, see Horace Mann Bond, *The Education of the Negro in the American Social Order* (Englewood Cliffs, N.J.: Prentice-Hall, 1934); Meyer Weinberg, *A Chance to Learn: A History of Race and Education in the United States* (New York: Cambridge University Press, 1977), chaps. 1–3,7. And as for contemporary discrepancies in school funding by race, see Andrew Hacker, *Two Nations: Black and White, Separate, Hostile, Unequal* (New York: Scribner's, 1992), p. 173; Kozol, *Savage Inequalities;* E.D. Hirsch, Jr., "Good Genes, Bad Schools," *New York Times*, October 29, 1994.
48. *Gazette of the United States*, April 27, 1789, quoted in Frank Mott, *Jefferson and the Press* (Baton Rouge: Louisiana State University Press, 1943), p. 15.
49. Mott, *Jefferson and the Press*, pp.167–168.
50. In the Spring of 1996, *Wall Street Journal* circulation exceeded 1.8 million, *USA TODAY* 1.6, the *New York Times* 1.1, and the *Los Angeles Times* 1.0. See *New York Times*, April

17, 1996; April 30, 1996. Also see, Harold Stanley and Richard Niemi, eds., *Vital Statistics on American Politics* (Washington, D.C.: C Q Press, 1994); *New York Times*, September 22, 1991; C. Everett Ladd, *The American Polity* (New York: Norton, 1985), pp. 486–487.

51. Leo Bogart, *Commercial Culture: The Media System and the Public Interest* (New York: Oxford University Press, 1995), p. 283. For good general references concerning media history, see Ladd, *The American Polity*, p. 488; Edward Chester, *Radio, Television, and American Politics* (New York: Sheed and Ward, 1969); Lawrence Lichty and Topping Malachi, *American Broadcasting* (New York: Hastings House, 1975); Michael Schudson, *Discovering the News* (New York: Basic Books, 1978).

52. *Near v. Minnesota*, 283 U.S. 679 (1931).

53. *New York Times v. United States*, 403 U.S. 713 (1971).

54. See *Curtis Publishing Co. v. Butts* 388 U.S. 130 (1967). In *Rosenbloom v. Metromedia* 403 U.S. 29 (1971), this category was broadened to include private individuals who happened to be involved in matters of "public or general interest;" although the Burger court narrowed the latter definition some in decisions such as *Gertz v. Robert Welch, Inc.* 418 U.S. 323 (1974), *Time, Inc. v. Firestone* 424 U.S. 448 (1976), and *Hutchinson v. Proxmire* 443 U.S. 111 (1979).

55. *Philadelphia Newspapers, Inc. v. Hepps*, 475 U.S. 767 (1986).

56. *New York Times v. Sullivan*, 376 U.S. 279 (1964).

57. For someone who is not a "public figure," or for a public figure when the story is not deemed to be "of legitimate public concern," the plaintiff need not prove the media's recklessness or awareness of the story's falsity. Instead, the plaintiff need only show that the story was false and damaging. See *Gertz v. Robert Welch, Inc.*, 418 U.S. 323 (1974); *Dun and Bradstreet, Inc. v. Greenmoss Builders, Inc.*, 472 U.S. 749 (1985).

58. For more on media's legally determined freedoms, see A. E. Howard, "The Press in Court," *Wilson Quarterly 6* (Special Issue 1982), pp. 86–93.

59. Doris Graber, *Mass Media and American Politics* (Washington, D.C.: CQ Press, 1994), chap. 3; Shanto Iyengar and Donald Kinder, *News That Matters* (Chicago, University of Chicago, 1987); Edward Epstein, *News from Nowhere* (New York: Vintage, 1973), pp. 16–17; David Paletz and Robert Entman, *Media Power Politics* (New York: Free Press, 1981), chap. 2; Howard Kahane, *Logic and Contemporary Rhetoric* (Belmont, Calif.: Wadsworth, 1980), pp. 228–234.

60. For example, see Iyengar and Kinder, *News That Matters*, pp. 33 and 60; W. Russell Neuman, "The Threshold of Public Attention," *Public Opinion Quarterly* (Summer 1990), pp. 159–176; Robert Entman, *Democracy without Citizens* (New York: Oxford University, 1989), p. 86; Jeffrey Berry, *The Interest Group Society* (Glenview, Ill.: Scott, Forseman, 1989), p. 110; Larry Bartels, "Messages Received," *American Political Science Review* 87 (June 1993), pp. 267–285.

61. Roper Organization, *Trends in Attitudes Towards Television and Other Media* (New York: Television Information Service, 1983), p. 8; Robert Bowen, *The Changing Television Audience in America* (New York: Columbia University Press, 1984); Warren Agee, Phillip Ault, and Edwin Emery, *Main Currents in Mass Communications* (New York: Harper & Row, 1986); Stanley and Niemi,*Vital Statistics on American Politics* , p. 53; Richard Zoglin, "Is TV Ruining Our Children?" *Time* (October 5, 1990); Stephen Ansolabehere, Roy Behr, and Shanto Iyengar, *The Media Game* (New York: Macmillan, 1993), pp. 13–14; Thomas Dye, *Who's Running America?* (Englewood Cliffs, N.J.: Prentice-Hall, 1995), pp. 122–123.

62. Kathleen Hall Jamieson and Karyn Kohrs Campbell, *The Interplay of Influence. Mass Media and Their Publics in News, Advertising, Politics* (Belmont, Calif: Wads won 1983),

p. 4; *New York Times,* June 27, 1989; Stanley and Niemi, *Vital Statistics on American Politics*, p. 53.

63. Pew Center for the People and The Press, *Survey* (May 1996); *Multimedia Audiences Report,* (New York: Mediamark Research, Spring 1992).

64. *The Ayer Directory of Publications* (Fort Washington, Pa.: IMS Press, annual); Stanley and Niemi,*Vital Statistics on American Politics* , p. 53.

65. Graber, *Mass Media and American Politics,* pp. 373–380; Jamieson and Campbell, *The Interplay of Influence*, pp. 11–12; James Boylan, "News People," *Wilson Quarterly 6* (Special Issue 1982), pp. 71–85.

66. See *New York Times,* December 24, 1990; June 19, 1992.

67. Benjamin Compaine, Christopher Sterling, Thomas Guback et al., *Who Owns the Media* (White Plains, N.Y.: Knowledge Industry, 1982).

68. *New York Times*, December 15, 1979.

69. *New York Times,* September 22, 1991; Compaine, *Who Owns the Media*, pp. 36–37; Bogart, *Commercial Culture:* pp. 58–60; James Rowe, "Chains Seen Buying More Papers," *Washington Post*, June 1, 1986, p. F2.

70. For example, see Bogart, *Commercial Culture*, chap. 2; *New York Times*, August 18, 1996.

71. Similar restrictions also exist for radio stations (e.g., companies in the largest markets can own only up to a total of eight stations, with no more than five on either the AM or FM bands). See Telecommunications Act of 1996; Kirk Victor, "Media Monsters," *National Journal*, March 2, 1996, pp. 480–484; *New York Times*, March 13, 1992; February 2, 1996.

72. *New York Times,* June 2, 1991.

73. Michael Parenti, *Inventing Reality* (New York: St. Martin's Press, 1985), p. 27; *Media Report to Women,* September 1, 1981, p. 4.

74. Peter Dreier and Steve Weinberg, "Interlocking Directorates," *Columbia Journalism Review* (November-December 1979), pp. 51–68; Ben Bagdikian, *The Media Monopoly* (Boston: Beacon Press, 1983); Dye, *Who's Running America?* chap. 4; Herbert Schiller, *Mass Communication and American Empire* (Boulder, Colo.: Westview, 1992).

75. William Greider, *Who Will Tell the People: The Betrayal of American Democracy* (New York: Simon & Schuster, 1992), p. 299.

76. For example, see *New York Times*, November 18, 1992; *Time*, November 30, 1992, p. 23; American Society of Newspaper Editors, *The Changing Face of the Newsroom* (Washington, D.C.: ASNE, 1989), p. 33; William Schneider and I. A. Lewis, "Views on the News," *Public Opinion* (August-September 1985), p. 7; G. Cleveland Wilhoit and David Weaver, *The American Journalist* (Bloomington: Indiana University, 1991); S. Robert Lichter, Stanley Rothman, and Linda Lichter, *The Media Elite* (New York: Hastings House, 1990), p, 47.

77. See William Lyons, John Scheib, and Lilliard Richardson, *American Government: Politics and Political Culture* (New York: West, 1995), p. 282.

78. Fred W. Friendly, *Due to Circumstances Beyond Our Control* (New York: Random House, 1967), pp. 281–282.

79. Ibid., pp. 271–272.

80. For example, see Laurel Campbell, "Commercial Timeouts Creep Up," Memphis *Commercial Appeal*, April 21, 1996, p. D1; *Advertising Age*, September 25, 1991.

81. *New York Times*, August 18, 1996; Dye, *Who's Running America?* p. 114; Parenti, *Democracy for the Few*, p. 166; Bogart, *Commercial Culture*, p. 267.

82. *New York Times*, August 17,1986 (press); *New York Times,* July 6,1988 (radio); Bogart, *Commercial Culture*, pt. II; Roger Noll, Merton Peck, and John McGowan, *Economic Aspects of Television Regulation* (Washington, D.C.: Brookings Institution, 1973), p.16; "Broadcasting and Cable," *Broadcasting* 96 (February 12, 1979): 23.

83. Bogart, *Commercial Culture*, p. 120. And, despite downturns, the 1996 profit rates of publicly traded newspapers were still twice that of the average Fortune 500 company. See *New York Times*, July 8, 1996.

84. For example, see U.S. Department of Commerce, Bureau of the Census, *Statistical Abstracts of the United States, 1982–1983* (Washington, D.C.: GPO, 1984), p. 562; Bogart, *Commercial Culture*, pp. 117–121.

85. For further indications of just how profitable the mass media have become, see Desmond Smith, "Mining the Golden Spectrum," *The Nation* (May 26, 1979); *New York Times*, December 12, 1977.

86. For example, see Bogart, *Commercial Culture*, pp. 103–121. One of the most developed examples of such delegation, a practice called "barter syndication," is detailed in *New York Times*, January 18, 1986; July 29, 1990.

87. *New York Times*, December 18, 1976.

88. Bogart, *Commercial Culture*, pt. II; N.R. Kleinfield, "The Networks' Advertising Dance," *New York Times*, July 29, 1990; Greider, *Who Will Tell the People*, chap 13.

89. Quoted in *New York Times*, August 6,1978.

90. *New York Times Magazine*, April 8, 1979, p. 52, Iver Peterson, "At Los Angeles Times, a Debate on News-Ad Interaction," *New York Times* November 17, 1997.

91. Ben Bagdikian, "Fires, Sex, and Freaks," *New York Times Magazine* (October 10, 1976).

92. Quoted in *New York Times*, October 1, 1993. Also see Carl Bernstein, "The Idiot Culture," *The New Republic*, June 8, 1992, pp. 24–25. For a discussion of subsequent newsroom morale, see William Glaberson, "Survey Finds Newsrooms Discontented," *New York Times*, November 23, 1992.

93. For example, see Entman, *Democracy without Citizens*, p. 111; Ron Powers, *The Newscasters* (New York: St. Martin's Press, 1977).

94. For example, see James Fallows, *Breaking the News: How the Media Undermine American Democracy* (New York: Pantheon, 1996).

95. Excerpted from 1958 speech to the Radio and Television News Directors Association, quoted in *New York Times*, July 27, 1990.

96. See Iver Petersen, "Study Finds Less Traditional News as Outlets Seek Move Relevant Content," *New York Times*, March 16, 1998.

97. For example, see Harold Stanley and Richard Niemi, eds., *Vital Statistics on American Politics* (Washington, D.C.: C Q Press, 1990), p. 57; James Q. Wilson, "Stage Struck," *New Republic*, June 21, 1993, pp. 31–32; *Newsweek*, March 2, 1992, pp. 24–26; Gregory Katz, "Issues Distant Second to 'Horse Race' Stories," *USA TODAY*, April 22, 1988, p. 6A; Harrigan, *Empty Dreams, Empty Pockets*, pp. 101–103. Michael J. Robinson, "The Media at Mid-Year," *Public Opinion* 3 (June/July 1980): 41–45.

98. For analysis of these trends in local television, see Randall Rothenberg, "More of Less From Local TV Stations," *New York Times*, November 2, 1990. And for a description of similar developments in the press portion of the mass media, see James Squires, *Read All About It! The Corporate Takeover of America's Newspapers* (New York: Random House, 1993).

99. *New York Times*, June 26,1977.

100. Ibid., May 20,1984.

101. For example, see Randall Rothenberg, "A Millions Channels and Nothing On," *New York Times*, October 23, 1996.

102. Bogart, *Commercial Culture*, pp. 99–101.

103. Frank Rich, "Media Amok," *New York Times*, May 18, 1996.

104. Ibid.

105. For example, see Bill Kovach, "Big Deals, With Journalism Thrown In," *New York Times*, August 3, 1995. Also see Frank Rich, "Good Night, David," *New York Times*, October 28,

1995. For a regular source of such exposes, see *EXTRA!*, the publication of Fairness and Accuracy in Reporting (FAIR).

106. See Frank Rich, "More Mogul Madness," *New York Times*, November 14, 1996.

107. Daniel Bell, quoted in Mitchell Levita, "Homelessness in America," *New York Times Magazine,* June 10, 1990, p. 91.

108. For example, see Noam Chomsky, *Necessary Illusions: Thought Control in Democratic Societies* (Boston: South End Press, 1989); Douglas Kellner, *Television and the Crisis of Democracy* (Boulder, Colo.: Westview Press, 1990).

109. For example, see Edward Herman and Noam Chomsky, *Manufacturing Consent: The Political Economy of the Mass Media* (New York: Pantheon Books, 1989); Andrew Kohut, "The Vocal Minority in American Politics," (Washington, D.C.: Times Mirror Center for the People and the Press, 1993); John Culhane, "Television Taboos," *New York Times*, February 20,1977.

110. Harrigan, *Empty Dreams, Empty Pockets*, pp. 104–108; Jonathan Tasini, "Lost in the Margins: Labor and the Media," A Special FAIR Report (Washington, D.C.: Fairness and Accuracy in Reporting, 1990); William Puette, *Through Jaundiced Eyes: How the Media View Organized Labor* (Ithaca, N.Y.: ILR Press, 1992); Parenti, *Inventing Reality*, chap. 6.

111. Parenti, *Inventing Reality*, chap. 6.

112. For example, see Larry Sabato, *Feeding Frenzy: How Attack Journalism Has Transformed American Politics* (New York: Free Press, 1991).

113. For example, see Morris Janowitz, *The Community Press in an Urban Setting* (Glencoe, Ill.: Free Press,1954); David Paletz, Peggy Reichert, and Barbara McIntyre, "How the Media Support Local Governmental Authority," *Public Opinion Quarterly* 35 (Spring 1971), pp. 80–92.

114. Quoted in Kahane, *Logic and Contemporary Rhetoric*, p. 236.

115. See Michael Parenti, *Make-Believe Media* (New York: St. Martin's, 1992); Parenti, *Inventing Reality*, chap. 1; Herbert Schiller, *The Mind Managers* (Boston: Beacon Press, 1973); Claus Mueller, *The Politics of Communication* (London: Oxford University Press, 1973).

   For examples of anti-establishment television shows getting little air time, see Erik Barnouw, *The Television Writer* (New York: Hill and Wang, 1962), p. 27; Robert Cirino, *Don't Blame the People* (New York: Vintage, 1972), pp. 303–306.

116. Ralph Miliband, *The State in Capitalist Society* (New York: Basic Books, 1969), p. 238.

117. *New York Times*, January 17, 1992; *Washington Post*, January 24, 1992; Parenti, *Inventing Reality*, chap. 2; Bagdikian, *The Media Monopoly*; Herbert Gans, *Deciding What's News* (New York: Vintage, 1979); James Aronson, *The Press and the Cold War* (Boston: Beacon Press, 1970).

118. Epstein, *News from Nowhere*; Timothy Crouse, *The Boys on the Bus* (New York: Ballantine, 1973); Sabato, *Feeding Frenzy* ; Greider, *Who Will Tell the People*, chap. 13; Graber, *Mass Media and American Politics*, p. 48; Ansolabehere, *The Media Game*, pp. 50–55;Harrigan, *Empty Dreams, Empty Pockets*, pp. 100–101, 114–116.

119. Leonard Matthews, quoted in *New York Times*, January 2, 1980.

120. Michael Parenti, *Democracy for the Few* (New York: St. Martin's Press, 1983), p. 193.

121. Bogart, *Commercial Culture*, pp. 101–102.

122. Tom Wicker, *On Press* (New York: Viking, 1978). Also see Todd Gitlin, "When the Right Talks, TV Listens," *The Nation* (October 15,1983), pp. 333–340.

123. *Economist*, December 5, 1987.

124. See *New York Times*, July 15, 1990; *Newsweek*, February 26, 1990, p. 4. For a more general account, see Ronald Collins, *Dictating Content: How Advertising Pressure Can Corrupt a Free Press* (Washington, D.C.: Center for the Study of Commercialism, 1993).

125. Kahane, *Logic and Contemporary Rhetoric*, p. 212; Bogart, *Commercial Culture*, chap. 4.

126. Lawrence Soley and Robert Craig, "Advertising Pressures on Newspapers: A Survey," *Journal of Advertising*, 21–4 (December 1992), pp. 1–10. For more examples, see Bogart, *Commercial Culture*, pp. 96–99.

127. For example, see Constance Hays, "Editors Urge Limits on Input By Advertisers," *New York Times*, June 23, 1997.

128. Vogel, "Business's New Class Struggle;" Bogart, *Commercial Culture*, pp. 94–95; *New York Times*, May 6, 1992.

129. David Vogel, "Business's New Class Struggle," *Nation*, December 15, 1979, pp. 609, *New York Times*, August 10, 1986.

130. William Domhoff, *The Powers That Be* (New York: Vintage, 1979), pp. 183–191; Stuart Ewen, *Captains of Consciousness* (New York: McGraw-Hill, 1976).

131. Bruce Howard, "The Advertising Council," *Ramparts* (December 1974-January 1975), pp. 25–26.

132. For example, see Carol Matlack, "Eyes On The Prizes," *National Journal*, February 23, 1991, p. 480; Burling Lowrey, "The Media's Honoraria," *Washington Post*, April 26, 1989.

133. For example, see Frank Rich, "Why Foster Lives," *New York Times*, October 11, 1995.

134. Communications Act of 1934, 27 USC 151(1934).

135. For a summary of the media's socializing role, see Noam Chomsky, "Ideological Conformity," *The Nation* (January 27,1979).

136. Roger Hatch and Frank Watkins (eds.), *Reverend Jesse L. Jackson: Straight from the Heart* (Philadelphia: Fortress, 1987), p. 318.

137. Hanes Walton, Jr., *Invisible Politics: Black Political Behavior* (Albany: State University of New York Press, 1985), p. 72.

138. As of 1993, that amounted to 181 radio stations and 19 television stations, out of the 11,021 total stations nationwide. See Geraldine Fabrikant, "Slow Gains by Minority Broadcasters," *New York Times*, May 31, 1994

139. *New York Times*, July 23, 1993; April 17, 1996; Clint Wilson and Felix Gutierrez, *Minorities and the Media* (Beverly Hills, Calif.: Sage, 1985); Hatch and Watkins, *Reverend Jesse L. Jackson*, p. 98; Parenti, *Inventing Reality*, p. 11).

140. *New York Times*, April 12, 1985; March 22, 1988; April 15, 1994; April 17, 1996; Christopher Campbell, *Race, Myth and the News* (Thousand Oaks, Cal.: Sage, 1995), p. 4. The numbers are somewhat better in radio and especially television; but, blacks remain underrepresented in both.

141. For example, see Felicity Barringer, "Editors Debate Realism vs. Retreat in Newsroom Diversity," *New York Times*, April 16, 1998.

142. Hatch and Watkins, *Reverend Jesse L. Jackson*, p. 319; Parenti, *Make-Believe Media*, chap. 8; Andrea Adelson, "How TV Is Creating New Perceptions About Blacks," *New York Times*, February 7, 1991.

143. Hatch and Watkins, *Reverend Jesse L. Jackson*.

144. Ibid., p. 296.

145. Kahane, *Logic and Contemporary Rhetoric*, p. 219.

146. William Raspberry, "Politics, Blacks, and the Press," in Richard Lee (ed.), *Politics and the Press* (Washington, D.C.: Acropolis, 1970), pp. 119–128. Also see Campbell, *Race, Myth and the News*, chap. 3.

147. Emma Bowen, quoted in *New York Times*, November 19, 1978.

148. For example, see Walter Goodman, "Missing From the Picture: Black Middle Class in the News," *New York Times*, May 22, 1990; Ishmael Reed, "Tuning Out Network Bias," *New York Times*, April 9, 1991; Martin Gilens, "Race and Poverty in America: Public Misperceptions and the American News Media," paper presented at the annual meeting of the American Political Science Association, Chicago, September 1995.

149. Randall Miller (ed.), *Ethnic Images in American Film and Television* (Philadelphia: Balch Institute, 1978); Bradley Greenberg, *Life on Television* (New York: Free Press, 1980); Anthony Jackson, ed., *Black Families and the Medium of Television* (Ann Arbor: University of Michigan's Bush Program in Child Development and Social Policy, 1982); John O'Connor, "On TV, Less Separate, More Equal," *New York Times*, April 29, 1990; Campbell, *Race, Myth and the News*, chap. 4.

150. Hatch and Watkins, *Reverend Jesse L. Jackson*, p. 320.

151. *New York Times*, January 8, 1978.

152. Robert Allen, *Black Awakening in Capitalist America: An Analytical History* (Garden City, N.Y.: Anchor/Doubleday, 1969), p. 182.

153. *The Crisis* (June-July 1985), p. 33; *New York Times* July 12, 1989.

154. *New York Times*, November 30, 1992.

155. *New York Times*/CBS poll, reported in *ibid.*, July 18,1986.

156. William Brink and Lou Harris, *Black and White* (New York: Simon & Schuster, 1967); Peter Goldman, *Report from Black America* (New York: Simon & Schuster, 1970); Milton Morris and Carolyn Cabe, "The Political Socialization of Black Youth," *Public Affairs Bulletin* (May-June 1972); Charles Bullock and Harrell Rodgers, *Black Political Attitudes* (Chicago: Markham, 1972); David Sears and John McConahay, *The Politics of Violence* (Boston: Houghton Mifflin, 1973); Lou Harris, *The Anguish of Change* (New York: Norton, 1974); Milton Morris, *The Politics of Black America* (New York: Harper & Row, 1975), pp. 124–135; Paul Abramson, *The Political Socialization of Black America* (New York: Free Press, 1977); Arthur Miller, "The Institutional Focus of Political Distrust," paper presented at the annual meeting of the American Political Science Association, August 1979.

157. Hatch and Watkins, *Reverend Jesse L. Jackson*, p. 323.

158. Franklin, *From Slavery to Freedom*, p. 412.

159. For example, see Patricia Turner, *I Heard It Through the Grapevine: Rumor in African American Culture* (Berkeley: University of California Press, 1993).

160. Ibid., p. 414.

161. Ibid., p. 415.

162. In 1989, for instance, there were 250 weeklies and 4 dailies, with total circulation estimated to be roughly 5 million. See *New York Times*, July 24, 1989.

163. For example, see Alex Jones, "Sense of Muscle for Black Journalists," *New York Times*, August 21, 1989.

164. See Roger Cohen, "Black Media Giant's Fire Still Burns," *New York Times*, November 19, 1990.

165. See *New York Times*, May 19, 1997. "Minorities" includes both blacks and Hispanics, and they owned 37 television stations and 293 radio stations as of 1995, down 10% from 1994.

166. For example, see William Schmidt, "Black Talk Radio: A Vital Force Is Emerging to Mobilize Opinion," *New York Times*, March 31, 1989.

167. Allan Morrison, "The Crusading Press,"in *The Negro Handbook* (Chicago: Johnson, 1966), p. 380. Also see Jeremy Gerard, "Minority Role in Broadcasting Yields Far Bigger Effect on Radio Than TV," *New York Times*, August 1, 1990; Sam Howe Verhovek, "Black Journalists Look to Advance: Group Says White Managers View Race in Newsroom Differently," *New York Times*, July 23, 1993.

168. James H. Brewer, "The Futile Trumpet," masters thesis, Virginia State University, 1959; Martin Dann (ed.), *The Black Press, 1827–1890* (New York: Capricorn, 1972); Edwina Mitchell, *The Crusading Black Journalist* (St. Louis: Farmer Press, 1972); Hanes Walton, Jr., Review of Andrew Buri, "Robert L. Vann of the Pittsburgh Courier," *American Historical Review* (December 1975), p. 1409.

169. Manning Marable, *How Capitalism Underdeveloped Black America* (Boston: South End Press, 1983), p. 197.

170. Franklin, *From Slavery to Freedom*, pp. 237–238.

171. Adolph Reed, Jr., *The Jesse Jackson Phenomenon* (New Haven, Conn.: Yale University Press, 1986), pp. 5–55.

172. Franklin, *From Slavery to Freedom*, p. 414. Also see Charles S. Johnson, *Growing Up in the Black Belt* (Washington, D.C.: American Council of Education, 1941); E. Franklin Frazier, *The Negro Church in America* (New York: Schocken, 1974).

173. Frazier, *The Negro Church in America*, pp. 47–50; Charles V. Hamilton, *The Black Preacher in American Politics* (New York: Morrow, 1972); Benjamin Mays and Joseph Nicholson, *The Negro's Church* (New York: Arno, 1969); "The National Black Survey, 1972–74," as summarized in Walton, *Invisible Politics*, pp. 47–48; Reed, *Jesse Jackson Phenomenon*, chap. 4; Doug McAdam, *Political Process and the Development of Black Insurgency* (Chicago: University of Chicago Press, 1982), p. 129; Everett Carll Ladd, *Negro Political Leadership in the South* (New York: Atheneum, 1969), p. 239; M. Elaine Burgess, *Negro Leaders in a Southern City* (Chapel Hill: University of North Carolina Press, 1960).

174. M. Kilson, "New Black Political Class," in Joseph Washington (ed.), *Dilemmas of the Black Middle Class* (Philadelphia: University of Pennsylvania Press, 1980), p. 87; Reed, *Jesse Jackson Phenomenon*, chap. 4. For an insightful prediction of such a transformation, see W. E. B. Du Bois, *The Souls of Black Folk* (Chicago: McClung, 1903), pp. 113–114.

175. For example, see Allison Davis et al., *Deep South* (Chicago: University of Chicago Press, 1941).

176. Marable, *How Capitalism Underdeveloped Black America*, chap. 7; "The Failure of the Negro Church," *Messenger* (October 1919), p. 6; V. F. Calverton, "Orthodox Religion: Does It Handicap Negro Progress?" *Messenger* (July 1927), pp. 221–236; LeRoi Jones, *Home* (New York: Morrow, 1966), pp. 94–95, 138–139; Gayraud Wilmore, *Black Religion and Black Radicalism* (Garden City, N.Y.: Anchor/Doubleday, 1973); Harold Cruse, *The Crisis of the Negro Intellectual* (New York: Morrow, 1967), pp. 90, 322; August Meier and Elliott Rudwick, *CORE: A Study in the Civil Rights Movement* (Urbana: University of Illinois Press, 1975), pp. 120, 270–271; Harold Cruse, *Rebellion or Revolution?* (New York: Morrow, 1968), pp. 60–62, 128.

177. Gary T. Marx, "Religion: Opiate or Inspiration of Civil Rights Militancy among Negroes?" *American Sociological Review* (February 1967), pp. 67–69.

178. Numan Bentley, *Massive Resistance* (Baton Rouge: Louisiana State University Press, 1969), pp. 294–301; James Graham Cook, *The Segregationists* (Englewood Cliffs, N.J.: Prentice-Hall, 1962); Martin Luther King, Jr., *Stride toward Freedom*, (New York: Harper & Row, 1958), pp. 34–36. For conflicting views, see Vincent Harding, "Religion and Resistance among Antebellum Negroes, 1800–1860," in August Meier and Elliott Rudwick (eds.), *The Making of Black America*, vol. 2 (New York: Atheneum, 1969); Hart Nelson and Anne Nelson, *The Black Church in the Sixties* (Lexington: University of Kentucky Press, 1975); Joe Feagin, "The Black Church: Inspiration or Opiate?" *Journal of Negro History* (October 1975); Charles Henry, Culture and African-American Politics (Indianapolis: Indiana University Press, 1990), chap. 4.

179. For an overview of the black church's role in contemporary electoral politics, see Katherine Tate, *From Protest to Politics: The New Black Voters in American Politics* (Cambridge, Mass.: Harvard University Press, 1994), pp. 95–103. For examples of the more militant positions, see C. Eric Lincoln, *The Black Church Since Frazier* (New York: Schocken Books, 1974); C. Eric Lincoln, *The Black Muslims in America* (Boston: Beacon Press, 1973); George Breitman (ed.), *Malcolm X Speaks* (New York: Grove Press, 1965); James Cone, *Black Theology and Black Power* (New York: Harper & Row, 1969); James Cone, *God of the Oppressed* (New York: Harper & Row, 1978); James Cone, *For My Peo-*

ple: Black Theology and the Black Church (Maryknoll, N.Y.: Orbis, 1984); James Cone, *A Black Theology of Liberation* (Maryknoll, N.Y.: Orbis, 1986); James Cone, *Speaking the Truth: Ecumenism, Liberation, and Black Theology* (Grand Rapids, Mich.: Eerdmans, 1986).

180. *New York Times*, November 19,1978. A more recent example of such advocacy is the Coalition Against Black Exploitation. See *New York Times*, July 13, 1990.

181. See William Schmidt, "A Small Newsletter Makes Big Waves Well Beyond Chicago," *New York Times*, June 26, 1989.

182. Holt, *Underachieving School*, p. 34.

183. For example, see Lawrence Levine, *The Opening of the American Mind* (Boston: Beacon Press, 1996); James Banks, "Social Studies, Ethnic Diversity, and Social Change," in Willie, *The Education of African Americans*; James Stewart, "The Field and Function of Black Studies," in Willie, *The Education of African Americans*; Kenneth Meier, James Stewart, and Robert England, *Race, Class, and Education: The Politics of Second-Generation Discrimination* (Madison: University of Wisconsin Press, 1989).

184. As of 1997, for example, 17 states had actually had their school financing systems declared unconstitutionally discriminatory by their state supreme courts. See *National Journal*, January 13, 1990, p. 84; *New York Times*, March 11, 1990; June 6, 1990; May 15, 1997.

185. Jesse Jackson, quoted in Hatch and Watkins, *Reverend Jesse L. Jackson*, pp. 320–321.

186. National Advisory Commission on Civil Disorders, *Report* (New York: Bantam, 1968), p. 389.

187. *DeSoto County Board of Supervisors v. North Mississippi Communications, Inc.* 951 F2nd 652 (1992).

188. Smaller variations of this plan actually have been proposed. For example, see Alvin Perlmutter, "The 1% Solution," *New York Times*, December 24, 1994; Karen DeWitt, "Public Broadcasters Propose Alternative to U.S. Financing," *New York Times*, May 3, 1995; Henry Morgenthau, "Airwaves for Sale," *New York Times*, March 4, 1994.

189. There is also some evidence that subscriber stations like Home Box Office (HBO) have been somewhat freer to push the boundaries of the political, economic, and social status quo. For example, see Bill Carter, "HBO as a Modern-Day Dickens," *New York Times*, November 1, 1992.

PART FOUR
CONCLUSIONS

Chapter 10

Shaping the Future

The whole history of the progress of human liberty shows all concessions yet made to her august claims have been of struggle. . . . The struggle may be a moral one; or it may be a physical one; or it may be both moral and physical, but it must be a struggle. Power concedes nothing without a demand. It never did and it never will.[1]

To begin with, has the governing structure designed by the Founding Fathers succeeded in protecting American inequality? There is clear evidence that inequality has been preserved and that the political-economic system described in Chapters 5–9 has impeded change.

On the eve of the Revolutionary War, 10 percent of the local population controlled 40 percent of all taxable assets in Newburyport, Massachusetts. A comparable 10 percent controlled 44 percent of the assets in Albany, New York; 47 percent in New York City; 50 percent in Portsmouth, New Hampshire; 57 percent in Boston; 62 percent in Charleston, South Carolina; and 90 percent in Philadelphia. Twelve persons owned three-fourths of all the land in New York State. Seven persons owned 1.7 million acres in Virginia. Approximately 500 men owned virtually the entire eastern seaboard.[2]

Today, the top 10 percent of American adults owns some 80 percent of all the nation's corporate stock. Meanwhile, each of the households in America's top one percent own nearly $7 million worth of wealth on average, and as a group they hold a clear majority of the nation's business assets. Such wealth holdings will provide this elite group with enough unearned income to keep them in the nation's top 5 percent of income earners even if they never work another day in their lives.[3]

Using a revised version of systems theory as a basic empirical framework, I have attempted to examine the relationship between America's political and economic processes. I found that the American political and economic systems are intricately intertwined, especially in the postindustrial era. There is a clear-cut economic class structure in the United States, and it is reinforced in various ways by the American government, educational system, and mass media. The resulting political-economic system seriously constrains any attempts at, or even demands for, structural change. This arrangement, then, first, and foremost comes to serve the interests of a small number of economic elites by protecting their positions of privilege.

How has that political economy affected African Americans? The existing system is inherently conservative and has functioned to lock in a history of individual and institutional racism—legacies of slavery. As a result, blacks have rarely held any of the dominant economic positions, and they have been underrepresented at most all levels of the political system as well. This understanding must guide the development of both policy and tactical agendas for transforming these political and economic structures.

The transformation to a more equitable political economy will not materialize out of thin air. It will only emerge when progressive groups and individuals come together to create it through the application of political power, both within and outside the present system. The initial task is to provide a general outline of what is required in order to exercise that political power effectively.

In the political pursuit of a more just society, progressive forces must first pool their power resources, such as votes, time, money, and skills. Second, they must understand the existing political-economic system if they are to successfully alter it in fundamental ways. To accomplish this, they will need to know where to focus their efforts, to know what to demand when victories are won, and to know how to institutionalize those gains so that they can be built upon over the long term. Given limited power resources, there is simply little room for inefficiency on the occasions when power opportunities do emerge. Finally, progressive reformers must act.

So far I have drawn on past and present experience to further understanding of the political-economic system. Now it is time to suggest a path of action. To that end, I shall first clarify the general goal, then review and selectively expand the specific structural changes proposed throughout the book, outline a basic political plan, and finally assess the prospects for change.

Realize, however, that there are no blueprints for revolutions. Instead, they emerge dynamically as groups and individuals react to circumstances and seize moments of political opportunity. Social scientists can only provide guideposts based upon their own measures and interpretations of historical trends and current realities.

GENERAL GOAL

As prospective delegates began to mobilize for the 1968 Black Power Conference in Philadelphia, a representative of the Clairol Corporation sent them the following message:

> Forget black militancy and all this foolish talk of revolution! Rely on the American businessman, for it is only he who has the power—and now the will—to promote black "self development."[4]

As indicated at the outset of this book, my primary goal has not been to see more African Americans incorporated into the existing economic mainstream, stripping class inequities of their racial component. Racially proportionate dependence, exploitation, and insecurity do not constitute purpose enough. Instead, the most basic goal is for all American citizens to have maximum control over their own lives, rather than creating a new hierarchical system to replace the old. As a delegate to the 1967 Black Power Conference in Newark put it, "I don't want to be exploited by a black man any more than I want to be exploited by a white man. You've got to change the whole system."[5]

By focusing on the reduction of political and economic barriers to this self-determination, however, I have not lost sight of other important impediments to fundamental change, white racism being the most obvious. As mentioned in the introduction, altering political and economic structures is necessary but not sufficient to achieve the primary goal of racial justice in the United States of America. Racist individuals in positions of power will indeed continue to discriminate even in a less hierarchical political economy. Nevertheless, these structural changes will accomplish two important ends. First, they will help clear the way for more equal economic and political opportunity, especially if and when racism diminishes. Second, they will take some of the sting out of existing racism by forcibly providing more equity for most African Americans. Thus the institutionalization of past racism can be reduced, even if dismantling white racism continues to prove difficult.

PROGRAM

> We can no longer rely on pressuring and cajoling political units toward desired actions. We must be in a position to change those political units when they are not responsive.[6]

Political Structures

Chapters 6–9 suggested ways to begin opening the political process so as to facilitate rather than impede fundamental change. Taken together, these alterations promise a considerably more open process. However, the people actually engaged in the exercise of political power will have to decide what to settle for at any particular point in time on the road to such a system. And once a more democratic arrangement is attained, they must be enlightened enough to utilize their increased power in a progressive manner.

Judicial Arena.   In a nation that prides itself in subscribing ultimately to the rule of law as opposed to the rule of individuals, it is imperative that those fundamental laws and their enforcers be as just as possible from the outset. Toward that end, the following policies were proposed:

1. Positive constitutional rights, such as housing, health care, a job at a livable wage, and an adequate guaranteed annual income for those unable to work

2. Random appointment of all judges, from lists both approved by their peers and weighted to ensure that blacks and other previously excluded groups would have more equal demographic representation on the bench
3. More racially integrated law enforcement agencies, some even placed under the judicial, as opposed to the executive, branch of government
4. More neighborhood control over choosing, overseeing, and disciplining the police who implement the law at the street level in residential areas

Electoral Arena.   Within the fundamental rights and liberties established and protected in the judicial arena, the American citizenry makes laws that affect how the nation's resources are allocated. This is generally done indirectly by means of a process of representative democracy; however, voters also make laws directly at the state and local levels by initiative and referendum. Thus, for the purposes of direct and indirect democracy, it is important to create an electoral mechanism that will be as open and fair as possible. In that pursuit, the following changes were proposed:

1. Increasing voter turnout by relaxing registration laws and possibly by requiring participation
2. National ballot initiatives
3. Deprivatizing corporate decision making by requiring that workers and other community members be represented on corporate boards of directors, placing more government limitations on corporate decisions, and facilitating worker ownership of the firms in which they work
4. Federal preclearance of all new election laws anywhere in the country
5. Public financing of all electoral campaigns, with supporting constitutional amendments as necessary
6. An end to the purchase of media time and space for campaign advertising, an allocation of free media time and space in its place, and supporting constitutional amendments as necessary
7. A bona fide multiparty system facilitated by using a proportional representation formula for electing representatives, simplified and lenient national standards for petitioning one's candidates onto the ballot, minor-party representatives on the Federal Election Commission, and a relatively equal allocation of public funding and free media time to all established political parties
8. Further opening the party nomination processes by assigning nominating convention delegates strictly by proportional representation (no longer requiring any minimum percentage of a state's primary vote in order to receive delegates) and by affirmative efforts to increase race, sex, and class representation among the delegates
9. A parliamentary system to strengthen political parties and thus help facilitate the passage of legislation outlined in the winning coalition's platforms

Legislative Arena.   Even if the electoral arena becomes more open and fair, elected representatives must be able to implement the platforms on which they were elected if representative democracy is to be meaningful. Consequently, beyond converting to a parliamentary system, the following proposals involve reducing many of the other checks and balances that presently obstruct those democratic opportunities:

1. Standing rules that limit debate in both the House and Senate
2. Simplified rules that would make it easier for congressional majorities to extract bills from committees
3. An end to the presidential veto
4. Proportional interest representation devices such as cumulative voting and leadership rotation
5. Bureaucrats with policy-related discretion to be both assigned randomly outside the area from which they live at the time of their initial appointments as well as rotated periodically
6. Affirmative action efforts that would increase the number of blacks chosen for executive, staff, and bureaucratic positions in federal, state, and local government
7. An expanded federal Justice Department with more leeway to observe and intervene in the local implementation of federal laws
8. Ombudsmen to serve as liaisons between service recipients and bureaucratic agencies
9. A strong Legal Aid program to assist all citizens in bringing and fending off lawsuits
10. A strong Consumer Protection Agency to help consumers press their rights in the private marketplace

Information Arena.   Lastly, it is quite clear that none of this will come to pass if people are not aware of the problems and alternatives and if the nation's political culture is not broadened to incorporate more egalitarianism. It is also clear that simply democratizing the political process without such changes will only make it easier for the majority to continue to help maintain the inequities of the current political economy. Therefore, the following reforms were suggested in the educational and media processes by which information and culture are transferred:

1. Random selection of school boards and trustees
2. An alteration of school curricula and practices to emphasize both the interrelationship of politics and economics and a more balanced analysis of both American and other nations' systems and histories, as well as rewards for behavioral traits such as creativity, independence, critical analysis, and cooperation
3. A formula by which no school would have less than 90 percent of what the richest school had to spend, subsidized by a progressive income tax on wage earners and their employers
4. More black representation in media decision making, including black commissioners on the Federal Communications Commission, greater affirmative action hiring and promotion efforts in the mass media, and start-up money for black media outlets
5. Significant limits on media ownership, for example, no person being allowed to own more than 5 percent of any medium or to hold media shares in a market where he or she has other investments
6. The pooling and random assignment of all media advertisements across time slots that provide the audience size and demographics desired
7. Expansion and further political insulation of publicly funded media outlets

8. Increasing popular access to media by facilitating a broader use of public-service advertisements, as well as more equal access to low-frequency cable channels
9. A First Amendment right to media access

As has been stressed throughout the book, it is critical to address the political and economic systems simultaneously, as they are intricately intertwined.[7] Thus conservative economic structures must also be altered if the inequities described in Chapters 3–5 are to be rectified. The preferred economic component of the new program is less capitalistic and more socialistic in nature—eliminating the dominance of an owning class by much more evenly dispersing the control of capital.

Economic Structures

"Why are there 40 million poor people in America?" And when you begin to ask that question you are raising questions about the economic system, about a broader distribution of wealth. When you ask that question, you begin to question the capitalistic economy. . . . But one day we must come to see that an edifice which produces beggars needs restructuring.[8]

At about the very same time that Martin Luther King, Jr., made that pronouncement, a young delegate to the 1967 Newark Black Power Conference took it a step further when he stated, "The capitalist system hasn't worked for us in the four hundred years we've been under it. . . . Capitalism is the most successful system of enforced exploitation in the world, I agree. It's the latest model of slavery."[9]

Socialists reject the economic system of capitalism. As Manning Marable put it, "The road to black liberation must also be a road to socialist revolution."[10]

In general, socialists argue that capitalism generates a small capital-owning class that possesses the controlling shares of the nation's wealth and power. As a consequence, the political and economic systems come to function primarily in the owners' interests. Robert Allen warns that "simple transference of business ownership into black hands . . . is in itself no guarantee that this will benefit the total community. Blacks are capable of exploiting one another just as easily as whites."[11]

Socialist Alternatives. According to socialists, a new economic system must be fashioned that will democratize the ownership of capital and thus allow all citizens to have more control over the political and economic decisions that affect their lives. Samuel Bowles and Herbert Gintis have described such democratization of ownership as a precondition to self-actualization, meaning one's physical, emotional, aesthetic, cognitive, and spiritual development. They also see it helping society to gain more justice and democracy, as well as a more rational and appropriate use of its natural resources. The needs of people would begin to receive more weight than the need for profits as the central guide to society's economic and political decisions, for what is good for General Motors is not necessarily good for America as a whole, or even for GM's workforce.[12]

Stated more concretely, a socialist society would be distinguishable first and foremost by worker control of the means of production. That, however, has come to mean at least two significantly different things, depending on the analyst. Some put their emphasis on democratizing the decisions of existing corporations, while others maintain that the means of production must also be owned either directly or indirectly by the workers themselves.

> We must speak out for racial justice. And we must work for an economic policy that takes lives of working people seriously; an economic strategy that encourages joint ventures between local governments and local plants, building mutual commitments among manufacturers, consumers and communities; for new strategies that will give workers and local government the technical assistance and financial backing to keep plants open and profitable.[13]

Economic Democracy.   Members of the Congressional Black Caucus and prominent black spokespersons such as Coretta Scott King, for example, have called for more centralized government planning of the existing American economy, in particular to create full employment.[14] Ralph Nader, on the other hand, has proposed what he terms his Corporate Democracy Act, which would require that all corporations be chartered by the federal government and be subject to regular independent audits; and that the majority of a corporation's board of directors be chosen independently of the stockholders and a "community impact analysis" be undertaken and approved should an industrial enterprise intend to expand or relocate. Countries like West Germany, for example, already have *codetermination laws,* which mandate worker representation on the boards of large corporations.[15]

In point of fact, however, these are only *left liberal* approaches, as much of the means of production would remain in the hands of the small owning class, at least at the outset. The owners of capital could still exert ultimate influence by the threat to withhold essential investments. The workers, nonetheless, would indeed have more control than they do at present.[16]

Socialism.   The more traditional socialist approach is to move towards collective ownership of at least the major means of production. As Manning Marable describes one such scenario:

> Socialism . . . would involve radical changes. . . . The state would assume the ownership of major corporations, and their direction would be left in the hands of those best qualified to make decisions at the point of production, the working class. Socialism would mean the expropriation of wealth from the capitalist class, and the guarantee of employment, decent housing, education, and health care to all citizens.[17]

Full conversion to a socialist economic system would involve most, if not all, of the following:

1. *Wage labor,* as presently defined, would come to an end for there would no longer be a separate capital-owning class. Workers would directly, or at least indirectly, own the companies where they worked and thus by definition work for themselves.
2. With no separate owning class, the extraction of *surplus value* would also come to an end, as the people actually working in the businesses would collectively receive the full market value of what they were producing.

3. The *workplace would be democratized* in the sense the worker-owners would have far greater control over such decisions as what products they were to produce, where, at what pace, under what conditions, for what wages, and under what kind of management system.
4. Some centralized *economic planning* would be necessary, such as for allocating scarce basic natural resources, coordinating the nation's large primary industries, and determining which worker-entrepreneurs get start-up loans to form other businesses. Nevertheless, the planners would be elected more democratically than elected representatives are at present.
5. Government also would see to it that *distribution of products* would be based more on people's needs, with guaranteed rights to food, shelter, clothing, and both medical and social services.
6. Without a profit-maximizing capital-owning class continually increasing production and then using advertising to stimulate contrived markets for those products, there would be less production of socially unnecessary goods and thus more *leisure time* for artistic, athletic, and cultural activities.
7. Finally, the *educational system* would have to help prepare people for creative work as well as for a more active political life, to help purge them of a variety of social prejudices, and to teach them to structure their personal needs within the requirements of society.[18]

Implementation could include having the federal government employ the power of eminent domain in order to nationalize the most basic major industries, such as steel, autos, and oil. The tax system could be used to dismantle monopolies, and raise money in order to spur and sustain cooperative businesses. As a vehicle for the latter, a National Consumer Cooperative Bank already exists and could be significantly expanded with renewed assistance from the federal government.[19] In addition, federal, state, and local governments already have the experience of owning and operating significant components of the nation's education, utilities, and mass transportation industries, as well as providing most of our police, fire, sanitation, and military services.[20]

Socialist Dilemmas.   There are some obvious challenges here as well. For example, should these socializing efforts come to fuller fruition, critics point to the inefficiencies and repressiveness of virtually all of history's self-styled socialist or communist states.[21] Nevertheless, there are also a number of reasons to believe that an American adaptation would not have to end up that way.

In response to questions concerning efficiency, the American farming industry has been governmentally planned and sustained for years without any glaring problems with inefficiency. Bowles and Gintis have argued that overall American production is actually likely to improve under socialism, given the rationality of centralized planning, the increased size of the work force in a full-employment economy, and such work incentives as full partnership in the firm, more generally meaningful work, and far more leisure time.[22] Even in mixed economies like those in West Germany and Scandinavia, far less inequality is tolerated vis-a-vis the United States, yet they remain prosperously competitive.[23]

Contrary to the dominant ideology's myth that human beings prefer not to work and thus must be frightened into doing so by adequate economic insecurity, empirical evidence suggests just the opposite. Public opinion polls actually indicate that virtually all Americans would prefer to work for a living.[24] And, as the following examples confirm, productivity often is enhanced by such protective arrangements.[25]

In the Milwaukee city and county governments, for example, workers have enjoyed pay incentives, school subsidies, parental leave, child care, and job sharing opportunities, as well as 4-day work weeks and flex-time options. Not only have such benefits been humane, but the subsequent security seems to have contributed to the development of a cooperative and productive work force.[26]

Sweden, at least until quite recently, guaranteed all of its citizens national health insurance, virtually free education, unemployment compensation at a rate of 90 percent of income, a generous pension system, and 18 months of paid parental leave. Meanwhile, it still had barely more than a 1 percent unemployment rate most of the time, was one of the world's most competitive economies, and had a national standard of living that was seldom exceeded by any other nation.[27]

As for repression, David Mermelstein contends that socialism in the United States would be qualitatively different from that in any other place it has existed. The United States is already economically well developed and thus would not require the sacrifices that have been necessary for economic development in most emerging socialist countries. The people cherish the principles of individual liberty and democracy. And fewer freedom-restricting security measures would be necessary as no hostile capitalistic powers of any real consequence would be threatening the country's existence.[28] Attorney Gerry Spence goes on to delineate a number of additional ways in which worker ownership would actually lead to fuller constitutional liberty and justice in the United States.[29]

Nonetheless, socialists are generally quick to admit that they are not promising an overnight utopia. Socialism is viewed as a gradual process, not as an immediate event.[30] Consequently, racism and other social pathologies, for example, will not cease the moment the means of production are finally controlled by the workers, nor will the frustration, anger, despair, self-hatred, and alienation that have built up over many generations disappear with the first dividend check or the first trip to the corporate boardroom. What is promised, however, is considerably more equality and more popular control over the economic and political decisions that affect people's lives. At the very least, socialism would significantly reduce the way in which the inherent inequalities in the present economic system amplify racial discrimination.[31]

POLICY AGENDA

Effective movement toward any one of these political or economic changes would be constructive. However, to build and maintain a mass-based political coalition, some relatively immediate rewards for those who participate must be made apparent. As Charles V. Hamilton has argued, people usually need to see a connection between a political process and a concrete political product before they can be counted on to contribute their participation.[32] So while the structural changes are being sought for long-term benefits, it is important not to ignore short-term gains, especially in light of the difficult socioeconomic position of many in the coalition.

What to push for first? A full-employment policy could certainly help establish a solid foundation for the political coalition. Putting the unemployed to work building roads, sewers, mass transportation systems, hospitals, housing, and day care centers would address a number of problems at once. The Equal Rights Amendment, a gay rights act, guaranteed annual income, and universal health care also would help. But realistically, most of these are not likely to come about without some structural alterations, such as public financing of electoral campaigns or some reduction of legislative checks and balances on the political side and a viable cooperative bank, regulation of plant closings, and significant federal wealth, gift, and inheritance taxes on the economic front. Justice is not simply an end that can be defined and imposed. Rather, it is a process that must be institutionalized. As a consequence, both short- and long-term changes must be pressed simultaneously.[33]

STRATEGIES AND TACTICS

> . . . With blacks possessing neither effective bureaucratic strength nor maximal political organization, no proven strategies and tactics of social change should be discarded for the forseeable future.[34]

What will be proposed now is a variant of what has come to be called a "rainbow coalition." The central idea is that fundamental political and economic change is not likely to increase significantly and endure until a sizable working coalition is formed from a variety of groups being treated unjustly under the present political economy. Each will have its own particular agenda; but, at very least, all ultimately have a common interest in altering the political and economic structures discussed throughout this book. The first step will require each of the subgroups to close ranks, organizing among themselves so that they better understand their own special needs and can enter as strong functioning components of the coalition. The second step entails forming the coalition itself in order to pursue a multifront strategy, using all available political resources.

> The concept of Black Power rests on a fundamental premise: Before a group can enter the open society, it must first close ranks.[35]

Organizing the Black Community.   In recent years, a variety of progressive black organizations have existed at both the national and local levels. They have included working- and lower-class groups such as the League of Revolutionary Black Workers (Detroit), the United Brothers (Newark), the Black United Front (District of Columbia), the North City Congress (Philadelphia), the United Front (Boston), the Black United Conference (Denver), and the Black Congress (Los Angeles), culminating in the formation of the National Black United Front in 1981. In addition, there is the Peoples' Alliance, as well as more middle-class groups that could also help organize the black community for the struggle ahead, including the National Bar Association, the NAACP, the National Urban League, the Progressive Black Baptist Alliance, and even the Delta Sigma Theta sorority and Alpha Phi Alpha fraternity. More recently there was the Million Man March in Washington and the various local organizations that have spun off from it.

Such groups need to continue organizing; and regardless of some major disagreements, they need to bring their memberships together into a loose coalition for the purpose of pursuing structural changes that will allow their members to maximize control over their lives. National conventions designed to aggregate these many interests and formulate a *national black agenda* have included the 1972 National Black Political Convention in Gary, the 1976 Black Issues Conference in Charlotte, the 1980 Richmond Conference on a Black Agenda, Baltimore's 1994 National African-American Leadership Summit, and the 1996 National Political Convention held in St. Louis.[36]

> I propose to . . . build a new functional Rainbow Coalition of the Rejected spanning lines of color, sex, age, religion, race, region, and national origin. The old minorities—Blacks, Hispanics, women, peace activists, environmentalists, youth, the elderly, small farmers, small businesspersons, poor people, gays, and lesbians—if we remain apart, will continue to be a minority. But, if we come together, the old "minorities" constitute a "new majority."[37]

A Rainbow Coalition.   Although questions have been raised about the viability of Jesse Jackson's own rainbow coalition movement,[38] the idea remains conceptually attractive. Quite frankly, it appears to be the only long-term vehicle on the horizon, no matter who leads it. Besides the numerical advantages, there is a real commonality of interest that can be tapped. Former senator Edward Brooke argued that

> [black] economic interests are clearly aligned with those of the majority of Americans. Inflation, unemployment, inequitable taxation, inadequate health care and housing are not black issues, but issues affecting millions of Americans who suffer the agonies of our economy without ever sharing its abundance.[39]

Manning Marable put it even more strongly when he stated:

> If there is no attempt on the part of white labor to engage in extensive self-criticism and to construct a common program for struggle against capital with non-whites, the final emancipation of the American working class will be unattainable.[40]

As an example of his point, Marable noted that the subordinate position of black workers lowers everybody's wages. When blacks are forced to accept less pay just to have a job, this bids down the wage rate in general.[41]

The roots of such a movement run deep. The abolitionist, early feminist, and free-soil movements all drew on a diversity of supportive groups. At the turn of the century, the Populist movement in the rural areas and the urban political machines were clear examples of such coalitions at work, despite unequal input and treatment of their various components. And in the early twentieth century, the Unemployment Councils and parts of the early labor and black rights movements also drew diverse group support. Yet the specific roots of the present-day effort can be traced rather directly to movements that gathered force in the 1950s and 1960s: black power, feminist, antiwar, environmental, Hispanic, Native American, New Left, and gay.

The challenge has been to link such movements together in pursuit of mutual interests, and certain issues have facilitated that endeavor. For example, many of these groups joined forces in the 1950s and 1960s to press for passage of the Civil Rights and Voting Rights acts, and Martin Luther King's subsequent Poor People's Campaign was one of the best examples of such an alliance. Thereafter, the neoconservative backlash embodied by the likes of Richard Nixon, Ronald Reagan, and George Bush only fueled the fires. An increasing number of these groups, for example, pulled together to defeat the Supreme Court nominations of archconservatives Harrold Carswell, Clement Haynesworth, and Robert Bork and to protest against unemployment, the nuclear arms race, and U.S. foreign policy in South Africa and Central America. Meanwhile, the Rainbow Coalition itself drew 756 delegates to its national unity convention in April 1986, and 1988 presidential candidate Jesse Jackson amassed an electoral coalition that included 4.4 million blacks, 2.1 million whites, and more than 200,000 Hispanics—54 percent of the total group being women.[42]

> Common ground between the Black movement—in both its integrationist and Black nationalist tendencies—and predominantly white progressive movements, is the principle of equality. . . . Equality implies a theory of justice which assumes that all parties within the state should have free access to the state apparatus, can reform existing economic and social institutions, and can enact laws that promote a more humane society.[43]

Clearly, there are many obstacles.[44] For instance, most of these groups are far from internally united and organized, and they often contain members who are suspicious of the motives of other groups.[45] Much cultural sensitivity is required. Group interests conflict.[46] White males tend to dominate such coalitions.[47] And, as Melvin King found out in his unsuccessful mayoral bid in Boston, the owning class can employ far more money, and the mass media are conditioned not to take such movements seriously.[48]

Nevertheless, there are advantages. Rather than demanding integration and conformity, for example, the rainbow concept actually encourages diversity. In the end, this is essentially multiracial politics, not deracialized politics. In addition, such coalitions have a track record of successfully forming around individual policy issues in the past. And quite frankly, in a large heterogeneous society in which political compromise is an absolute necessity, this would appear to be the most promising vehicle for effectively brokering such compromises.[49]

Yet, as Jesse Jackson put it, "Ultimately the poor do not just want friends, they want to be empowered."[50] Where to begin?

> [The black community] should not rely on exclusively legal campaigns, nor should it restrict itself to all-out street warfare. Instead it must devise a strategy of calculated confrontation, using a mixture of tactics to fit a variety of contingencies. . . . Tactical innovation should be the order of the day, and anything workable goes . . . from legal struggle, to electoral politics, to direct action campaigns, to force. In short, what is required is a coordinated, multifaceted, multilateral struggle.[51]

A Multifront Strategy. A rainbow coalition can become an ongoing protest organization outside of the context of individual crises. Beyond that, it could help organize more traditional political efforts, as a variety of progressive groups have regularly seen the need for working within the system at the same time. Hopefully, a rainbow coalition can serve to unite these efforts. Past gains must be protected, and a new agenda must be set.

Litigation. As suggested in Chapter 6, the Bill of Rights and certain federal civil rights and voting rights laws do offer some protection. Thus legal efforts must continue, with the purpose of guaranteeing that hard-won gains from the past are fairly and fully enforced. But much structural change is also needed if new, more positive rights and fuller justice are to be forthcoming. To achieve those structural changes, legislators must be confronted.

Lobbying. Elected and appointed officials must be pressed to enforce existing laws; they must also be pressured to change the political and economic structures themselves. Letters and telegrams must be sent, and phone calls must be made. And the officials must be informed and persuaded on a face-to-face basis wherever possible. Yet only so much can be expected from the elected and appointed products of the present arrangement. More diverse and progressive-thinking individuals have to be placed in legislative and administrative positions—and that can be set in motion through the ballot box.[52]

Voting. Calculated nonvoting can send a message of overall disapproval. Unfortunately, it can also be interpreted as apathy, indifference, or even contentment. Thus the low-cost tactic of registering and voting is strongly encouraged. But the only valuable vote is a rationally cast vote, which also requires attentiveness to the campaign process. Within that campaign process, talented progressive-thinking people must seek office, and others of like mind must support their efforts with time and money.[53]

Structural impediments to this pursuit exist, of course. Chapter 7 pointed out that existing practices filter out candidates with radically new agendas and that the owning class begins with sizable advantages in its efforts to keep it that way. In addition, many crucial decisions are presently being made outside of government in the private sector.

Economic Power. To exert pressure on private-sector decision makers, employees and consumers can band together to pressure noncooperating businesses. Employees can organize labor unions and demand seats on boards of directors, management input, and employee stock ownership plans, striking if necessary in order to achieve them. In addition, mass protests can be launched. In April 1980, for example, a variety of progressive groups came together across the country in what was called Big Business Day. They marched and spoke out against a number of offensive corporate practices. The NAACP also created the Annual Black Dollar Week, encouraging African-American consumers to remind businesses to be socially responsible if they wish to continue to enjoy black patronage.[54]

As a specific example of consumer power, although not challenging economic structures as such, Jesse Jackson's Operation PUSH organized an Economic Justice Campaign designed to force private companies to have more black-owned franchises and distributorships, to provide more research money to black colleges, to implement affirmative action policies for hiring and promoting managers, and to use black advertising agencies, black media sources for those ads, black banks, black insurance companies, and black contractors, on a regular basis. In July 1981, for instance,

PUSH began a boycott against the Coca-Cola company. Not only were people urged not to purchase Coke products, but a number of grocery stores pulled the products from their shelves, and Coke machines were physically removed from a number of government buildings. In the end, the Coca-Cola Corporation agreed to create 32 black distributorships, to lend nearly $2 million to small entrepreneurs in the black community, and to deposit more money in black-owned banks. Comparable campaigns were subsequently launched against Anheuser Busch, Burger King, Avon, Quaker Oats, General Foods, Nike, and the Southland Corporation (owners of 7-Eleven convenience stores).

Economic boycotts also have been launched at the local level. African Americans in Brattleboro, North Carolina, for example, formed the Concerned Citizens of Brattleboro after a police brutality complaint. They then staged a boycott of white-owned businesses in the community and actually drove some out of business, as they pressed for the appointment of a black police chief and the end of racially motivated police brutality. Their successes encouraged comparable efforts in other small towns in the region.[55]

Direct Action. Besides going outside the traditional political process to place direct pressure on private corporations, direct-action techniques can be directed toward governmental decision makers as well. Martin Luther King, Jr., spoke of the need to create a crisis in order to force a dialogue. Such crisis-creating tactics have taken both legal and illegal forms, ranging from lawful protest assemblies and marches to sit-ins and freedom rides to arson and physical violence.[56] Because the American system craves stability, a host of concessions have been won over the years as the system strove to end such turmoil.

Education. Groups, especially whites, must be educated to look beyond their immediate stakes in the status quo, with emphasis on common interests and a common ideoogy concerning the requisites of justice. In addition, progressive political education must be institutionalized—particularly in light of the limits of mainstream schooling and the mass media discussed in Chapter 9. Labor unions, for example, have long employed a Committee on Political Education (COPE) to disseminate pertinent political information to their members and help to organize their political forces. Another example has been the Center for Popular Economics, run from the University of Massachusetts and providing progressive education and training for labor leaders.[57]Comparable seminars, workshops, and newsletters must be institutionalized at the grass-roots level across the entire population.

By way of summary, Sheila Collins points to the rainbow coalition initiated by Jesse Jackson as a reasonable starting point:

> Jackson's genius lay in linking nonelectoral forms of political mobilization and protest with traditional electoral politics, and in sensing those areas of convergence that could unite the interests of disparate groups around a common program. Although embryonic and fragile, the Rainbow Coalition represents the construction of a new kind of politics appropriate to the historical, cultural realities, and changing socioeconomic context of late twentieth-century America.[58]

PROSPECTS

> Blacks are the weather vane for this society. Because of racism, we are in the front and bear the brunt of social and economic deterioration and in the rear of social and economic development. [But] whatever is happening to blacks today will be happening to whites tomorrow.[59]

Mounting Crises

Enduring Problems.   In the last analysis, most social and economic problems boil down to people—often very poor people. And, the largest concentrations of these indigent people can be found in America's central cities. As the urban underclass has become an ever larger percentage of postindustrial city populations, however, these cities have become less fiscally capable of dealing with the entire array of related problems. The subsequent escalation in urban impoverishment tends to occur in vicious cycles that lead to periodic bouts of violent social unrest.

More than one out of every five postindustrial city residents lives below the federal government's poverty line. Beyond that, those figures actually understate the level of indigence by failing to count many who are poor and by masking the fact that inner-city residents are becoming poorer and less likely to escape their plights. They have become a veritable *permanent underclass* whose ranks are growing and whose position is deteriorating even further.[60]

They can be shuffled from slum rentals to public housing to living with relatives to heating grates on the streets and back again, even from city to city, but they do not disappear. At any point in time, some cities will have to accommodate most of them. And, of course, there are times when the various safety valves all fail.[61]

> I read that report . . . of the 1919 riot in Chicago, and it is as if I were reading the report of the investigating committee on the Harlem riot of 1935, the report of the investigating committee on the Harlem riot of 1943, the report of the McCone Commission on the 1968 Watts riot.
>
> I must again in candor say to you members of this the Kerner Commission—it is a kind of Alice in Wonderland—with the same moving picture re-shown over and over again, the same analysis, the same recommendations, and the same inaction.[62]

The Fires Return.   In the spring and summer of 1977, a decade after the Kerner Commission had reported on the ghetto unrest of the 1960s, a number of media sources gave special coverage to the city ghettos "ten years later." What they found amidst some rather cosmetic gains was continuing segregation, unemployment, housing deterioration, and incomes that were not catching up with those of whites.[63] Such findings led a task force of the National Advisory Commission on Criminal Justice Standards and Goals to conclude, "The present tranquility is deceptive . . . Many of the traditional indicators for disorders are clearly present and need but little stimulus to activate them."[64] They also led Secretary of Labor Ray Marshall to warn:

> What this leads to is an inflammable mixture in the urban areas. We have a concentration not only of a whole generation of blacks that may never have jobs, but disaffected Viet

Nam vets (a high percentage of them are minorities), ex-convicts, and who knows how many illegal aliens.[65]

And then, as predicted, the urban unrest began anew. The list below notes more than two dozen such disturbances that have occurred since 1977.

July 1977: A *New York City* power failure sets off massive looting, some beginning within 30 seconds of the blackout. Ultimately, 3,700 are arrested.

April 1980: Youths in *Wichita* clash with police, and in the rampage that ensues, cars are burned, bricks are thrown at passing cars, and sniping occurs. In the end, 52 are injured and 29 arrested.

May 1980: Unrest in *Miami* includes beatings, maimings, burnings, looting, and sniping; with 18 dead, more than 200 seriously wounded, 750 arrested, and more than $100 million in property damage.

July 1980: Violence erupts in *Chattanooga*, Tennessee and *Orlando*, Florida, including rock throwing, sniping, and numerous fire bombings, with dozens of injuries and arrests.

December 1981: Comparable racial violence occurs in *Gainesville*, Florida.

January 1983: Another *Miami* incident involves three days of sniping, rock throwing, beatings, robbery, lootings, vandalism, etc., leaving 1 dead, 25 injured, and 45 arrested.

April 1983: Crowds throw stones, bottles, and bricks at police cars in *Montgomery*, Alabama.

May 1983: Youths throw rocks and bottles at *Miami* police, besides committing sporadic vandalism.

July 1983: *New York City* youths rampage after a concert in Central Park, with as many as 1,000 of them robbing and assaulting concert goers as well as patrons of a posh Central Park restaurant. Arson and looting occur. Whites are advised to avoid the neighborhood or risk being violently attacked. In the end, 13 are injured and 300 arrested.

October 1985: Police face a barrage of rocks, bottles, and sniper fire in *Auburn*, Georgia.

February 1987: In *Tampa*, Florida stores are looted, cars and trash fires are set, and stones are thrown at police.

September 1988: Rocks are hurled at whites and two stores are burned in the black Cedar Grove neighborhood of *Shreveport*, Louisiana.

January 1989: Angry crowds fir at *Tampa* police for two consecutive nights.

August 1989: Extensive vandalism and looting sweep *Vineland*, N.J.

September 1989: Thousands of black youths attack police and loot *Virginia Beach* stores. The National Guard is called in to restore order. The melee leaves some 50 people hospitalized and 650 arrested.

December 1990: Arson and vandalism sweep *Miami*'s Puerto Rican neighborhood of Wynwood.

May 1991: Hispanic youths attack police and burn police cars in *Washington, D.C.*

June 1991: Sporadic violence once again rocks *Miami*'s Liberty City and Overton areas. Dozens are arrested and three police officers are injured.

July 1991: Following a spirited protest demonstration, angry black teens smash store windows in downtown *New Brunswick*, N.J.

August 1991: Some 61 people, including 43 police officers are injured, as racial violence envelopes the Crown Heights section of *Brooklyn*. Rocks and bottles are thrown at police and several police cars are burned.

October 1996: In *St. Petersburg*, racial unrest leaves 11 injured, 28 buildings burned, and requires the National Guard to quell. One month later, similar unrest recurs.

November 1996: Rocks, bottles and fire bombs are thrown during racial clashes in *Leland*, Mississippi.

In 1990, Milwaukee city councilman Michael McGee even organized a group called the Black Panther Community Militia dressed in black military fatigues. He then demanded that the city allocate $100 million to provide jobs for unemployed Milwaukee residents or his group might be forced to take more violent steps such as poisoning the water supply or bombing the city's Bradley Center.[66]

As these individual incidents indicate, postindustrial city ghettoes are indeed an "inflammable mixture" providing a barometer of the nation's socioeconomic distress and fiscal limitations. Yet in a very real sense these events are just the tip of the iceberg. Violent crime has been soaring, racial polarization continues, people continue to lose their middle-income jobs, governmental tax bases decline—the list goes on.[67]

Nevertheless, not until the cities begin to burn is the situation viewed as a "crisis," and even then only in the specific cities exhibiting the unrest. As a result, solutions come to be incremental and discrete. Yet if the vicious cycle continues, it is uncertain just how much trauma the American fabric can withstand and how much more government can spend on placating the rebellious poor and still maintain the integrity of the present socioeconomic system.

Alternative Futures

> Current and future economic and social conditions require fundamental altering of political values, structures, and processes.[68]

With several of the nation's most serious social and economic problems continuing to worsen, it would seem that national policy is ultimately headed in either one of two directions. As a number of the problems appear inherent in capitalism itself, the nation will likely be forced to choose either (1) to retain capitalism—warts and all—by allowing more effective repression of the increasingly turbulent underclasses; or (2) to opt for a different economic arrangement with a gradual socialization of capital ownership and the elimination of the underclasses as they presently exist; or alternatively, they can continue to stumble along until the social order breaks down and the decision is made in the streets.

> The question is whether or not the economic crisis will be used to reorganize society along increasingly regimented lines, or alternately, whether the crisis can be used to build a popular, socialist movement which will in the short run protect the living standard of working people and in the long run prepare the way for the eventual reorganization of our society along more humane lines.[69]

Friendly Fascism

> Believe, Obey, Fight.
>   —an oft-quoted fascist slogan

At the far right extreme of the ideological spectrum we find a political value structure called fascism. Traditional fascism encompasses at least five important tenets: conflict theory, elitism, antirationalism, totalitarianism, and ultranationalism.

Conflict Theory. By their very nature, people strive to dominate other people, and nations strive to dominate other nations.

Elitism. People are born unequal, and thus some are capable of providing greater service to society than others. What will arise, then, is a natural grouping of political and economic elites who, on the basis of their abilities and wills, are the ones who will and should possess a disproportionate share of the nation's wealth and power.

Antirationalism. Products of the Western Enlightenment period (e.g., science, technology, and liberal democracy) have not reduced national and international problems. Life is far too complex and unpredictable for people to continue to place such faith in rationality while they search for solutions. Therefore, important truths, rather than the products of rationalism, are simply random facts that exist to serve a desired political purpose. Consequently, as Mussolini exhorted, people should "feel, not think"; while, the born elites will discern truth by virtue of their superior instincts.

Totalitarianism. The emerging elites then should and will attempt to organize and control virtually every aspect of human existence, including life-styles, culture, education, work, and so forth. And, they must crush any opposition to their quest for total control of both society and the individual.

Ultranationalism. Just as a nation is composed of a pyramid of competing people headed by whichever person has the most ability and will, the same is true internationally. In that arena, the nation with the most talent, discipline, and the strongest will to act will ultimately emerge victorious. If therefore the citizens of a nation led by such a leader believe, unite, obey, and fight, that nation's destiny can be achieved. Consequently, national solidarity and international imperialism is a sign of vitality, and war an opportunity for a spiritual creativity of sorts. Conversely, if a nation shirks this responsibility, it will be overrun by the forces of history.

Beyond the tenets of the ideology itself, it is also important to take note of the social context within which fascism generally has arisen. Fascism has tended to emerge primarily in industrialized capitalist countries suffering from a combination of international humiliation and domestic economic difficulties. Meanwhile, left-wing social movements arise among the lower classes attempting to force some redistribution of the nation's wealth and power. Soon the combination of this left-wing militancy and the political and economic concessions attained as a result, threaten both the status of the middle class and the dominant position of the capital-owning class. At that juncture, a charismatic leader emerges to lead a broad-based reactionary movement.

Kenneth and Patricia Dolbeare contend that fascism involves the "elaborate organization and management of daily life in the name of efficiency, mutual sacrifice, and national survival."[70] This is accomplished by a combination of "symbolic manipulations," such as scapegoating, as well as " . . . widespread coercion, police surveillance, brutal attacks on dissidents, and deliberate arbitrariness, backed up by a network of spying and reporting on each other by citizens generally, all under the guise of national security."[71]

> . . . before . . . the fascist upheaval, Capitalism dominates, but it is Capitalism in which there are certain mutations: it is a Capitalism with restricted limits of accumulation, where economic dead weights abound, where the destruction of capital increases, and where there are more parasitic and reactionary strata.[72]

If economic hardship continues to mount at home, sizable components of the working, middle, and upper classes could well turn their wrath toward the societal costs involved in what many might see as "overindulging a shiftless and parasitic minority of citizens wallowing in the urban ghettoes." Such people also might be seen as "making the streets unsafe"; and, "their petty protests arousing senseless feelings of guilt among the hardworking majority." Beyond that, many in the middle and upper classes might feel that "social services for these degenerates, concocted in the rarified air of some ivory tower, only sap needed capital away from potentially productive private investments."

The priorities for change would be rather simple as we proceeded down the ideological path ever further to the right. Encouraging the accumulation and investment of capital would clearly become the top priority in governmental budgeting, from the federal to the local level. Social welfare services would be further reduced so that "nonproducers" would be maintained at no more than subsistence level at most, and as many of those services as possible would be provided privately—allowing private elites more control.[73] The police would be "unleashed" so as more effectively to be able to enforce the law, and the judicial system would be streamlined to avoid burdensome technicalities and delays. Practices such as preventive detention would be allowed, and the rights of the accused would be reduced in order not to interfere with the efficient prosecution of those arrested.[74]

In addition, expect to see members of the repressed groups holding positions such as police officer, prison guard, mayor, and judge, with little choice but to strictly enforce these increasingly oppressive laws. That conveys a sense of sensitivity and impartiality while at the same time protecting the interests of the wealthy in particular. Such *local rule* is a device which has been used repeatedly by nations engaged in international colonization. At very least, it confuses the issues at hand.[75]

Prospects.   As long as the general public views poverty and subsequent lower-class unrest as purely "their" problems, the situation most likely will continue to deteriorate. The response will be either to offer these people "help" (liberalism on the ideological left) or to force them to "cut it more on their own" (conservatism on the ideological right). If a fundamental choice must be made, however, between the socialist direction further to the ideological left or the fascist direction further to the ideological right, such a narrow view of the problem, especially within the dominant American political culture that dates back to the Founding Fathers, may well lead at least temporarily down the road to the right.

There are already indications of such a drift, for example, the *ultranationalism* aroused during the Iranian hostage crisis, the invasion of Grenada, the invasion of Panama, and the Gulf War;[76] the potential for *totalitarianism* when right-wing zealots patrol college classrooms,[77] when the United States jails a far higher proportion of its citizens than any other nation on earth, when constant dollar per-capita expenditure for police protection nearly triples between 1930 and 1960 and then more than doubles from 1960 to the present,[78] when police ransack newsrooms in search of evidence, journalists are jailed for refusal to reveal their sources of information, when the U.S. Treasury Department demands records of travel agents suspected of arranging illegal travel to Cuba, when an increasing number of retail companies refuse to allow even charitable solicitations on their premises for fear that they would then have to allow union organizers the same opportunity to interact with patrons and workers;[79] the *antirationalism* that is evident in schoolbooks being burned, the right-wing ravings heard over much of talk radio, the resurgence of the Ku Klux Klan, the reactionary "patriot movement" of highly armed private "militias," the subtle racism in recent presidential campaigns, the religious right's politics of good and evil;[80] and the *elitism* that is embodied in the reemergence of sweatshops and child labor in the United States,[81] as well as the reduction and privatization of ever more social services, including the Welfare Reform Act of 1996.[82]

The increased visibility of *black conservatives* is another outgrowth of this recent national shift to the ideological right. Showered with public attention by conservative whites and the white media,[83] the list of prominent black conservatives has included the likes of Thomas Sowell, Robert Woodson, Walter Williams, Shelby Steele, Stephen Carter, and Glenn Loury, not to mention the election of J. C. Watts and Gary Franks to the U.S. House of Representatives and the elevation of Clarence Thomas to the U.S. Supreme Court. Like their white conservative counterparts, they tend to oppose governmental intervention in the capitalist marketplace. They also espouse the traditional view that the American system is open to anyone willing to work hard enough. The obvious corollary is that those failing are failing because of their own weaknesses, while governmental social programs only create and perpetuate dependence on the part of those too unmotivated to compete. Similarly, most oppose affirmative action and favor much stricter and harsher law enforcement.[84]

In the long run, however, the implications of such a rightward shift may well prove unacceptable, even to the bulk of America's white middle and working classes. If increasingly desperate poor people are abandoned or repressed, particularly if a significant number come to be seen as elderly whites and small children,[85] this is likely to do damage to a good many previously well-insulated consciences. In addition, if civil liberties are retracted from the ghettoized poor, this could certainly have a spillover effect. Moves such as abridging protection from unwarranted searches and seizures by police, or possibly even declaring a form of martial law, would put a sizable crimp in everyone else's freedom as well.

Should such a scenario play out to its logical extremes, it might not be long before the non-owning classes stop turning blame on each other and start to see the impositions of big government more as a surrogate for the small group of wealthy capitalists who benefit most from the existing arrangement. At that point, their socioeconomic divisions might well diminish, and they might actually begin to form a multiclass, multiracial mass movement that would seriously challenge the legitimacy and very existence of the current political-economic system.[86]

Socialist Trends

Socialist structural alterations have already begun to occur in the economic system. Workers and citizens of all races have come together to demand, and in some cases achieve, greater control over their lives.

> It is worth remembering that our national highway system was not built by the Kiwanis Club. The Chamber of Commerce did not send astronauts to the moon. Social Security

was not a neighborhood project. Contrary to folklore, the U.S. computer industry . . . began and rose out of the Pentagon, not somebody's garage. The U.S. aerospace industry was an economic winner picked long ago by the Federal Government.[87]

Industrial Policy.   Even within the existing private enterprise system, various levels of government have been weighing industrial policies designed to allow boards of business, labor, and government officials to do more centralized planning of the economy. In particular, they would determine which industries government should assist. In all likelihood they would recommend supporting major declining industries, fast growers, large employers, exporters, and technological pioneers by utilizing such means as trade barriers, subsidies, technical assistance, favorable regulatory treatment, tax abatements, and subsidized loans. Such national planning has been done for years in agriculture and a variety of defense-related industries.[88]

As small first steps, the federal government's 1984 Tariff and Trade Act listed guidelines American steel companies were to follow in reinvesting their capital if they wanted continued governmental protection from foreign competitors. The National Institute of Standards and Technology, and the National Science Foundation, have spent millions of dollars annually to spur research and development projects; while the federal government joined the "Big Three" American auto makers in a project to jointly develop a more reliable, energy-efficient automobile—similar to efforts by Japan's Ministry of International Trade and Industry. There also has been the creation of the Advanced Technology Program, which selectively subsidizes risky high-tech commercial research; the Manufacturing Extension Partnership, which helps smaller businesses incorporate new technologies; and a host of other such federal entities. Meanwhile, various states have acted to protect in-state companies from hostile takeovers in order to reduce the potential for economic disruption, while both states and localities have been funding local technological development ventures.[89]

Local Content Legislation.   There also has been some serious congressional discussion, as well as some action, on *local content legislation*. This legal approach, for example, requires that a fixed percentage of certain manufactured products be made in the United States if they are to be sold here. At least indirectly, one effect of increasing local content legislation would be constraint on the mobility of multinational corporations.[90]

> We must speak out against plant closings that happen without prior notice; against economic royalism while thousands of workers lose their jobs; against factories fleeing to third world countries, where workers' health and safety is ignored and union organizing is forbidden.[91]

Regulating Plant Closings.   To contain corporate mobility more directly, some relatively strong legislation has been proposed, and some actually has been adopted in Wisconsin, Maine, Michigan, and at least 16 other states. As discussed in Chapter 7, one of the boldest examples was Oregon's Employment Stability Bill of 1981, which would have required businesses with more than 50 employees (1) to give 1 year's notice before closing or making any significant layoff, (2) to compensate the community they leave by paying 85 percent of any "adjustment costs," (3) to pay for the relocation of all workers, (4) to pay benefit premiums for 1 year after closing, and

(5) to give the Oregon Bureau of Labor and Industry the first option to buy the company. Ohio's so-called Schwarzwalder Bill would have required virtually the same thing of its departing firms, but it called for a two-year notice.[92]

Meanwhile, at least a half dozen members of Congress have introduced national variants of such legislation, and in 1988 the federal government passed a law that requires 60-day notice before many sizable plants can close.[93] In the summer of 1991, the National Labor Relations Board issued guidelines for when companies must negotiate with their unions before moving to new locations.[94] And, the United States Supreme Court has upheld state-mandated severance benefits.[95]

Eminent Domain.   *Eminent domain* has long been available as a mechanism whereby government could forcibly acquire private property for public use. The property is simply condemned, a fair market price is paid to the owner, and the space is then used for whatever public purpose the government has designed. The state of Hawaii even used eminent domain to acquire parts of large family estates so that land would be available for badly needed private housing construction.[96] Thus the legal groundwork would seem to be in place for one of the newest innovations in eminent domain application.

Going a step further, cities have begun to consider the right of eminent domain as a way to prevent large corporations from deserting them. The government of New Bedford, Massachusetts, for example, designed a plan whereby it would condemn a cutting-tools plant, purchase it, and then sell it to an organization that would keep it in New Bedford—another company, a public-private partnership, or a group made up of plant managers and union employees. As another example, the Pittsburgh area's Tristate Conference on Steel—a combination of steelworkers, religious leaders, and other residents—designed a plan that included a regional authority that could use eminent domain to allow steelworkers to buy a number of ailing steel mills in the region, modernize the mills, and run them.[97]

Unitary Taxes.   Despite considerable corporate opposition, *unitary taxation* has existed in more than a dozen states, has been facilitated by the Multistate Tax Commission,[98] and has been upheld by the United States Supreme Court.[99] In these states, all of the international profits of multinational corporations are taxed according to the proportion of that corporation that is represented by the subsidiaries operating within that state. At very least, that too adds some modest constraints on multinational corporate investment.

Prompting Corporate Responsibility.   In a 1986 pastoral letter entitled "Economic Justice For All," the National Conference of Catholic Bishops called for "making economic decisions more accountable to the common good." Governments at the federal, state, and local levels have been taking a few tentative steps towards inducing such social responsibility on the part of their private employers. Cleveland Mayor Carl Stokes, for example, used $50 million in city deposits as leverage to induce banks to make small business loans to black entrepreneurs.[100] A number of cities have since mandated that businesses receiving grants, tax breaks, and city contracts provide a prescribed level of wages and benefits.[101] Hawaii has attained nearly universal health insurance coverage by requiring their businesses to provide it.[102] Meanwhile, Congress has passed the Family and Medical Leave Act, requiring employers to allow time off so workers can deal with family medical emergencies. In addition, Senator Edward Kennedy recently introduced legislation in the United States Congress that would reduce federal taxes on "most favored companies"—companies that provided sufficient benefits to their employees. Meanwhile, others in Congress have actually proposed laws that would mandate benefits such as child care, health insurance, and pensions.[103]

In 1997, as another case-in-point, a Presidential task force was created to address the problem of sweatshop labor utilized by American-based clothiers. Comprised of representatives from human rights groups, labor unions, and apparel industry giants such as Reebok and Nike, the companies ultimately agreed on a code of conduct which would regulate the wages and working conditions of the various clothing factories they used around the world. This also included the creation of an association of monitors who would inspect the factories to verify compliance.[104]

> We want to set up worker control, not only for ourselves but for our children, so they'll have jobs and an economic future in our community.[105]

Worker Cooperatives.   Besides simply constraining the decisions of corporations belonging to the owning class, there are now dozens of fully worker-owned cooperative businesses in operation across the land. In particular, such states as Massachusetts and Maine paved the way with important legal revisions, and these businesses have been assisted by organizations such as the National Center for Employee Ownership and the Industrial Coop Association.

Such collective ventures date back as far as the 1880s when the Knights of Labor first created 135 industrial cooperatives.[106] More recently, one success story has been the Workers' Owned Sewing Company of Windsor, North Carolina, where primarily black women employees took control of the entire business. Other examples have included Avis Car Rental and Republic Engineered Steel, as well as food industry companies such as Sunkist, Ocean Spray, Agway, and Land-O-Lakes.[107]

Employee Stock-Ownership Plans.   In addition, some 10,000 *employee stock-ownership plans* (ESOPs) exist, involving more than 11 million workers; and, more than one-fifth of these firms employ at least 1,000 people.[108] For example, 10,000 steelworkers in Weirton, West Virginia, agreed in September of 1983 to spend $386 million in order to buy their plant. And even though they subsequently have chosen to sell a portion of their stock publicly, this still leaves the Weirton Works as one of the larger worker-controlled enterprises in the United States. Workers have also purchased significant portions of companies as large as Publix Supermarkets, Epic Healthcare, Science Applications, Kroger Foods, J.C. Penney, McDonnell Douglas, Ashland Oil, Morgan Stanley, The Journal Company, and Colt Industries, as well as Pan American, Trans World, Republic, and United Airlines. In addition, the AFL-CIO has set aside an Employee Partnership Fund that lends money to workers who seek to buy their factories.[109]

Worker Self-Management.   As another method of gaining at least some control, self-management is also finding its way onto shop floors. For example, at the General

Motors battery plant in Fitzgerald, Georgia, worker-management teams have been choosing their leaders and helping to determine their own budgets, schedules, and proficiency and maintenance standards. They have also had some disciplinary juris-diction. A New York Stock Exchange survey found that some 14 percent of U.S. com-panies with more than 100 employees had similar plans, while a federal study found that 44 percent of firms with more than 500 employees included their workers in dis-cussions of plant operations. In addition, the federal government's 1993 Conference on the Future of the American Workplace strongly endorsed this practice. Analysts warn, however, that many of these changes have been largely cosmetic, with the tougher and more important decisions still remaining in the hands of management.[110]

Control Through Unions.   Nonetheless, workers are beginning to bargain collec-tively for even more control. For example, the United Food and Commercial Work-ers persuaded several meat-packing companies to agree that if they closed a union plant, they would not open a nonunion one for at least five years. The United Rubber Workers got the four largest tire producers to guarantee that if they shut down a plant, they would give six months' notice and grant full pensions after 25 years of work (or after five years if the worker was over the age of 55), assure preferential hir-ing at other plants, and guarantee workers the right to negotiate ways of saving the plant or the method by which it was to be closed. Beyond that, the United Auto Workers and General Motors/Toyota agreed that workers would both participate in corporate decision making and have access to corporate financial data; and before any layoffs could occur, salaries of executives and managers had to be cut, and all outside contract work had to be called in.[111] All of this is but a prelude to the kind of worker control that could emerge should workers begin to pool and strategically invest their hundreds of billions of dollars in pension funds. The largest teachers' pension fund, for example, has issued guidelines corporate boards must follow if they are to continue to receive pension fund investments.[112] Meanwhile, the AFL-CIO has actually pooled resources from hundreds of pension funds to create the Housing Investment Trust, which invests more than $100 million annually to finance low-income housing.[113]

Mass Mobilization.   As for mass mobilizing, the AFL-CIO reinvigorated itself with the election of John Sweeney as president. Among other things, the union launched a massive membership drive and began spending millions in election cam-paigns.[114] Yet even prior to that, a number of labor unions joined forces to wage national campaigns against the antiunion postures of J. P. Stevens Company and Lit-ton Industries.[115] Progressive laborites united with consumer advocates, liberals, and other leftists to form both the National Coalition and the All-Peoples' Congress, with goals such as citizen participation in corporate decision making and severance pay-ments from firms choosing to leave an area.[116] Various churches backed United Steel Worker unionists in their attempts to fight plant shutdowns in Youngstown and Pitts-burgh.[117] The North American Farm Alliance was established in 1983 as a coalition of farmers; union members; blacks; women; and peace, religious, and environmental groups united to fight "pro-corporate governmental farm policies."[118] In addition, corporate shareholders have been pooling their proxy votes in order to press corporations to democratize their governing structures and behave in a more socially responsible manner.[119]

There also have been the emergence and growth of such progressive organizations as the Democratic Socialists of America, Fair Share, Citizens' Action, the Gray Panthers, Working Today, National Peoples' Action, the Association of Community Organizations for Reform Now (ACORN), the Institute for Policy Studies and their Conferences on Alternative State and Local Politics, various tenant groups, the Center for the Study of Democratic Societies, Detroit's League of Revolutionary Black Workers, and so on. In 1986, for instance, ACORN negotiated an agreement whereby Boatman's Bank would invest $50 million a year in home loans to residents in low-income St. Louis neighborhoods, besides providing low-cost checking accounts and cashing government checks at no cost. This is only one of the dozens of such successes since 1970 alone.[120]

In addition, progressive electoral groups have sent socialists into elected positions, ranging from congressional representative (Bernard Sanders of Vermont) to president of a major industrial union (William Winpinsinger of the International Association of Machinists). At the local level, there is a long history of socialist mayors and councilpersons as well as public ownership of capital. Earlier in the century, for example, socialists held power in Dayton, Schenectady, Davenport, Milwaukee, Oakland, Berkeley, and dozens of other cities. As a matter of fact, 1911 witnessed the election of more than 70 socialist mayors and 1,200 socialist officeholders across 340 American cities.[121] Most recently, socialists have been elected mayors of Burlington, Vermont, and Santa Monica, California.[122]

European Models.   Finally, European countries provide model legislation for a good deal of this transformation. For example, as suggested earlier, centralized industrial planning and regulation of plant relocations have existed there for some time. In addition, many European governments have taken further progressive steps. For example, most have been taxing and spending at much higher rates than in the United States in order to provide a far more elaborate welfare state, including national health insurance and much more extensive mass transportation. In addition, the majority of public utility companies, as well as rail and air transportation, have been nationalized, as have sizable shares of the manufacturing and banking industries.

The collective farms of Czechoslovakia and Hungary provide models of economic success against great odds. As a matter of fact, despite the privatization trend occurring across Eastern Europe following the collapse of state-centered communism, these collective enterprises have endured and remained quite popular.[123]

The classic comprehensive example is Mondragon, Spain. That city pioneered worker-owned cooperatives, allowing employees direct "one person-one vote" control over their corporations. In fact, they actually developed a large cooperative complex with a development bank, credit unions, schools, research and development firms, leisure clubs, housing, and agricultural extension services.[124]

Lastly, the Swedes pioneered a concept that conceivably allowed for a gradual and peaceful transition to this type of socialism. They proposed taxing individuals and corporate profits in order to create a fund with which unions—representing 90 percent of all Sweden's workers—could gradually buy up the nation's corporate stock.[125]

Unifying Issues

> . . . race has persistently obstructed the development of class politics across more than one hundred years of American political history.[126]

A number of issues taking shape may begin to unite the nation's nonelite blacks and whites, making them increasingly aware of their common interests in structural change. For example, Chapter 5 spelled out at length the declining socioeconomic position of most of the nation. Let us consider this in human terms.

Terry Hatfield, age 34, lost his job as a shipping department foreman when a Cleveland-area plant closed. When his unemployment benefits expired, he and his family were in trouble. The last source of income for Terry, his wife Susan, and their two children (ages 4 and 5) was a welfare check of $327 a month. Unable to continue to pay their rent of $300 a month and with their electricity cut off by the utility company for overdue bills, the Hatfields sold what they could and moved into a pair of tents. "It definitely breaks your pride," Terry said. "No one could have told me when the plant closed that I'd still be out of work a year and a half later." And even after the recession started taking its toll on their neighbors, forcing them also to go on welfare and food stamps, the Hatfields still assumed that poverty was somehow the fault of those afflicted. "I used to think, What's their problem?" Susan said. "Now I realize the problem."[127]

Then there is also the predicament faced by a growing number of elderly people. Confronted with cuts in Social Security and Medicare, they are often compelled to rely on their children for basic subsistence needs. This, in turn, can create economic hardship for their middle-and working-class offspring. Yet all the elderly are not that fortunate.

Robert (last name withheld at his request) is a World War II veteran with two purple hearts and a former road construction worker. At age 82, he now sells drugs out of his one-bedroom North Memphis apartment to supplement his only other source of income—the $475 Social Security check he receives each month. "I know it ain't right, but what else am I goin' to do to live?"[128]

Ninety-one-year-old Mattie Schultz lived in San Antonio, Texas, on a combined social security and veteran's benefit check of $233 per month. Too proud to accept public welfare or private charity, Mattie was arrested and jailed for shoplifting $15 worth of food to keep from starving. Humiliated, all she could say was that she just wished God would close her eyes.[129]

Howard and Fannie Spears resided in St. Louis. Howard was 93 years old and blind; his wife was 88. Unable to pay $800 in overdue utility bills, their gas was shut off. In the winter, forced to heat their apartment with a small electric heater, ice began to form on their floor and walls. On December 22, three days before Christmas, Howard froze to death. His wife was taken to the hospital, treated, and then released.[130]

> It is inevitable that the U.S. economy will grow more slowly . . . [and] some people will obviously have to do with less. . . . The basic health of the U.S. economy is based on the basic health of its corporations and banks. . . . Yet it will be a hard pill for many Americans to swallow—the idea of doing with less so that big business can have more. It will be particularly hard to swallow because it is quite obvious that if big businesses are the most vis-

ible victims of what ails the Debt Economy, they are also in large measure the cause of it.[131]

Not long after *Business Week* presented that assessment, as previously indicated, a research team at the University of Michigan completed an extensive five-year study that indicated that seven out of every ten Americans stood a better than even chance of falling below the federal poverty level at some point in their lives. They concluded, "It is not merely some vague minority called "the poor" who stand in economic peril, it is the majority of Americans."[132] Meanwhile, Fordham University's "Index of Social Well Being" has been falling rather steadily since the middle 1970s.[133] If present trends continue, it may not be long before more and more people identify with Mattie Schultz, the Hatfields, and the Spears, and begin to believe that there is something fundamentally wrong.[134]

Emerging Consciousness

> Any substantial decline of the middle class—even if it is partially psychological—would be ominous for the United States as a whole.[135]

Both capitalist Lee Iacocca and socialist Howard Zinn agree that fundamental change is not likely to commence until middle-class faith in the current system is shaken. Iacocca noted:

> It's the middle class that gives us stability and keeps the economy rolling. As long as a guy is making enough money to meet his mortgage payments, eat fairly well, drive a car, send his kids to college, and go out with his wife once a week for dinner and a show, he's satisfied. And if the middle class is content, we'll never have a civil war or a revolution.[136]

Zinn observed:

> In a highly developed society, the Establishment cannot survive without the obedience and loyalty of millions of people who are given small rewards to keep the system going. . . . These people—the employed, the somewhat privileged—are drawn into alliance with the elite. They become the guardians of the system, buffers between the upper and lower classes. If they stop obeying, the system falls.[137]

As a result of a history of oppression, many African Americans have become alienated. In 1967, for example, only 14 percent of Newark blacks *not* involved in that city's ghetto unrest felt that local government could be trusted. The figure was a mere 5 percent for those who participated in the turmoil.[138] Meanwhile, Harris polls indicate that nationwide, the number of alienated blacks increased from 46 percent at the time of those ghetto disturbances to more than 70 percent thereafter—a figure so large that it had to include much of the black middle class.[139] Beyond that, blacks' trust in governmental institutions has declined faster than the national average.[140]

The only group that is more alienated is lower-class whites. In 1969, for example, when 40 percent of African Americans felt "what I think doesn't count for much anymore," that figure was 60 percent for lower-class whites; and whereas less than a third of all blacks felt that "people in power don't care about us," half the lower-class whites felt that way.[141] Like their black counterparts, these whites saw themselves living in deteriorating housing, attending inferior schools, and being stereotyped in the mass media, yet they did not feel that they were receiving even the limited attention blacks were receiving from the government or from the "limousine liberals."[142]

Tables 10.1 and 10.2 show that such alienation has continued and has reached well beyond the black and white lower classes. The size of the numbers indicates that many in the U.S. middle class also seem to feel that they have been left out of a system perceived to be functioning primarily to serve the interests of the rich, while many also display a shrinking amount of confidence in society's major institutions. As faith in societal institutions has continued to decline,[143] a full 80 percent of Americans feel that "government is run for the benefit of a few big interests," up from 29 percent in 1964.[144]

Alienation also can be seen in the mounting disillusionment with the country's major political parties.[145] In addition, it is visible in the low rates of voter turnout mentioned in Chapter 7. Americans vote at lower rates than virtually any other functioning democracy in the world, and that rate actually has been declining over the last several decades.[146]

Some attitude and value changes do appear to be emerging out of all this, however. For one thing, the difference between the way blacks and whites perceive national problems has been lessening.[147] In terms of personal values, rugged individualism seems to be giving way to an increased recognition of people's interdependence; the obsession with private property appears to be giving way to growing concern for the nation's common property; and blind allegiance to the so-called work ethic does not appear to be nearly as strong as it previously was perceived to be.[148]

In terms of the existing distribution of wealth and income, three-quarters of the American public generally agrees that "there is too much power concentrated in the hands of a few big companies," while two-thirds believe "business corporations make

TABLE 10.1

AMERICAN ALIENATION, 1966–1995

	Percentage of Respondents Agreeing with Statement					
	1966	1971	1977	1985	1990	1995
The rich get richer and the poor get poorer	45	62	77	79	82	79
Most people with power try to take advantage of people like yourself	28	33	60	65	64	72
What you think doesn't count very much anymore.	37	44	61	62	62	71
The people running the country don't really care what happens to you	26	41	60	57	53	60
You're left out of things going on around you	9	20	35	48	44	51
Harris "Alienation Index"	29	40	59	56	61	67

Source: Adapted from Louis Harris polls, 1966–1995.

TABLE 10.2

CONFIDENCE IN INSTITUTIONS, 1966–1995

Percentage of Respondents Declaring "A Great Deal of Confidence"

	1966	1971	1975	1980	1985	1990	1995
Medicine	73	61	43	34	39	35	26
The military	61	27	24	28	32	43	43
Higher education	61	37	36	36	35	35	27
Major corporations	55	27	19	16	17	14	21
The U.S. Supreme Court	50	23	28	27	28	32	32
The Congress	42	19	13	18	16	12	10
Organized religion	41	27	32	22	21	20	24
The executive branch of government	41	23	13	17	19	14	9
Television news	—	—	35	29	23	27	16
The press	29	18	26	19	16	18	11
Law firms	—	—	16	13	12	—	9
Organized labor	22	14	14	14	13	14	8
Wall Street	—	—	—	12	—	9	13
The White House	—	—	—	18	30	21	13
Harris "Confidence Index"	100	58	55	49	51	50	43

Source: Adapted from Louis Harris polls, 1966–1995

*In response to the question "As far as people in charge of running (READ LIST) are concerned, would you say you have a great deal of confidence, only some confidence, or hardly any confidence at all in them?"

too much profit."[149] A *Journalism Quarterly* article found that more than 40 percent of "middle class" Americans agreed that "capitalism must be altered before any significant improvements in human welfare can be realized."[150] Even political conservatives have been forced to concede inherent problems in the existing economic system.[151]

As for solutions, in the middle of the highly conservative "Reagan Revolution," nearly two-thirds of the public indicated that they felt financial resources "should be more evenly distributed among a larger percentage of the people."[152] By the end of the 1980s, the Center for Media and Public Affairs found roughly three in ten Americans preferring that the United States "move toward socialism."[153] Another poll found two-thirds of the public in favor of employee ownership and control of large corporations, with nearly half favoring direct public control of all natural resources.[154]

> As the contradictions of late twentieth-century capitalism deepen, more and more of the white electorate will be tainted with the aversive stain once reserved for blacks and "dirty immigrants." As white feminists, workers, farmers, peace and environmental activists, and gays and lesbians are shunned by the institutions they once gave their loyalty and are branded "un-American" . . . they will begin to accept their place in that "other America" represented by the brightly colored hues of the Rainbow Coalition—a creature half in, half out of the two-party system, part social protest movement, part electoral machine—a political amphibian in the process of evolving.[155]

Critical Realignment

Regardless of who leads it or under what banner it occurs, one of the first indications that this progressive political coalition is truly beginning to form may be a "critical re-alignment" in the nation's electoral politics. As discussed in Chapter 7 above, the United States has never had the sort of capitalist-socialist party dichotomy found in most every other industrial or postindustrial democracy in the world. Both the Industrial Revolution and the Great Depression set off party realignments here; but for a variety of reasons including regionalism, race, and the nature of both the nation's two-party system and its conservative political culture, capitalism itself never became the critical dividing issue.[156]

That may soon change. As postindustrial frustrations rise, the emerging class consciousness discussed above may ultimately be strong enough to overcome both the host of social issues that currently divide the non-owning classes, as well as their long-standing faith in "laissez faire" capitalism. Once the rich have been allowed to get ever richer and "friendly fascism" has played itself out, the nonowners may well come to find that little has trickled down, and they are even poorer and less secure than they were before.

When the next major socioeconomic crisis hits, one of the two major parties may be compelled to break ranks and propose overtly socialist alternatives in order to appeal to the large majority of Americans. Instead of being divided as black and white, male and female, straight and gay, religious and less religious, immigrants and natives, gun owners and nongun owners, the middle and working classes may well be driven by their common interests to put those divisions aside and develop a political and economic system more responsive to the most basic economic needs of postindustrial society in the twenty-first century.[157]

NOTES

1. Frederick Douglass, quoted in Howard Zinn, *A People's History of the United States* (New York: Harper & Row, 1980), p. 179.
2. Jackson Turner Main, *The Social Structure of Revolutionary America* (Princeton, N.J.: Princeton University Press, 1965); Sam Bass Warner, *The Private City* (Philadelphia: University of Pennsylvania Press, 1968).
3. See reference sources, calculations, and discussion in chap. 4 and 5 above.
4. Quoted in Robert Allen, *Black Awakening in Capitalist America: An Analytical History* (Garden City, N.Y.: Anchor/Doubleday, 1969), p. 164.
5. Ibid., p. 158.
6. Quoted in Francis Broderick and August Meier (eds.), *Negro Protest Thought in the Twentieth Century* (Indianapolis: Bobbs-Merrill, 1965), p. 425.
7. Also see, for example, Aldon Morris, "The Future of Black Politics: Governance versus Process and Formality," *National Political Science Review* 3 (1991), pp. 168–174.
8. Martin Luther King, Jr., "The President's Address to the 10th Anniversary Convention of the Southern Christian Leadership Conference (August 16, 1967)," in Robert Scott and Wayne Brockreide (eds.), *The Rhetoric of Black Power* (New York: Harper & Row, 1969),

pp. 161–162. For further discussion of King's socialist leanings, see James Cone, *For My People: Black Theology and the Black Church* (Maryknoll, N.Y.: Orbis, 1984), p. 96.

9. Quoted in Allen, *Black Awakening*, p. 159.

10. Manning Marable, *How Capitalism Underdeveloped Black America* (Boston: South End Press, 1983), p. 256. Also see W. E. B. Du Bois, "Is Man Free?" *Scientific Monthly* (May 1948); W. E. B. Du Bois, "There Must Come a Vast Social Change in the United States," *National Guardian*, July 11,1951; Wilson Record, *Race and Radicalism* (Ithaca: Cornell University Press, 1964); Phillip Foner (ed.), *The Black Panthers Speak* (Philadelphia: Lippincott, 1970); Earl Ofar, "Marxist-Leninism: The Key to Black Liberation," *Black Scholar* 4 (1972), pp. 35–46; I. A. Baraka, "Why I Changed My Ideology: Black Nationalism and Socialist Revolution," *Black World* 24 (1975), pp. 30–42; Cedric Robinson, *Black Marxism: The Making of the Black Radical Tradition* (London: Zed Books,1983); Lloyd Hogan, "the Role of Land and African-Centered Values in Black Economic Development," in James Jennings, ed., *Race, Politics, and Economic Development* (New York: Verso, 1992).

11. Allen, *Black Awakening*, p. 153.

12. Samuel Bowles and Herbert Gintis, "Schooling for a Socialist America," in David Gordon (ed.), *Problems in Political Economy* (Lexington, Mass.: Heath, 1977), pp. 263–270; Kenneth Dolbeare and Patricia Dolbeare, *American Ideologies* (Boston: Houghton Mifflin, 1976), chap. 8.

13. Jesse Jackson, quoted in *New York Times*, January 28, 1987.

14. Coretta King and others have advocated this position in organizations like the Full Employment Action Council.

15. *Village Voice*, September 29, 1975.

16. For further development of such "left liberal" approaches, see Gar Alperovitz and Jeff Faux, *Rebuilding America: A Blueprint for the New Economy* (New York: Pantheon, 1984); Samuel Bowles et al., *Beyond the Wasteland* (Garden City, N.Y.: Anchor/Doubleday, 1983); J. Morton Davis, *Making America Work Again* (New York: Crown, 1983); Martin Carnoy and Derek Shearer, *Economic Democracy* (Armonk, N.Y.: Sharpe, 1980); Neil Jacoby, *Corporate Power and Social Responsibility* (New York: Macmillan, 1973); David Mahoney, *New York Times*, February 7, 1983; Wassily Leontief, quoted in *New York Times*, April 6,1983.

17. Marable, *How Capitalism Underdeveloped Black America*, p. 16.

18. See Bowles and Gintis, "Schooling for a Socialist America"; William Tabb, "A Pro-People Policy," in William Tabb and Larry Sawers (eds.), *Marxism and the Metropolis* (New York: Oxford University Press, 1984); William Tabb, "Economic Democracy and Regional Restructuring: An Internalization Perspective," in Larry Sawers and William Tabb (eds.), *Sunbelt/Snowbelt* (New York: Oxford University Press, 1984); Richard Child Hill, "Fiscal Crisis, Austerity Politics, and Alternative Urban Policies," in Tabb and Sawers, *Marxism and the Metropolis;* Bowles, *Beyond the Wasteland.*

19. On August 20, 1978, Congress created the National Consumer Cooperative Bank (Public Law 95–351). See *New York Times,* June 27, 1982. For an updated history, see the National Cooperative Bank's web page at www.ncb.com/day/a9a.htm.

20. For a detailed fictional account of how such a revolution and transformation might take place, see Kenneth Dolbeare and Janette Hubbell, *USA 2012: After the Middle-Class Revolution* (Chatham, N.J.: Chatham House, 1996).

21. Friedrich Hayek, *The Road to Serfdom* (Chicago: University of Chicago Press, 1944); Charles Lindbloom, *Politics and Markets* (New Haven: Yale University Press, 1977).

22. Bowles and Gintis, "Schooling for a Socialist America."

23. Youssef Ibrahim, "Welfare's Snug Coat Cuts Norwegian Cold," *New York Times,* December 13, 1996; Holly Sklar, *Chaos or Community?* (Boston: South End Press, 1995), pp. 148–149; Malcolm Sawyer and Frank Wasserman, "Income Distribution in the OECD Countries," *OECD Economic Outlook* (July 1976), p. 14; Lester Thurow, Zero-Sum Society (New York: Basic Books, 1980); Lindbloom, Politics and Markets, chap. 20.

24. Alperovitz and Faux, *Rebuilding America,* pp. 113–121.

25. For more evidence, see Barry Bluestone and Bennett Harrison, *The Deindustrialization of America* (New York: Basic Books, 1982), pp. 232–234; Karl Frieden, *Workplace Democracy and Productivity* (Washington, D.C.: National Center for Economic Alternatives, 1980); James O'Toole, *Making America Work* (New York: Continuum, 1981); Alperovitz and Faux, *Rebuilding America,* pp. 99–109.

26. *New York Times,* October 6, 1989. Also see Paul Bernstein, "Worker-Owned Plywood Firms Steadily Outperform Industry," *World of Work Reports* (May 1977); Bluestone and Harrison, *The Deindustrialization of America,* p. 260; Alperovitz and Faux, *Rebuilding America,* pp. 243–255.

27. Daniel Pedersen, "The Swedish Model," *Newsweek,* March 5, 1990, pp. 30–31.

28. David Mermelstein, "Austerity, Planning, and the Socialist Alternative," in Roger Alcaly and David Mermelstein (eds.), *The Fiscal Crisis of American Cities* (New York: Vintage, 1977), pp. 360–361.

29. Gerry Spence, *With Justice For None: Destroying An American Myth* (New York: Penguin Books, 1989), chap. 16.

30. Bowles and Gintis, "Schooling for a Socialist America," p. 265.

31. For further references on socialism, see David McLellan, *The Thought of Karl Marx* (New York: Harper & Row, 1971); Shlomo Avineri, *The Social and Political Thought of Karl Marx* (New York: Cambridge University Press, 1969); Robert Tucker (ed.), *The Marx-Engels Reader* (New York: Norton, 1978); Bruce Brown, *Marx, Freud, and the Critique of Everyday Life* (New York: Monthly Review Press, 1973); Michael Harrington, *Socialism* (New York: Saturday Review Press, 1972); David McLellan, Marxism after Marx (Boston: Houghton Mifflin, 1979); R. N. Berki, *Socialism* (New York: St. Martin's Press, 1975); Chantal Mouffe, "Toward a Liberal Socialism?", *Dissent* (Winter 1993), pp. 81–87; Christopher Pierson, *Socialism after Communism: the New Market System* (University Park: Pennsylvania State University Press, 1995). For more examples of socialist thought as applied by black scholars, see the later writings of W. E. B. Du Bois, as well as the writings of scholars such as Herbert Aptheker, Robert Allen, Manning Marable, Phillip Foner, and James Cone.

32. Charles V. Hamilton, "The Patron-Recipient Relationship and Minority Politics in New York City," *Political Science Quarterly* (Summer 1979).

33. For example, see William Fletcher and Eugene Newport, "Race and Economic Development: The Need for a Black Agenda," in Jennings, *Race, Politics, and Economic Development;* Dona Cooper Hamilton and Charles V. Hamilton, "The Dual Agenda of African-American Organizations since the New Deal: Social Welfare Policies and Civil Rights," *Political Science Quarterly* 107 (Fall 1992), pp. 435–452.

34. Ronald Walters, "Black Politics: Mobilization for Empowerment," in Winston Van Horne (ed.), *Race: Twentieth Century Dilemmas—Twenty-First Century Prognoses* (Madison: University of Wisconsin, 1989), p. 267.

35. Kwame Ture and Charles V. Hamilton, *Black Power* (New York: Random House, 1967, p. 44. More recently, see Robert Smith, *We Have No Leaders: African Americans in the Post Civil Rights Era* (Albany, Y.Y.: SUNY Press, 1996).

36. See Ron Walters, *Black Presidential Politics in America: A Strategic Approach* (Albany, N.Y.: SUNY Press, 1988), pp. 86–109; *New York Times,* June 15, 1994; September 18, 1996.

37. Jesse Jackson, quoted in Sheila Collins, *The Rainbow Challenge: The Jackson Campaign and the Future of U.S. Politics* (New York: Monthly Review Press, 1986), p. 83. Also see Melvin King, "The Rainbow Coalition," in Jeffrey Elliott (ed.), *Black Voices in American Politics* (Orlando, Fla.: Harcourt Brace Jovanovich, 1986); Marable, *How Capitalism Underdeveloped Black America,* p. 258; Charles V. Hamilton, "Deracialization: Examination of a Political Strategy," *First World* (March–April 1977).

38. Bob Faw and Nancy Skelton, Thunder in America (Austin: Texas Monthly Press, 1986); Adolph Reed, Jr., The Jesse Jackson Phenomenon (New Haven, Conn.: Yale University Press, 1986); New York Times, December 4, 1987.

39. *Focus* (October 1973), p. 2.

40. Marable, *How Capitalism Underdeveloped Black America,* p. 51.

41. Ibid., chap. 1.

42. *New York Times,* June 13,1988.

43. Marable, *How Capitalism Underdeveloped Black America,* p. 17. Also see W. E. B. Du Bois, *The Education of Black People* (New York: Monthly Review Press, 1973).

44. For example see Wilbur Rich, ed., *The Politics of Minority Coalitions: Race, Ethnicity, and Shared Uncertainties* (New York: Praeger, 1996).

45. *New York Times,* January 5,1984; Collins, *Rainbow Challenge,* chap. 6; Paula McClain and Joseph Stewart, *"Can We All Get Along?": Racial and Ethnic Minorities in American Politics* (Boulder, Colo.: Westview Press, 1995), chap. 5.

46. For example, see Susan Tolchin, *The Angry American: How Voter Rage Is Changing the Nation* (Boulder, Colo.: Westview, 1996); McClain and Stewart, *"Can We All Get Along?",* chap. 5. One of the classic examples of such conflict has arisen around the issue of affirmative action. For example, see Rochelle Stanfield, "The Wedge Issue," *National Journal,* April 1, 1995, pp. 790–793; Carl Cohen, *Naked Racial Preference: The Case Against Affirmative Action* (New York: Rowman and Littlefield, 1995); Andrew Kull, *The Color-Blind Constitution* (Cambridge: Harvard University Press, 1992); Christopher Edley, *Not All Black And White: Affirmative Action, Race, and American Values* (New York: Hill and Wang, 1996); Bob Herbert, "The Wrong Target," *New York Times,* April 5, 1995; Clint Bolick, "Beyond Race: The Future of Affirmative Action," paper presented at the annual meeting of the American Political Science Association, Washington, D.C., September 2–5, 1993.

47. Harry Holloway, "Negro Political Strategy," *Social Science Quarterly* (December 1968), pp. 545–546.

48. King, "The Rainbow Coalition."

49. For example, see John Harrigan, *Empty Dreams, Empty Pockets: Class and Bias in American Politics* (New York: Macmillan, 1993), pp. 177–179; Bill Whalen, "When a Fist Turns into a Handshake," Insight, June 11, 1990, pp. 8–17; Stanley Greenberg and Theda Skoepol, eds., *The New Majority: Toward a Popular Progressive Politics* (New Haven: Yale Univ., 1997).

50. Interview in *Playboy* (January 1984), p. 77.

51. Allen, *Black Awakening,* p. 280. Also see Katherine Tate, *From Protest to Politics: The New Black Voters in American Politics* (New York: Russell Sage, 1994), chap. 8.

52. Charles V. Hamilton, "Racial, Ethnic, and Social Class Politics and Administration," *Public Administration Review* (October 1972). Also see Carol Swain, *Black Faces, Black Interests: The Representation of African Americans in Congress* (Cambridge, Mass.: Harvard University Press, 1993); Ture and Hamilton, *Black Power;* Bernard Boxill, "Is

Further Civil Rights Legislation Irrelevant to Black Progress?" in Van Horne, *Race*, pp. 12–48.

53. For example, see Rufus Browning, *Protest is Not Enough* (Berkeley: University of California Press, 1984).

54. For example, see the *Tri-State Defender*, April 5–9, 1992, p. 1.

55. Peter Kilborn, "Blacks Make Boycott Hurt A Small Town," *New York Times*, August 18, 1994.

56. This author does not advocate the use of violence, especially against other human beings—at least not within a system with as many other avenues available as the present U.S. system.

57. *New York Times*, August 12, 1979.

58. Collins, *Rainbow Challenge*, p. 19.

59. Jesse Jackson, quoted in Roger Hatch and Frank Watkins (eds.), *Reverend Jesse L. Jackson: Straight from the Heart* (Philadelphia: Fortress, 1987), pp. 38–39.

60. Laura Waxman and Lilia Reyes, Status Report on Hunger and Homelessness in America's Cities (Washington, D.C.: U.S. Conference of Mayors, January 1, 1989); Marcus Pohlmann, *Governing the Postindustrial City* (New York: Longman, 1993), chap. 3.

61. See Christopher Jencks and Paul Peterson, eds., *The Urban Underclass* (Washington, D.C.: Brookings, 1991); William Julius Wilson, *The Truly Disadvantaged* (Chicago: University of Chicago, 1987).

62. Kenneth B. Clark, quoted in *Report of the National Advisory Commission on Civil Disorders*, reprint (New York: Bantam, 1968), p. 29.

63. *New York Times*, July 24, 1977; or *U.S News and World Report*, August 29, 1977, pp. 50–51. For an even more recent example, see *New York Times*, January 1, 1985.

64. Quoted in *New York Times*, March 3, 1977. Also see U.S. Commission on Civil Rights report on the Miami unrest, in *New York Times*, June 9, 1982.

65. Quoted in *New York Times*, May 14, 1977.

66. *Ibid.*, July 1, 1990; April 6, 1990.

67. For a recent compendium, see Wesley Skogan, *Disorder and Decline* (New York: Free Press, 1990).

68. Charles V. Hamilton, "Political Access, Minority Participation, and the New Normalcy," in Dunbar, ed., *Minority Report* (1984), p. 23.

69. Mermelstein, "Austerity, Planning, and the Socialist Alternative," p. 361. Also for wide-ranging predictions concerning the urban future, see Gary Gappert and Richard Knight, eds., *Cities in the 21st Century* (Beverly Hills, Calif.: Sage, 1982).

70. Dolbeare and Dolbeare, *American Ideologies*, p. 224.

71. Ibid. For further discussion, see DeFelice, *Interpretations of Fascism*, chap. 14; Carl Cohen, ed., *Communism, Fascism, and Democracy* (New York: Random House, 1962); Kenneth Dolbeare, *Political Change in the United States* (New York: McGraw Hill, 1974); William Ebenstein, *Fascism at Work* (New York: Free Press, 1969); Daniel Guerin, *Fascism and Big Business* (New York: Monthly Review, 1969); Paul M. Hayes, *Fascism* (New York: Free Press, 1973); Anthony James Joes, *Fascism in the Contemporary World* (Boulder, Colo.: Westview, 1978); Walter Laqueur, *Fascism* (Berkeley: University of California Press, 1976); Benito Mussolini, *Fascism* (Rome: Ardita, 1935); Benito Mussolini, *The Corporate State* (Florence: Vallechi, 1936); Franz Neumann, *Behemoth* (New York: Harper and Row, 1966); Ernst Nolte, *Three Faces of Fascism* (New York: Holt, Rhinehart, and Winston, 1966); William Reich, *The Mass Psychology of Fascism* (New York: Farrar, Straus and Giroux, 1970); David Schoenbaum, *Hitler's Social Revolution* (New

York: Doubleday/Anchor, 1967); S. J. Woolf, ed., *The Nature of Fascism* (New York: Vintage, 1969).

72. Renzo DeFelice, *Interpretations of Fascism* (Cambridge, Mass.: Harvard University Press, 1977), p. 53.

73. Milton Friedman, *Capitalism and Freedom* (Chicago: University of Chicago Press, 1962), pp. 133–135; Theodore Lowi, *The End of Liberalism* (New York: Norton, 1979).

74. For example, see William Mayer, *The Changing American Mind* (Ann Arbor: University of Michigan Press, 1992); S. C. Craig, The Malevolent Leaders: Popular Discontent in America (Boulder, Colo.: Westview, 1993); Times Mirror Poll, released September 20, 1994.

75. *New York Times*, April 23, 1990.

76. For documentation of contemporary militaristic attitudes, see Bruce Russett and Donald DeLuca, "Don't Tread on Me," *Political Science Quarterly* 96 (Fall 1981), pp. 381–389.

77. For example, see *New York Times*, October 4, 1985.

78. Ibid.; May 26, 1986.

79. For an example of the latter, see Kirk Johnson, "A New Grinch Turns Up at the Mall: Retailers, Fearful of Union Organizers, Bar the Salvation Army," *ibid.*, December 16, 1995.

80. For example, see John Tierney, "A San Francisco Talk Show Takes Right-Wing Radio to a New Dimension," ibid., February 14, 1995; Francis Clines, "Cool to Dole's Campaigning, Talk Radio Tries to Start a Fire," ibid., September 21, 1996; Michael Janofsky, "Keeping a Closer Watch on Paramilitary Groups is Urged," ibid., April 11, 1996; Richard Serrano, "In Wake of Oklahoma Tragedy, Support for Militias Grows," ibid., April 21, 1996.

81. Bob Herbert, "The Sweatshop Lives," *New York Times*, December 28, 1994; Alan Finder, "Despite Tough Laws, Sweatshops Flourish," ibid., February 6, 1995; Joe Sexton, "A Factory Reinvents the Sweatshop," ibid., May 29, 1995; Kenneth Noble, "Los Angeles Sweatshops Are Thriving, Experts Say," ibid., August 5, 1995; Bob Herbert, "Sweatshop Beneficiaries," ibid., July 24, 1995; Steven Greenhouse, "Sweatshop Raids Cast Doubt on Ability of Garment Makers to Police Factories," ibid., July 18, 1997; Steve Greenhouse, "U.S. Says Many Government Shops Break the Law," ibid., October 17, 1997.

Kirk Victor, "Kids on the Job," *National Journal*, July 14, 1990, pp. 1712–1713; Gina Kolata, "More Children Are Employed, Often Perilously," *New York Times*, June 21, 1992, Memphis *Tri-State Defender,* December 20–20, 1997.

82. For example, see Gary Orfield and Carole Ashkinaze, *The Closing Door: Conservative Policy and Black Opportunity* (Chicago: University of Chicago Press, 1991); Frances Fox Piven and Richard Cloward, *The New Class War* (New York: Pantheon, 1985); Fred Block, et al., *The Mean Season* (New York: Pantheon, 1987).

For general discussion of these overall trends and prospects, see Bertram Gross, *Friendly Fascism* (New York: Evans, 1980); Dan Carter, *The Politics of Rage: George Wallace , the Origins of the New Conservatism, and the Transformation of American Politics* (New York: Simon and Schuster, 1995); Sara Diamond, *Roads to Dominion: Right-Wing Movements and Political Power in the United States* (New York: Guilford Press, 1995); Joseph Davey, *The New Social Contract: America's Journey from a Welfare State to a Police State* (New York: Praeger, 1995); Thomas and Mary Edsall, *Chain Reaction: The Impact of Race, Rights, and Taxes on American Politics* (New York: Norton, 1992); Michael Omi and Howard Winant, *Racial Formation in the United States* (New York: Routledge, 1986), chap. 10; Paul Sniderman and Thomas Piazza, *The Scar of Race* (Cambridge Mass.: Harvard University Press, 1993); Martin Carnoy, *Faded Dreams: The Politics and Economics of Race in the United States* (New York: Cambridge University Press,

1994); Kevin Phillips, *Arrogant Capital: Washington, Wall Street, and the Frustration of American Politics* (Boston: Back Bay Books, 1995).

83. See Georgia Persons, ed., *Dilemmas of Black Politics: Issues of Leadership and Strategy* (New York: Harper Collins, 1993), pp. 198–204; Deborah Toler, "Black Conservatives: Part One," *The Public Eye Newsletter* 7 (December 1993); Jane Mayer and Jill Abramson, *Strange Justice: The Selling of Clarence Thomas* (Boston: Houghton Mifflin, 1994).

84. For example, see Mack Jones, "The Political Thought of the New Black Conservatives," in Franklin Jones, et al., *Readings in American Political Issues* (Dubuque, Ia.: Kendall/Hunt, 1987); Cornell West, "Assessing Black Neoconservatism," in Floyd Hayes, ed., *The Turbulent Voyage: Readings in African-American Studies* (San Diego, Calif.: Collegiate Press, 1992); Martin Kilson, "The Gang That Couldn't Shoot Straight," *Transition* 62 (1993); Lewis Randolph, "The New African-American Conservatives or The Same Old Song With A Few New Twists?" unpublished paper presented at the First National Conference on Civil and Human Rights of African Americans, Memphis, Tennessee, August 1995.

    For original works by these black conservatives, see Joseph Perkins, ed., *A Conservative Agenda for Black Americans* (Washington, D.C.: Heritage Foundation, 1990); *The Fairmont Papers* (San Francisco: Institute for Contemporary Studies, 1981); Walter Williams, *The State Against Blacks* (New York: New Press, 1982); Thomas Sowell, *Markets and Minorities* (New York: Basic Books, 1981); Shelby Steele, *The Content of Our Character: A New Vision of Race in America* (New York: St. Martin's, 1990); Stephen Carter, *Reflections of an Affirmative Action Baby* (New York: Basic Books, 1991).

85. One in four children currently lives below the federal poverty level, and two-thirds of those indigent children live in homes where one or both parents have a job. See Bob Herbert, "One in Four," *New York Times*, December 16, 1996. Also see, for example, ibid., November 30, 1996; December 23, 1996; Jonathan Kozol, *Amazing Grace: The Lives of Children and the Conscience of a Nation* (New York: Crown Publishing, 1995).

86. For further discussion of the subject, see Robert Cherry, "Economic Theories of Racism," in Gordon, *Problems in Political Economy*, pp. 170–182; Norman Fainstein and Susan Fainstein, *Urban Political Movements* (Englewood Cliffs, N.J.: Prentice-Hall, 1974).

87. From "Our Do-Nothing Government," *New York Times*, March 30, 1992, an article written by an anonymous Republican who had served in both the Reagan and Bush administrations.

88. *National Journal*, March 7, 1992, pp. 576–577; Alperovitz and Faux, *Rebuilding America*, especially chaps. 7–16; Ira Maganizer and Robert Reich, *Minding America's Business* (New York: Harcourt Brace Jovanovich, 1982); Thurow, *The Zero-Sum Society*; Bluestone and Harrison, *The Deindustrialization of America*, pp. 244–257.

89. *National Journal*, July 9, 1994, pp. 1612–1617; May 21, 1994, p. 1176; December 11, 1993, p. 2952; *New York Times*, September 16, 1983; January 12, 1984; June 10, 1984; April 19, 1990; July 30, 1991; March 2, 1992; September 30, 1993; October 11, 1993. For a blueprint which estimates the costs of creating full employment, for example, see Philip Harvey, *Securing the Right to Employment* (Princeton, N.J.: Princeton University Press, 1989). And for a warning about the potential for elite abuse in such policies, see William Darity, "The Managerial Class and Industrial Policy," *Industrial Relations* 25 (Spring 1986), pp. 212–227.

90. *New York Times*, November 4, 1983; November 11, 1983; February 4, 1984.

91. Quoted in ibid., January 28, 1987.

92. Bruce Nissen, *Fighting for Jobs: Case Studies of Labor-Community Coalitions Confronting Plant Closings* (Albany, N.Y.: SUNY Press, 1995); Bluestone and Harrison, *The Deindustrialization of America*, pp. 235–243; Bennett Harrison and Barry Bluestone,

"The Incidence and Regulation of Plant Closings," in Sawers and Tabb, *Sunbelt/Snowbelt*, pp. 368–402; Tabb, "Pro-People Urban Policy," p. 371.

93. See *New York Times*, August 3, 1988. However, see *New York Times*, February 25, 1993; August 3, 1993 for indications of how its various exemptions appear to have significantly limited its impact.

94. See ibid., June 15, 1991.

95. *Fort Halifax Packing Company v. Coyne* 86 U.S. 341 (1987).

96. *New York Times*, June 3,1984.

97. Ibid., June 10,1984.

98. See Bluestone and Harrison, *The Deindustrialization of America*, p. 234

99. *Mobil Oil Corporation v. Vermont* 445 U.S. 425 (1980); reaffirmed again in both 1983 and 1994. See Linda Greenhouse, "Court Backs Tax Method of California," *New York Times*, June 21, 1994.

100. Carl Stokes, *Promises of Power* (New York: Simon and Schuster, 1973).

101. See *New York Times*, April 4, 1996; *Washington Post*, November 12, 1996.

102. *New York Times*, July 23, 1991.

103. Ibid., April 16, 1996; April 13, 1987; September 20, 1984; Susan Fainstein, Norman Fainstein, and P. Jefferson Armistead, "San Francisco: Urban Transformation and the Local State," in Susan Fainstein, Norman Fainstein, and Richard Child Hill et al., *Restructuring the City* (White Plains, N.Y.: Longman, 1983).

104. See Steven Greenhouse, "Apparel Industry Group Moves to End Sweatshops," *New York Times*, April 9, 1997.

105. *New York Times*, January 25, 1980. For more coverage of the Rath Meatpacking Company buyout, see *New York Times*, November 2, 1983.

106. Joseph Roebuck, *A History of American Labor* (New York: Free Press, 1966), p. 160; Bluestone and Harrison, *The Deindustrialization of America*, p. 257.

107. *New York Times*, April 17, 1984; February 10, 1994.

108. U.S. Department of Commerce, Bureau of the Census, *Statistical Abstracts of the United States 1995* (Washington, D.C.: GPO, 1995), p. 553.

109. Corey Rosen, Katherine Klein, and Karen Young, *Employee Stock Ownership in America: The Equity Solution* (Lexington, Mass.: Lexington Books, 1985); Bluestone and Harrison, *The Deindustrialization of America*, pp. 252–262; Dotson Rader, "The Town That Saved Itself," *Parade Magazine*, April 24, 1988, pp. 8–10; *New York Times*, January 15, 1984; March 15, 1985; April 24, 1988; June 19, 1989; September 18, 1989; February 20, 1990; April 16, 1990; December 9, 1993. Much of this information is now compiled and circulated by the National Center for Employee Ownership.

110. Alperovitz and Faux, *Rebuilding America*, pp. 99–109; *New York Times*, June 25, 1980; February 13, 1983; February 23, 1983; January 15, 1984; July 27, 1993; December 5, 1994.

111. Jeremy Rifkin and Randy Barber, *The North Will Rise Again: Pensions and Power in the 1980s* (Boston: Beacon Press, 1978). Also see *New York Times*, May 23, 1980; April 7, 1981; August 28, 1989; March 17, 1991; June 6, 1991.

112. The pension fund is the Teachers Insurance and Annuity Association/College Retirement Equities Fund (TIAA/CREF). See *New York Times* October 6, 1993.

113. For example, see ibid., March 15, 1994.

114. For example, see Peter Kilborn, "AFL-CIO Picks Militant As President: Sharp Turn Seen For Labor in U.S." ibid., October 26, 1995; Kirk Victor, "Labor's New Look," *National Journal*, October 14, 1995, pp. 2522–2527; Julie Kosterlitz, "Laboring Uphill," ibid., March 2, 1996, pp. 474–478; *New York Times*, February 17–18, 1997; May 30, 1997. Julie Kosterlitz, "Unions of the World Unite," ibid., May 16, 1998, p. 1134.

115. *Nation*, July 9–16, 1983, pp. 39–41.

116. *New York Times*, January 19, 1980.

117. *Washington Post National Weekly Edition*, June 4, 1984, pp. 17–18; *New York Times*, January 1, 1985; January 18, 1985.

118. *Guardian*, June 20, 1984, p. 8.

119. For examples of these "proxy wars," see *New York Times*, March 5, 1989.

120. Ibid., May 5, 1986. Also see David Walls, *The Activist's Almanac* (New York: Simon and Schuster, 1993); Paul Martin Du Bois and Frances Moore Lappe, *The Quickening of America* (San Francisco: Jossey-Bass, 1994); Janice Perlman, "Grassrooting the System," *Social Policy* 7 (September/October 1976); John Herbers, "Citizen Activism Gaining in the Nation," *New York Times*, May 15, 1982; Bennett Harrison, "Regional Restructuring and Good Business Climates," in Larry Sawers and William Tabb, eds., *Sunbelt/Snowbelt* (New York: Oxford University Press, 1984); Peter Dreier, "The Tenant's Movement," in William Tabb and Larry Sawers, eds., *Marxism and the Metropolis* (New York: Oxford University Press, 1984); William Tabb, " A Pro-People's Urban Policy," in Tabb and Sawers, *Marxism and the Metropolis*; Joe Feagin, "Sunbelt Metropolis and Development Capital," in Sawers and Tabb, *Sunbelt/Snowbelt*, pp. 123–124; Piven and Cloward, *The New Class War*; Dan Luria and Jack Russell, *Rational Reindustrialization* (Detroit: Widgetripper, 1981); Harry Boyte, *The Backyard Revolution* (Philadelphia: Temple University Press, 1980); Dan Georgakas and Marvin Surkin, *Detroit: I Do Mind Dying* (New York: St. Martin's, 1975).

121. James Weinstein, *The Decline of Socialism in America, 1912–1925* (New York: Random House, 1967); James Weinstein, *The Corporate Ideal in the Liberal State, 1900–1918* (Boston: Beacon Press, 1968); Bruce Stave, *Socialism and Cities* (Port Washington, N.Y.: Kennikat, 1975); Frederick Howe, *The City: The Hope of Democracy* (New York: Scribner's, Sons 1905).

122. Allan Gold, "Exit a Socialist, to Let History Judge," *New York Times*, March 2, 1989; W.J. Conway, *Challenging Boundaries of Reform: Socialism in Burlington* (Philadelphia: Temple University Press, 1990).

123. *New York Times*, October 6, 1991.

124. Kenneth Hoover, "Mondragon's Answers to Utopia's Problems," *Utopian Studies* 3, pp. 1–20; Anna Guitierrez-Johnson and William Whyte, "the Mondragon System of Worker Production Coops," *Industrial and Labor Relations Review* 31 (October 1977), pp. 18–30; Carnoy and Shearer, *Economic Democracy*, pp. 149–152.

125. See *New York Times*, October 6, 1991.

126. Robert Huckfeldt and Carol Kohfeld, *Race and the Decline of Class in American Politics* (Champagne-Urbana: University of Illinois Press, 1989), p. 188.

127. *Akron Beacon Journal*, June 26, 1983, pp. 1, 7.
    For more examples, see Jon Nordheimer, "From Middle Class to Jobless," *New York Times*, April 13, 1992; Dirk Johnson, "Family Struggles to Make Do After Fall From Middle Class," ibid., March 11, 1994; Michael Winerip, "Downsizing Statistics Don't Show the Pain," ibid., February 27, 1996; Robin Pogrebin, "Now the Working Class, Too, Is Foraging for Empty Cans," ibid., April 29, 1996; Bob Herbert, "Families on the Edge," ibid., September 23, 1996.

128. Reginald Bundy, "Dealing Elderly," *Tri-State Defender*, April 27-May 1, 1996, p. 1A.

129. *New York Times*, July 30, 1979.
    For more examples, see Alan Finder, "In Fearful Thrift, Elderly Forage in Garbage Bins," *New York Times*, November 17, 1994.

130. *Quad City Times*, December 23, 1983, p. 5. In August of 1995, more than 500 predominantly poor residents of Chicago suffered heat-related deaths.

For more case studies, see William Schmidt, "Hard Work Can't Stop Hard Times," *New York Times*, November 25, 1990.

131. *Business Week*, October 12, 1974.

132. See James Morgan, *Panel Study on Income Dynamics* (Ann Arbor: University of Michigan Press, 1977); *New York Times*, July 10, 1977.

133. The index is based on governmental statistics for 16 different social problems, including infant mortality, unemployment, poverty, homicides, teen suicides, child abuse, alcohol-related traffic fatalities, drug abuse, high school dropout rates, and so on. Compiled by Fordham's Institute for Innovation in Social Policy, the index stood at 77.5 in 1973 and fell to an all-time low of 37.5 in 1994. See *New York Times*, October 14, 1996; October 5, 1992.

134. For example, see Michael Kagay, "From Coast to Coast, Affluent to Poor, Poll Shows Anxiety Over Jobs," ibid., March 11, 1994; "Americans and Their Money," *Money Magazine*, April, 1995; *Time*/CNN Poll, January 20, 1996; Louis Uchitelle and N. R. Kleinfield, "Huge White-Collar Layoffs Batter Egos, Dreams, Work Ethic," Memphis *Commercial Appeal*, March 10, 1996, p. C3.

135. From a November 1986 *Time* magazine editorial, quoted in Kevin Phillips, *Boiling Point: Democrats, Republicans, and the Decline of Middle-Class Prosperity* (New York: Harper-Perennial, 1993), p. 3.

136. Lee Iacocca, *Iacocca: An Autobiography* (New York: Bantam, 1984), p. 319.

137. Zinn, *People's History*, p. 574. Also see, for example, Jean Jacques Rousseau, *Social Contract* (New York: Penguin, 1968); Seymour Martin Lipset, *Political Man: The Social Bases of Politics* (Baltimore: Johns Hopkins Press, 1981).

138. Joe Feagin and Harlan Hahn, *Ghetto Revolts* (New York: Macmillan, 1973), p. 41. For similar findings on the Watts unrest, see David Sears and John McConahay, *The Politics of Violence* (Boston: Houghton Mifflin, 1973).

139. ABC-Harris survey, March 1980. Also see Ellis Cose, *The Rage of the Priveleged Class* (New York: Harper-Collins, 1993); Rochelle, Stanfield, "Black Frustration," *National Journal*, May 16, 1992, pp. 1162–1166; Tricia Rose, *Black Noise: Rap Music and Black Culture in Contemporary America* (Hanover, N.H.: Wesleyan University Press, 1994).

140. Robert Smith and Richard Seltzer, *Race, Class, and Culture: A Study in Afro-American Mass Opinion* (Albany, N.Y.: State University of New York Press, 1992); Arthur Miller, "Political Issues and Trust in Government," *American Political Science Review* (September 1974).

141. Brink and Harris, *Black and White*, p. 135.

142. Barbara Mikulski, "Who Speaks for Ethnic America?" *New York Times*, September 29, 1970; Pete Hamill, "The Revolt of the White Lower Middle Class," *New York* (April 14, 1969), pp. 26–29; Paul Wilkes, "As the Blacks Move In, the Ethnics Move Out," *New York Times Magazine* (January 24, 1971). For more recent data, see Harrigan, *Empty Dreams*, p. 110.

143. For example, also see Cedric Herring, *Splitting the Middle: Political Alienation, Acquiesence, and Activism Among America's Middle Layers* (New York: Praeger, 1989); Survey by the Roper Organization, October 17–24, 1992; Virginia Hodgkinson, Murray Weitzman, and the Gallup Organization, Inc., *Giving and Volunteering in the United States: 1994 Edition* (Washington, D.C.: Independent Sector, 1994); Survey of the Times Mirror Center for the People and the Press, May 20, 1995.

144. See Phillips, *Boiling Point*, pp. xix-xx. Also see *New York Times,* March 10, 1998, Miller, "Political Issues and Trust"; Michael Harrington, *The New American Poverty* (New York: Viking Penguin, 1984), chap. 3; Arthur Levine, *When Dreams and Heroes Died* (San

Francisco: Jossey-Bass, 1980); Andrew Levison, "The Rebellion of Blue Collar Youth," *Progressive* (October 1972), pp. 38–42.

145. For example, see Stanley Greenberg, *Middle Class Dreams: The Politics and Power of the New American Majority* (New York: Times Books, 1996); Theodore Lowi, "The Party Crasher," *New York Times Magazine*, August 23, 1992; Kevin Phillips, "Under the Electoral Volcano," *New York Times*, November 7, 1994 .

146. Murray Levin, *The Alienated Voter* (New York: Holt, Rinehart and Winston, 1960); Donald Warren, *The Radical Center* (South Bend, Ind.: University of Notre Dame Press, 1976); Arthur Hadley, *The Empty Polling Booth* (Englewood Cliffs, N.J.: Prentice-Hall, 1978); Eliza Newlin Carney, "Opting Out of Politics," *National Journal,* January 17, 1998, pp. 106–111.

147. Gallup poll for the Joint Center for Policy Studies (1986), cited in National Urban League, *The State of Black America, 1987* (New York: National Urban League, 1987), p. 13.

148. Jennifer Hochschild, *Facing Up to the American Dream: Race, Class, and the Soul of the Nation* (Princeton, N.J.: Princeton University Press, 1995); Kenneth Dolbeare, *Democracy at Risk* (New York: Chatham, 1984), p. 34; Daniel Rogers, *New York Times*, April 16, 1980.

149. Donald Kellermann, *The People, The Press, and Politics 1990* (Los Angeles: Time Mirror Center for the People and the Press, 1990), p. 28; Phillips, *Boiling Point*, pp. 233–244.

150. Robert Peterson, Gerald Albaum, George Kozmetsky, et al., "Attitudes Towards Capitalism," *Journalism Quarterly* 60 (Spring 1984), p. 61. Also see Ralph Miliband, *Divided Societies: Class Struggle in Contemporary Capitalism* (New York: Oxford University Press, 1989).

151. Paul Starobin, "Rethinking Capitalism," *National Journal*, January 18, 1997, pp. 106–109; Kevin Phillips, *The Politics of Rich and Poor* (New York: Harper, 1990); Phillips, *Arrogant Capital*.

152. Gallup Poll, December 1984.

153. Report of the Center for Media and Public Affairs (November 1989), quoted in Georgie Anne Geyer, "The Sorrow of El Salvador," Memphis *Commercial Appeal*, November 25, 1989.

154. Collins, *Rainbow Challenge*, p. 55.

155. Collins, *Rainbow Challenge*, p. 301.

156. See Walter Burnham, *Critical Elections and the Mainsprings of American Politics* (New York: Norton, 1970). For more on realignments, see James Sundquist, *Dynamics of the Party System* (Washington, D.C.: Brookings Institute, 1983); Byron Shafer, ed., *The End of Realignment?* (Madison: University of Wisconsin Press, 1991); Peter Nardulli, "The Concept of Critical Realignment, Electoral Behavior, and Political Change," *American Political Science Review* 89 (March 1995), pp. 10–22; David Lawrence, *The Collapse of the Democratic Presidential Majority* (Boulder, Colo.: Westview Press, 1996); Harvey Schantz, *American Presidential Elections: Process, Policy, and Political Change* (Albany, N.Y.: SUNY Press, 1996).

157. For example, see Phillips, *The Politics of Rich and Poor*; Hamilton, "Political Access;" Michael Kazin, "The Workers' Party?" *New York Times*, October 19, 1995. Or, for predictions of somewhat more incremental progressive change, see Mario Cuomo, *Reason to Believe* (New York: Simon and Schuster, 1995); Jacob Weisberg, *In Defense of Government: The Fall and Rise of Public Trust* (New York: Scribner, 1996); E.J. Dionne, *They Only Look Dead: Why Progressives Will Dominate the Next Political Era* (New York: Simon and Schuster, 1996); James Carville, *We're Right, They're Wrong: A Handbook for Spirited Progressives* (New York: Random House, 1996).

Bibliography

Abramson, Paul. *The Political Socialization of Black America.* New York: Free Press, 1977.

Adams, John. *Works.* New York: AMS Press, 1971.

Agee, Warren, Phillip Ault, and Edwin Emery. *Main Currents in Mass Communications.* New York: Harper & Row, 1986.

Allen, Robert. *Black Awakening in Capitalist America: An Analytical History.* Garden City, N.Y.: Anchor/Doubleday, 1969.

Almond, Gabriel, and G. Bingham Powell. *Comparative Politics: A Developmental Approach.* Boston: Little, Brown, 1966.

Alperovitz, Gar, and Jeff Faux. *Rebuilding America: A Blueprint for the New Economy.* New York: Pantheon, 1984.

Anderson, Charles. *The Political Economy of Social Class.* Englewood Cliffs, N.J.: Prentice Hall, 1974.

Anderson, Martin. *The Federal Bulldozer.* Cambridge, Mass.: MIT Press, 1964.

Anderson, Stanley. *Ombudsmen for American Government.* Englewood Cliffs, N.J.: Prentice Hall, 1968.

Ansolabehere, Stephen, Roy Behr, and Shanto Iyegar. *The Media Game.* New York: Macmillan, 1993.

Ansolabehere, Stephen, and Shanto Iyengar. *Going Negative: How Attack Ads Shrink and Polarize the Electorate.* New York: Free Press, 1995.

Aronson, James. *The Press and the Cold War.* Boston: Beacon Press, 1970.

Astin, Alexander. *The Myth of Equal Access to Higher Education.* Atlanta: Southern Education Foundation,1975.

Avineri, Shlomo. *The Social and Political Thought of Karl Marx.* New York: Cambridge University Press, 1969.

Bachrach, Peter, and Morton Baratz. "Decisions and Nondecisions: An Analytical Framework." *American Political Science Review* (September 1963).

Bachrach, Peter, and Morton Baratz. "Two Faces of Power." *American Political Science Review* (December 1962).

Bacon, Betty (ed.). *How Much Truth Do We Tell Our Children?* Minneapolis: MEP Publications, 1988.

Bagdikian, Ben. "Fires, Sex, and Freaks." *New York Times Magazine* (October 10,1976).

Bagdikian, Ben. *The Media Monopoly.* Boston: Beacon Press, 1983.

Balbus, Isaac. "The Concept of Interest in Pluralist and Marxian Analysis." *Politics and Society* (February 1971).

Baldus, David, George G. Woodworth, and Charles Pulaski. *Equal Justice and the Death Penalty.* Boston: Northeastern University Press, 1990.

Ball, Terence, and Richard Dagger. *Political Ideologies and the Democratic Ideal.* New York: Harper Collins, 1991.

Bane, Mary Jo, and David Ellwood. *Welfare Realities: From Rhetoric to Reform.* Cambridge, Mass.: Harvard University, 1994.

Baran, Paul, and Paul Sweezy. *Monopoly Capital.* New York: Monthly Review Press, 1966.

Barker, Sir Ernest. *Social Contract: Essays by Locke, Hume, and Rousseau.* London: Oxford University Press, 1960.

Barker, Lucius (ed.). *Black Electoral Politics.* New Brunswick, N.J.: Tansaction, 1990.

Barker, Lucius, and Mack Jones. *African Americans and the American Political System.* Englewood Cliffs, N.J.: Prentice Hall, 1994.

Barker, Lucius, and Jesse McCorry. *Black Americans and the Political System.* Cambridge, Mass.: Winthrop, 1976.

Barker, Lucius and Ronald Waters (eds.). *Jesse Jackson's 1984 Presidential Campaign.* Urbana: University of Illinois Press, 1989.

Barlett, Donald, and James Steele. *Who Really Pays Taxes?* New York: Simon and Schuster, 1994.

Barnouw, Clyde. *The Television Writer.* New York: Hill and Wang, 1962.

Barrow, Clyde. *Universities and the Capitalist State.* Madison: University of Wisconsin, 1990.

Bates, Timothy. *Banking on Black Enterprise: The Potential of Emerging Firms for Revitalizing Urban Economies.* Washington, D.C.: Joint Center for Political and Economic Studies, 1993.

Bates, Timothy. *Black Capitalism.* New York: Praeger, 1973.

Beard, Charles. *An Economic Interpretation of the Constitution.* New York: Macmillan, 1962.

Becker, Theodore, and Vernon Murray. *Government Lawlessness in America.* New York: Oxford University Press, 1971.

Bell, Daniel. *The Cultural Contradictions of Capitalism.* New York: Basic Books, 1976.

Bell, Derrick. *And We Are Not Saved: The Elusive Quest for Racial Reform.* New York: Basic Books, 1987.

Bell, Derrick. *Faces at the Bottom of the Well: The Permanance of Racism.* New York: Basic, 1992.

Bennett, Lerone. *The Challenge of Blackness.* Chicago: Johnson Publishers, 1972.

Bentley, Arthur. *The Process of Government.* Chicago: University of Chicago Press, 1908.

Bentley, Numan. *Massive Resistance.* Baton Rouge: Louisiana State University Press, 1969.

Berg, John. *Unequal Struggle: Class, Gender Race, and Power in the U.S. Congress.* Boulder, Colo.: Westview Press, 1994.

Berki, R. N. *Socialism.* New York: St. Martin's Press, 1975.

Berle, Adolph. *The Twentieth Century Capitalist Revolution.* Orlando, Fla.: Harcourt Brace Jovanovich, 1954.

Berle, Adolph, and Gardner Means. *The Madern Corporation and Private Property.* New York: Commerce Clearing House, 1932.

Berry, Jeffrey. *The Interest Group Society.* Glenview, Ill.: Scott, Forseman, 1989.

Best, Michael, and William Connolly. *The Politicized Economy.* Lexington, Mass.: Heath, 1982.

Bickel, Alexander. *The Least Dangerous Branch.* Indianapolis: Bobbs-Merrill, 1962.

Black, Randall. *Private Pressure on Public Law: The Legal Career of Justice Thurgood Marshall.* New York: Kennikat, 1973.

Blackwell, James. *The Black Community.* New York: Dodd, Mead, 1975.

Blaustein, Albert, and Robert Zangrando. *Civil Rights and the Black American.* New York: Washington Square Press, 1968.

Block, Fred, Richard Cloward, Barbara Ehrenreich, and Francis Fox Piven. *The Mean Season: The Attack on the Welfare State.* New York: Pantheon, 1987

Bluestone, Barry, and Bennett Harrison. *Capital and Communities.* Washington, D.C.: Progressive Alliance, 1980.

Bluestone, Barry, and Bennett Harrison. *The Deindustrialization of America.* New York: Basic Books, 1982.

Bogart, Leo. *Commercial Culture: The Media System and the Public Interest.* New York: Oxford University Press, 1995.

Bolling, Richard. *House Out of Order.* New York: Dutton, 1965.

Bond, Horace Mann. *The Education of the Negro in the American Social Order.* Englewood Cliffs, N.J.: Prentice-Hall, 1934.

Bositis, David. *The Congressional Black Caucus in the 103rd Congress.* Lanham, Md.: University Press of America, 1994.

Bottomore, J.B. (ed.). *Karl Marx: Early Writings.* London: Watts, 1963.

Bowen, Robert. *The Changing Television Audience in America.* New York: Columbia University Press, 1984.

Bowles, Samuel, and Herbert Gintis. *Schooling in Capitalist America.* New York: Basic Books, 1976.

Bowles, Samuel, David Gordon, and Thomas Weisskopf. *Beyond the Wasteland.* Garden City, N.Y.: Anchor/Doubleday, 1983.

Bowser, Benjamin, and Raymond Hunt (eds.). *Impacts of Racism on White Americans.* Newbury Park, Cal.: Sage, 1996.

Boyte, Harry. *The Backyard Revolution.* Philadelphia: Temple University Press, 1980.

Brady, David. *Critical Elections and Congressional Policy Making.* Stanford: Stanford University Press, 1988.

Breitman, George (ed.). *The Last Year of Malcolm X.* New York: Merit, 1967.

Breitman, George (ed.). *Malcolm X Speaks.* New York: Grove Press, 1965.

Brenner, M. Harvey. *Estimating the Social Costs of National Economic Policy: Implications for Mental and Physical Health, and Criminal Aggression.* Washington D.C.: GPO, 1976.

Brink, William, and Lou Harris. *Black and White.* New York: Simon & Schuster, 1967.

Broderick, Francis, and August Meier (eds.). *Negro Protest Thought in the Twentieth Century.* Indianapolis: Bobbs-Merrill, 1965.

Brown, Bruce. *Marx, Freud, and the Critique of Everyday Life.* New York: Monthly Review Press, 1973.

Bullard, Robert. *Confronting Environmental Racism: Voices from the Grassroots.* Boston: South End, 1993.

Bullard, Robert (ed.). *Unequal Protection: Environmental Justice and Communities of Color.* San Francisco: Sierra Club, 1994.

Bullock, Charles, and Harrell Rodgers. *Black Political Attitudes.* Chicago: Markham, 1972.

Burgess, M. Elaine. *Negro Leaders in a Southern City.* Chapel Hill: University of North Carolina Press, 1960.

Burnham, Walter. *Critical Elections and the Mainsprings of American Politics.* New York: Norton, 1970.

Bush, Rod (ed.). *The New Black Vote.* San Francisco: Synthesis Publications, 1984.

Butters, Keith, Lawrence Thompson, and Lynn Bollinger. *Effect of Taxation on Investments by Individuals.* Cambridge, Mass.: Riverside Press, 1953.

Calverton, V. F. "Orthodox Religion: Does it Handicap Negro Progress?" *Messenger* (July 1927).

Campbell, Christopher. *Race, Myth, and the News.* Thousand Oaks, Cal.: Sage, 1995.

Carnoy, Martin. *Faded Dreams: The Politics and Economics of Race in America.* New York: Cambridge University Press, 1994.

Carnoy, Martin, and Derek Shearer. *Economic Democracy.* Armonk, N.Y.: Sharpe, 1980.

Carr, Leslie. *Color-Blind Racism.* Beverly Hills, Calif.: Sage, 1997.

Carter, Dan. *From George Wallace to Newt Gingrich: Race in the Conservative Revolution.* Baton Rouge, La: Louisiana University Press, 1996.

Carter, Dan. *The Politics of Rage: George Wallace, the Origins of the New Conservatism, and the Transformation of American Politics.* New York: Simon and Schuster, 1995.

Carter, Stephen. *Reflections of an Affirmative Action Baby.* New York: Basic Books, 1991.

Carville, James. *We're Right, They're Wrong: A Handbook for Spirited Progressives.* New York: Random House, 1996.

Chicago Tribune Staff. *The American Millstone: An Examination of the Nation's Permanent Underclass.* Chicago: Contemporary Books, 1986.

Chomsky, Noam. *Necessary Illusions: Thought Control in Democratic Societies.* Boston: South End Press, 1989.

Cigler, Allan, and Burdett Loomis (eds.). *Interest Group Politics.* Washington D.C.: CQ Press, 1994.

Cirino, Robert. *Don't Blame the People.* New York: Vintage, 1972.

Clark, Kenneth. *The Dark Ghetto.* New York: Harper & Row, 1965.

Clawson, Dan, Alan Neustadtl, and Denise Scott. *Money Talks.* New York: Basic Books, 1992.

Cloward, Richard, and Francis Fox Piven. *Why Americans Don't Vote.* New York: Pantheon, 1988.

Colby, Gerald. *Du Pont: Behind the Nylon Curtain.* New York: Lyle Stuart, 1985.

Cole, Leonard. *Blacks in Power.* Princeton, N.J.: Princeton University Press, 1976.

Coleman, Richard, and Lee Rainwater. *Social Standing in America,* 1978. New York: Basic Books, 1978.

Coles, Robert. *Teachers and the Children of Poverty.* Washington, D.C.: Potomac Institute, 1970.

Coles, Robert, and Jon Erickson. *The Middle Americans.* Boston: Little, Brown, 1971.

Collier, Peter, and David Horowitz. *Rockefellers: An American Dynasty.* New York: Holt, Rinehart and Winston, 1976.

Collins, Ronald. *Dictating Content: How Advertising Pressure Can Corrupt a Free Press.* Washington D.C.: Center for the Study of Commercialism, 1993.

Collins, Sheila. *The Rainbow Challenge: The Jackson Campaign and the Future of American Politics.* New York: Monthly Review Press, 1986.

Compaine, Benjamin, Christopher Sterling, Thomas Guback, and Kendrick Noble Jr. *Who Owns the Media.* White Plains, N.Y.: Knowledge Industry, 1982.

Cone, James. *Black Theology and Black Power.* New York: Harper & Row, 1969.

Cone, James. *A Black Theology of Liberation.* Maryknoll, N.Y.: Orbis, 1986.

Cone, James. *For My People: Black Theology and the Black Church.* Maryknoll, N.Y.: Orbis, 1984.

Cone, James. *God of the Oppressed.* New York: Harper & Row, 1978.

Cone, James. *Speaking the Truth: Ecumenism, Liberation, and Black Theology.* Grand Rapids, Mich.: Eerdmans, 1986.

Connolly, William. "Appearances and Reality in Politics." *Political Theory* (November 1979).

Conway, W.J. *Challenging Borders of Reform: Socialism in Burlington.* Philadelphia: Temple University Press, 1990.

Cook, Fay Lomax., and Edith Barrett. *Support for the American Welfare System: The Views of Congress and the Public.* New York: Columbia University, 1992.

Cook, James Graham. *The Segregationists.* Englewood Cliffs, N.J.: Prentice- Hall, 1962.

Cose, Ellis. *The Rage of the Privileged Class.* New York: Harper, 1993.

Cox, C. Benjamin, and Byron Massialas. *Social Studies in the United States.* New York: Harcourt, Brace and World, 1967.

Crouse, Timothy. *The Boys on the Bus.* New York: Ballantine, 1973.

Cruse, Harold. *The Crisis of the Negro Intellectual.* New York: Morrow, 1967.

Cruse, Harold. *Plural but Equal: Blacks and Minorities in America's Plural Society.* New York: Morrow, 1987.

Cruse, Harold. *Rebellion or Revolution?* New York: Morrow, 1968.

Cuomo, Mario. *Reason to Believe.* New York: Simon and Schuster, 1995.

Dahl, Robert. *Dilemmas of Pluralist Democracy.* New Haven, Conn.: Yale University Press, 1982.

Dahl, Robert. *Pluralist Democracy in the United States.* Chicago: Rand McNally, 1967.

Dahl, Robert. *Who Governs?* New Haven, Conn.: Yale University Press, 1961.

Dahl, Robert, and Charles Lindbloom. *Politics, Economics, and Welfare.* Chicago: University of Chicago Press, 1976.

Dann, Martin (ed.). *The Black Press, 1827–1890.* New York: Capricorn, 1972.

Danziger, Sheldon and Peter Gottschalk. *America Unequal.* Cambridge, Mass.: Harvard University Press, 1995.

Davey, Joseph. *The New Social Contract: America's Journey from a Welfare State to a Police State.* New York: Praeger, 1995.

Davidson, Chandler (ed.). *Minority Vote Dilution.* Washington, D.C.: Howard University Press, 1984.

Davidson, Roger, and Walter Oleszek. *Congress Against Itself.* Bloomington: Indiana University Press, 1977.

Davis, Abraham, and Barbara Graham. *The Supreme Court, Race, and Civil Rights.* Thousand Oaks, Cal.: Sage, 1995.

Davis, Allison, Burleigh Gardner, and Mary Gardner. *Deep South.* Chicago: University of Chicago Press, 1941.

Davis, Angela. *Women, Culture, Politics.* New York: Random House, 1990.

Davis, Frank. *The Economics of Black Community Development.* Chicago: Markham, 1972.

Davis, George, and Glegg Watson. *Black Life in Corporate America: Swimming in the Mainstream.* Garden City, N.Y.: Doubleday, 1985.

Davis, J. Morton. *Making America Work Again.* New York: Crown, 1983.

Dawson, Michael. *Behind the Mule: Race and Class in African-American Politics.* Princeton: Princeton University Press, 1994.

De Felice, Renzo. *Interpretations of Fascism.* Cambridge, Mass.: Harvard University Press, 1977.

De Lone, Richard. *Small Futures: Children, Inequality, and the Limits of Liberal Reform.* Orlando, Fla.: Harcourt Brace Jovanovich, 1979.

De Mott, Benjamin. *The Imperial Middle: Why Americans Can't Think Straight About Class.* New York: William Morrow, 1990.

De Vries, Walter, and Lance Tarrance. *The Ticket-splitter.* Grand Rapids, Mich.: Eerdmans, 1972.

Diamond, Sara. *Roads to Dominion: Right-Wing Movements and Political Power in the United States.* New York: Guilford Press, 1995.

Dionne, E. J. *They Only Look Dead: Why Progressives Will Dominate the Next Political Era.* New York: Simon and Schuster, 1996.

Doberman, Martin. *Paul Robeson.* New York: Knopf, 1989.

Dolbeare, Kenneth. *Democracy at Risk.* New York: Chatham, 1984.

Dolbeare, Kenneth, and Patricia Dolbeare. *American Ideologies.* Boston: Houghton Mifflin, 1976.

Dolbeare, Kenneth, and Janette Hubbell. *USA 2012: After the Middle Class Revolution.* Chatham, N.J.: Chatham House, 1996.

Domhoff, G. William. *Who Rules America Now?* New York: Simon and Schuster, 1983.

Domhoff, G. William. *Higher Circles: The Governing Class in America.* New York, Random House, 1971.

Domhoff, G. William. *The Bohemian Grove and Other Retreats: A Study in Ruling Class Cohesiveness.* New York: Harper and Row, 1975.

Domhoff, William. *Power Structure Research.* Beverly Hills: Sage, 1980.

Domhoff, William. *The Powers That Be.* New York: Vintage, 1979.

Domhoff, William. *Who Rules America?* Englewood Cliffs, N.J.: Prentice- Hall, 1967.

Downie, Leonard, Jr. *Justice Denied.* New York: Praeger, 1971.

Drake, St. Clair, and Horace Cayton. *Black Metropolis.* Orlando, Fla.: Harcourt Brace Jovanovich, 1945.

Drew, Elizabeth. *Politics and Money.* New York: Macmillan, 1983.

Drimmer, Melvin (ed.). *Black History: A Reappraisal.* Garden City, N.Y.: Anchor/Doubleday, 1969.

Drucker, Peter. *The Unseen Revolution.* New York: Harper & Row, 1976.

D'Sousa, Dinesh. *The End of Racism.* Washington, D.C.: American Enterprise Institute, 1995.

Du Bois, Paul Martin and Francis Moore Lappe. *The Quickening of America.* San Fransisco: Josey Bass, 1994.

Du Bois, W. E. B. *Black Reconstruction.* New York: Russell, 1935.

Du Bois, W. E. B. *Black Reconstruction in America,* 1860–880. New York: Atheneum, 1971.

Du Bois, W. E. B. *The Education of Black People.* New York: Monthly Review Press, 1973.

Du Bois, W. E. B. "Is Man Free?" *Scientific Monthly* (May 1948).

Du Bois, W. E. B. *The Souls of Black Folks.* Chicago: McClung, 1903.

Du Bois, W. E. B. "There Must Come a Vast Social Change in the United States." *National Guardian,* July 11, 1951.

Dunbar, Leslie (ed.). *Minority Report: What Has Happened to Blacks, Hispanics, American Indians, and Other Minorities in the Eighties.* New York: Pantheon, 1984.

Duncan, Greg. *Years of Poverty, Years of Plenty.* Ann Arbor, Mich.: University of Michigan, 1984.

Dye, Thomas. *The Politics of Equality.* Indianapolis: Bobbs-Merrill, 1971.

Dye, Thomas. *Who's Running America?* Englewood Cliffs, N.J., Prentice-Hall, 1990.

Dymally, Mervyn (ed.). *The Black Politician: His Struggle for Power.* Belmont, Cal.: Wadsworth, 1971.

Easton, David. *A Framework for Political Analysis.* Englewood Cliffs, N.J.: Prentice-Hall, 1965.

Easton, David. *The Political System.* Chicago: University of Chicago Press, 1971.

Easton, David, and K. H. Guddat. *Writings of the Young Karl Marx on Philosophy and Society.* Garden City, N.Y.: Doubleday, 1967.

Ebenstein, William. *Fascism at Work.* New York: Free Press, 1969.

Edelman, Murray. *The Symbolic Uses of Politics.* Urbana: University of Illinois Press, 1964.

Edsall, Thomas. *The New Politics of Inequality.* New York: Norton, 1984.

Edsall, Thomas, and Mary Edsall. *Chain Reaction: The Impact of Race, Rights, and Taxes on American Politics.* New York: Norton, 1992.

Edwards, Helen. *Black Faces in High Places.* Orlando, Fla.: Harcourt Brace Jovanovich, 1971.

Edwards, Richard (ed.). *The Capitalist System.* Englewood Cliffs, N.J.: Prentice-Hall, 1978.

Elliot, Jeffrey (ed.). *Black Voices in American Politics.* Orlando, Fla.: Harcourt Brace Jovanovich, 1986.

Entman, Robert. *Democracy without Citizens.* New York: Oxford University, 1989.

Epstein, Edward. *News from Nowhere.* New York: Vintage, 1973.

Ewen, Stuart. *Captains of Consciousness.* New York: McGraw Hill, 1976.

Ewen, Stuart. *PR! A Social History of Hype.* New York: Basic, 1996.

Fainstein, Norman, and Susan Fainstein. *Urban Political Movements.* Englewood Cliffs, N.J.: Prentice-Hall, 1974.

Fallows, James. *Breaking the News: How the Media Undermine American Democracy.* New York: Pantheon, 1996.

Farrand, Max (ed.). *The Records of the Federal Convention of 1787.* New Haven, Conn.: Yale University Press, 1937.

Faw, Bob, and Nancy Skelton. *Thunder in America.* Austin: Texas Monthly Press, 1986.

Feagin, Joe. "The Black Church: Inspiration or Opiate?" *Journal of Negro History* (October 1975).

Feagin, Joe, and Harlan Hahn. *Ghetto Revolts.* New York: Macmillan, 1973.

Fine, Sidney. *Laissez-Faire and the General-Welfare State.* Ann Arbor: University of Michigan, 1964.

Flaming, Karl. "Black Powerlessness in Policy-making Positions." *Sociological Quarterly* (Winter 1972).

Foner, Phillip (ed.). *The Black Panthers Speak.* Philadelphia: Lippincott, 1970.

Ford, Henry Jones. *The Rise and Growth of American Politics.* New York: Macmillan, 1898.

Foster, Lorn (ed.). *The Voting Rights Act: Consequences and Implications.* New York: Praeger, 1985.

Frank, Robert, and Phillip Cook. *The Winner-Take-All Society.* New York: Free Press, 1995.

Franklin, John Hope. *From Slavery to Freedom: A History of Negro Americans.* New York: Knopf, 1980.

Fraser, Douglas. *Economic Dislocations: Plant Closings, Plant Relocations, and Plant Conversion, report prepared for the U.S. Congress,* Joint Economic Committee, Washington, D.C., 1979.

Frazier, E. Franklin, and C. Eric Lincoln. *The Negro Church in America.* New York: Schocken, 1973.

Frieden, Bernard, and Marshall Kaplan. *The Politics of Neglect.* Cambridge, Mass.: MIT Press, 1975.

Frieden, Karl. *Workplace Democracy and Productivity.* Washington D.C.: National Center for Economic Alternatives, 1980.

Friedman, Milton. *Capitalism and Freedom.* Chicago: University of Chicago Press, 1962.

Friendly, Fred W. *Due to Circumstances Beyond Our Control.* New York: Random House, 1967.

Friesema, Paul. "Black Control of Central Cities: The Hollow Prize." *Journal of the American Institute of Planners* (March 1969).

Froebel, Folker, Jurgen Heinrichs, and Otto Kreye. *The New International Division of Labour.* Cambridge, Mass.: Cambridge University Press, 1980.

Frye, Marilyn. *The Politics of Reality.* Freedom, Calif.: The Crossings Press, 1983.

Galbraith, J. K. *The New Industrial State.* Boston: Houghton Mifflin, 1967.

Gans, Herbert. *Deciding What's News.* New York: Vintage, 1979.

Gans, Herbert. *More Equality.* New York: Pantheon, 1972.

Gilder, George. *Wealth and Poverty*. New York: Basic Books, 1981.

Gitlin, Todd. "When the Right Talks, TV Listens." *The Nation* (October 15,1983).

Glasgow, Douglas. *The Black Underclass*. San Francisco: Jossey-Bass, 1980.

Goings, Kenneth. "The NAACP Comes of Age: The Defeat of Judge John J. Parker," in Winfted B. Moore, Joseph Tripp, and Lyon Tyler (eds.), *Developing Dixie: Modernization in a Traditional Society*. Westport, Conn.: Greenwood Press, 1988.

Goldberg, David. *Racist Culture: Philosophy and the Politics of Meaning*. Cambridge: Blackwell, 1993.

Goldman, Peter. *Report from Black America*. New York: Simon & Schuster, 1970.

Gomes, Ralph, and Linda Faye Williams (eds.). *From Exclusion to Inclusion: The Long Struggle for African American Political Power*. Westport, Conn.: Greenwood Press, 1992.

Goodwin, Leonard. *Do the Poor Want to Work?* Washington, D.C.: Brookings Institution, 1972.

Gordon, David (ed.). *Problems in Political Economy*. Lexington, Mass.: Heath, 1977.

Gordon, Lewis. *Bad Faith and Antiblack Racism*. Atlantic Highlands, N.J.: Humanities Press, 1995

Gosnell, Harold. *Machine Politics: Chicago Model*. Chicago: University of Chicago Press, 1934,1968.

Graber, Doris. *Mass Media and American Politics*. Washington D.C.: CQ Press, 1994.

Graham, Hugh Davis. *Civil Rights and the Presidency: Race and Gender in American Politics, 1960–1972*. New York: Oxford University Press, 1992.

Grantham, Dewey (ed.). *The Political Status of the Negro in the Age of FDR*. Chicago: University of Chicago Press, 1973.

Green, Mark J., and Robert Massie, Jr. (eds.), *The Big Business Reader*. New York: Pilgrim Press, 1983.

Green, Robert. *The Urban Challenge: Poverty and Race*. Chicago: Follett, 1977.

Greenberg, Bradley (ed.). *Life on Television*. New York: Free Press, 1980.

Greenberg, Edward. *Capitalism and the American Political Ideal*. New York: Sharpe, 1985.

Greenberg, Stanley, and Theda Skoepol (eds.). *The New Majority: Toward a Popular Progressive Politics*. New Haven, Conn.: Yale University Press, 1997.

Greenburg, Jack. *Crusaders in the Courts: How A Dedicated Band of Lawyers Fought for the Civil Rights Revolution*. New York: Basic Books, 1994.

Greider, William. *Who Will Tell the People: The Betrayal of American Democracy*. New York: Simon and Schuster, 1992.

Grier, William and Price Cobb. Black Rage. New York: Basic Books, 1969.

Grofman, Bernard, Lisa Handley, and Richard Niemi. *Minority Representation and the Quest for Voting Equality*. New York: Cambridge University Press, 1992.

Grofman, Bernard, and Chandler Davidson (eds.). *Controversies in Minority Voting: The Voting Rights Act in Perspective*. Washington, D.C.: Brookings Institute, 1992.

Gross, Bertram. *Friendly Fascism*. New York: Evans, 1980.

Grossman, Joel. *Lawyers and Judges: The ABA and the Politics of Judicial Selection*. New York: Wiley, 1965.

Guerin, Daniel. *Fascism and Big Business*. New York: Monthly Review, 1969.

Hacker, Andrew. *Two Nations: Black and White, Separate, Hostile, Unequal.* New York: Scribner's, 1992.

Hadley, Arthur. *The Empty Polling Booth.* Englewood Cliffs, N.J.: Prentice-Hall, 1978.

Hagan, David. *Capitalism and Schooling,* dissertation, University of Chicago, 1978.

Hamill, Pete. "The Revolt of the White Lower Middle Class." *New York* (April 14, 1969).

Hamilton, Charles V. *The Bench and the Ballot: Southern Federal Judges and Black Votes.* New York: Oxford University Press, 1973.

Hamilton, Charles V. *The Black Preacher in American Politics.* New York: Morrow, 1972.

Hamilton, Charles V. *The Black Experience in American Politics.* New York: Putnam, 1973.

Hamilton, Charles V. "Conduit Colonialism and Public Policy." *Black World* (October 1972).

Hamilton, Charles V. "Deracialization: Examination of a Political Strategy." *First World* (March–April 1977).

Hamilton, Charles V. "The Patron-Recipient Relationship and Minority Politics in New York City." *Political Science Quarterly* (Summer 1979).

Hamilton, Charles V. "Racial, Ethnic, and Social Class Politics and Administration." *Public Administration Review* (October 1972).

Hamilton, Charles V., and Stokely Carmichael. *Black Power.* New York: Random House, 1967

Hamilton, Charles V., and Stokely Carmichael. *Black Power: The Politics of Liberation in America.* New York: Vintage Books, 1967.

Hamilton, Richard. *Class and Politics in the United States.* New York: Wiley, 1972.

Hans, Valerie, and Neil Vidmar. *Judging the Jury.* New York: Plenum Press, 1986.

Harrett, Rodney. *College and University Trustees.* Princeton, N.J.: Educational Testing Service, 1969.

Harrigan, John. *Empty Dreams, Empty Pockets: Class and Bias in American Politics.* New York: Macmillan, 1993.

Harrington, Michael. *The New American Poverty.* New York: Viking Penguin, 1984.

Harrington, Michael. *Socialism.* New York: Saturday Review Press, 1972.

Harris, Abram. *The Negro as Capitalist.* New York: Haskell, 1936.

Harris, Lou. *The Anguish of Change.* New York: Norton, 1974.

Harrison, Bennett and Barry Bluestone. *The Great U-Turn: Corporate Restructuring and Polarizing of America.* New York: Basic Books, 1988.

Harty, Sheila. *Hucksters in the Classroom.* Washington, D.C.: Center for Study of Responsive Law, 1979.

Harvey, Philip. *Securing the Right to Employment.* Princeton, N.J.: Princeton University Press, 1989.

Hatch, Roger, and Frank Watkins (eds.). *Reverend Jesse L. Jackson: Straight from the Heart.* Philadelphia: Fortress, 1987.

Hawley, Willis. *Strategy for Effective Desegregation: A Synthesis of Findings.* Nashville, Tenn.: Center for Education and Human Development Policy, 1987.

Hayek, Friedrich. *The Road to Serfdom.* Chicago: University of Chicago Press, 1944.

Hayes, Floyd. (ed.). *The Turbulent Voyage: Readings in African-American Studies.* San Diego, Cal.: Collegiate Press, 1992.

Hayes, John. *Lonely Fighter.* Secaucus, N.J.: Lyle Stuart, 1979.

Hayes, Paul M. *Fascism.* New York: Free Press, 1973.

Herman, Edward S. *Corporate Control, Corporate Power.* New York: Cambridge University Press, 1981.

Herman, Edward, and Noam Chomsky. *Manufacturing Consent: The Political Economy of the Mass Media.* New York: Pantheon Books, 1989.

Herring, Cedric, *Splitting the Middle: Political Alientation, Acquiesence, and Activism Among America's Middle Layers.* New York: Praeger, 1989.

Hess, David, and Judith Torney. *The Development of Political Attitudes in Children.* Garden City, N.Y.: Doubleday, 1968.

Hesse, Herman. *Beneath the Wheel.* New York: Fanar, Strauss & Giroux, 1968.

Hill, Herbert, and James Jones (eds.). *Race in America: The Struggle for Equality.* Madison: University of Wisconsin Press, 1993.

Hochschild, Jennifer. *Facing Up to the American Dream: Race, Class, and Soul of a Nation.* Princeton, N.J.: Princeton University, 1995.

Hodgkinson, Virginia, Murray Weitzman, and the Gallup Organization, Inc. *Giving and Volunteering in the United States: 1994 Edition.* Washington, D.C.: Independent Sector, 1994.

Holloway, Harry. "Negro Political Strategy." *Social Science Quarterly* (December 1968).

Holt, John. *The Underachieving School.* New York: Pitman, 1969.

Hoover, Kenneth. *Ideology and Political Life.* Monterey, Cal.: Brooks/Cole Press, 1987.

Howard, Joseph C. "Why We Organize." *Journal of Public Law,* vol. 20 (1971).

Howard, M.C., and J.E. King. *The Political Economy of Marx.* New York: Longman, 1985

Huckfield, Robert, and Carol Kohfeld. *Race and the Decline of Class in American Politics.* Champagne-Urbana: University of Illinois Press, 1989.

Hunter, Floyd. *Community Power Structure.* Chapel Hill, N.C.: University of North Carolina Press, 1953.

Hurley, Andrew. *Environmental Inequalities: Class, Race, and Industrial Pollution in Gary, Indiana, 1945–1980.* Chapel Hill: University of North Carolina Press, 1995.

Iacocca, Lee. *Iacocca: An Autobiography.* New York: Bantam, 1984.

Iyengar, Shanto, and Donald Kinder. *News That Matters.* Chicago, University of Chicago, 1987.

Jackson, Anthony (ed.). *Black Families and the Medium of Television.* Ann Arbor: University of Michigan's Bush Program in Child Development and Social Policy, 1982.

Jacob, Herbert. *Justice in America.* Boston: Little, Brown, 1972.

Jacob, Herbert. *Urban Justice.* Englewood Cliffs, N.J.: Prentice-Hall, 1973.

Jacoby, Neil. *Corporate Powers and Social Responsibility.* New York: Macmillan, 1973.

Jamieson, Kathleen Hall, and Karyn Kohrs Campbell. *The Interplay of Influence: Mass Media and Their Publics in News, Advertising, and Politics.* Belmont, Cal.: Wadsworth, 1983.

Jencks, Christopher. *Inequality: A Reassessment of the Effect of Family and Schools in America.* New York: Basic Books, 1972.

Jencks, Christopher. *Rethinking Social Policy.* Cambridge, Mass.: Harvard University Press, 1992.

Jencks, Christopher, and Paul Peterson (eds.). *The Urban Underclass.* Washington D.C.: Brookings Institute, 1991.

Jennings, James (ed.). *Race, Politics, and Economic Development.* New York: Verso, 1992.

Jennings, James, and Melvin King. *From Access to Power: Black Politics in Boston.* Cambridge, Mass.: Schenkman, 1986.

Jennings, James, and Paul Peterson (eds.). *The Urban Underclass.* Washington, D.C.: Brookings, 1991.

Johnson, Charles S. *Growing Up in the Black Belt.* Washington, D.C.: American Council of Education, 1941.

Joes, Anthony James. *Fascism in the Contemporary World.* Boulder, Colo.: Westview, 1978.

Jones, LeRoi. *Home.* New York: Morrow, 1966.

Kahane, Howard. *Logic and Contemporary Rhetoric.* Belmont, Calif.: Wadsworth, 1980.

Katz, Michael. *The Undeserving Poor: From the War on Poverty to the War on Welfare.* New York: Pantheon, 1989.

Katznelson, Ira, and Mark Kesselman. *The Politics of Power.* Orlando, Fla.: Harcourt Brace Jovanovich, 1987.

Katznelson, Ira, and Margaret Weir. *Schooling for All: Race, Class, and the Decline of the Democratic Ideal.* New York: Basic Books, 1985.

Kaufman, Bel. *Up the Down Staircase.* Englewood Cliffs, N.J.: Prentice-Hall, 1964.

Kaus, Mickey. *The End of Equality.* New York: Basic Books, 1992.

Keech, William. *The Impact of Negro Voting.* Chicago: Rand McNally, 1968.

Keller, Edmund. "The Impact of Black Mayors on Urban Policy." *Annals of the American Academy of Political and Social Science* (September 1978).

Keller, S. *Beyond the Ruling Class.* New York: Random House, 1963.

Kellerman, Donald. *The People, The Press & Politics 1990.* Los Angeles: Times Mirror, 1990.

Kellner, Douglas. *Television and the Crisis of Democracy.* Boulder, Colo.: Westview Press, 1990.

Kimball, Penn. *The Disconnected.* New York: Columbia University Press, 1972.

Kinder, Donald, and Lynn Sanders. *Divided by Color: Racial Attitudes and Democratic Ideals.* Chicago: University of Chicago Press, 1996.

King, Desmond. *Separate and Unequal: Black Americans and the United States Federal Government.* New York: Oxford University Press, 1995.

King, Martin Luther, Jr. "The President's Address to the 10th Anniversary Convention of the Southern Christian Leadership Conference (August 16, 1967)," in Robert Scott and Wayne Brockreide (eds.), *The Rhetoric of Black Power.* New York: Harper & Row, 1969.

King, Martin Luther, Jr. *Stride toward Freedom.* New York: Harper & Row, 1958.

Kline, Mary Jo (ed.). *Alexander Hamilton.* New York: Harper & Row, 1973.

Kohl, Herbert. *36 Children.* New York: New American Library, 1967.

Kolko, Gabriel. *The Roots of American Foreign Policy.* Boston: Beacon Press, 1969.

Kolko, Gabriel. *Wealth and Power in America.* New York: Praeger, 1962.

Kornhauser, William. *The Politics of Mass Society.* New York: Free Press, 1959.

Kozol, Jonathan. *Death at an Early Age.* Boston: Houghton Mifflin, 1967.

Kozol, Jonathan. *The Night Is Dark and I Am Far from Home.* Boston: Houghton Mifflin, 1975.

Kozol, Jonathan. *Savage Inequalities: Children in America's Schools.* New York: Crown Publishers, 1991.

Kristol, Irving. *Two Cheers for Capitalism.* New York: Basic Books, 1978.

Ladd, Everett Caril. *Negro Political Leadership in the South.* New York: Atheneum, 1969.

Ladd, Everett Caril. *Transformations of the American Party System.* New York: Norton, 1978.

Laffer, Arthur, and James Seymour. *The Economics of the Tax Revolt.* Orlando, Fla.: Harcourt Brace Jovanovich, 1979.

Lampman, Robert. *The Share of Top Wealth-holders in National Wealth.* Princeton, N.J.: Princeton University Press, 1962.

Laqueur, Walter. *Fascism* Berkeley: University of California Press, 1976.

Lashley, Marilyn and Melanie Njeri Jackson. *African Americans and the New Policy Consensus: Retreat of the Liberal State?* Westport, Conn.: Greenwood Press, 1994.

Latham, Earl. "The Group Basis of Politics." *American Political Science Review* (June 1952).

Lawrence, David. *The Collapse of the Democratic Presidential Majority.* Boulder, Colo.: Westview Press, 1996.

Lawson, Stephen. *In Pursuit of Power.* New York: Columbia University Press, 1985.

Lawson, Steven. *Black Ballots: Voting Rights in the South, 1944–1969.* New York: Columbia University Press, 1976.

Leggett, John. *Class, Race, and Labor.* New York: Oxford University Press, 1968.

Leigh, Nancy Green. *Stemming Middle Class Decline: The Challenge to Economic Development Planning.* New Brunswick, N.J.: CUPR, 1994.

Lerner, Gerda (ed.). *Black Women in White America.* New York: Pantheon, 1972.

Lessing, Doris. *The Golden Notebook.* New York: Simon & Schuster, 1962.

Levin, Jack, and Jack McDevitt. *Hate Crimes: The Rising Tide of Bigotry and Bloodshed.* New York: Plenum Press, 1993.

Levin, Murray. *The Alienated Voter.* New York: Holt, Rinehart and Winston, 1960.

Levine, Arthur. *When Dreams and Heroes Died.* San Fransisco: Jossey-Bass, 1980.

Levine, Lawrence. *The Opening of the American Mind.* Boston: Beacon Press, 1996.

Levinson, Sanford (ed.). *Power and Community.* New York: Pantheon, 1970.

Levison, Andrew. "The Rebellion of Blue Collar Youth." *Progressive* (October 1972).

Levison, Andrew. *The Working Class Majority.* Baltimore: Penguin, 1974.

Levitan, Sar, and Isaac Shapiro. *America's Contradictions.* Washington, D.C.: Johns Hopkins University, 1987.

Levy, Frank. *Dollars and Dreams: The Changing American Income Distribution.* New York: Norton, 1988.

Levy, Frank. "The Vanishing Middle Class and Related Issues." *PS* (Summer 1987).

Lewinsohn, Paul. *Race, Class, and Party.* New York: Grosset & Dunlap, 1965.

Lichter, Robert, and Richard Noyles. *Good Intentions Make Bad News: Why Americans Hate Campaign Journalism.* Boston: Rowland and Littlefield, 1995.

Lichter, S. Robert, Stanley Rothman, and Lilliard Richardson. *The Media Elite.* New York: Hastings House, 1990.

Lincoln, C. Eric. *The Black Church Since Frazier.* New York: Schocken Books, 1974.

Lincoln, C. Eric. *The Black Muslims in America.* Boston: Beacon Press, 1973. Lindbloom, Charles. Politics and Markets. New York: Basic Books, 1977.

Lindbloom, Charles. "The Science of Muddling Through." *Public Administration Review* (Spring 1959).

Locke, John, "Second Treatise on Civil Government," in Maurice Cranston (ed.), *Locke on Politics, Religion, and Education.* New York: Collier, 1965.

Lowi, Theodore. *The End of Liberalism.* New York: Norton, 1979.

Lundberg, Ferdinand. *The Rich and the Super-rich.* Secaucus, N.J.: Lyle Stuart, 1968.

Lundberg, Ferdinand. *The Rockefeller Syndrome.* Secaucus, N.J.: Lyle Stuart, 1975.

Luria, Dan, and Jack Russell. *Rational Reindustrialization.* Detroit: Widgetripper, 1981.

Lynd, Staughton. "Slavery and the Founding Fathers," in Melvin Drimmer (ed.), *Black History: A Reappraisal.* Garden City, N.Y.:Anchor/ Doubleday, 1969.

Lyman, Stanford. *The Black American in Sociological Thought.* New York: Capricorn, 1972.

MacKinnon, Catherine. *Toward A Feminist Theory of the State.* Cambridge, Mass.: Harvard University Press, 1989.

MacPherson, C. B. *The Political Theory of Possessive Individualism.* New York: Oxford University Press, 1973.

Maganizer, Ira, and Robert Reich. *Minding America's Business.* New York: Harcourt Brace Jovanovich, 1982.

Main, Jackson Turner. *The Social Structure of Revolutionary America.* Princeton, N.J.: Princeton University Press, 1965.

Malcom X. *The Autobiography of Malcom X.* New York: Grove Press, 1965.

Mandel, Ernest. *Late Capitalism.* London: New Left Books, 1975.

Mandel, Ernest. *Marxist Economic Theory.* New York: Monthly Review Press, 1962.

Manley, John. "Neo-pluralism." *American Political Science Review* (June 1983).

Marable, Manning. *How Capitalism Underdeveloped Black America.* Boston: South End Press, 1983.

Marx, Gary T. "Religion: Opiate or Inspiration of Civil Rights Militancy among Negroes?" *American Sociological Review* (February 1967).

Marx, Karl. *Das Kapital,* ed. Frederick Engels. Moscow: Progress Publishers, 1965.

Marx, Karl. *The Grnndrisse,* tr. Martin Nicolaus. Baltimore: Penguin, 1973.

Marx, Karl. *The Poverty of Philosophy,* ed. Frederick Engels. Moscow: Progress Publishers, 1966.

Marx, Karl. "Profit of Capital," in J. B. Bottomore (ed.), *Karl Marx: Early Writings.* London: Watts, 1963.

Marx, Karl. *Value, Price, and Profit.* New York: International Publishers, 1935.

Marx, Karl, and Frederick Engels. *Articles from the Nene Rheinische,* tr. S. Rvazanskava, ed. B. lsaacs. Moscow: Progress Publishers, 1964.

Marx, Karl, and Frederick Engels. *The German Ideology,* tr. and ed. S. Rvazanskava. Moscow: Progress Publishers, 1964.

Massey, Douglas, and Nancey Denton. *American Apartheid: Segregation and the Making of the Underclass.* Cambridge: Harvard University, 1993.

Mayer, Jane, and Jill Abramson. *Strange Justice: The Selling of Clarence Thomas.* Boston: Houghton Mifflin, 1994.

Mays, Benjamin, and Joseph Nicholson. *The Negro's Church.* New York: Arno, 1969.

McAdam, Doug. *Political Process and the Development of Black Insurgency.* Chicago: University of Chicago Press, 1982.

McClain, Paula, and Joseph Stewart. "Can We All Get Along?": *Racial and Ethnic Minorities in American Politics.* Boulder, Colo.: Westview Press, 1995.

McGahey, Richard. "Industrial Policy." *Review of Black Political Economy* (Summer–Fall 1984).

McGuire, Kevin. *The Supreme Court Bar: Legal Elites in the Washington Community.* Charlottesville: University of Virginia, 1993.

McLellan, David. *Marxism after Marx.* Boston: Houghton Mifflin, 1979.

McLellan, David. *The Thought of Karl Marx.* New York: Harper & Row, 1971.

McMurtry, John. *The Structure of Marx's World View.* Princeton, N.J.: Princeton University Press, 1978.

Medsger, Betty. "The Free Propaganda That Floods the Schools." Progressive (December 1976).

Meier, August, and Elliott Rudwick (eds.), *The Making of Black America,* vol. 2. New York: Atheneum, 1969.

Meier, August, and Elliott Rudwick. *CORE: A Study in the Civil Rights Movement.* Urbana: University of Illinois Press, 1975.

Meier, Kenneth, James Stewart, and Robert England. *Race, Class, and Education: The Politics of Second Generation Discrimination.* Madison: University of Wisconsin Press, 1989.

Melman, Seymour. *Profits without Production.* New York: Knopf, 1983.

Menchik, Paul. *Conference on Research in Income and Wealth.* New York: National Bureau of Economic Research, 1979.

Meranto, Phillip, Oneida Meranto, and Matthew Lippman. *Guarding the Ivory Tower.* Denver: Lucha, 1985.

Mermelstein, David. "Austerity, Planning, and the Socialist Alternative," in Roger Alcaly and David Mermelstein (eds.), *The Fiscal Crisis of the American Cities.* New York: Vintage, 1977.

Mermelstein, David (ed.). *The Economic Crisis Reader.* New York: Random House, 1975.

Meyers, M. (ed.). *The Mind of the Founder.* Indianapolis: Bobbs-Merrill, 1973.

Milbraith, Lester, and M. L. Goel. *Political Participation.* Chicago: Rand McNally, 1977.

Miliband, Ralph. *Divided Societies: Class Struggle in Contemporary Capitalism.* New York: Oxford University Press, 1989.

Miliband, Ralph. *The State in Capitalist Society.* New York: Basic Books, 1969.

Miller, Randall (ed.). *Ethnic Images in American Film and Television.* Philadelphia: Balch Institute, 1978.

Mills, C. Wright. *The Power Elite.* New York: Oxford University Press, 1956.

Mishel, Lawrence, and Jared Bernstein. *The State of Working America, 1994–95.* Washington, D.C.: Economic Policy Institute, 1994.

Mitchell, Edwina. *The Crusading Black Journalist.* St. Louis: Farmer Press, 1972.

Mohr, Richard. *Gays/Justice.* New York: Columbia University, 1988.

Molnar, Alex. *Giving Kids the Business: The Commercialization of America's Schools.* Boulder, Colo.: Westview Press, 1996.

Monroe, Sylvester, and Peter Goldman. *Brothers.* New York: Newsweek/ William Morrow, 1988.

Moore, Winfred, et al. (eds.). *Developing Dixie: Modernization in a Traditional Society.* Westport, Conn.: Greenwood Press, 1988.

Morgan, James. *Panel Study on Income Dynamics.* Ann Arbor: University of Michigan Press, 1977.

Morris, Milton. *The Politics of Black America.* New York: Harper & Row, 1975.

Morris, Milton, and Carolyn Cabe. "The Political Socialization of Black Youth." *Public Affairs Bulletin* (May–June 1972).

Morrison, Allan. "The Crusading Press," in *The Negro Handbook.* Chicago: Johnson, 1966.

Mott, Frank. *Jefferson and the Press.* Baton Rouge: Louisiana State University Press, 1943.

Mouffe, Chantal. "Toward a Liberal Socialim?" *Dissent,* (Winter 1993).

Mueller, Claus. *The Politics of Communication.* London: Oxford University Press, 1973.

Mussolini, Benito. *The Corporate State.* Florence: Vallechi, 1936.

Mussolini, Benito. *Fascism.* Rome: Ardita, 1935.

Mydral, Gunnar. *An American Dilemma.* New York: Harper, 1944.

Navarro, Vincent. *Dangerous to Your Heath.* New York: Monthly Review Press, 1993.

Nedelsky, Jennifer. *Private Property and the Limits of American Constitutionalism: The Madisonian Framework and its Legacy.* Chicago: University of Chicago, 1990.

Nelson, Hart, and Anne Nelson. *The Black Church in the Sixties.* Lexington: University of Kentucky Press, 1975.

Nelson, Joel. *Post-Industrial Capitalism: Exploring Economic Inequality in America.* Beverly Hills, Cal.: SAGE Publications, 1995.

Neumann, Franz. *Behemoth.* New York: Harper and Row, 1966.

Newfield, Jack, and Paul DuBrul. *The Permanent Government.* New York: Pilgrim Press, 1981.

Newman, Katherine. *Declining Fortunes: The Withering of the American Dream.* New York: Basic, 1993.

Nieman, Donald. *Promises to Keep: African-Americans and the Constitutional Order, 1776 to the Present.* New York: Oxford, 1991.

Nissen, Bruce. *Fighting for Jobs: Case Studies of Labor-Community Coalitions Confronting Plant Closings.* Albany, N.Y.: SUNY Press, 1995.

Noll, Roger, Merton Peck, and John McGowan. *Economic Aspects of Television Regulation.* Washington, D.C.: Brookings Institution, 1973.

O'Connor, James. *The Fiscal Crisis of the State.* New York: St. Martin's Press, 1973.

Oliver, Melvin, and Thomas Shapiro. *Black Wealth/White Wealth.* New York: Routledge, 1995.

Omi, Michael, and Howard Winant. *Racial Formation in the United States.* New York: Routledge, 1989

O'Reilly, Kenneth. *Nixon's Piano: Presidents and Racial Politics from Washington to Clinton.* New York: Free Press, 1995.

Orfield, Gary, and Carol Ashkinaze. *The Closing Door: Conservative Policy and Black Opportunity.* Chicago: University of Chicago, 1991.

O'Toole, James. *Making America Work.* New York: Continuum, 1981.

Paletz, David, and Robert Entman. *Media Power Politics.* New York: Free Press, 1981.

Parenti, Michael. *Democracy for the Few.* New York: St. Martin's Press, 1983.

Parenti, Michael. *Inventing Reality*. New York: St. Martin's Ptess, 1985.

Parenti, Michael. *Make-Believe Media*. New York: St. Martin's , 1992.

Parker, Frank. *Black Votes Count*. Chapel Hill: University of North Carolina Press, 1990.

Parsons, Talcott. "A Revised Analytical Approach to the Theory of Social Stratification," in R. Bendix and S. M. Lipset (eds.), *Class, Status, and Power*. New York: Free Press, 1953.

Parsons, Talcott, and Kenneth Clark (eds.). *The Negro American*. Boston: Houghton Mifflin, 1966.

Pechman, Joseph. *Who Paid the Taxes, 1966–1985?* Washington, D.C.: Brookings Institute, 1985.

Perkins, Joseph (ed.). *A Conservative Agenda for Black Americans*. Washington, D.C.: Heritage Foundation, 1990.

Perry, Huey, and Wayne Parent (eds.). *Blacks and the American Political System*. Gainesville: University of Florida, 1995.

Persons, Georgia (ed.). *Dilemmas of Black Politics: Issues of Leadership and Strategy*. New York: Harper Collins, 1993.

Petracca, Mark (ed.). *The Politics of Interests: Interest Groups Transformed*. Boulder, Colo.: Westview Press, 1992.

Phillips, Kevin. *Arrogant Capital: Washington, Wall Street, and the Frustration of American Politics*. Boston: Back Bay Books, 1995.

Phillips, Kevin. *Boiling Point: Democrats, Republicans, and the Decline of Middle-Class Prosperity*. New York: Harper, 1993.

Phillips, Kevin. *The Politics of Rich and Poor*. New York: Harper, 1990.

Pierson, Christopher. *Socialism after Communism: the New Market System*. University Park: Pennsylvania State University Press, 1995.

Pinderhughes, Diane. *Race and Ethnicity in Chicago Politics: A Reexamination of Pluralist Theory*. Urbana: University of Illinois Press, 1987.

Pinkney, Alphonso. *The Myth of Black Progress*. New York: Cambridge University Press, 1984.

Piven, Frances Fox, and Richard Cloward. *The New Class War*. New York: Pantheon, 1982.

Piven, Frances Fox, and Richard Cloward. *Regulating the Poor*. New York: Vintage, 1971.

Pohlmann, Marcus. *Governing the Postindustrial City*. White Plains, N.Y.: Longman Press, 1993.

Pohlmann, Marcus. *Political Power in the Postindustrial City*. Millwood, N.Y.: Associated Faculties Press, 1986.

Pohlmann, Marcus, and Michael Kirby. *Racial Politics at the Crossroads: Memphis Elects Dr. W. W. Herenton*. Knoxville: University of Tennessee Press, 1996.

Polsby, Nelson. *Community Power and Political Theory*. New Haven, Conn.: Yale University Press, 1980.

Powell, Thomas. *The Persistence of Racism in America*. New York: University Press of America, 1992

Powers, Ron. *The Newscasters*. New York: St. Martin's Press, 1977.

Preston, Michael B., Lenneal J. Henderson, Jr., and Paul L. Puryear (eds.), *The New Black Politics: The Search For Political Power*. White Plains, N.Y.: Longman, 1982.

Puette, William. *Through Jaundiced Eyes: How the Media View Organized Labor*. Ithaca, N.Y.: ILR Press, 1992.

Quinney, R. (ed.). *Capitalist Society.* New York: Dorsey, 1979.

Ranney, Austin. *Curing the Mischief of Faction.* Berkeley: University of California Press, 1975.

Ransford, H. Edward. *Race and Class in American Society.* Cambridge, Mass.: Schenkman, 1977.

Ransom, Roger, and Richard Sutch. *One Kind of Freedom.* Cambridge: Cambridge University Press, 1977.

Raspberry, William. "Politics, Blacks, and the Press," in Richard Lee (ed.), *Politics and the Press.* Washington, D.C.: Acropolis, 1970.

Rauch, Jonathan. *Demosclerosis.* New York: Times Books, 1994.

Record, Wilson. *The Negro and the Communist Party.* New York: Atheneum, 1971.

Record, Wilson. *Race and Radicalism.* Ithaca, N.Y.: Cornell University Press, 1964.

Redman, Eric. *The Dance of Legislation.* New York: Simon & Schuster, 1973.

Reed, Adolph, Jr. *The Jesse Jackson Phenomenon.* New Haven, Conn.: Yale University Press, 1986.

Reich, Robert. *The Work of Nations: Preparing Ourselves for 21st Century Capitalism.* New York: Knopf, 1991

Reich, William. *The Mass Psychology of Fascism.* New York: Farrar, Straus, and Giroux, 1970.

Reid, Samuel. *The New Industrial Order.* New York: McGraw-Hill, 1976

Reiman, Jeffrey. *The Rich Get Richer and the Poor Get Prison.* New York: Macmillan, 1990.

Reimer, Everett. *School Is Dead.* Garden City, N.Y. Doubleday, 1971.

Rexroat, Cynthia. *The Declining Economic Status of Black Children.* Washington D.C.: Joint Center for Political and Economic Studies, 1994.

Richardson, Marilyn. *Maria W. Stewart, America's First Black Woman Political Writer: Essays and Speeches.* Bloomington, Ind.: Indiana University, 1987.

Riddlesperger, James, and Donald Jackson (eds.). *Presidential Leadership and Civil Rights Policy.* Westport, Conn.: Greenwood, 1995.

Rifkin, Jeremy, and Randy Barber. *The North Will Rise Again: Pensions and Power in the 1980s.* Boston: Beacon Press, 1978.

Rifkin, Jeremy. *The End of Work: The Decline of the Global Labor Force and the Dawn of the Post-Market Era.* New York: Putnam, 1994.

Robinson, Cedric. *Black Marxism: The Making of the Black Radical Tradition.* London: Zed Books, 1983.

Robinson, Donald. *Slavery in the Structure of American Politics.* New York: Harcourt Brace and Jovanovich, 1971.

Robinson, Paulette, and Billy Tidwell (eds.). *The State of Black America 1995.* New York: National Urban League, 1995.

Rodgers, Harrell. *Poor Women, Poor Families: The Economic Plight of America's Female-Headed Households.* New York: Sharpe, 1990.

Roebuck, Joseph. *A History of American Labor.* New York: Free Press, 1966.

Roper Organization. *Trends in Attitudes Towards Television and Other Media.* New York: Television Information Service, 1983.

Rose, Tricia. *Black Noise: Rap Music and Black Culture in Contemporary America.* Hanover, N.H.: Wesleyan University Press, 1994.

Rosen, Corey, Katherine Klein, and Karen Young. *Employee Stock Ownership in America: The Equity Solution.* Lexington, Mass.: Lexington Books, 1985.

Rosenberg, Gerald. *The Hollow Hope: Can Courts Bring About Social Change?* Chicago: University of Chicago, 1991.

Rossiter, Clinton. *Conservatism in America.* New York: Vintage, 1962.

Rossiter, Clinton (ed.). *The Federalist Papers.* New York: New American Library, 1961.

Rovetch, Emily (ed.). *Like It Is.* New York: Dutton, 1981.

Rowan, Carl. *Just Between Us.* New York: Random House, 1974.

Sabato, Larry. *Feeding Frenzy: How Attack Journalism Has Transformed American Politics.* New York: Free Press, 1991.

Samuelson, Paul, and William Nordhaus. *Economics.* New York: McGraw-Hill, 1985.

Sawers, Larry, and William Tabb (eds.), *Sunbelt/Snowbelt.* New York: Oxford University Press, 1984.

Schantz, Harvey. *American Presidential Elections: Process, Policy, and Political Change.* Albany, N.Y.: SUNY Press, 1996.

Schattschneider, E. E. *Party Government.* New York: Holt, Rinehart and Winston, 1942.

Schattschneider, E. E. *The Semi-Sovereign People.* New York: Holt, Rinehart and Winston,1960.

Scherer, Frederic. *Industrial Market Structure and Economic Performance.* Chicago: Rand McNally, 1980.

Schiller, Herbert. *Mass Communication and American Empire.* Boulder, Colo.: Westview, 1992.

Schiller, Herbert. *The Mind Managers.* Boston: Beacon Press, 1973.

Schlozman, Kay Lehman, and John Tierney. *Organized Interests and American Democracy.* New York: Harper and Row, 1986.

Schor, Juliet. *The Overworked American: The Unexpected Decline of Leisure.* New York: Basic, 1991

Schuman, Howard, Charlotte Steeh, and Lawrence Boho. *Racial Attitudes in America.* Cambridge, Mass.: Harvard University Press, 1985.

Schumpeter, Joseph. *Capitalism, Socialism, and Democracy.* New York: Harper & Row, 1950.

Schwartz, Herman. *Packing the Courts: The Conservative Campaign to Rewrite the Constitution.* New York: Scribner, 1988.

Scott, Robert, and Wayne Brockreide (eds.). *The Rhetoric of Black Power.* New York: Harper & Row, 1969.

Sears, David, and John McConahay. *The Politics of Violence.* Boston: Houghton Mifflin, 1973.

Shafer, Byron (ed.). *The End of Realignment?* Madison: University of Wisconsin Press, 1991.

Shostak, Arthur. *Blue Collar.* New York. Random House, 1969.

Shull, Steven. *A Kinder, Gentler Racism? The Reagan-Bush Legacy.* Armonk, N.Y.: M.E. Sharpe, 1993.

Shull, Steven. *The President and Civil Rights Policy: Leadership and Change.* New York: Greenwood, 1989.

Sigelman, Lee, and Susan Welch. *Black Americans' Views of Racial Inequality: The Dream Deferred.* New York: Cambridge University Press, 1991.

Sinkler, George. *The Racial Attitudes of American Presidents.* Garden City, N.Y.: Doubleday, 1972.

Sklar, Holly. *Chaos or Community? Seeking Solutions, Not Scapegoats for Bad Economics.* Boston: South End, 1995.

Skogan, Wesley. *Disorder and Decline.* New York: Free Press, 1990.

Smead, Howard. *Blood Justice.* New York: Oxford University, 1986.

Smith, Adam. *The Wealth of Nations.* New York: Modern Library, 1969 (reprint).

Smith, Bob. *They Closed Our Schools.* Chapel Hill: University of North Carolina Press, 1965.

Smith, Christopher E. *Courts and the Poor.* Chicago: Nelson-Hall, 1991.

Smith, J. David. *The Eugenic Assault on America.* Fairfax, Va.: George Mason University Press, 1993.

Smith, James D., and Staunton K. Calvert. "Estimating the Wealth of Top Wealth-holders from Estate Tax Returns." *Proceedings of the American Statistical Association* (1965)

Smith, James D., and Stephen D. Franklin. "The Concentration of Wealth, 1922–1969." *American Economic Review* (May 1974).

Smith, James D., and Finis Welch. *Closing the Gap.* Santa Monica, Calif.: Rand, 1986.

Smith, Robert. *Racism in the Post–Civil Rights Era: Now You See it, Now You Don't.* Albany, New York: SUNY Press,1995

Smith, Robert and Richard Seltzer. *Race, Class, and Culture: A Study in Afro-American Mass Opinion.* Albany, N.Y.: State University of New York Press, 1992.

Sniderman, Paul, and Thomas Piazza. *The Scar of Race.* Cambridge: Harvard University, 1993.

Spence, Gerry. *With Justice for None: Destroying an American Myth.* New York: Penguin Books, 1989.

Squires, James. *Read All About It! The Corporate Takeover of America's Newspapers.* New York: Random House, 1993.

Stanley, Harold, and Richard Niemi. *Vital Statistics on American Politics.* Washington D.C.: CQ Press, 1994.

Steele, Lewis M. "Nine Men in Black Who Think White." *New York Times,* October 13, 1968.

Steele, Shelby. *The Content of Our Character: A New Vision of Race in America.* New York: St. Martin's, 1990.

Sternleib, George, and James Hughes. *Income and Jobs: USA.* New Brunswick, N.J.: Center for Urban Policy Research, 1984.

Stokes, Carl. *Promises of Power.* New York: Simon and Schuster, 1973.

Stone, Chuck. *Black Political Power in America.* Indianapolis: Bobbs-Merrill, 1964.

Sundquist, James. *Dynamics of the Party System.* Washington, D.C.: Brookings Institute, 1983.

Swain, Carol. *Black Faces, Black Interests: The Representation of African Americans in Congress.* Cambridge, Mass.: Harvard University Press, 1993.

Szatmary, David. *Shays' Rebellion: The Making of an Agrarian Insurrection.* Amherst: University of Massachusetts Press, 1980.

Tabb, William, and Larry Sawers (eds.), *Marxism and the Metropolis.* New York: Oxford University Press, 1978.

Tate, Katherine. *From Protest to Politics: The New Black Voters in American Elections.* Cambridge, Mass.: Harvard University Press, 1994.

Teixeira, Ruy. *The Disappearing American Voter.* Washington D.C.: Brookings Institution, 1992.

Teixeira, Ruy. *Why Americans Don't Vote: Turnout Decline in the United States, 1960–1984.* New York: Greenwood Press, 1987.

Terkel, Studs. *Division Street: America.* New York: Pantheon, 1967.

Terkel, Studs. Race: *How Blacks and Whites Think and Feel About the American Obsession.* New York: The New Press, 1992.

Terkel, Studs. *Working.* New York: Avon, 1974.

Terrell, Mary Church. *A Colored Woman in a White World.* Washington, D.C.: Ransdell, 1940.

Thurow, Lester. *Generating Inequality.* New York: Basic Books, 1975.

Thurow, Lester. *Zero-Sum Society.* New York: Basic Books, 1980.

Tolchin, Martin, and Susan Tolchin. *Buying into America.* New York: Times Books, 1987.

Toure, Kwame, and Charles V. Hamilton. *Black Power.* New York: Random House, 1967.

Truman, David B. *The Governmental Process: Political Interests and Public Opinion.* New York: Knopf, 1971.

Tucker, Robert C. (ed.). *The Marx-Engels Reader.* New York: Norton, 1978.

Turner, Julius. *Party and Constituency: Pressures on Congress.* Baltimore: Johns Hopkins Press, 1970.

Turner, Margaret Austin, Michael Fix, and Raymond Struyk. *Opportunities Denied, Opportunities Diminished: Racial Discrimination in Hiring.* Washington, D.C.: Urban Institute Press, 1991.

van den Berghe, Pierre L. *Race and Racism.* New York: Wiley, 1967.

Van Horne, Winston (ed.). *Race: Twentieth Century Dilemmas—Twenty-First Century Prognoses.* Milwaukee: University of Wisconsin Institute on Race and Ethnicity, 1989.

Vernon, Raymond. *Storm Over the Multinationals.* Cambridge, Mass.: Harvard University Press, 1977.

Vines, Kenneth. "Federal District Judges and Race Relations Cases in the South." *Journal of Politics* (May 1964).

Vivian, C. T. *Black Power and the American Myth.* Philadelphia: Fortress, 1970.

Walls, David. *The Activist's Almanac.* New York: Simon and Schuster, 1993.

Walters, Ronald. *Black Presidential Politics in America: A Strategic Approach.* Albany, N.Y.: SUNY Press, 1988.

Walton, Hanes, Jr. *Black Political Parties.* New York: Free Press, 1972.

Walton, Hanes, Jr. *Black Politics and and Black Political Behavior: A Linkage Analysis.* New York: Praeger, 1994.

Walton, Hanes, Jr. *Invisible Politics: Black Political Behavior.* Albany, N.Y.: State University of New York Press, 1985.

Wanninski, Jude. *The Way the World Works.* New York: Basic Books, 1978.

Ware, Gilbert (ed.). *From the Black Bar: Voices for Equal Justice.* New York: Putnam, 1976.

Warren, Donald. *The Radical Center.* South Bend, Ind.: University of Notre Dame Press, 1976.

Washington Joseph, (ed.). *Dilemmas of the Black Middle Class.* Philadelphia: University of Pennsylvania Press, 1980.

Washington, Linn. *Black Judges on Justice: Perspectives from the Bench.* New York: New Press, 1994.

Weinberg, Meyer. *A Chance to Learn: A History of Race and Education in the United States.* New York: Cambridge University Press, 1977.

Weinstein, James. *The Corporate Ideal in the Liberal State, 1900–1918.* Boston: Beacon Press, 1968.

Weinstein, James. *The Decline of American Socialism.* New York: Monthly Review Press, 1967.

Weinstein, James. *The Decline of Socialism in America, 1912–1925.* New York: Random House, 1967.

Weisberg, Jacob. *In Defense of Government: The Fall and Rise of Public Trust.* New York: Scribner, 1996.

Whitby, Kenny. *The Color of Representation: Congressional Behavior and Black Interests.* Ann Arbor, Mich.: University of Michigan Press, 1997.

Wicker, Tom. *On Press.* New York: Viking, 1978.

Wildavsky, Aaron. *The Politics of the Budgetary Process.* Boston: Little, Brown, 1974.

Wilhoit, G. Cleveland, and David Weaver. *The American Journalist.* Bloomington: Indiana University, 1991.

Wilkes, Paul. "As the Blacks Move In, the Ethnics Move Out." *New York Times Magazine* (January 24, 1971).

Williams, Henry. *Black Response to the American Left, 1917–1920.* Princeton, N.J.: Princeton University Press, 1973.

Williams, Linda Faye (ed.). *From Exclusion to Inclusion.* Westport, Conn.: Greenwood, 1992.

Williams, Walter. *The State Against Blacks.* New York: New Press, 1982.

Williams, William Appleman. *The Great Evasion.* Chicago: Quadrangle Books, 1964.

Willie, Charles, Antoine Garibaldi, and Wornie Reed (eds.). *The Education of African-Americans.* New York: Auburn House, 1991.

Wilmore, Gayraud. *Black Religion and Black Radicalism.* Garden City, N.Y.: AnchorDoubleday, 1973.

Wilson, Clint, and Felix Gutierrez. *Minorities and the Media.* Beverly Hills, Calif.: Sage, 1985.

Wilson, James Q. *Negro Politics.* New York: Free Press, 1965.

Wilson, William J. *The Declining Significance of Race.* Chicago: University of Chicago Press, 1980.

Wilson, William J. *The Truly Disadvantaged.* Chicago: University of Chicago Press, 1987.

Wirt, Frederick. *Politics of Southern Equality.* Hawthorne, N.Y.: Aldine, 1970.

Wolman, Harold, and Norman Thomas. "Black Interests, Black Groups and Black Influence in the Federal Political Process." *Journal of Politics* (November 1970).

Woodson, Carter. *The Education of the Negro Prior to 1861.* Washington, D.C.: Associated Publishers, 1919.

Woolf, S. J. (ed.). *The Nature of Fascism.* New York: Vintage, 1969.

Wright, Erik. "Race, Class, and Income Inequality." *American Journal of Sociology* (May 1978).

Yette, Samuel. *The Choice: The Issue of Black Survival in America.* Silver Spring, Md.: Cottage Books, 1971.

Zeitlin, Maurice. "Corporate Ownership and Control." *American Journal of Sociology,* (March 1974).

Zeitlin, Maurice (ed.). *American Society Inc.* Chicago: Rand McNally, 1970.

Zilg, Gerald. *Du Pont: Behind the Nylon Curtain.* Englewood Cliffs, N.J.: Prentice-Hall, 1974.

Zinn, Howard. *Declarations of Independence: Cross Examining American Ideology.* New York: Harper Collins, 1990.

Zinn, Howard. *A People's History of the United States.* New York: Harper & Row, 1980.

Zweigenhaft, Richard, and William H. Domhoff. *Blacks in the White Establishment? A Study of Race and Class in America.* New Haven: Yale University Press, 1991.

Index